A Comprehensive Welsh Gran

Reference Grammars
General Editor: Glanville Price

Published:

L. S. R. Byrne and E. L. Churchill's
A Comprehensive French Grammar
Fourth Edition
Rewritten by Glanville Price

A Comprehensive Russian Grammar
Terence Wade
Edited by Michael J. de K. Holman

A Comprehensive Welsh Grammar
David A. Thorne

In preparation:

A Comprehensive German Grammar

A Comprehensive Italian Grammar

A Comprehensive Portuguese Grammar

A Comprehensive Spanish Grammar

A Comprehensive Welsh Grammar

David A. Thorne

BLACKWELL
Oxford UK & Cambridge USA

First published 1993

Blackwell Publishers
108 Cowley Road, Oxford, OX4 1JF, UK

238 Main Street, Suite 501
Cambridge, Massachusetts 02142, USA

British Library Cataloguing in Publication Data
A CIP catalogue record for this book is available from the British Library.

Library of Congress Cataloging-in-Publication Data
Thorne, David, 1944–
    A comprehensive Welsh grammar/David Thorne.
        p. cm.
    Includes bibliographical references and index.
    ISBN 0–631–16407–3 (alk. paper). – ISBN 0–631–16408–1 (pbk.: alk. paper)
    1. Welsh language – Grammar.   I. Title.
PB2123.T48   1993
491.6′682421–dc20   92–39657
                                                                    CIP

Typeset in 10 on 12 pt Times
by Joshua Associates Ltd, Oxford
Printed in Great Britain by Page Bros Ltd, Norwich

This book is printed on acid-free paper

Contents

The Noun Phrase

The Verb

Compounds

Sentence and Clause Structure

Prepositions, Adverbs, Conjunctions, Interjections

Appendices

Preface

The earliest grammars of the Welsh language were written during the Renaissance period. In the intervening 450 years numerous grammars reflecting various needs and pursuing a variety of theoretical issues have appeared.

If any justification is required for producing another grammar of Welsh, it should be borne in mind that there have been few attempts at a comprehensive coverage of the grammar of Welsh current in the latter part of the twentieth century. This is what I have attempted in this volume. For the description of the common core of the language as well as for the varieties surrounding it, I have depended heavily on the work of a host of colleagues, the resources of the *University of Wales Dictionary* and unpublished descriptions of spoken Welsh presented for higher degrees of the University of Wales. The references included in the Bibliography will give some indication of my debt to contemporary authors and texts. Where a feature relates specifically to a particular dialect of Welsh, or to a particular register or to another period in the history of the language, a note has been included in the text to show that the description no longer refers to the contemporary standard language.

The grammar will not be able to answer all the questions that an advanced student of the language is likely to ask but it is hoped that this volume will go part of the way to meet the needs of students who wish to become acquainted with contemporary usage.

The research and writing has been supported by grants from the St

David's University College Pantyfedwen Fund and St David's University College Research Fund. My sincere thanks are due to Blackwell for commissioning and publishing the book, to Professor Glanville Price for suggesting that I take the Project on board, and to Professor D. Simon Evans of the Centre for Research and Scholarship at the University of Wales, Lampeter, for his support and encouragement.

Grammatical Abbreviations

The following grammatical abbreviations have been used:

abs.	absolute	n.m.	noun masculine
adj.	adjective	n.pl.	noun plural
adv.	adverb	O.	object
C.	complement	P.	predicator
comp.	comparative	pl.	plural
conj.	conjunction	pluperf.	pluperfect
dial.	dialect	prep.	preposition
equ.	equative	pres.	present
fem.	feminine	pret.	preterite
indic.	indicative	pron.	pronoun
imper.	imperative	S.	subject
imperf.	imperfect	sing.	singular
impers.	impersonal	subj.	subjunctive
masc.	masculine	sup.	superlative
N.	noun	vb.	verb
neut.	neuter	v.n.	verb-noun
n.f.	noun feminine		

Introduction

The Sounds of Welsh

1 Between slant lines / / (indicating phonemes) and within square brackets [ ] (indicating allophones) the symbols of the International Phonetic Alphabet are used. The consonantal system is set out in table 1. (See also **6**.)

Table 1

	Bilabial	Labio-dental	Dental	Alveolar	Lateral	Palato-Alveolar	Palatal	Velar	Uvular	Glottal
Plosive	p b			t d				k g		
Affricate						tʃ dʒ				
Fricative		f v	θ ð	s z	ɫ	ʃ			χ	h
Liquid				r̥ r	l					
Nasal	m			n				ŋ		
Glide	w						j			

2 The voiced alveolar fricative /z/ is a feature of the sound system of southern spoken Welsh, but does not occur at all in north Wales, /s/ being substituted for it in borrowings. It is also outside the system of standard Welsh. In southern Welsh /z/ commonly occurs in borrowings from English:

[zu]	'zoo'
[fɛzant]	'pheasant'
[zɛbra]	'zebra'

Finally it realizes the English pluralizing morpheme in borrowed forms:

[bɑbiz]	'babies'
[rɑzɛrz]	'razors'
[plʊmz]	'plums'

It is also attached to some native words such as

[drɪdunz]	'starlings'

and to plural forms to produce a double plural:

[mɪlgi]	'greyhound'
[mɪlgun]	'greyhounds'
[mɪlgunz]	double plural
[gwiθur]	'worker'
[gwiθwir]	'workers'
[gwiθwirz]	double plural

In other southern Welsh forms, the English pluralizing morpheme is realized by /s/:

[kwɪls]	'quills'
[teils]	'tiles'
[kʊrljuns]	'curlews'

This may suggest that /z/ was not established in the dialects when these forms became current in their vocabulary.

3 The affricates /ʧ, ʤ/ are also classed as borrowed sounds by Welsh speakers. They occur almost exclusively in borrowed forms, although the sounds have developed in Welsh as a result of the assimilation of /t+j/ and /d+j/. Similarly /ʃ/ has evolved in the language by assimilation of /s+j/. There is a tendency in all dialects of Welsh to interchange /ʧ/ and /ʃ/:

[ʧauns/ʃauns]	'chance'
[ʧʊps/ʃʊps]	'wet'
[ʧep/ʃep]	'cheap'

In native words [ʧ] occurs only medially and finally:

[kɪʧ]	2 sing. imper.	'grasp'
[kɪʧo]	v.n.	'grasp'
[sgɪʧɛ]	n.pl.	'shoes'

In borrowings it can occur initially, medially and finally:

[ʧalk]	'chalk'
[maʧɛn]	'match'
[waʧ]	'watch'

/ʤ/, on the other hand, occurs only initially in native words:

| [ʤaul] | 'devil' |
| [ʤogɛl] | 'safe' |

In borrowings it again occurs initially, medially and finally:

[ʤam]	'jam'
[ʤɪʤo]	'judge'
[gɑʤ]	'gauge'

4 The glottal fricative /h/ may appear initially and medially:

haf	'summer'
hawdd	'easy'
arholi	'examine'
cyhoeddi	'publish'
brenhinol	'royal'

Medially /h/ is normally tied to the stress pattern, occurring before a stressed vowel and following either another vowel or a nasal consonant or /r/. By adding a syllable, stress moves and /h/ disappears in:

cynghanedd 'harmony'   pl. *cynganeddion*

/h/ moves with the stress in:

dihareb   'proverb'   pl. *diarhebion*

In other forms, stress moves but /h/ is retained:

arholiad   'examination'   pl. *arholiadau*

cyhuddiad   'accusation'   pl. *cyhuddiadau*
cyhoedd 'public',   *cyhoeddusrwydd* 'publicity'

Although /h/ does not occur in the dialects of south-east Wales, it does function as a prosodic stress marker in these dialects. The same dialects lack also the voiceless alveolar trill /ɹ̥/, which occurs only initially; /r/ occurs in place of /ɹ̥/ in south-east Wales.

5 The non-fricative lateral /l/ is described as clear or neutral in southern Welsh, but in north Wales generally the non-fricative lateral has a marked dark quality.

6 The simple vowels are described in figure 1, in which 'high' and 'low' refer to tongue position, and 'front' and 'back' to the front and back of the mouth.

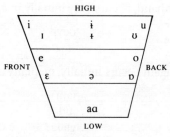

Figure 1

/i, ɨ, e ɑ, o, u/ are phonologically long
/ɪ, ɨ, ɛ, a, ɒ, ʊ, ə/ are phonologically short.

The phonemic inventory of southern Welsh lacks the two high central vowels current in north Wales. In south Wales these central vowels are realized by the high front vowels /i, ɪ/. The difference is illustrated by the following pairs:

SW	NW		
[bis]	[bɨs]	*bys*	'finger'
[bɪr]	[bɨr]	*byr*	'short'
[sir]	[sɨr]	*sur*	'sour'
[ɬin]	[ɬɨn]	*llun*	'picture'

7 In the orthography (see section **19**, table 3) /i, ɨ, ɪ, ɨ/ may all be symbolized by *y*. The sounds are said to be clear. /ə/ is also represented by *y*; the sound is described as dark or obscure.

8 In south-east Wales /ɑ/ has an allophone, a half-open front vowel [æ] which occurs in monosyllables and stressed final syllables:

[kæ]	*cae*	'field'
[tæd]	*tad*	'father'
[kəm'ræg]	*Cymraeg*	'Welsh'
[gla'næ]	*glanhau*	'clean'

[æ] varies considerably in quality and in some areas is diphthongized towards [ə]; the vowel also occurs in mid-Wales.

9 In the Teifi Valley and again in north Pembrokeshire this central vowel /ə/ occurs in monosyllables where other varieties of southern Welsh select /ɪ/:

[brən]	*bryn*	'hill'
[bəθ]	*byth*	'ever'
[kləsd]	*clust*	'ear'
[kən]	*cyn*	'before'
[gwərð]	*gwyrdd*	'green'
[hən]	*hyn*	'this'
[hwən]	*chwyn*	'weeds'

10 In the western portion of Pembrokeshire the central vowel all but disappears from the dialect to be replaced by a high vowel:

[kəvan]	[kivan]	*cyfan*	'whole'
[mənið]	[mini/muni]	*mynydd*	'mountain'
[əsgol]	[ɪsgol]	*ysgol*	'school'

11 The diphthongs of south Wales fall into two groups according to their second element. They are described in figures 2 and 3. These, and the diagrams in **13** below, indicate the direction of movement of diphthongs: e.g. 'ai→' indicates a diphthong that starts as 'a' and finishes as 'i'.

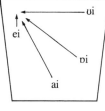
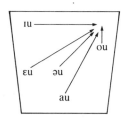

Figure 2   Figure 3

12 In south Cardiganshire we find in addition the diphthongs /ae/, /oe/ in monosyllables and stressed final syllables:

[poen]	*poen*	'pain'
[koed]	*coed*	'trees'
[kad'noed]	*cadnoed*	'foxes'
[kae]	*cae*	'field'
[saeθ]	*saeth*	'arrow'
[bro'gaed]	*brogaed*	'frogs'

13 The diphthongs of north Wales fall into three groups and are described in figures 4–6.

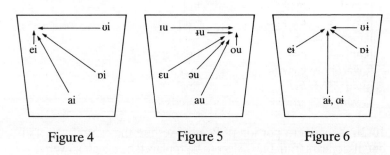

Figure 4   Figure 5   Figure 6

14 The first elements of diphthongs are short over a considerable area of south Wales, but exceptions have been noted particularly in monosyllables. In north Wales in open and closed monosyllables and stressed ultima, the first element of /ɒi, ʊi/ is long; in the same word position, but in open syllables only, the first element of /au, ɛu/ is long. The diphthongs /ai/ and /ɑi/ contrast in monosyllables only and examples of phonemic contrast are few:

[hail]	*haul*	'sun'
[hɑil]	*hael*	'generous'
[kai]	*cau*	'shut'
[kɑi]	*cae*	'field'

15 Although the orthography of Welsh is largely phonemic the relation between phoneme and grapheme is not always straightforward. The consonants are set out in table 2.

16 In English loans the grapheme *j* is used for /dʒ/:

[dʒam]	*jam*	'jam'
[gɑrɛdʒ]	*garej*	'garage'

Table 2

/p/	p	/t/	t	/k/	c
/b/	b	/d/	d	/g/	g
/m/	m	/n/	n	/ŋ/	ng
/f/	ff, ph	/θ/	th	/s/	s
/ɬ/	ll	/ʃ/	si, sh	/χ/	ch
/h/	h	/v/	f	/ð/	dd
/l/	l	/r/	r	/ɾ̥/	rh
/w/	w	/j/	i		

[dʒel]	*jêl*	'jail'
[dʒɒb]	*job*	'job'

Geiriadur Prifysgol Cymru (The University of Wales Dictionary) uses *ts* for /ʧ/ in forms like:

[ʧain]	*tsaen*	'chain'
[ʧips]	*tsips*	'chips'
[waʧ]	*wats*	'watch'
[maʧɛn]	*matsen*	'match'

but the pedagogic *Cymraeg Byw* (Living Welsh: a register of Welsh designed to assist the learner to master the language) proposes *tsh* to give a slightly different spelling.

Sh or *s* is used to denote /ʃ/ finally:

[bruʃ]	*brwsh, brws*	'brush'

but in all other positions the sound is represented by *si*:

[ʃɒp]	*siop*	'shop'
[bruʃo]	*brwsio*	'brush'
[pɛnʃun]	*pensiwn*	'pension'
[ʃarad]	*siarad*	'speak'

17 *ng* represents both /ŋ/ and /ŋg/:

[aŋori]	*angori*	'anchor'
[baŋgor]	Bangor	

18 /f/ is denoted by *ff* initially except where /f/ realizes spirant mutation of *p*; *ph* denotes spirant mutation of *p*, see **47**. The only exceptions are Biblical proper nouns: *Pharisead* 'Pharisee', *Philistiad* 'Philistine', *Philipi* 'Philippi', *Philipiaid* 'Philippians', *Philemon* 'Philemon', *Phrygia* 'Phrygia'.

19 The vowels and diphthongs and their orthographic equivalents are noted in table 3.

Table 3

/i/	/ɪ/		i, y			
/e/	/ɛ/		e			
/ɑ/	/a/		a			
/o/	/ɒ/		o			
/u/	/ʊ/		w			
/ɨ/	/ɨ/		u, y			
/ə/			y			
/ei/	ei	/ɨu/	iw, yw, uw	/eɨ/	eu
/ai/	ai	/ɛu/	ew	/aɨ/	au
/ɒi/	oi	/au/	aw	/ɑɨ/	ae
/ʊi/	wy	/ou/	ow	/oɨ/	oe
		/ɨu/	yw, uw	/ʊɨ/	wy
		/əu/	yw		

Alphabet

20 Each letter or digraph has a traditional name which is noted below in Welsh spelling:

a	â
b	bî
c	èc
ch	èch
d	dî
e	ê
f	èf
ff	èff
g	èg
ng	èng
h	âets

i	î
l	èl
ll	èll
m	èm
n	èn
o	ô
p	pî
ph	ffî
r	èr
rh	rhi, rho
s	ès
t	tî
th	èth
u	û
w	w
y	y

Note

In some words *ng* is sounded *ng-g*: *dangos* 'show'; Bangor etc. In the Welsh alphabet *ng* follows *g* directly (e.g. *llegach, lleng, lleiaf*), but forms sounded *ng-g* are listed in dictionaries between -*nf*- and -*nh*- (*danfon, dangos, danheddog*).

Length, Stress and Accents

21 The orthography echoes all the northern Welsh contrasts but does not reflect length distinctions. Monosyllabic proclitics have a short vowel:

fy	'my'
dy	'your'
yn	'in'
a	'and'
y	'the'

otherwise in open monosyllables the simple vowel is always long:

da	'good'
lle	'place'
tri	'three'
llw	'oath'

22 In monosyllables ending in *p*, *t*, *c*, *m*, *ng*, the simple vowel is normally short:

cap	'cap'
cam	'step'
llong	'ship'
lloc	'fold, pen'
het	'hat'

English borrowings such as

siâp	'shape'
gât	'gate'
tâp	'tape'
grŵp	'group'
sêt	'seat'
ffrâm	'frame'

have a long vowel and length is indicated by a circumflex accent. In two forms,

côt	'coat'
grôt	'groat'

the vowel is long in northern Welsh and short in southern varieties.

23 Certain verbal forms that have been subject to coalescence or contraction and where the vowel is pronounced long, carry the circumflex accent:

ŷm	(<*ydym*)	'we are'
bûm	(<*buum*)	'I have been'
bôm	(<*byddom*)	'we may be'
bônt	(<*byddont*)	'they may be'

24 Other verbal forms, where the vowel preceding -*nt* is long as a result of the contraction of two short vowels, also carry the circumflex:

cânt	'they shall get'
ânt	'they go, they shall go'
gwnânt	'they make, they shall make'
rhônt	'they give, they shall give'
dônt	'they come, they shall come'

25 In monosyllables ending in *b*, *d*, *g*, *f*, *ff*, *dd*, *ch*, *th*, *s*, the simple vowels are usually long and are not marked:

mab	'son'
gwag	'empty'
haf	'summer'
hoff	'favourite'
rhaff	'rope'
sach	'sack'
peth	'thing'

26 The vowel is short in

os	'if'
och	'ugh'
fflach	'flash'
rhag	'lest'

27 *Heb* 'without' has a short vowel in northern dialects but a long vowel in southern dialects.

28 Vowels in monosyllables ending in *l*, *n*, *r*, vary in length. The long simple vowel is marked by a circumflex:

ffŵl	'fool'
(*y*)*stên*	'pitcher'
sêr	'stars'
blêr	'untidy'
(*y*)*stôl*	'stool'
siôl	'shawl'

i and *u* are usually long and are left unmarked except where length is contrastive:

min	'edge'
hir	'long'
llun	'picture'

A short vowel occurs in a few exceptions:

ffwr	'fur'
swil	'shy'
prin	'scarce'
bil	'bill'

Where length is contrastive in monosyllables, the long vowel is normally marked by a circumflex while the short vowel is left unmarked:

âr	'tilth'	*ar*	'on'

mân	'tiny'	*man*	'place'
ffôn	'phone'	*ffon*	'stick'
cân	'song'	*can*	'flour'
tâl	'payment'	*tal*	'tall'
llên	'literature'	*llen*	'curtain'
gwâr	'civilized'	*gwar*	'nape of the neck'
ôd	'snow'	*od*	'odd'
brân	'crow'	*bran*	'bran'

A circumflex is also used on *ŷd* 'corn', *tŷ* 'house', *iâ* 'ice', *iâr* 'hen'.

29 Examples of marking the short vowel with the diacritic ` are rare:

nod	'target'
nòd	'nod'
clos	'yard'
clòs	'close'
pin	'pine'
pìn	'pin'
sgil	'behind'
sgìl	'skill'

30 No consistency as regards vowel length is to be found preceding *ll*: the vowel is usually short in northern Welsh and long in southern Welsh but variation is common.

31 When a consonantal cluster follows a vowel in a monosyllable, the vowel is short:

sant	'saint'
perth	'hedge'
corff	'body'
pant	'valley'
cwrt	'court'

32 A vowel preceding -*llt*, -*sb*, -*sg*, -*st*, is long in north Wales but short in south Wales:

gwallt	'hair'
swllt	'shilling'
tyst	'witness'
llesg	'feeble'
cosb	'punishment'

33 In stressed penultima the short vowel is marked by doubling the following *n* or *r* and the long vowel is left unmarked:

canu	'sing'	*cannu*	'whiten'
caru	'love'	*carreg*	'stone'
tonau	'tunes'	*tonnau*	'waves'
Tori	'Tory'	*torri*	'break'

With one exception (see **34**) *n* and *r* are doubled only in stressed syllables:

ennill	'win'	*enillodd*	'he won'

but never before a semivowel or a consonant:

gyrru	'drive'	*gyrwyr*	'drivers'
torri	'break'	*toriad*	'break'

34 The strong secondary stress on the negative prefix *an-*, however, does support a double consonant:

annedwydd	'unhappy'
annaturiol	'unnatural'
annoeth	'unwise'
annheilwng	'unworthy'

In all polysyllables quoted so far in this section, stress falls on the penult.

35 Where stress occurs finally and is not marked by -*h*-, it can be shown by means of the diacritic ´, or a circumflex:

parhau	'continue'
parhad	'continuation'
mwynhau	'enjoy'
mwynhad	'enjoyment'
eglurhad	'explanation'
crynhoi	'gather'
gwacáu	'empty'
dwysáu	'intensify'
rysáit	'recipe'
agosáu	'approach'
dicléin	'consumption'
tristáu	'grieve'
carafán	'caravan'

gwacâd	'evacuation'
arwyddocâd	'significance'
canŵ	'canoe'
parêd	'parade'
tatŵ	'tatoo'
sigâr	'cigar'
balŵn	'balloon'
cartŵn	'cartoon'

36 Final stress is not always marked:

Cymraeg	'Welsh'
paratoi	'prepare'
cyfleu	'imply'
preswylfeydd	'dwelling places'
dileu	'delete'

37 Where the simple vowel is the result of contraction, or is the final stressed vowel, the circumflex accent is always selected, whether there be an *h* in the final syllable or not:

iachâ	'he/she cures'
iachâd	'cure'
caniatâ	'he/she permits'
bwytâf	'I shall eat'
casâf	'I shall hate'
parhânt	'they will continue'
nesânt	'they will draw near'
esmwythâ	'he/she will ease'
canfûm	'I perceived'
dramâu	'plays'
themâu	'themes'
operâu	'operas'
bwâu	'arches'

It also occurs in

amhûr	'impure'
amhêr	'insipid'

38 In unstressed syllables the vowel is always short:

lluddedig	'weary'
problem	'problem'
ychwanegu	'add'

ymbil	'implore'
cyfarwyddiadur	'directory'

39 In the following words primary stress falls on the penult and the vowel *w* is marked by a circumflex:

ymhŵedd	'beseech'
pŵer	'power'
(y)rŵan	'now'

40 The diphthong *ai* (when it realizes a contracted form of *a* + *ai*), the diphthong *oi* (when it realizes a contracted form of *o* + *ai*) and the diphthong *au* (when it realizes a contracted form of *a* + *au*) carry the circumflex:

gwnâi	(<*gwna-ai*)	'he could (would) do'
trôi	(<*tro-ai*)	'he could (would) turn'
rhôi	(<*rho-ai*)	'he could (would) give'
plâu	(<*pla-au*)	'plagues'

41 The circumflex is used on the initial element of the falling diphthong *wy* and on the second element of the rising diphthong *wy*, primarily to distinguish between words orthographically alike but different in meaning:

gŵydd	'goose', presence'
gwŷdd	'trees, loom'
gŵyr	'he/she knows; crooked'
gwŷr	'men'

Where *g-* has been subject to soft mutation (see **47**) the circumflex distinguishes between:

ŵyl		'he/she weeps'
wŷl	(<*gwŷl*)	'he/she sees'
ŵyn		'lambs'
wyn	(<*gwyn*)	'white'
wŷn	(<*gwŷn*)	'ache'
ŵyr		'grandson'
wŷr	(<*gwŷr*)	'men'

42 In some borrowed words stress falls on the pre-penultima:

testament	'testament'
sacrament	'sacrament'
polisi	'policy'

ambiwlans	'ambulance'
melodi	'melody'
paragraff	'paragraph'

In *cárnifal* 'carnival' the stress is marked and in *swôleg* 'zoology' the unstressed vowel carries a circumflex. With the addition of a syllable stress reverts to the penult:

paragraffau	'paragraphs'
testamentau	'testaments'
swolegol	'zoological' (also *swôlegol*)

Diaeresis

43 The diaeresis consists of two dots placed over a vowel and is used to denote a stressed penultimate vowel:

gweddïo	'pray'
elïau	'ointments'
crëwr	'creator'
saernïo	'fashion'
crëyr	'heron'
copïo	'copy'
düwch	'gloom'
ffansïol	'fanciful'
gwäell	'knitting-needle'
sïo	'hiss'
cwmnïau	'companies'
twrcïod	'turkeys'
gïau	'sinews'
ysbïwr	'spy'
gwnïad	'sewing'
academïau	'academies'
saernïaeth	'construction'
heresïau	'heresies'
Llandybïe	

In *naif* 'naïve' the stressed ultima carries the diaeresis. Note also the diaeresis in the following:

troëdig	'repugnant'
tröedigaeth	'conversion'

Hyphen

44 The hyphen is inserted:

(i) to link loose compounds (see **332–333**) formed from *cyd-*, 'co-, fellow, joint':

cyd-Gristnogion	'fellow Christians'
cyd-aelod	'fellow member'
cyd-etifedd	'joint-heir'

(ii) to link loose compounds formed from *cyd-*, *cam-* 'wrong, mis-', and a monosyllable:

cyd-fyw	'live together'
cyd-ddwyn	'bear with others'
cyd-gwrdd	'meet together'
cyd-fynd	'accompany, concur'
cam-farn	'unjust judgement, error'
cam-drin	'abuse'
cam-drefn	'disorder'
cam-dro	'bad turn'

(iii) in strict and loose compounds to separate the constituents *dd-d*, *d-d*, *t-h*:

lladd-dy	'slaughter house'
cybydd-dod	'avarice'
cyd-dyfu	'grow together'
hwynt-hwy	3 pl. reduplicated personal pron.

(iv) in loose compounds to link elements that are equally stressed:

di-fai	'without blame'
di-boen	'without pain'
di-flas	'without taste'
bardd-bregethwr	'preacher-poet'
di-ben-draw	'endless'
ail-law	'second hand'
di-asgwrn-cefn	'spineless'
môr-forwyn	'mermaid'
chwit-chwat	'shilly-shallying'

(v) on occasion to link the different elements of a place-name:

Llanarmon-yn-Iâl

Llanbedr-y-fro
Cil-y-cwm
Clas-ar-Wy
Llys-y-frân
Llys-faen
Llanrhaeadr-ym-Mochnant
Rhyd-y-mwyn
Tal-y-bont
Morfa-mawr
Nant-y-moel
Ystrad-ffin
Ynys-y-bŵl

(vi) in combinations such as:

is-lywydd	'vice-president'
is-bwyllgor	'sub-committee'
lled-orwedd	'half-lying'
lled-wyro	'half-inclined'
ôl-nodiad	'postscript'
cyn-gadeirydd	'former chairman'
cyn-oesoedd	'early ages'
chwaer naill-ran	'half-sister'
dyn naill-fraich	'one-armed man'

Apostrophe

45 The apostrophe is used:

(i) with the definite article following a vowel or diphthong (see **158**):

y gŵr a'r wraig   'the husband and the wife'
mae'r plant yn cysgu   'the children are sleeping'

(ii) it is used as shortened form of the adverbial *y(r)* after a vowel where there is a close relationship between the two words between which it is placed:

Heddiw, yn y man lle'r adeiladwyd yr hen gastell ni cheir ond adfeilion.
'Today, in the place where the old castle was built one will find only ruins'

(iii) it is used in *'n* for the verbal adjunct *yn* and the predicative *yn* (see **278**) following a vowel or diphthong:

mae hi'n canu	'she is singing'
'rwyf i'n gweithio	'I am working'
canai'n swynol	'he/she sang sweetly'

(iv) it is used to signify that a final consonant that is normally present has been lost:

cry' for *cryf* 'strong'
gwelan' for *gwelant* 'they will see'
hapusa' for *hapusaf* 'happiest'

(v) in poetry and prose it is used in the form *f'* for *fy* 'my' and *d'* for *dy* 'your' before words beginning with a vowel (see also **108, 215**):

Dydd arall o derm f'einioes treiglo wnaeth
'Another day of my life's term has passed'
(John Morris Jones (1894–1929))

Eiliad dy farwolaeth oedd eiliad d' enedigaeth di
'The moment of your death was the moment of your birth'
(Alan Llwyd (1948–   ))

Where *fy* 'my' is lost completely following a vowel, the apostrophe is appended to the following word:

Mae iaith bereiddia'r ddaear hon
  Ar enau 'nghariad i.
'The sweetest language in this world
  Is on my lover's lips'
(John Morris Jones (1894–1929))

Yn awr prinder y gweryd
Cei orau 'mord, bynciwr mud.
'At the time of the earth's scarcity
You will have my table's best, mute songster'
(T. Llew Jones (1915–   ))

(vi) it is used to signify the loss of a vowel or syllable initially and medially:

Deunaw oed dy i'engoed teg
'Eighteen years your fair youthfulness'
(Dic Jones (1934–   ))

Canaf i gerdd ddihafal
'Deryn Du mewn derwen dal
'I shall praise a blackbird's
Incomparable song in a tall oak'
(T. Llew Jones (1915–))

l'engoed, *'deryn* are compressed forms of *ieuengoed* 'youth', *aderyn* 'bird'.

(vii) in poetry and prose it is used with the infixed forms of the prefixed and affixed personal pronouns (see **217**):

Â'th lais dilledaist y llwyn
'With your voice you clothed the shrub'
(T. Llew Jones (1915–))

Casâf Ef a'i ddeddfau a'i bobl
'I hate Him and his laws and his people'
(John Bunyan, 1962: 36)

Fe'm cyffrowyd ac fe'm synnwyd
'I was excited and I was amazed'
(*Y Faner*, 19 Ionawr 1991: 21)

Capitals

46 Capitals are called in Welsh *priflythrennau* or *llythrennau bras*, small letters *llythrennau bach*. Capital letters are used:

(i) at the beginning of sentences

(ii) to specify proper names (for example, persons, places, titles of printed works, days of the week, the names of the months – but not usually the seasons; the planets – but not the earth, the sun or the moon; the names of government institutions and movements):

Silvan Evans
Llanelli
Y Faner
Traddodiad Llenyddol Morgannwg 'The Literary Tradition of Glamorgan'
Y Nos, y Niwl a'r Ynys 'The Night, the Mist and the Island'
Geiriadur Prifysgol Cymru 'The University of Wales Dictionary'

ar y Sul 'on Sunday'
Tachwedd 'November'
Neifion 'Neptune'
Y Swyddfa Gymreig 'The Welsh Office'
Llyfrgell Genedlaethol Cymru 'The National Library of Wales'
Urdd Gobaith Cymru 'The Welsh League of Youth'

(iii) with adjectives formed from proper nouns:

cyfnod y Tuduriaid   'the Tudor period'
y Methodistiaid Calfinaidd   'the Calvinistic Methodists'

(iv) in abbreviations:

GPC
Geiriadur Prifysgol Cymru   'The University of Wales
                                 Dictionary'

LlGC
Llyfrgell Genedlaethol Cymru 'The National Library of Wales'

(v) for titles:

Syr John Rhŷs   'Sir John Rhŷs'
yr Esgob Burgess   'Bishop Burgess'

Mutation

Introduction

47 Welsh, like all the Celtic languages, shows initial consonant mutation. The term 'mutation' refers to the substitution of an initial consonant in a word for another consonant, under various morphological or syntactic conditions.

In Welsh, mutations are traditionally grouped into three sets: Soft Mutation, Nasal Mutation, Spirant Mutation.

The changes that occur as a result of mutation are listed in table 4 for ease of reference.

Spirant mutation also requires the addition of *h-* to words with initial vowels.

Throughout the sections on initial consonant mutation the radical form is noted within parentheses on the right-hand side of the page.

The Soft Mutation

48 The initial consonant of feminine singular nouns following the article is subject to mutation:

y gyllell	'the knife'	(*cyllell*)
y fam	'the mother'	(*mam*)

Table 4

Initial consonant	Soft mutation	Nasal mutation	Spirant mutation
p	b	mh	ph
t	d	nh	th
c	g	ngh	ch
b	f	m	
d	dd	n	
g	—	ng	
ll	l		
rh	r		
m	f		

y fuwch	'the cow'	(*buwch*)
o'r ardd	'from the garden'	(*gardd*)
i'r dref	'to the town'	(*tref*)

Pobl 'people' is a feminine singular noun and as such the initial consonant is subject to soft mutation following the article:

y bobl	'the people'	(*pobl*)

The mutation in the plural form following the article, however, is highly irregular, because plural nouns are not normally subject to soft mutation following the article:

pobloedd	*y bobloedd*

The initial consonant of an adjective following *pobl, pobloedd* is subject to mutation (see **50**):

pobl dda	'a good people'
pobloedd fawrion	'a mighty people'

The radical also occurs following *pobloedd*.
    The dual plural is also subject to mutation following the article:

gefell	'twin'	*yr efeilliaid*	(*gefeilliaid*)

Examples of the dual plural are rare.
    Ll- and *rh-* are not subject to mutation following the article in feminine singular nouns:

y llysywen	'the eel'

o'r llyfrgell	'from the library'
i'r rhyd	'to the ford'
y rhaff	'the rope'

Many names of places, mountains etc., are feminine singular nouns preceded by the article, which causes mutation:

Y Waun, Y Gelli, Y Foel, Yr Wyddfa, Y Fan

The article may be understood and omitted, but the noun is still subject to mutation:

Felindre, Faerdre, Gilfach-wen, Waun-fawr

Sometimes the mutation is irregular because no article is understood before the feminine singular noun:

Gelli'r Ynn, Waunarlwydd, Gorseinon

The radical forms are *Celli, Gwaun, Cors*.

Note

The borrowed fem. sing. nouns in *g-*, *gêm* 'game', *gôl* 'goal', resist mutation following the article: *y gêm* 'the game', *y gôl* 'the goal'.

49 The masculine and feminine numerals *dau*, *dwy* 'two' mutate following the article:

y ddwy	'the two' (feminine)	(*dwy*)
y ddwy chwaer	'the two sisters'	(*dwy*)
y ddau	'the two' (masculine)	(*dau*)
y ddau afal	'the two apples'	(*dau*)

Mutation also occurs in *deu-* and *dwy-* in compounds:

y ddwyfron	'the breasts'	(*dwyfron*)
y ddeuddyn	'the persons'	(*deuddyn*)

Note

Dwylo 'hands' and *deuddeg* 'twelve' resist mutation following the article: *y dwylo* 'the hands', *y deuddeg* 'the twelve'.

50 The initial consonant of an adjective following a feminine singular noun is subject to mutation:

rhaglen ddiddorol	'an interesting programme'	(*diddorol*)
triniaeth lawfeddygol	'surgical treatment'	(*llawfeddygol*)
gwraig olygus	'an attractive woman'	(*golygus*)

The same rule persists when more than one adjective follows the fem. sing. noun:

cyfres fer flasus	'a short interesting series'	(*ber, blasus*)
merch fach welw	'a small pale girl'	(*bach, gwelw*)
cath ddu raenus	'a sleek black cat'	(*du, graenus*)

The radical is often found following -*s*:

nos da	'good night'
yr wythnos diwethaf	'last week'

After a fem. sing. noun *braf* 'fine' is not mutated in the literary language:

noson braf	'a fine evening'

Braf, however, is subject to soft mutation in some varieties of southern Welsh. *Braf* also resists mutation following *mor* (see **52**):

Mor braf yw clywed emyn Cymraeg
'So pleasant is it to hear a Welsh hymn'
      (Siôn Eirian, 1979: 26–7)

and also following the predicative *yn* (see **54**):

Byddai hynny'n braf er cymaint y boen
'That would be fine despite the pain'
      (Kate Roberts, 1976: 75)

In varieties of northern Welsh, *bach* 'small' does not mutate following fem. sing. nouns. Adjectives that follow a proper noun may undergo mutation when the reference is to a particular individual, as the equivalent of *N* + the + *adj.*:

Arthur Fawr	'Arthur the Great'	(*mawr*)
Hywel Dda	'Hywel the Good'	(*da*)
Selyf Ddoeth	'Solomon the Wise'	(*doeth*)

The adjective, however, frequently resists mutation:

Ieuan Du   *Gwilym Tew*   *Gwenno Llwyd*   *Rhodri Mawr*

Proper nouns may mutate following a fem. sing. noun:

Gŵyl Ddewi	'St David's Day'	(*Dewi*)
Ffair Fartin	'St Martin's fair-day'	(*Martin*)
Eglwys Rufain	'The Roman Catholic Church'	(*Rhufain*)

Examples occur of the proper noun resisting mutation:

Gŵyl Dewi	'St David's Day'
Ynys Môn	'Anglesey'
Dinas Dafydd	'David's City'

On mutation of the adjective following the plural noun *pobloedd* see **48**.

51 When a compound (see **333**) is formed by placing an adjective before a noun (masc. or fem.), the noun is subject to mutation:

(i) strict compounds:

crom	'bowed'	+ *bach*	'hook'	> *cromfach*	'bracket'
glas	'young'	+ *llanc*	'youth'	> *glaslanc*	'youth'
haf	'summer'	+ *dydd*	'day'	> *hafddydd*	'summer's day'
hwyl	'sail'	+ *pren*	'tree'	> *hwylbren*	'mast'

(ii) loose compounds:

hen	'old'	+ *lle*	'place'	> *hen le*	'old place'
gwir	'true'	+ *dyn*	'man'	> *gwir ddyn*	'true man'
melys	'sweet'	+ *llais*	'voice'	> *melys lais*	'sweet voice'
annwyl	'dear'	+ *gwlad*	'country'	> *annwyl wlad*	'dear country'
rhyw	'some'	+ *prynhawn*	'afternoon'	> *rhyw brynhawn*	'some afternoon'

Rhyw is used with verb-nouns to denote that an action is imprecise or wide of the mark; it triggers mutation:

Rwy'n rhyw led-gredu fod y methiant hwn yn anochel   (*lled-gredu*)
'I half suspect that this failure is inevitable'
    (Bryan Martin Davies, 1988: 12)

Byddai Mererid yn aml yn rhyw ganu wrthi ei hun   (*canu*)
'Mererid would frequently sing a little to herself'
    (Rhiannon Davies Jones, 1989: 36)

Nouns following *amryw* (<*am* + *rhyw*) 'several', *cyfryw* (<*cyf* + *rhyw*) 'such', *unrhyw* (<*un* + *rhyw*) 'any' mutate:

amryw bethau	'several things'	(*pethau*)
y cyfryw rai	'such ones'	(*rhai*)
unrhyw bryd	'any time'	(*pryd*)

In poetry and to a lesser extent in prose, most adjectives may occur before the noun they modify, but this is a literary device; the noun is subject to mutation:

Daw arall ddydd ac arall ddwylo   (*dydd, dwylo*)
'Another day and other hands will come'
   (Rhiannon Davies Jones, 1977: 172)

mawrion weithredoedd Duw   (*gweithredoedd*)
'the great works of God'
   (Acts 2: 11)

Rhyw ddedwydd lonydd le   (*lle*)
Llonydd le ar dyle neu dwyn . . .   (*lle*)
'Some happy peaceful place
A peaceful place on hill or knoll'
   (David James Jones, Gwenallt (1899–1968))

An adjective occurring between the article and a fem. sing. noun mutates:

y ddu nos	'the dark night'	(*du*)
y lwyd wawr	'the grey dawn'	(*llwyd*)

When the noun is understood and omitted the mutation remains:

y fechan	'the little (girl)'	(*bechan*)
y lonnaf	'the happiest (woman)'	(*llonnaf*)

52 Adjectives following *cyn, mor* (see **198–199**) mutate:

Mor deg oedd ac mor osgeiddig   (*teg, gosgeiddig*)
'It was so fair and so graceful'
   (Rhiannon Davies Jones, 1987: 171)

Yr oedd gwallt ei ben yn wyn fel gwlân,
cyn wynned â'r eira   (*gwynned*)
'The hair on his head was white like wool,
as white as snow'
   (*Y Faner*, 23/30 Rhagfyr 1988: 7)

Braf 'fine, pleasant' resists mutation (see **50**).
Ll- and *rh-* do not mutate following *cyn, mor*:

mor llydan	'so broad'	*mor rhwydd*	'so easy'
cyn llawned â	'as full as'	*cyn rhwydded â*	'as easy as'

53 When the equative (see **199** (iii)) is used to express surprise it mutates unless preceded by the conjunction *a* 'and':

Fyrred yw bywyd!   (*byrred*)
'How short life is!'

Leied a ddywedir am yrfa S L ym Mhrifysgol
Lerpwl!   (*lleied*)
'How little is said of S L's career at Liverpool
University!'
> (*Y Faner*, 17 Chwefror 1989: 5)

Surprise may not be intended but mutation still occurs:

Gynted ag y deuent i gyffiniau Nant Conwy
dechreuai hewian arni   (*cynted*)
'As soon as they would come to the Nant Conwy
area she would begin to nag her'
> (Rhiannon Davies Jones, 1989: 103)

54 Nouns and adjectives following the predicative *yn* (see **278**)
mutate:

Rwy'n ddyn rhesymol   (*dyn*)
'I am a reasonable man'
> (Robat Gruffudd, 1986: 260)

Roedd y caffe'n wag   (*gwag*)
'The café was empty'
> (Emyr Humphreys, 1981: 80)

Ll- and *rh-* do not mutate following the predicative *yn*:

Byddai'n rhaid iddynt fynd adref
'It would be necessary for them to go home'
> (Kate Roberts, 1972: 23)

Yr oeddem ninnau'r plant yn llygaid ac yn glustiau i gyd
'We children were all eyes and ears'
> (Rhiannon Davies Jones, 1977: 101)

Braf 'fine' keeps the radical following the predicative *yn* (see **50**).

55 The superlative (see **201**) used adverbially mutates:

Dere draw gyntaf y gelli di   (*cyntaf*)
'Come over as quickly (lit. 'the quickest') as you can'

Mae hi'n aros gyda ni fynychaf   (*mynychaf*)
'She stays with us usually (lit. 'most frequently')'

Nouns following the superlative may select either mutation or the
radical consonant:

Ardderchocaf frenin . . . ac anrhydeddus
ddeiliaid   (*brenin*)
'Most splendid king . . . and honourable subjects'
    (Rhiannon Davies Jones, 1987: 177)

Mynnai rhai iddo ganu'r 'Deryn Pur' yn olaf cân ar ei
wely angau
'Some insisted that he sang "Deryn Pur" as a final
song on his death bed'
    (Hywel Teifi Edwards, 1989: 132)

eithaf Gymro   (*Cymro*)
'virtuous (lit. 'utmost') Welshman'

eithaf peth
'advantageous thing'

Prif 'chief' always precedes the noun and causes mutation, but there
is no mutation following *cyntaf* 'first':

prif ddynion   (*dynion*)
'chief men'

y cyntaf peth
'the first thing'

56 *Po* (see **201** (ii), **418**) is followed by the mutation of the
superlative:

gorau po gyntaf   (*cyntaf*)
'the sooner the better'

Po fwyaf o ddiod a gaiff mwyaf o grefydd fydd yn
ei siarad   (*mwyaf*)
'The more drink he has the more religion he will
talk'
    (John Bunyan, 1962: 42)

Cadarna'r mur po arwa'r garreg   (*garwa*)
'The stronger the wall, the rougher the stone'
    (Proverb)

Formerly *po* was followed by the radical:

Po callaf y dyn, anamlaf ei eiriau
'The wiser the man, the fewer his words'
    (Proverb)

Po mwyaf y gwaharddodd efe iddynt, mwy o lawer
y cyhoeddasant
'The more he forbade them, the more they published'
(Mark 7: 36) (1955 translation)

57 Fem. sing. nouns mutate following the numeral *un* 'one':

un ferch	'one girl'	(*merch*)
un gath	'one cat'	(*cath*)
un wraig	'one wife'	(*gwraig*)

Ll- and *rh-* in fem. sing. nouns do not mutate following *un*:

un llaw	'one hand'	*un rhwyd*	'one net'

An adjective following *un* substituting for a fem. sing. noun mutates:

Heblaw bod yn gyfrol bwysig, mae hon hefyd
yn un ddiddorol i bori ynddi   (*diddorol*)
'Apart from being an important volume, it is
also an interesting one to browse in'
(Aneirin Talfan Davies, 1976: 200)

un ryfedd yw hi   'she is a strange one'   (*rhyfedd*)

When *un* has the meaning 'similar', both masc. and fem. sing. nouns
mutate:

Yr oedd tyrfa o Siapaneaid o'r un feddwl â mi   (*meddwl*)
'There was a party of Japanese of similar mind to me'
(*Y Faner*, 16 Chwefror 1990: 9)

Mae'r plentyn yr un ben â'i dad   (*pen*)
'The child has a head like his father's'
(The child is as clever as his father)

When *un* means 'the one and the same', fem. sing. nouns mutate:

Ceir glosau Cymraeg o'r un ganrif ar eiriau
Lladin yn y testun   (*canrif*)
'Welsh glosses from the same century occur
on Latin words in the text'
(Geraint Bowen, 1970: 16)

Rhannai'r ddau yr un uchelgais, yr un gwely,
a'r un gred ddiniwed   (*cred*)

'The two shared the same ambition, the same bed,
and the same naïve belief'

(Eigra Lewis Roberts, 1981: 53)

58 Fem. sing. nouns are mutated following the feminine numeral *dwy* 'two':

dwy ferch	'two girls'	(*merch*)
dwy lwy	'two spoons'	(*llwy*)
dwy gath	'two cats'	(*cath*)

59 Masc. sing. nouns are mutated following the masculine numeral *dau* 'two':

dau frawd	'two brothers'	(*brawd*)
dau lo	'two calves'	(*llo*)

Some forms resist mutation following *dau* (see **160**); the following are frequently found:

dau cant	*deucant*	'two hundred'
dau pen	*deupen*	'two ends'
dau tu	*deutu*	'two sides'
	deuparth	'two parts, two thirds'
dau cymaint		'twice as much'

60 Numerals occasionally follow plural nouns and are mutated, but this is a literary device:

tafodau fil	'thousand tongues'	(*mil*)
brodyr dri	'three brothers'	(*tri*)

61 Feminine ordinal numbers are mutated following the article:

y bedwaredd bennod	'the fourth chapter'	(*pedwaredd*)
y drydedd salm ar hugain	'the twenty-third psalm'	(*trydedd*)
y bedwaredd	'the fourth'	(*pedwaredd*)
y drydedd ar hugain	'the twenty-third'	(*trydedd*)

62 Masc. and fem. nouns are mutated following the ordinal *ail* 'second':

ei ail wraig	'his second wife'	(*gwraig*)
yr ail blentyn	'the second child'	(*plentyn*)
ail gar	'a second car'	(*car*)

Fem. sing. nouns are mutated following the other ordinals:

y drydedd ferch	'the third girl'	(*merch*)
y bedwaredd gaseg	'the fourth mare'	(*caseg*)
y bumed waith	'the fifth time'	(*gwaith*)
y seithfed ddafad ar hugain	'the twenty-seventh sheep'	(*dafad*)
pumed car	'a fifth car'	
y trydydd mab	'the third son'	

63 Nouns are mutated following the 2 sing. prefixed pronoun *dy* 'thy, your' and the 3 sing. masc. prefixed pronoun *ei* 'his' (see **214**):

> *Sut mae dy dad?*   (*tad*)
> 'How is your father?'
> > (Gweneth Lilly, 1984: 24)

> *Beth yw dy wleidyddiaeth di, Owen?*   (*gwleidyddiaeth*)
> 'What are your politics, Owen?'
> > (Emyr Humphreys, 1986: 21)

> *Fe hoffai fynd i newid ei grys*   (*crys*)
> 'He would like to go to change his shirt'
> > (R. Cyril Hughes, 1976: 201)

64 Nouns are mutated following the 2 sing. infixed pronoun *'th* 'thy, your' and the 3 sing. masc. infixed pronoun *'i, 'w* 'his' (see **217**):

> *Mae dy lygaid di mor las a'th wallt di mor felyn*   (*gwallt*)
> 'Your eyes are so blue and your hair so fair'
> > (Rhiannon Davies Jones, 1985: 6)

> *Casâf Ef a'i ddeddfau a'i bobl*   (*deddfau, pobl*)
> 'I hate Him and his laws and his people'
> > (John Bunyan, 1962: 36)

> *Ces beth gwaith i'w berswadio*   (*perswadio*)
> 'I had some trouble persuading him'
> > (Robat Gruffudd, 1986: 241)

65 Nouns are mutated following *wele* 'behold', *dyma* 'here is', *dyna* 'there is':

> *Wele ragflas o rai o gredoau pwysicaf Luther*   (*rhagflas*)
> 'Behold a foretaste of some of Luther's most
> important beliefs'
> > (R. Geraint Gruffydd, 1988: 4)

Dyma eiriau o lythyr gan Humphrey Foulkes   (*geiriau*)
'Here are words from a letter by Humphrey Foulkes'
   (Gwyn Thomas, 1971: 22)

Dyna gri llawer y dyddiau hyn   (*cri*)
'That is the cry of many these days'
   (*Y Faner*, 14 Ebrill 1989: 4)

66 Nouns following the interrogative pronoun *pa* 'what' (see **235**) mutate:

Pa ddewis sydd gan ddyn . . .?   (*dewis*)
'What choice does a man have . . .?'
   (Eigra Lewis Roberts, 1988: 81)

Pa fath o bobl, yng nghanol yr unfed ganrif ar
bymtheg, a oedd yn awyddus i ddysgu Cymraeg, a
beth oedd eu cymhellion?   (*math*)
'What sort of people, in the middle of the
seventeenth century, were keen to learn Welsh,
and what were their motives?'
   (Geraint Bowen, 1970: 39)

67 Nouns following *naill* '(the) one':

Mae'r naill genhedlaeth yn dilyn y llall   (*cenhedlaeth*)
'One generation follows the other'
   (R. Gerallt Jones, 1977: 41)

| *dyn naill-fraich* | 'a one-armed man' | (*braich*) |
| *chwaer naill-ran* | 'a half-sister' | (*rhan*) |

Note
Mutation does not occur in the compounds *neilltu* 'one side', *neillparth* 'one part'.

68 In the following genitival construction the second element mutates:

(i) feminine singular noun + singular noun:

| *carreg filltir* | 'milestone' | (*milltir*) |
| *cot law* | 'raincoat' | (*glaw*) |

(ii) feminine singular noun + verb-noun:

| *gwialen bysgota* | 'fishing-rod' | (*pysgota*) |
| *ffon gerdded* | 'walking-stick' | (*cerdded*) |

(iii) feminine singular noun + plural noun:

sioe flodau	'flower show'	(*blodau*)
siop lyfrau	'book shop'	(*llyfrau*)

(iv) feminine singular noun + noun denoting matter or measure:

odyn galch	'lime kiln'	(*calch*)
potel beint	'pint bottle'	(*peint*)

69 Mutation follows the prepositions *am, ar, at, dan, dros, drwy, heb, hyd, i, o, gan, wrth*:

am bunt	'for £1'	(*punt*)
o law i law	'from hand to hand'	(*llaw*)
heb waith a heb dir	'without work and without land'	(*gwaith, tir*)
ar fwrdd y gegin	'on the kitchen table'	(*bwrdd*)
at ddrws y tŷ	'towards the house door'	(*drws*)
dan fawd y wraig	'under the wife's thumb'	(*bawd*)
dros glawdd yr ardd	'over the garden hedge/wall'	(*clawdd*)
drwy ddŵr a thân	'through fire and water'	(*dŵr*)
hyd farw	'until death'	(*marw*)
wrth glwyd yr ardd	'at the garden gate'	(*clwyd*)
fe'm trawyd gan bêl	'I was hit by a ball'	(*pêl*)

70 When the object of the simple verb is not preceded by the article or any other word but follows immediately after either (a) the verb, or (b) the verb + an auxiliary pronoun, or (c) the subject, it is mutated:

Mi rof fwled trwy dy ben   (*bwled*)
'I'll put a bullet through your head'
    (Harri Williams, 1978: 67)

Codais goler fy nghot   (*coler*)
'I raised my coat collar'
    (Wil Roberts, 1985: 34)

Mae naw mlynedd er pan gawson ni ddillad newydd   (*dillad*)
'It's nine years since we had new clothes'
    (Kate Roberts, 1976: 26)

Cafodd Lloyd lwyddiant nodedig   (*llwyddiant*)
'Lloyd had a notable success'
    (Geraint H. Jenkins, 1983: 78)

71 The independent personal pronouns (see **211**) are mutated as objects of impersonal forms:

> *Poenir dithau*   (*tithau*)
> 'You will be punished'
> > (Luke 16: 25)

72 In an abnormal sentence (see **351**) the particle *a* causes mutation of the following verb:

> *Mi a rodiaf yn nerth yr Arglwydd Dduw*   (*rhodiaf*)
> 'I shall walk in the might of the Lord God'
> > (John Bunyan, 1962: 39)

> *Chwi a alwyd o'ch gorchwyl*   (*galwyd*)
> 'You were called from your tasks'
> > (Mair Wyn Hughes, 1983: 7)

The particle may be omitted but the verb is still subject to mutation:

> *Tymor arall ddaw ac fe fydd awdurdodau'r sir*
> *yn dweud fel arfer bod pethau am fod yn wahanol* (*daw*)
> 'Another season will come and the county authorities
> will say as usual that things will change'
>
> (*Golwg*, 8 Medi 1988: 15)

73 Verbs are mutated following the relative pronoun *a*:

> *Y dreth bwysicaf, a'r drymaf, oedd y Dreth Dir*
> *a basiwyd yn 1693*   (*pasiwyd*)
> 'The most important tax, and the heaviest, was the
> Land Tax that was passed in 1693'
> > (Geraint H. Jenkins, 1983: 58)

The interrogative pronouns *pwy* 'who', *beth*, *pa beth* 'what' may be followed by a relative clause:

> *Pwy a ddyrchefid yn esgob yn ei le tybed?*   (*dyrchefid*)
> 'Who would be elevated bishop in his place?'
> > (R. Cyril Hughes, 1975: 49)

> *Pa beth a roddwch i mi?* (1955 translation)   (*rhoddwch*)
> *Beth a rowch imi?* (1988 translation)   (*rhowch*)
> 'What will you give me?'
> > (Matt. 26: 15)

The relative pronoun is often omitted but the verb is still mutated:

> *Pwy all roi cyngor i mi?*   (*gall*)
> 'Who can give me advice?'
>> (Emyr Humphreys, 1986: 59)

> *Beth ddigwyddodd i'r côr?*   (*digwyddodd*)
> 'What happened to the choir?'
>> (Emyr Humphreys, 1986: 98)

74 The complement of *sydd*, *sy* (see **227**) is mutated whether or not preceded by the particle *yn/'n*:

Ef sydd yn ben	'He is chief'	(*pen*)
Hynny sydd orau	'That is best'	(*gorau*)
Yr hyn sydd raid sydd raid	'What must be must be'	(*rhaid*)

75 In copula clauses that select Complement + Predicate + Subject structure, *bod* (*b-* forms) is mutated following the complement (see **279**, **349** (iv)):

> *Crwydryn fu Liam erioed*   (*bu*)
> 'Liam had always been a wanderer'
>> (Gweneth Lilly, 1981: 9)

> *Chi fydd y ddwy smartia yn y briodas*   (*bydd*)
> 'You will be the smartest two at the wedding'
>> (Kate Roberts, 1976: 27)

> *Crydcymalau fyddai ei ran bellach*   (*byddai*)
> 'Rheumatism would be his part from now on'
>> (Marion Eames, 1982: 11)

> *Ofer fai ceisio'i ddilyn o orchest i orchest*   (*bai*)
> 'It would be extravagant to attempt to follow
> him from exploit to exploit'
>> (Hywel Teifi Edwards, 1989: 113)

76 *Sut?* 'What kind of?' causes mutation of the following noun:

> *Sut flwyddyn fyddai hi?*   (*blwyddyn*)
> 'What kind of year would it be?'
>> (T. Glynne Davies, 1974: 33)

> *A sut ornest a welwyd ar y Strade y Sadwrn diwethaf?*   (*gornest*)
> 'And what kind of contest was seen at Stradey last Saturday?'
>> (*Y Faner*, 20 Ionawr 1989: 21)

Sut fagwraeth gâi fy wyrion i?   (*magwraeth*)
'What kind of upbringing would my grandchildren
have?'
  (Emyr Humphreys, 1981: 24)

77 In informal texts and in varieties of spoken Welsh *sut?* 'how?',
pryd? 'when what time?', *faint?* 'how much, how many?', may cause
mutation of the following verb:

Sut fedraist ti dynnu dy hun oddi wrth y moch?   (*medraist*)
'How were you able to drag yourself away from
the pigs?'
  (Jane Edwards, 1976: 78)

Pryd fuost ti ym Mhlas Iolyn ddiwethaf?   (*diwethaf*)
'When were you at Plas Iolyn last?'
  (R. Cyril Hughes, 1975: 49)

Faint all plentyn dan bump ei gofio?   (*gall*)
'How much can a child under five remember?'
  (Emyr Humphreys, 1981: 39)

78 Singular and plural nouns undergo mutation after *ychydig* 'a
little, few':

ychydig gariad	'a little love'	(*cariad*)
ychydig bethau	'a few things'	(*pethau*)

79 A noun in apposition to a proper noun is subject to mutation:

Pyfog butain   (*putain*)
'Pyfog the whore'
  (Rhiannon Davies Jones, 1977: 99)

Islwyn Ffowc, lenor   (*llenor*)
'Islwyn Ffowc, author'
  (*Y Faner*, 30 Mawrth 1979: 15)

Iago fab Sebedeus   (*mab*)
'James son of Zebedee'
  (Matt. 4: 21)

Ioan Fedyddiwr   (*Bedyddiwr*)
'John the Baptist'

Gwilym druan   (*truan*)
'poor Gwilym'

Truan is also mutated following common nouns and in the construction *druan o*:

> *Fydd y taeog druan fyth uwch bawd sawdl*   (*truan*)
> 'The poor serf will never be better off'
>   (Rhiannon Davies Jones, 1977: 37)

> *Druan ohonom, druan o'n plant*   (*truan*)
> 'Poor us, our poor children'
>   (*Y Faner*, 21 Ebrill 1989: 7)

When the noun in apposition follows the auxiliary pronoun or a common noun it is mutated:

> *Treuliasom ni blant lawer i brynhawn hyfryd*
> *o haf yno*   (*plant*)
> 'We children spent many a happy summer's afternoon
> there'
>   (Aneirin Talfan Davies, 1972: 237)

> *Soniodd ef wedyn am ei gefndyr, feibion*
> *Gruffudd ap Rhys o Ddeheubarth*   (*meibion*)
> 'Then he spoke of his cousins, the sons of
> Gruffudd ap Rhys from Deheubarth'
>   (Rhiannon Davies Jones, 1977: 145)

The name of a female historical figure, following a common noun which denotes office or a title, is mutated:

> *y Forwyn Fair/y Wyry Fair*   'the Virgin Mary'   (*Mair*)

but in more recent examples the mutation is resisted:

> *y Frenhines Mari*   'Queen Mary'

See also **132**.

Note
The mutation is exceptional in *yr Arglwydd Dduw* 'the Lord God'.

80   The pre-verbal particles *mi, fe* (see **336**) cause mutation:

> *fe ddywed John Davies Mallwyd yn ei eiriadur*   (*dywed*)
> 'John Davies of Mallwyd states in his dictionary'
>   (Geraint Bowen, 1970: 13)

Mi garwn ymhelaethu arno yn y fan yma   (*carwn*)
'I would like to enlarge upon it here'
        (Geraint Bowen, 1970: 36)

See also **212** (iv).

Note
In varieties of spoken Welsh the particles may be omitted, but the
initial consonant of the verb is still subject to mutation.

81 *Peth*, *llawer*, *pob*, *cwbl*, *digon*, *dim* are mutated when used
adverbially:

Mae hi'n well beth na ni	'She is a little better than us'	(*peth*)
Nid yw ef gartref lawer	'He is not home much'	(*llawer*)
Mae ef yn galw yma bob dydd	'He calls here every day'	(*pob*)
Mae'n gwbl ddiwerth	'It's completely worthless'	(*cwbl*)
Gweithiodd ddigon	'He worked enough'	(*digon*)
Nid af i ddim i'r dref	'I will not go to town'	(*dim*)

In informal texts and in varieties of spoken Welsh *ddim* may:

(i) negate a copula sentence (see **349** (iv)):

Ddim pysgotwr oedd y diawl
'The blighter was not a fisherman'
        (*Y Faner*, 25 Mai 1979: 18)

(ii) negate a mixed sentence (see **337** (ii), **352**):

Ddim arna' i y mae'r bai eu bod nhw yn y militia
'It's not my fault that they are in the militia'
        (T. Glynne Davies, 1974: 244)

(iii) provide a negative response:

Does dim ots 'da chi yfed ar fy ôl i?
Ddim o gwbl
'You don't object to drinking after me?
Not at all'
        (John Rowlands, 1978: 82)

(iv) add further comment to a previous statement:

Mi wna i sgwennu – ddim bob dydd cofia
'I'll write – not every day remember'
        (T. Glynne Davies, 1974: 376)

Ddim ond 'nothing but, only' may occur in informal texts:

> *'Wyt ti'n mynd i aros efo ni yn hir, hir y tro yma, Dad?'*
> *'Ddim ond tan ddydd Llun'*
> 'Are you going to stay with us a long, long while this time, Dad?'
> 'Only until Monday'
> (Gwyn ap Gwilym, 1979: 24)

Ddim ond derives from *dim ond* and the latter is common in standard Welsh:

> *Dim ond unwaith y bûm i mewn ysbyty yn glaf*
> 'Only once have I been ill in hospital'
> (John Gruffydd Jones, 1981: 11)

82 Certain verbs are used parenthetically (with mutation) to express opinion or feeling:

> *Mae'r gwynt ar y Tywyn yma yn glustiau*
> *i gyd debyga i!*　　　　　　　　　　　　　　(*tebyga*)
> 'The wind on this shore is all ears
> I believe'
> (Rhiannon Davies Jones, 1977: 26)

> *i gyfeiriad y dwyrain feddyliwn i*　　　　　(*meddyliwn*)
> 'eastwards, I would think'
> (J. G. Williams, 1978: 50)

> *Nid peth felly yw eglwys dybiaf i*　　　　　(*tybiaf*)
> 'A church is not that sort of thing I should think'
> (John Jenkins, 1978: 31)

> *Dim ond Mr Callaghan a'i gefnogwyr, gredwn i,*
> *fuasai'n dymuno gweld ddoe . . . yn dychwelyd*　　(*credwn*)
> 'Only Mr Callaghan and his supporters, I believe,
> would wish to see yesterday . . . return'
> (*Y Faner*, 30 Mawrth 1979: 3)

83 Nouns or nominal groups functioning adverbially are mutated:

> *Laweroedd o weithiau y bûm yn addoli yma yn y*
> *goedwig*　　　　　　　　　　　　　　　　(*llaweroedd*)
> 'Many times had I been to worship here in the
> woods'
> (J. G. Williams, 1978: 85)

Ymwelodd droeon â Gwenfô   (*troeon*)
'He visited Wenfoe many times'
   (Aneirin Talfan Davies, 1976: 2)

Ddeunaw mis yn ôl oedd hi   (*deunaw*)
'Eighteen months ago it was'
   (Rhiannon Thomas, 1988: 38)

Ganrif yn ôl, lleiafrif bychan a brynai bapur newydd   (*canrif*)
'A century ago, it was a small minority that would
buy a newspaper'
   (Geraint Bowen, 1976: 81)

The radical is also retained:

*Blynyddoedd lawer cyn i'r Dr Nicholas gymryd at y pwnc 'r oedd
eraill yng Nghymru wedi'u cyffroi gan bosibiliadau daeareg*
'Years before Dr Nicholas took to the subject others in Wales
had been excited by the possibilities of geology'
   (Hywel Teifi Edwards, 1980: 89)

In denoting the time of an event with *dydd* 'day', *prynhawn* 'afternoon', *bore* 'morning', varieties of northern Welsh select mutation but the radical remains in southern varieties.

84 Nouns, adjectives and verb-nouns are subject to mutation following the conjunction *neu* 'or':

dyn neu fenyw	'man or woman'	(*menyw*)
eithriad neu ddwy	'an exception or two'	(*dwy*)
melyn neu las	'yellow or blue'	(*glas*)
ennill neu golli	'win or lose'	(*colli*)
plant neu rieni	'children or parents'	(*rhieni*)

The conjunction *ynteu* is often added to *neu* or used alone in the construction *ai/naill ai . . . ynteu*, 'either . . . or'; *ynteu* is followed by mutation:

*Ni wn p'un ai rhinwedd ynteu wendid yng ngwaith
T. Rowland Hughes ydyw . . .*   (*gwendid*)
'I do not know whether it is a virtue or a weakness
in the work of T. Rowland Hughes . . .'
   (Geraint Bowen, 1976: 122)

Ni wyddwn pa un ai cysgu ynteu grio yr oedd   (*crio*)
'I did not know whether he was sleeping or crying'
   (Rhiannon Davies Jones, 1985: 142)

Fel y troediem yn araf, araf, law yn llaw
neu ynteu fraich ym mraich teimlem wres y cyrff dynol   (*braich*)
'As we walked very slowly, hand in hand or arm in arm
we could feel the heat of human bodies'
    (Rhiannon Davies Jones, 1985: 35)

85 Nouns in the vocative are subject to mutation:

Darllenwch hwnna, gyfaill   (*cyfaill*)
'Read that, friend'
    (Alun Jones, 1981: 26)

Wraig, rhaid imi gael fy nghinio ar frys   (*gwraig*)
'Wife, I must have my dinner quickly'
    (Emyr Hywel, 1973–4: 29)

Llefara fardd   (*bardd*)
'Speak bard'
    (Emyr Humphreys, 1986: 42)

Examples of the mutation of proper nouns are rare:

Dyna dy dynged, Lywarch   (*Llywarch*)
'That is your fate, Llywarch'
    (*Y Traethodydd* CXLII, 1987: 162)

In formal contexts an interjection often precedes the noun and the noun is subject to mutation following the interjection:

Y mae'r Duw a addolwn ni yn alluog i'n hachub,
ac fe'n hachub o ganol y ffwrnais danllyd ac o'th
afael dithau, O frenin   (*brenin*)
'The God whom we worship is able to save us from
the midst of the blazing furnace and from your grasp,
O king'
    (Dan. 3: 17)

O Dduw, yr wyf yn diolch iti nad wyf i fel pawb arall   (*Duw*)
'O God, I thank thee that I am not like everybody else'
    (Luke 18: 12)

O Frenin, meddai, mae'r hyn a ddywed Carleg yn wir   (*Brenin*)
'O King, he said, what Carleg says is true'
    (Bryan Martin Davies, 1988: 33)

The interjection may be omitted:

> *Clyw air yr Arglwydd, frenin Jwda*   (*brenin*)
> 'Hear the word of the Lord, king of Judah'
> (Jer. 22: 2)

> *Fab dyn, llefara wrth henuriaid Israel*   (*mab*)
> 'Son of man, speak to the elders of Israel'
> (Ezek. 20: 3)

The radical may also occur in the vocative:

> *Tŷ Dafydd, fel hyn y dywed yr Arglwydd* (1988)
> *O dŷ Dafydd, fel hyn y dywed yr Arglwydd* (1955)
> 'House of David, thus saith the Lord'
> (Jer. 21: 12)

Examples occur in an earlier period of the radical following the interjection:

> *O meibion Israel* (1955)
> 'O sons of Israel'
> (Amos 2: 11)

The radical normally occurs in *cariad* 'darling':

> *Paid â phoeni, cariad*
> 'Don't worry, darling'
> (Emyr Humphreys, 1981: 27)

86 In varieties of northern Welsh the numerals *saith* 'seven' and *wyth* 'eight' cause mutation of *p-*, *t-*, *c-*:

saith bunt	'£7'	(*punt*)
wyth geiniog	'eight pence'	(*ceiniog*)

Southern Welsh normally retains the radical. See also **109**.

87 Verbs with initial *b-*, *d-*, *g-*, *m-*, *ll-*, *rh-*, are mutated following the negative pre-verbal particles *ni*, *na* (see **337, 338**):

> *Ni feiddiai wnio na gwau ar y Sul . . .*   (*beiddiai*)
> 'She did not dare to sew or knit on Sunday . . .'
> (T. Glynne Davies, 1974: 46)

> *Ni fu arnaf erioed ofn cysgodion*   (*bu*)
> 'I have never been afraid of shadows'
> (John Gruffydd Jones, 1981: 10)

> *Na feddylier na welsom chwarae llachar gan*
> *Bontypridd*   (*meddylier*)
> 'Don't think that we didn't see some sparkling
> play by Pontypridd'
>   (*Y Faner*, 3 Chwefror 1989: 21)

Ni may be omitted but the mutation remains:

> . *Wnes i ddim byd na ddylwn i*   (*gwnes*)
> 'I did not do anything I ought not to have done'
>   (Emyr Humphreys, 1981: 287)

Initial *b-* in forms of *bod* often resist mutation following *ni, na*:

> *Ni bu erioed atalfa ar dafod Gwenhwyfar*
> 'There had never been a check on Gwenhwyfar's tongue'
>   (Rhiannon Davies Jones, 1987: 159)

> *Ni bydd nos mwyach* (1988)
> 'There shall be no night in future'
>   (Rev. 22: 5)

> *Fe ddywedwyd mwy nag unwaith na bydd bardd yn gwybod beth*
> *y bydd am ei ddweud nes y bydd wedi ei ddweud*
> 'It has been said more than once that a poet will not know what
> he wishes to say until he has said it'
>   (Geraint Bowen, 1972: 35)

The particle *na* cannot be omitted preceding the imper. or in replies
(see **338**) and in such situations is followed by mutation.

In contemporary Welsh *na* is normally selected in relative clauses
but *ni* also occurs, especially in earlier Biblical prose:

> *Dros amser y mae'r pethau a welir, ond*
> *y mae'r pethau na welir yn dragwyddol* (1988)   (*gwelir*)
> *Y pethau a welir sydd dros amser, ond y pethau*
> *ni welir sydd dragwyddol* (1955)
> 'What is seen passes away; what is unseen is
> eternal'
>   (2 Cor. 4: 18)

> *Elfen annisgwyl yn y frwydr oedd darganfyddiad*
> *Dilys ei bod yn mwynhau dysgu a bod ganddi ddawn*
> *ni wyddai amdani cynt i drosglwyddo gwybodaeth*
> *i bobl ifainc*   (*gwyddai*)

'An unexpected element in the battle was Dilys's
discovery that she enjoyed teaching and that she had
a gift that she did not know about previously of
presenting knowledge to young people'
    (Rhiannon Thomas, 1988: 40)

Radical and mutation occur after *ni* in *rhaid*, *gwiw*, *gwaeth*:

Ni raid ond ei chymharu â Llywelyn Fawr,
Thomas Parry   (*rhaid*)
'We only need compare it to *Llywelyn Fawr*
by Thomas Parry'
    (Geraint Bowen, 1976: 229)

Ni waeth pwy oedd wrth y llyw   (*gwaeth*)
'No matter who was in authority'
    (*Y Faner*, 9 Medi 1988: 9)

Ni wiw   (*gwiw*)
'It would be useless'

Ni may be omitted before *gwaeth*, *gwiw* but the mutation remains.
The fact that *ni* is omitted may or may not be indicated by an
apostrophe:

'Waeth inni heb â sôn am geinder y mynegiant
yn unig   (*gwaeth*)
'It is no use mentioning only the elegance of
expression'
    (Geraint Bowen, 1976: 33)

Waeth mor chwerw ac annymunol ei feirniadaeth,
ni phetrusai ynghylch ymosod yn gyhoeddus arnynt   (*gwaeth*)
'No matter how bitter and unpleasant his censure,
he did not hesitate to attack them publicly'
    (Geraint Jenkins, 1980: 109)

Wiw dechrau sôn am theatr fach y Pike   (*gwiw*)
'It would be improper to start talking
about the Pike little theatre'
    (*Golwg*, 21 Rhagfyr 1989: 21)

Wiw i neb ddweud dim   (*gwiw*)
'It would be improper for anyone to say anything'

Nid may also be selected before *rhaid*, *gwiw*, *gwaeth*:

> *Nid rhaid treulio amser yn y ddarlith hon i ddangos . . .*
> 'It is not necessary to take up time in this lecture to show . . .'
>   (Geraint Bowen, 1976: 351)

> *Nid gwiw poeni am yfory*
> 'It is not proper to worry about tomorrow'
>   (Rhiannon Davies Jones, 1985: 30)

> *Nid gwaeth gennym*
> 'It does not matter to us'

88 *Mawr* is mutated in negative contexts:

> *Doedd fawr o wahaniaeth beth a ddigwyddai iddo*   (*mawr*)
> 'It mattered little what would happen to him'
>   (John Rowlands, 1978: 8)

> *Dydy picwarch fawr o arf*   (*mawr*)
> 'A pitchfork is not much of a weapon'
>   (Emyr Hywel, 1973–4: 34)

> *'Doedd Gruff fawr gwell na fawr gwaeth ei fyd*   (*mawr*)
> 'Gruff was not better or worse off'
>   (T. Glynne Davies, 1974: 194)

89 Adjectives functioning adverbially following another adjective are mutated:

gwych ryfeddol	'amazingly splendid'	(*rhyfeddol*)
cywir ddigon	'correct enough'	(*digon*)

When an adjective is used adverbially before another adjective, verb-noun or verb, the second element of the loose compound is subject to soft mutation:

gwir fawr	'truly large'	(*mawr*)
pur ddieithr	'quite strange'	(*dieithr*)
prysur weithio	'busily working'	(*gweithio*)

90 The adverbs *go* 'somewhat', *rhy* 'too', *hollol* 'entirely' are followed by mutation:

> *Croeso go gam a gâi gan ei lysfam*   (*cam*)
> 'He would receive a somewhat cool
> reception from his stepmother'
>   (R. Cyril Hughes, 1975: 27)

cerdd go gignoeth   (*cignoeth*)
'a somewhat cruel poem'
  (Aneirin Talfan Davies, 1972: 6)

dynes hollol wahanol   (*gwahanol*)
'an entirely different woman'
  (Kate Roberts, 1972: 22–3)

Roedd yntau'n rhy wan i frwydro'n ôl   (*gwan*)
'He was too weak to fight back'
  (John Rowlands, 1965: 7)

Ll- and *rh-* resist mutation following the adverb *pur* 'quite':

pur llwyddiannus	'quite successful'
pur rhydlyd	'quite rusty'
pur dda	'quite good' (*da*)

91 Following the interrogative particle *a* in direct and indirect questions the verb mutates:

A rodia dau ynghyd, heb fod yn gytûn? (1995)   (*rhodia*)
A gerdda dau gyda'i gilydd heb wneud
cytundeb? (1988)   (*cerdda*)
'Do two men travel together unless they have agreed?'
  (Amos 3: 3)

A wrthodwn yr abwyd?   (*gwrthodwn*)
'Will we refuse the bait?'
  (*Y Faner*, 4 Awst 1989: 5)

Aeth Mati ymlaen wedi iddi oedi tipyn, fel petai
heb fod yn sicr a ddylai ddweud   (*dylai*)
'Mati continued after she had hesitated a while as though
she was unsure whether she should say'
  (Kate Roberts, 1976: 26)

The particle may be omitted in informal texts and in speech but the verb still mutates:

Ddoi di acw i swper?   (*doi*)
'Will you come here to supper?'
  (Emyr Humphreys, 1986: 45)

Ga' i fynd i brynu cacen fêl?   (*ca'*)
'May I go and buy a honey cake?'
  (Gweneth Lilly, 1984: 10)

92   The interrogative particle *oni* causes mutation of *b-*, *d-*, *g-*, *m-*, *ll-*, *rh-*:

> *Oni fuom yn proffwydo yn dy enw di . . . ?*   (*buom*)
> 'Did we not prophesy in your name . . .?'
>   (Matt. 7: 22)

> *Oni ddylem ofyn pam y mae cynifer o bobl yn*
> *camddefnyddio alcohol?*   (*dylem*)
> 'Should we not ask why so many people misuse
> alcohol?'
>   (*Y Faner*, 14 Ebrill 1989: 8)

93   Verbs following the conjunction *oni* 'if not, unless' are mutated:

> *Oni lwydda i ennill ein diddordeb yn y cymeriadau*
> *. . . y mae'n methu*   (*llwydda*)
> 'Unless he succeeds in arousing our interest in
> the characters . . . he fails'
>   (Geraint Bowen, 1976: 106)

> *Ni châi unrhyw Gymro Cymraeg ddal unrhyw swydd*
> *yn ei wlad ei hun oni allai ddefnyddio'r Saesneg*   (*gallai*)
> 'No Welsh-speaking Welshman was allowed to hold
> any position in his own country unless he could
> use English'
>   (Geraint H. Jenkins, 1983: 98)

Initial *b-* in *bod*-forms resists mutation:

> *Yn y fan honno byddai Tâl yr hen of yn eistedd am ryw gyfran o*
> *bob dydd oni byddai'n storm*
> 'In that place Tâl the old blacksmith would sit for some part of
> every day unless it was stormy'
>   (Rhiannon Davies Jones, 1977: 40)

Os na may occur instead of *oni* in less formal texts and in varieties of spoken Welsh, and is followed by mutation:

> *Os na fedri di gael pàs efo fo, mi ddo i'n ôl*
> *yn gynnar*   (*medri*)
> 'If you are unable to get a lift with him, I will
> come back early'
>   (Rhiannon Thomas, 1988: 49)

> *Dywedodd wrthi y byddai'n rhaid iddi ei hel oddi yno*
> *os na ostyngai ei llais*   (*gostyngai*)

'She told her that she would have to send her packing
unless she lowered her voice'
    (Jane Edwards, 1976: 151)

94 Verbs following the conjunctions *pan* 'when', *er pan* 'since' are
mutated:

Fe fu amser pan fyddai drysau trên yn cael
eu hagor i chi   (*byddai*)
'There had been a time when train doors would
be opened for you'
    (Eigra Lewis Roberts, 1988: 82)

Doedd ganddi ddim esgus digonol pan ddaeth
Eurwyn ati   (*daeth*)
'She did not have an adequate excuse to offer
when Eurwyn came to her'
    (Rhiannon Thomas, 1988: 15)

Mae naw mlynedd er pan gawson ni ddillad newydd   (*cawson*)
'It's nine years since we had new clothes'
    (Kate Roberts, 1976: 26)

Mae tridiau er pan fuom ni ar Enlli   (*buom*)
'It's three days since we were on Bardsey'
    (Rhiannon Davies Jones, 1985: 17)

95 *Piau* 'who owns' (see **228**) may be mutated:

Ni biau'r porfeydd gwelltog   (*piau*)
'The grassy pastures are ours'
    (Rhiannon Davies Jones, 1977: 107)

Ef biau'r wobr   (*piau*)
'The prize is his'
    (J. Elwyn Hughes, 1989: 69)

Instances of the radical are common:

Fi piau hi
'It is I who own her'
    (Emyr Humphreys, 1986: 59)

Myfi piau dial (1988)
Myfi biau dial (1955)
'Vengeance is mine'
    (Heb. 10: 30)

The noun object after *piau* may be mutated:

> *Fe biau ragair Elfennau Cemeg (1937) gan*   (*rhagair*)
> *R. O. Davies*
> 'He wrote the preface to *Elfennau Cemeg* (1937)
> by R. O. Davies'
>> (Geraint Bowen, 1976: 245)

96 The second of two adjectives repeated is mutated:

> *Aeth ei gorff yn drymach, drymach*   (*trymach*)
> 'His body became heavier and heavier'
>> (Rhiannon Davies Jones, 1987: 194)

> *A Dafydd oedd yn myned gryfach, gryfach,*
> *ond tŷ Saul oedd yn myned wannach,*
> *wannach* (1955)   (*cryfach, gwannach*)
> 'And David waxed stronger and stronger,
> but the house of Saul waxed weaker and
> weaker'
>> (2 Sam. 3: 1)

> *Dewisais bob gair yn fanwl fanwl*   (*manwl*)
> 'I selected every word most carefully'
>> (*Y Faner*, 17 Chwefror 1978: 20)

97 The subject of *oes* (see **278** (vi)) may or may not be mutated:

(i) with mutation:

> *Nid oes ddiben manylu*   (*diben*)
> 'There is no point in going into detail'
>> (R. Geraint Gruffydd, 1988: 72)

> *Nid oes rithyn o wirionedd yn y*
> *ddamcaniaeth*   (*rhithyn*)
> 'There is no grain of truth in the theory'
>> (*Y Faner*, 14 Chwefror 1992: 32)

(ii) with the radical:

> *Nid oes cofeb i'r Parchedig John Kenrick*
> 'There is no memorial to the Reverend John Kenrick'
>> (*Y Faner*, 9 Medi 1988: 13)

> *Lle nad oes cyfraith, nid oes trosedd yn ei herbyn chwaith*
> 'Where there is no law, there is no transgression either'
>> (Rom. 4: 15)

98 Mutation of the subject of *oedd* (see **277**) is rare in contemporary prose:

Nid oedd fenyn ar y bara   (*menyn*)
'There was no butter on the bread'
    (Geraint Bowen, 1972: 55)

Nid oedd dir annibynnol y gallai dyn
sefyll arno   (*tir*)
'There was no independent ground upon
which a man could stand'
    (R. Geraint Gruffydd, 1988: 117)

Nid oedd ball ar eu syched am wybodaeth   (*pall*)
'There was no limit on their thirst for
knowledge'
    (Geraint H. Jenkins, 1983: 111)

99 *Byw* 'live' and *marw* 'die' may select mutation when used adjectivally without the predicative *yn* following initial *b-* in forms of *bod* 'to be':

Bu farw'r Tywysog Dafydd ap Llywelyn   (*marw*)
'Prince Dafydd ap Llywelyn died'
    (Rhiannon Davies Jones, 1987: 228)

Os buom farw gydag ef, byddwn fyw hefyd
gydag ef   (*marw, byw*)
'If we died with him, we shall also live with him'
    (2 Tim. 2: 11)

Bu fyw am ran olaf ei oes fel gwasanaethwr
ein duw Gwyllawg   (*byw*)
'He lived for the latter part of his life
as servant of our god Gwyllawg'
    (Bryan Martin Davies, 1988: 20)

The radical also occurs:

Fydd y Diafol ddim byw'n hir 'rwan!
'The devil will not live long now!'
    (Rhiannon Davies Jones, 1985: 59)

Trefna dy dŷ; canys marw fyddi, ac ni byddi byw (1955)
Trefna dy dŷ; oherwydd 'rwyt ar fin marw; ni fyddi fyw (1988)
'Set your house in order: for you shall die and not live'
    (Isa. 38: 1)

100 *Rhaid* may or may not be mutated following forms of *bod* 'to be':

(i) with mutation:

> *Nid oedd raid i neb ymboeni am dorri'r glaswellt*   (*rhaid*)
> 'No one had to worry about cutting the grass'
>   (*Y Faner*, 3 Medi 1988: 13)

> *Bu raid i Gwenhwyfar oddef y surni*   (*rhaid*)
> 'Gwenhwyfar had to suffer the gall'
>   (Rhiannon Davies Jones, 1987: 213)

> *My fydd raid imi fynd*   (*rhaid*)
> 'I shall have to go'
>   (Eigra Lewis Roberts, 1988: 22)

(ii) with the radical:

> *Fe fu rhaid i'r gwas mawr, Daniel Lloyd, ei hebrwng tua thre*
> 'The head man-servant, Daniel Lloyd, had to escort him home'
>   (T. Llew Jones, 1980: 29)

> *Bu rhaid i Owen Edwards ddisgwyl yn hir am lyfr Morris Jones*
> 'Owen Edwards had to wait a long time for Morris Jones's book'
>   (Geraint Bowen, 1976: 302)

101 Mutation occurs following an interpolation which may be

(i) An adverb or prepositional phrase:

> *Mae yma ormod o ailadrodd*   (*gormod*)
> 'There is here too much repetition'
>   (W. Rhys Nicholas, 1988: 108)

> *Gwelwyd hefyd waith celfydd iawn yn y*
> *gystadleuaeth Caligraffi*   (*gwaith*)
> 'Very skilled work was also seen in the
> calligraphy competition'
>   (*Y Faner*, 25 Awst 1988: 19)

> *Yr oedd John Prichard Prŷs o Langadwaladr yn*
> *rhagweld yn 1721 dranc yr iaith Gymraeg*   (*tranc*)
> 'John Prichard Prŷs from Llangadwaladr
> anticipated in 1721 the death of the Welsh
> language'
>   (R. Geraint Gruffydd, 1988: 156)

Mae e'n canmol, ymhlith eraill, Fyrddin a Thaliesin
am eu bod yn brydyddion Cristnogol   (*Myrddin*)
'He praises, amongst others, Myrddin and Taliesin
because they are Christian poets'
    (Gwyn Thomas, 1971: 60)

(ii) a conjugated preposition:

Mae ganddo rywbeth gwerth ei ddweud,
ac mae ganddo ddychymyg bardd   (*rhywbeth, dychymyg*)
'He has something that is worth saying,
and he has a poet's imagination'
    (W. Rhys Nicholas, 1977: 31)

Nid oes gennyf ddigon o ddiddordeb
yn y maes hwn   (*digon*)
'I don't have enough interest in this field'
    (*Barddas*, Gorff./Awst 1992: 6)

102 When a noun clause (see **353**) is introduced by *bod* 'to be', the
verb-noun may or may not be mutated:

(i) with mutation:

Fe ddywed S.L. fod ei dad yn ofni'r cyhoedd   (*bod*)
'S.L. states that his father feared the public'
    (D. Tecwyn Lloyd, 1988: 80)

Rwy'n credu fod pob un ohonom ni yn wylo'n
fewnol wrth fynd oddi ar y cae   (*bod*)
'I believe that every one of us was weeping
inside as we left the field'
    (R. Gerallt Jones, 1977: 42)

Efallai fod y frawddeg olaf . . . yn rhoi syniad
i ni am y gwendid   (*bod*)
'Perhaps the last sentence . . . gives us an idea
of the weakness'
    (Geraint Bowen 1976: 315)

Diau fod rhywbeth oeraidd i ni heddiw yn idiom
faterol Gwilym Tawe   (*bod*)
'Probably there is something cold for us today in
Gwilym Tawe's materialistic idiom'
    (Hywel Teifi Edwards, 1980: 79)

(ii) with the radical:

Teimlaf bod y cynllun hwn wedi gweithio'n llwyddiannus
'I feel that this plan has worked successfully'
(W. Rhys Nicholas, 1988: 115)

Rwyn meddwl bod na fwy o obaith yn awr
'I believe that there is more hope now'
(*Y Faner*, 16 Rhagfyr 1988: 5)

Efallai bod gennym ni yn 1989 fwy o achos gobeithio am heddwch byd nag oedd gan ddarllenwyr 1939
'Perhaps we in 1989 have more reason to hope for world peace than did readers in 1939'
(*Y Faner*, 6 Ionawr 1989: 4)

103 *Bod* may or may not be mutated following the preposition *er* 'despite, although' in adverbial clauses:

(i) with mutation:

'Roedd y pwyslais yn bennaf ar eirfa er fod cyferiadau at gynaniad, gramadeg a semanteg   (*bod*)
'The emphasis was primarily on lexis although there are references to pronunciation, grammar and semantics'
(*BBCS*, 33: 29)

O ran arddull a chywirdeb iaith maent oll yn gymharol gydradd er fod un neu ddau yn rhy flodeuog   (*bod*)
'From the point of view of style and correctness of language they are all more or less equal although one or two are too flowery'
(W. Rhys Nicholas, 1988: 15)

(ii) with the radical:

'Doedd hi ddim yn hollol olau eto er bod y wawr wedi torri
'It was not quite light yet although it was daybreak'
(Friedrich Dürrenmatt, 1958: 14)

Er bod peth beirniadu arno yma a thraw, gwyddent hwy ei gyfeillion fod gwreiddyn y mater ganddo

'Although there was some criticism of him here and there, his
friends knew that he had the root of the matter'
    (Jane Edwards, 1976: 132)

104 *Bod* is frequently mutated following *oni bai* in adverbial
clauses, but the radical also occurs:

Oni bai fod argraffwyr Cymreig yn Amwythig wedi
mabwysiadu'r dull hwn ni fuasai'r fasnach lyfrau
Gymraeg wedi ffynnu cystal   (*bod*)
'Had not Welsh printers in Shrewsbury adopted
this method the Welsh book trade would not have
prospered so well'
    (Geraint H. Jenkins, 1980: 92)

Taflodd yr anghenfil bicell danllyd at ei fynwes,
a buasai wedi ei drywanu oni bai fod gan y pererin
darian   (*bod*)
'The monster threw a fiery spear at his breast, and
would have wounded him had not the pilgrim had a shield'
    (John Bunyan, 1962: 65)

Fe fyddai wedi aros mwy ym Motryddan oni bai bod arni eisiau
bod yn Lleweni i groesawu ei thad
'She would have stayed longer at Botryddan had she not wanted
to be in Lleweni to welcome her father'
    (R. Cyril Hughes, 1975: 19)

Nid aethai Nan Nan ar gyfyl bwthyn Magda oni bai bod y siwrnai
i fyny'r Garthau yn dechrau mynd yn drech na hi
'Nan Nan would not have gone anywhere near Magda's cottage
were not the journey up Garthau beginning to get the better of
her'
    (Rhiannon Davies Jones, 1977: 49)

105 When *bod* follows immediately after the impersonal verb, it
may be mutated:

Gwelir fod Morris Jones yn rhoi pwyslais mawr
ar Gymraeg llafar   (*bod*)
'It is seen that Morris Jones places great
emphasis on spoken Welsh'
    (Geraint Bowen, 1976: 317)

The radical also occurs:

Ofnid bod y sefyllfa'n ffrwydrol
'It was feared that the situation was explosive'
(Geraint H. Jenkins, 1983: 92)

*Cyfrifid bod sgrifennu'n gyhoeddus am adloniant fel hyn hyd yn
oed yn waeth tramgwydd na mynd i'w weld a'i fwynhau*
'It was considered that to write publicly about entertainment in
this fashion was an even worse offence than going to see it and
enjoying it'
(D. Tecwyn Lloyd, 1988: 77)

106 The verb-noun is mutated following the preposition *i* in a noun
clause:

Carem ichi dderbyn y gwniadur hardd hwn   (*derbyn*)
'We would like you to accept this handsome
thimble'
(Lewis Carroll, 1982: 29)

Gwyddai iddo gael ei eni yn gymharol olygus   (*cael*)
'He knew that he had been born fairly good-looking'
(Rhydwen Williams, 1979: 8)

107 Mutation occurs following the preposition *i* in an adverbial
clause introduced by *am, gan, o achos, oherwydd, oblegid, er, wedi,
cyn, ar ôl, gyda, erbyn, nes, er mwyn, rhag, oddieithr, ond, hyd nes,
tan, efallai, hwyrach, rhag ofn, wrth*, for example:

Ty'd o'r drws 'na, Bethan, rhag iti gael annwyd   (*cael*)
'Come away from that door, Bethan, lest you catch cold'
(Islwyn Ffowc Elis, 1971: 26)

*Yr oedd yn nosi wrth i Farged gerdded i lawr y
mymryn stryd at y sgwâr*   (*cerdded*)
'It was getting dark as Marged walked along the
little street towards the square'
(T. Glynne Davies, 1974: 59)

*Go brin y byddai'n gorwedd arni yn y gwely
rhag ofn iddo rychu'i ddillad*   (*rhychu*)
'He would hardly lie on top of her in bed
for fear of creasing his clothes'
(John Rowlands, 1978: 87)

Yn aml iawn fe wyddai beth oedd neges yr ymofynnydd
cyn iddo ofyn am ddim   (*gofyn*)
'Frequently he would know the enquirer's errand
before he asked for anything'
    (R. Cyril Hughes, 1975: 133)

The Nasal Mutation

108 Nasal mutation occurs following the 1 sing. prefixed personal
pronoun *fy* 'my':

fy mhlant	'my children'	(*plant*)
fy mlodau	'my flowers'	(*blodau*)
fy nhraed	'my feet'	(*traed*)
fy nannedd	'my teeth'	(*dannedd*)
fy nghar	'my car'	(*car*)
fy ngwraig	'my wife'	(*gwraig*)

Sibrydiodd yn fy nghlust   (*clust*)
'She whispered in my ear'
    (Rhiannon Davies Jones, 1985: 49)

Fe laddwyd fy nhad cyn imi gael fy ngeni   (*tad, geni*)
'My father was killed before I was born'
    (Rhiannon Thomas, 1988: 35)

Y broblem ddynol oedd fy mhrif ddiddordeb   (*prif*)
'The human problem was my main interest'
    (Geraint Bowen, 1972: 135)

In speech initial *f-* is frequently omitted:

'y nhad	'my father'	(*tad*)
'y nghwrw	'my beer'	(*cwrw*)

Diolch am 'y nhynnu i allan   (*tynnu*)
'Thank you for pulling me out'
    (Emyr Humphries, 1986: 44)

'y may also be omitted but the mutation remains (see also **45** (v)):

Huw, 'nghariad i . . .   (*cariad*)
'Huw, my love . . .'
    (Eigra Lewis Roberts, 1988: 19)

Mi rwyt ti'n iawn, mi rydw i wedi 'mrifo . . .   (*brifo*)
'You are correct, I have been hurt . . .'
   (Rhiannon Thomas, 1988: 125)

In varieties of southern spoken Welsh the pronoun is realized by [ən] and may be followed by the soft mutation:

[ən dɑd]	'my father'	(*tad*)
[ən vam]	'my mother'	(*mam*)

109 Following the numerals *pum* 'five', *saith* 'seven', *wyth* 'eight', *naw* 'nine', *deng* 'ten', *deuddeng* 'twelve', *pymtheng* 'fifteen', *deunaw* 'eighteen', *ugain* 'twenty', *can* 'hundred' (and their compund forms), the words *blynedd* 'year', *blwydd* 'a year old', *diwrnod* 'day' mutate:

y deng mlynedd ar hugain cyntaf   (*blynedd*)
'the first thirty years'

deugain mlynedd	'forty years'	(*blynedd*)
pum mlynedd	'five years'	(*blynedd*)
wyth mlwydd oed	'eight years old'	(*blwydd*)

In *diwrnod* the radical often follows *pum, saith, wyth*:

pum diwrnod / saith diwrnod / wyth diwrnod

On *pum* see **202** n. 1.
On *deng* see **202** n. 2.
On *deuddeng, pymtheng* see **203** n. 1.
On *can* see **203** n. 3.

Note
Saith muwch (1955) (Gen. 41: 27), *wyth nyn* (1955) (Jer. 41: 15), are archaisms and are rendered *saith buwch* 'seven cows', *wyth dyn* 'eight men' in the 1988 translation of the Welsh Bible. In Middle Welsh soft mutation followed *saith*, but examples in contemporary Welsh are rare: *saith fasgedaid* 'seven basketfuls' (Matt. 15: 37; Mark 8: 9); *saith gythraul* 'seven devils' (Luke 8: 2); *saith ben* 'seven heads' (Rev. 17: 7); *saith bla* 'seven plagues' (Rev. 15: 1) (all 1988).
  See also **86**.

110 In composite numerals (see **203**) *blynedd* 'year' and *blwydd* 'a year old' mutate after *un* 'one':

un mlynedd ar hugain	'twenty-one years'	(*blynedd*)
un mlwydd ar ddeg oed	'eleven years old'	(*blwydd*)

111 Nouns are subject to mutation following the preposition *yn* 'in':

yn nyfnder gaeaf	*(dyfnder)*
'in the depths of winter'	

yn Nhestament Newydd 1567	*(Testament)*
'in the New Testament of 1567'	

Yn becomes *ym* before a radical *m-*, or *mh-*:

ym Maesteg	'in Maesteg'	
ym mhoced ei got	'in his coat pocket'	*(poced)*

Yn becomes *yng* before *ng-* or *ngh-*:

yng ngwres yr haul	*(gwres)*
'in the heat of the sun'	

yng nghanu'r gynulleidfa	*(canu)*
'in the congregation's singing'	

yng Nghaernarfon	*(Caernarfon)*
'in Caernarfon'	

Note

In varieties of spoken Welsh the soft mutation rather than the nasal mutation may follow the prep. *yn*: *yn Gaergybi* 'in Caergybi'; *yn boced ei got* 'in his coat pocket'; *yn Gaerdydd* 'in Cardiff'.

The Spirant Mutation

112 Spirant mutation occurs following the numerals *tri* 'three' and *chwe* 'six':

tri phen	'three heads'	*(pen)*
tri thŷ	'three houses'	*(tŷ)*
tri chae	'three fields'	*(cae)*
chwe phennill	'six verses'	*(pennill)*
chwe thorth	'six loaves'	*(torth)*
chwe chath	'six cats'	*(cath)*

Yr oedd tri phorth o du'r dwyrain	*(porth)*
'There were three gates to the east'	
(Rev. 21: 13)	

chwe throsgais	*(trosgais)*
'six converted tries'	
(*Y Faner*, 20 Medi 1991: 19)	

y tri chasgliad cyntaf a gyhoeddodd   (*casgliad*)
'the first three volumes that he published'
    (Derec Llwyd Morgan, 1983: 17)

daeth allan . . . Goliath, dyn o Gath, ac
yn chwe chufydd a rhychwant o daldra   (*cufydd*)
'. . . Goliath came out, a man from Gath,
whose height was six cubits and a span'
    (1 Sam. 17: 4)

113 Following the 3 sing. fem. prefixed pronoun *ei* ('*i*) 'her':

ei phlant	'her children'	(*plant*)
ei thad	'her father'	(*tad*)
ei chartref	'her home'	(*cartref*)

atgofion am 'i phlentyndod   (*plentyndod*)
'memories of her childhood'
    (Jane Edwards, 1980: 20)

Ei thrydedd briodas â Morys Wyn o Wydr
yw'r pwnc   (*trydedd*)
'Her third marriage to Morys Wyn of Gwydr
is the subject'
    (W. Rhys Nicholas, 1984: 92)

Medrodd Martha sôn am ei charwriaeth hithau   (*carwriaeth*)
'Martha could also speak of her courtship'
    (Kate Roberts, 1972: 25)

114 Following the 3 sing. fem. infixed possessive pronouns *'i* and *'w* 'her':

Yr ail dro yr eisteddodd i synfyfyrio uwchben
ei bywyd yr oedd ugain mlynedd yn hŷn, a'i
phlant i gyd wedi priodi   (*plant*)
'The second time she sat to reflect on her life
she was twenty years older, and all her children
had married'
    (Kate Roberts, 1972: 21)

a rhyw wraig, a'i henw Martha, a'i derbyniodd ef
i'w thŷ (1955)   (*tŷ*)
'and a certain woman called Martha received him
into her house'
    (Luke 10: 38)

Ddaw run o'i thraed hi ar y cyfyl   (*traed*)
'Not one of her feet will come to the
vicinity'
    (Jane Edwards, 1980: 53)

Nid oes yma neb i'w chlywed   (*clywed*)
'There is no one here to hear her'
    (Eigra Lewis Roberts, 1988: 15)

Cafodd y gwylanod wledd i'w chofio   (*cofio*)
'The seagulls had a feast to remember'
    (Rhiannon Thomas, 1988: 39)

115 Verbs with initial *p-*, *t-*, *c-* undergo mutation following the
negative pre-verbal particles *ni*, *na* (see **337**, **338**):

Ni phlesiai Williams Ddiwygwyr mwyaf
brwd y Coleg   (*plesiai*)
'Williams did not please the College's
most passionate Reformers'
    (*Llên Cymru*, 1989: 34)

Ni thâl iddo wneud sant o un ac adyn o'r llall   (*tâl*)
'It does not pay him to make a saint of one
and a scoundrel of the other'
    (Geraint Bowen, 1972: 69)

Ni chymerodd Tom ei gyngor   (*cymerodd*)
'Tom did not take his advice'
    (T. Llew Jones, 1980: 11)

The particle *na* cannot be omitted preceding the imper., or in replies
(see **338**). Although *ni* is often omitted the verb is still subject to
mutation:

Chododd o mo'i ben o'r croesair   (*cododd*)
'He did not raise his head from the crossword'
    (Rhiannon Thomas, 1988: 65)

116 The conjunction *na* projects mutation to initial *p-*, *t-*, *c-*
following the comparative adjective:

Bydd yn haws na phaentio'r wal   (*paentio*)
'It will be easier than painting the wall'

Go brin y gellid rhoi harddach blodyn ar fedd
T. H. Parry Williams na thrwy ofyn am Soned Goffa
iddo   (*trwy*)
'One could hardly place a fairer flower on the
grave of T. H. Parry Williams than by asking for a
sonnet in his memory'
    (W. Rhys Nicholas, 1977: 58)

Mae'n llai o dreth ar rywun na cheisio barddoni   (*ceisio*)
'It is less strain on someone than attempting
to write poetry'
    (Geraint Bowen, 1972: 77)

Na also functions as a negative co-ordinating conjunction and
causes aspirate mutation of initial *p-*, *t-*, *c-*:

Ceir heddiw ddramâu heb iddynt na phlot na thema
bositif   (*plot*)
'There are plays today with neither a plot nor
a positive theme'
    (Geraint Bowen, 1972: 133)

Yr wyf yn gwbl sicr na all nac angau nac einioes,
nac angylion na thywysogaethau . . . na dim byd
arall a grewyd ein gwahanu ni oddi wrth gariad
Duw   (*tywysogaethau*)
'I am convinced that neither death nor life, nor
angels nor principalities . . . nor anything else
created can separate us from the love of God'
    (Rom. 8: 38–9)

Dyna pam hefyd na wnaeth hi ddim i geisio
dod o hyd iddo, na cheisio cael dim at ei chadw   (*ceisio*)
'That is the reason she made no attempt either
to try and discover his whereabouts or to ask for
anything towards her keep'
    (Kate Roberts, 1972: 20)

117 Following the prepositions *â* 'with', *gyda* 'with, together with',
tua 'towards, about':

Y mae cynllunydd y siaced lwch yn derbyn
tua phum punt ar hugain   (*pum*)

'The designer of the dust jacket receives
about twenty-five pounds'
    (Geraint Bowen, 1972: 60)

*Gyda chynifer o gystadleuwyr, y mae'n anodd
iawn bod yn bendant ynglyn â threfn teilyngdod
y cerddi*   (*cynifer, trefn*)
'With so many competitors, it is very difficult
to arrange the poems strictly in order of merit'
    (W. Rhys Nicholas, 1977: 14)

Yr oedd yn ei gasáu â châs perffaith   (*câs*)
'He hated him with perfect hatred'
    (Emyr Humphreys, 1986: 113)

118 Following the conjunction *a* 'and':

llyfrau a phamffledi a chylchgronau   (*pamffledi, cylchgronau*)
'books and pamphlets and periodicals'
    (Geraint Bowen, 1976: 252)

Trwy'r iaith a thrwy'r gymdeithas y rhed y trydan   (*trwy*)
'It is through the language and through the community
that the electricity flows'
    (Ned Thomas, 1985: 7)

*Syrthiasant i freichiau ei gilydd a cherdded
allan o'r fynwent gyda'i gilydd*   (*cerdded*)
'They fell into each other's arms and walked
from the cemetery together'
    (Geraint Bowen, 1972: 54)

119 Following the conjunction *â* 'as':

*Y cyfan a wnes i wedyn oedd rhoi ffurf
fodern i'r hanes sydd bron mor hen â phechod
ei hun!*   (*pechod*)
'All that I did then was to give the story
that is almost as old as sin itself a modern
form!'
    (Geraint Bowen, 1972: 138)

*Yn y diwedd maent bron mor fyw imi â phobl
rwyn cyfarfod â hwy bob dydd*   (*pobl*)

'Eventually they are almost as real to me
as people that I meet every day'
    (Geraint Bowen, 1972: 134)

Cyn goched â thân   (*tân*)
'As red as fire'

Mor ddi-ddal â cheiliog y gwynt   (*ceiliog*)
'As unreliable as a weathercock'

120 Following the conjunction *o* 'if':

Ac o phecha neb, y mae i ni Eiriolwr gyda'r Tad,
Iesu Grist, y Cyfiawn (1955)   (*pecha*)
Ond os bydd i rywun bechu, y mae gennym Eiriolwr
gyda'r Tad, sef Iesu Grist, y cyfiawn (1988)
'But should anyone sin, we have one to
plead our cause with the Father, Jesus Christ,
the just'
    (1 John 2: 1)

O thyn neb yn ôl, nid yw fy enaid yn ymfodloni
ynddo (1955)   (*tyn*)
'If any man draw back, my soul has no pleasure
in him'
    (Heb. 10: 38)

O cherwch fi, cedwch fy ngorchmynion (1955)
Os ydych yn fy ngharu i, fe gadwch
fy ngorchmynion i (1988)   (*cerwch*)
'If you love me you will obey my commands'
    (John 14: 15)

Note
In contemporary prose *os* has supplanted *o*, but *o* occurs in older
editions of the Bible (see **415**).

121 Following the interrogative particle *oni*:

Oni phroffwydasom yn dy enw di? (1955)   (*proffwydasom*)
'Have we not prophesied in your name?'
    (Matt. 7: 22)

Oni thywelltaist fi fel llaeth a'm ceulo
fel caws?   (*tywelltaist*)

'Did you not pour me out like milk and curdle
me like cheese?'
  (Job 10: 10)

*Oni chlywodd am y gamdybiaeth feirniadol honno a
elwir Bwriadaeth?* (*clywodd*)
'Has he not heard of that critical misconjecture
called Teleology?'
  (*Taliesin*, Hydref 1988: 81)

122 Following the conjunction *oni* 'if not, unless':

*Bydd yn edifar gennych oni phrynwch gar
dibynadwy* (*prynwch*)
'You will be sorry unless you buy a reliable
car'

*Oni thaenir yr efengyl yn eu plith, sut y
gallant gael eu dwyn i wir ras Duw?* (*taenir*)
'Unless the gospel is spread in their midst,
how can they be brought to God's true grace?'
  (*Llên Cymru*, 1989: 32)

*Deddfwyd nad oedd neb i ddal swydd wladol oni
chymunai yn Eglwys Loegr* (*cymunai*)
'It was enacted that no one was to hold state
office unless he took communion in the Church of England'
  (Gwyn Thomas, 1971: 19)

Os na may occur instead of *oni* in less formal texts and in varieties of
spoken Welsh, and is followed by mutation:

*Os na phlanwch chi'r had yn fuan, bydd
hi'n rhy hwyr* (*planu*)
'Unless you plant the seed soon, it will
be too late'

*Bydd hi'n rhy hwyr i fynd ar wyliau
eleni, os na threfnwch chi bethau ar unwaith* (*trefnwch*)
'It will be too late to go on holiday this year,
unless you organize things immediately'

*Os na chafodd ciwcymbars fawr o le mewn
llenyddiaeth Gymraeg hyd yma – mae hynny ar
fin newid* (*cafodd*)

'If cucumbers have not had much attention in Welsh
literature so far – that is about to change'
(*Golwg*, 6 Hydref 1988: 3)

Dydi pobl ifanc heddiw ddim yn fodlon os na
chân nhw falu a dinistrio   (*cân*)
'Young people today are unhappy unless they are
allowed to break and destroy'
(Eigra Lewis Roberts, 1980: 93)

123 Following the conjunction *oni/hyd oni* 'until':

Ni fwytâf hyd oni thraethwyf fy negesau (1955)   (*traethwyf*)
'I will not eat until I have told mine errand'
(Gen. 24: 33)

Nid oedd i'w ollwng hyd oni chytunai ddychwelyd   (*cytunai*)
'He was not to be released until he agreed
to return'

124 Following the adverb *tra* 'very':

cylchgrawn tra phwysig   (*pwysig*)
'a very important journal'
(D. Tecwyn Lloyd, 1988: 95)

Mae'n dra thebyg i Joseph ddechrau cael hwyl
ar lymeitian tipyn bach unwaith eto   (*tebyg*)
'It is very likely that Joseph had started to enjoy
the odd tipple once more'
(T. Llew Jones, 1980: 96)

Wŷr Athen, yr wyf yn gweld ar bob llaw eich bod
yn dra chrefyddgar   (*crefyddgar*)
'Men of Athens, I see all around that you are
very religious'
(Acts 17: 22)

125 A vowel is preceded by *h-*:

(i) following the 3 sing. fem. prefixed pronoun *ei* 'her':

Edrychodd ar ei horiawr   (*oriawr*)
'She looked at her watch'
(Eigra Lewis Roberts, 1988: 58)

Saesneg oedd ei hiaith gyntaf   (*iaith*)
'English was her first language'
   (Ned Thomas, 1985: 7)

(ii) following the 3 sing. fem. infixed possessive pronouns *'i* and *'w*:

Ymhen hanner awr yr oedd y baned wedi'i hyfed   (*yfed*)
'Within half an hour the contents of the cup
had been drunk'
   (Rhiannon Thomas, 1988: 106)

Roedd ganddo lawer stori ddifyr i'w hadrodd   (*adrodd*)
'He had many interesting tales to tell'

(iii) following the 3 sing. masc. and fem. infixed object pronouns *'i*:

*Fe'i hawdurdodwyd gan yr esgobion . . . yn unol ag
Act 1536*   (*awdurdodwyd*)
'It was authorized by the bishops . . . in accordance
with the 1536 Act'
   (R. Geraint Gruffydd, 1988: 32)

*Bu farw Morgan fis Medi 1604 ac fe'i holynwyd
gan Richard Parry*   (*olynwyd*)
'Morgan died in September 1604 and he was
succeeded by Richard Parry'
   (R. Geraint Gruffyd, 1988: 35)

*Yn 1703 y cyhoeddwyd G. B. C. ond fe'i hysgrifennwyd
cyn hynny*   (*ysgrifennwyd*)
'G. B. C. was published in 1703 but it was written
before then'
   (Gwyn Thomas, 1971: 19)

(iv) following the 1 pl. prefixed pronoun *ein* 'our':

y mae hyn yn ein hatgoffa o'r syniad   (*atgoffa*)
'this reminds us of the idea'
   (Geraint Bowen, 1972: 18)

yn ein heglwysi plwy   (*eglwysi*)
'in our parish churches'
   (Rhiannon Davies Jones, 1985: 19)

(v) following the 1 pl. infixed pronoun *'n*:

*Yr un math o draddodiad yn union yw'n
henglynion beddargraff ni*   (*englynion*)

'Our own epitaphic stanzas belong to
exactly the same sort of tradition'
    (W. Rhys Nicholas, 1977: 30)

Rhaid inni adael i'n hastudiaeth o ffeithiau
byd natur reoli ein gwybodaeth wyddonol   (*astudiaeth*)
'We must allow our study of the facts of the world
of nature to control our scientific knowledge'
    (R. Geraint Gruffydd, 1988: 116)

(vi) following the 1 sing. infixed pronoun *'m*:

Fe'm hysgogwyd lawer gwaith i droi i'r
Bywgraffiadur   (*ysgogwyd*)
'I was impelled many times to turn to the
Biographical Dictionary'
    (*Y Faner*, 26 Awst 1988: 14)

(vii) following the 3 pl. prefixed pronoun *eu* 'their':

Fe fu amser pan fyddai drysau trên yn
cael eu hagor i chi   (*agor*)
'There was a time when train doors
would be opened for you'
    (Eigra Lewis Roberts, 1988: 82)

Nid yw'r cyfieithwyr wedi eu henwi ar
yr wynebddalen   (*enwi*)
'The translators are not named on
the title page'
    (R. Geraint Gruffydd, 1988: 54)

(viii) following the 3 pl. infixed pronoun *'u*:

Cwynent am eu blinder a'u hafiechyd   (*afiechyd*)
'They complained of their weariness
and their illness'
    (Jane Edwards, 1976: 87)

Fedrai hi mo'u hwynebu nhw heno   (*wynebu*)
'She could not face them tonight'
    (Rhiannon Thomas, 1988: 8)

(ix) with *ugain* after *ar*:

un ar hugain	'twenty-one'	(*ugain*)
saith ar hugain	'twenty-seven'	(*ugain*)

126   In prepositions such as *gan* (*can*), *gyda* (*g*) (*cyda* (*g*)), *ger (cer)*, *dros* (*tros*), *drwy* (*trwy*), *dan* (*tan*), and the adverbs *drosodd* (*trosodd*), *drwodd* (*trwodd*), *draw* (*traw*) the original radicals may be restored after *a* 'and' and take mutation:

yma a thraw	'here and there'	(*traw*)
drosodd a throsodd	'over and over'	(*trosodd*)
drwodd a thrwodd	'through and through'	(*trwodd*)

Daeth Dilys i gasáu boreau Sul, a chydag amser . . .   (*cydag*)
'Dilys came to loathe Sunday mornings, and
with time . . .'
    (Rhiannon Thomas, 1988: 103)

gan y tân, a chan y mwg, a chan y brwmstan (1955)   (*can*)
'By the fire, and by the smoke, and by the
brimstone'
    (Rev. 9: 18)

gerbron fy Nhad, a cherbron ei angylion ef   (*cer*)
'in the presence of my father, and in the presence
of his angels'
    (Rev. 3: 5)

A than ymddiddan ag ef aeth i mewn   (*tan*)
'And talking with him he went in'
    (Acts 9: 27)

. . . a thrwy Ddyffryn Clwyd i gyffiniau Wrecsam   (*trwy*)
'. . . and through the Vale of Clwyd to the
Wrexham area'
    (Rhiannon Davies Jones, 1985: 9)

Newch chi ystyried sefyll dros eich hawlia
a thros eich cydweithwyr?   (*tros*)
'Will you consider making a stand for your rights
and for your fellow-workers?'
    (*Taliesin*, Hydref 1988: 23)

Although the phrases *a chwedyn* 'and afterwards', *a chwedi* 'and after' cannot be explained as mutation of the original radical following the conjunction *a*, they probably derive from *ac wedyn*, *ac wedi* with *c* wrongly attached to *wedyn*, *wedi*:

yn yr oesoedd cynt a chwedyn   (*wedyn*)
'in earlier times and afterwards'
    (R. Geraint Gruffydd, 1988: 148)

A chwedi iddynt blethu coron o ddrain (1955)   (*wedi*)
'And after they had plaited a crown of thorns'
(Matt. 27: 29)

The Mutation of Proper Nouns

127 Welsh place-names are normally mutated in the literary language:

(i) Soft

    Rhydychen *neu* Gaergrawnt   (Caergrawnt)
        (R. Geraint Gruffydd, 1988: 27)

    o Wynedd   (Gwynedd)
        (*Y Faner*, 11 Tachwedd 1988: 17)

    o Frymbo   (Brymbo)
        (*Y Faner*, 7 Hydref 1988: 22)

    i Ddulyn   (Dulyn)
        (*Y Faner*, 4 Mawrth 1988: 15)

    o Feirionnydd   (Meirionnydd)
        (Gwyn Thomas, 1971: 77)

    hyd Gernyw   (Cernyw)
        (Rachel Bromwich and D. Simon Evans,
        1988: xxvii)

(ii) Nasal

    yng Nghaeredin   (Caeredin)
        (*Y Faner*, 19 Chwefror 1988: 20)

    ym Mhorthmadog   (Porthmadog)
        (*Y Faner*, 17 Chwefror 1988: 5)

    yn Nhrefeca   (Trefeca)
        (R. Geraint Gruffydd, 1988: 125)

    ym Mronant   (Bronant)
        (*Y Faner*, 4 Mawrth 1988: 15)

    yn Ninbych   (Dinbych)
        (*Y Faner*, 6 Ionawr 1989: 8)

(iii) Spirant

    Milffwrdd *a* Chaergybi   (Caergybi)
        (Robat Gruffudd, 1986: 236)

    Llanbedr Pont Steffan *a* Phumsaint   (Pumsaint)
        (*Y Faner*, 4 Mawrth 1988: 12)

    tua Phenyberth   (Penyberth)
        (Rhiannon Davies Jones, 1985: 7)

128 Examples of Welsh place-names resisting mutation are rare in the literary language:

    Pennant oedd y rhan uchaf a Carregnewid y rhan isaf
    'Pennant was the highest part and Carregnewid the lowest part'
    (*Y Faner*, 19 Chwefror 1988: 12)

On mutation following the conjunction *a* 'and' see **118**.
Mutation is frequently resisted in speech.

129 Foreign place-names may be mutated:

(i) Soft

    o Blymouth   (Plymouth)
        (Gwyn Thomas, 1971: 71)

    o Dunis   (Tunis)
        (Gwyn Thomas, 1971: 158)

    i Faseru   (Maseru)
        (*Y Faner*, 20 Ionawr 1989: 11)

(ii) Nasal

    yng Nghaliffornia   (Califfornia)
        (*Y Faner*, 7 Hydref 1988: 16)

    ym Mhrâg   (Prâg)
        (John Rowlands, 1972)

    yng Ngenefa   (Genefa)
        (Ned Thomas, 1985: 32)

    ym Mlackpool   (Blackpool)
        (*Barn*, Ionawr/Chwefror 1992: 82)

(iii) Spirant

Syria *a* Chreta   (Creta)
    (Marian Henry Jones, 1982: 125)

Sbaen *a* Chroatia   (Croatia)
    (R. Geraint Gruffydd, 1988: 24)

Prydain *a* Phortiwgal   (Portiwgal)
    (Marian Henry Jones, 1982: 124)

130 Examples of foreign place-names resisting mutation are common:

yn Twickenham
    (*Y Faner*, 19 Mawrth 1988: 22)

yn Castelgandolfo
    (*Y Faner*, 14 Hydref 1988: 5)

yn Cabŵl
    (*Y Faner*, 3 Chwefror 1989: 10)

yn Berlin
    (Robat Gruffudd, 1986: 12)

yn Plombières
    (Marian Henry Jones, 1982: 260)

o Berlin
    (Robat Gruffudd, 1986: 132)

o Glasgow
    (Hywel Teifi Edwards, 1980: 63)

i Clapham Junction
    (*Y Faner*, 23/30 Rhagfyr 1988: 27)

i Barbados
    (Robat Gruffudd, 1986: 128)

131 Personal names may be mutated in formal texts:

(i) Soft

i Ddewi Wyn   (Dewi)
    (Hywel Teifi Edwards, 1989: 27)

i Fathew   (Mathew)
    (R. Geraint Gruffydd, 1988: 49)

   at Ruffudd Hiraethog   (Gruffudd)
      (Geraint Bowen, 1970: 44)

   gan Lew Llwyfo   (Llew)
      (Hywel Teifi Edwards, 1989: 64)

   gan Forgan   (Morgan)
      (Geraint Bowen, 1970: 153)

(ii) Nasal

   yn Naniel Owen   (Daniel)
      (Geraint Bowen, 1972: 176)

(iii) Spirant

   Robert *a* Chatrin Llwyd   (Catrin)
      (Geraint Bowen, 1970: 33)

   Ceiriog *a* Chrwys   (Crwys)
      (W. Rhys Nicholas, 1977: 66)

   Gwynn Jones *a* Pharry Williams   (Parry Williams)
      (Derec Llwyd Morgan, 1972: 13)

   Pantycelyn *a* Thwm o'r Nant   (Twm)
      (Geraint H. Jenkins, 1983: 12)

   gyda Chulhwch   (Culhwch)
      (Rachel Bromwich and D. Simon Evans,
      1988: xxviii)

132 Mutation of personal names is frequently resisted:

   William Abraham (1842–1922) *neu* Mabon
      (D. Tecwyn Lloyd, 1988: 30)

   Rhydderch *a* Cynfelin Goch
      (Geraint Bowen, 1970: 289)

   at Gwalchmai
      (Hywel Teifi Edwards, 1980: 7)

   gan Morgan Llwyd
      (Gwyn Thomas, 1971: 49)

   yn Gruffydd Robert
      (Geraint Bowen, 1970: 81)

In informal texts and in speech personal names usually resist mutation:

> *yr hen* Peilat
> 'the old Pilate'
>> (*Y Faner*, 19 Chwefror 1988: 8)

> *i* Dilys
>> (Rhiannon Thomas, 1988: 16)

> *i* Dafydd Iwan
>> (*Golwg*, 24 Tachwedd 1988: 24)

> *yr hen* Dewi
> 'the old Dewi'
>> (*Y Faner*, 24 Chwefror 1989: 8)

On mutation following prepositions see **69**.
On mutation of the noun following an adjective see **51**.
On mutation following conjunctions see **84**, **118**.

133 Brand names may also select mutation:

> *racsyn o* Gortina   (Cortina)
> 'a wretched Cortina'
>> (*Taliesin*, Hydref 1988: 23)

> *hen* Gortinas   (Cortinas)
> 'old Cortinas'
>> (*Golwg*, 17 Tachwedd 1988: 23)

> *Fe dalwch fwy o lawer am* Fercedes   (Mercedes)
> 'You will pay much more for a Mercedes'
>> (*Y Cymro*, 7 Rhagfyr 1988: 10)

The radical also occurs:

> *yn ei* Deimlar *newydd*
> 'in his new Daimler'
>> (*Taliesin*, Rhagfyr 1988: 61)

On mutation of nouns following the 3 sing. masc. prefixed pronoun see **63**.

134 In formal texts the initial consonant of book titles, periodicals and literary works may be mutated:

(i) Soft

    ei Gerdd Dafod   (*Cerdd*)
        (Geraint Bowen, 1976: 135)

    i Weledigaetheu y Bardd Cwsc   (*Gweledigaetheu*)
        (Geraint Bowen, 1976: 332)

    yr ail Ddrych   (*Drych*)
        (Geraint Bowen, 1970: 269)

    i Lyfr Gweddi Gyffredin 1621   (*Llyfr*)
        (Geraint H. Jenkins, 1983: 152)

    drwy Eiriadur Prifysgol Cymru   (*Geiriadur*)
        (Geraint Bowen, 1970: 115)

(ii) Nasal

    yng Nghwrs y Byd   (*Cwrs*)
        (*Y Faner*, 6 Ionawr 1989: 8)

    ym Mhurdan Patrig   (*Purdan*)
        (Gwyn Thomas, 1971: 184)

    yn Nhrawsganu Gynan Garwyn   (*Trawsganu*)
        (Rachel Bromwich and D. Simon Evans,
        1988: xxiii)

    yn Nrych 1740   (*Drych*)
        (Geraint Bowen, 1970: 269)

(iii) Aspirate

    Cymru *a* Chyfres y Fil   (*Cyfres*)
        (Geraint Bowen, 1976: 190)

Regional and Stylistic Variation

135 The emergence of new sounds (see **3**) has had repercussions on the language. Both /tʃ/ and /dʒ/ have been integrated into the mutation system and in some dialects are subject to soft mutation and nasal mutation:

[tʃɒklad	də dʒɒklad	ən nʃɒklad]
'chocolate	your chocolate	my chocolate'

[dʒoni	i ðjoni]
'goodness	his goodness'

[dʒɒb	ənʒɒb i]
'job	my job'

[ʧɒp	ənʒhɒp i]
'chop	my chop'

Aspirate mutation of /ʧ/ is confined to varieties of northern Welsh:

[ʧɒklad	i θjɒklad]
'chocolate	her chocolate'

In dialects that select /h/ (see **4**), the 3 sing. fem. prefixed pron. *ei* [i] and the 3 pl. prefixed pron. *eu* [i] (see **214**) may trigger mutation in /m-, n-, l-, r-, j-, w-/:

[mam	i mham]
'mother	her/their mother'

[nain	i nhain]
'grandmother	her/their grandmother'

[lamp	i lhamp]
'lamp	her/their lamp'

[rɑs	i rhɑs]
'race	her/their race'

[jɑr	i hjɑr]
'hen	her/their hen'

[waʧ]	i whaʧ]
'watch	her/their watch'

136 Varieties of Welsh that are low on the formality cline tend not to select mutation so consistently as varieties high on the cline. A dialect lexicon (see for example C. M. Jones (1987) II: 1–423) yields numerous examples.

The same tendency is discernible in informal texts:

Yn anffodus nid yw hinsawdd 100 gradd F. yn cydfynd â Celtaid gwallt golau
'Unfortunately a climate of 100 degrees F. does not agree with fair-headed Celts'
(*Y Faner*, 2 Rhagfyr 1988: 10)

Gyda côd ysgrifenedig, fe fyddai'n rhaid i ni fod yn ystyriol o leiafrifoedd ethnig eraill yng ngwledydd Prydain
'With a written code we would have to consider other ethnic minorities in the countries of Britain'
  (*Golwg*, 8 Rhagfyr 1988: 13)

seren llenyddol
'a literary star'
  (*Sbec*, 25 Chwefror–3 Mawrth 1989: 8)

dwy gyfres mwyaf llwyddiannus mis Awst
'August's two most successful series'
  (*Barn*, Hydref 1990: 4)

tri cynhyrchydd
'three producers'
  (*Barn*, Gorffennaf 1992: 9)

On mutation following the prepositions *â*, *gyda* see **117**.
On mutation of the adjective following the fem. sing. noun see **50**.
On mutation following the numeral *tri* see **112**.

Mutation following Prefixes

137 The prefixes listed below are followed by mutation and the classification is based on the mutation selected. These prefixes often occur as the first element of a strict compound (s.c.) or loose compound (l.c.) (see **332–333**).

138 Soft Mutation

ad-, **at-**: 'very, second, bad, re-'

  s.c.: *atgas* 'unpleasant'; *adladd* 'aftergrass'; *adflas* 'tang'; *adlais* 'echo'; *adfyd* 'adversity'; *adlam* 'rebound'.
  l.c.: *adennill* 'recover'; *ad-dalu* 'repay'; *adfeddiannu* 'repossess'; *adnewyddu* 'renovate'; *aduno* 'reunite'.

add-: 'very'

  s.c.: *addfwyn* 'gentle'; *addoer* 'chilling'.

af-: negative prefix

> s.c.: *afiach* 'sick'; *aflan* 'unclean'; *afraid* 'unnecessary'; *afrwydd* 'difficult'.
> l.c.: *afresymol* 'unreasonable'; *aflafar* 'harsh'; *aflonydd* 'restless'.

all-: 'other, ex-, extra-'

> s.c.: *alltud* 'foreigner'; *allfro* 'foreign land'; *allblyg* 'extrovert'.

am-, ym-: 'around'

> s.c.: *amdo* 'shroud'; *amgylch* 'circumference'; *amwisg* 'shroud'; *amdorch* 'garland'.

> 'mutual'
> s.c.: *ymladd* 'fight'; *ymweld* 'visit'; *ymdrechu* 'endeavour'.

> reflexive prefix
> s.c.: *ymolchi* 'wash oneself'; *ymburo* 'purify oneself'; *ymddwyn* 'behave oneself'; *ymlâdd* 'tire oneself'

> 'various'
> s.c.: *amryw* 'many'; *amyd* 'mixed corn'.

> 'very'
> s.c.: *amwyn* 'very white'; *amdrwsgl* 'very clumsy'; *amdlawd* 'very poor'.

ar-: 'on, near'

> s.c.: *arddwrn* 'wrist'; *arfoll* 'pledge'; *arfal* 'grist'; *argel* 'refuge'; *argae* 'dam'.

can-, cyn-: 'with, after'

> s.c.: *canlyn* 'follow'; *canllaith* 'tender'; *cynhebrwng* 'funeral'.

cyd-: 'co-, common, inter-'

> s.c.: *cytbwys* 'equal'; *cydradd* 'equal in rank, value, etc.'; *cydymaith* 'companion'.
> l.c.: *cydberthynas* 'correlation'; *cyd-destun* 'context'; *cyd-Gymro* 'fellow Welshman'; *cyd-weithiwr* 'fellow-worker'.

cyf-, cy-: 'equal'

> s.c.: *cyfwerth* 'of equal value'; *cyfradd* 'of equal rank'; *cyfiaith* 'of the same language'.

intensive prefix
s.c.: *cyfaddas* 'proper'; *cyfaddef* 'admit'; *cyfagos* 'near'; *cyflawn* 'complete'.

cyfr-: intensive prefix 'wholly, utterly, very'

s.c.: *cyfrgoll* 'total loss'; *cyfrdrist* 'extremely sad'; *cyfrddoeth* 'most wise'.
l.c.: *cyfrgolledig* 'damned'.

cynt-, **cyn(h)-**: 'former, past, ex-, pre-'

s.c.: *cynfyd* 'primitive world'; *cynsail* 'precedent'; *cynhaeaf* 'autumn'; *cynddail* 'first leaves'.
l.c.: *cyn-faer* 'former mayor'; *cyn-aelod* 'former member'; *cyn-gadeirydd* 'former chairman'.

di-: 'extreme'

s.c.: *dinoethi* 'expose'; *diddanu* 'amuse'; *didol* 'separate'; *dioddef* 'suffer'.

negative prefix with adjectives and verbs
s.c.: *diflas* 'tedious'; *diwerth* 'worthless'; *diboen* 'painless'.
l.c.: *di-flas* 'tasteless'; *di-boen* 'painless'; *di-baid* 'unceasing'; *didrafferth* 'without trouble'; *di-ddadl* 'unquestionable'; *di-arddel* 'disown'; *digroeni* 'flay, skin'.

dir-: intensive prefix

s.c.: *dirboen* 'agony'; *dirfawr* 'vast'; *dirgymell* 'urge'; *dirnad* 'understanding'; *dirgrynu* 'vibrate'.

dis-: intensive prefix

s.c.: *distaw* 'silent'.

negative prefix
s.c.: *disgloff* 'nimble'.

dy-: 'to, together'

s.c.: *dyfynnu* 'quote'; *dygyfor* 'commotion'.

dy-: 'bad'

s.c.: *dybryd* 'atrocious'.

e- (eh-), ech-: 'out of, free from'

sc.: *echdoe* 'the day before yesterday'; *echnos* 'the night before last'; *echryd* 'dread'.

negative prefix
s.c.: *eofn* 'fearless'; *ehangder* 'expanse'

go-, (gwo-), gwa-: 'sub-, rather, fairly'

s.c.: *goblyg* 'fold'; *gobennydd* 'cushion'; *gogan* 'deride'; *golosg* 'charcoal'.
l.c. (with adjectives): *go dda* 'fairly good'; *go fawr* 'fairly big'; *go ddrwg* 'fairly bad'; *go dywyll* 'fairly dark'; see **90**.

gor-: intensive prefix

s.c.: *gorbarod* 'over-ready'; *gorbwyso* 'over-emphasize'; *gorbrudd* 'very depressed'; *gorlawn* 'overfull'.

'too, over'
l.c.: *gorofalus* 'over-careful'; *gorgynnil* 'too thrifty'.

hy-: 'easy, good, complete' (dark y)

s.c.: *hyglyw* 'audible'; *hyblyg* 'flexible'; *hyfryd* 'pleasant'; *hydraul* 'easily worn out'.

rhag-: 'fore, pre-'

s.c.: *rhagfarn* 'prejudice'; *rhagrith* 'hypocrisy'; *rhagluniaeth* 'providence'.
l.c.: *rhagfynegi* 'foretell'; *rhagymadrodd* 'introduction'.

rhy-: 'too, very'

s.c. (dark y): *rhyfedd* 'strange'; *rhydyllu* 'perforate'.
l.c. (clear y): *rhy fawr* 'too big'; *rhy dda* 'too good'; *rhy drist* 'too sad'; see **90**.

rhyng-: 'inter-'

l.c.: *rhyngwladol* 'international'; *rhyngosodiad* 'interpolation'.

tan-: 'under'

l.c.: *tangyflogaeth* 'under-employment'; *tanysgrifiad* 'subscription'; *tanddaearol* 'subterranean'.

traf-: intensive prefix

    s.c.: *traflyncu* 'devour'.

traws-, tros-: 'trans'

    s.c.: *trosglwyddo* 'transfer'.
    l.c.: *trawsblannu* 'transplant'; *trawsfeddiannu* 'usurp'.

try-: 'through, thorough'

    s.c.: *tryloyw* 'transparent'; *tryfrith* 'speckled'; *trywanu* 'stab'.

ym-: reflexive prefix

    s.c.: *ymatal* 'refrain'; *ymddangos* 'appear'; *ymgodymu* 'cope'.

139 Spirant Mutation

a-: intensive prefix

    s.c.: *achul* 'thin'; *athrist* 'very sad'.

dy-: intensive prefix

    s.c.: *dychryn* 'fright'.

    pejorative prefix
    s.c.: *dychan* 'satire'.

go-: 'rather, slightly'

    s.c.: *gochel* 'shun'; *gochanu* 'praise'; *gochrwm* 'stooping'.

gor-, gwar-:

    s.c.: *gorffen* (*gor* + *pen*) 'finish'; *gorchudd* 'cover'; *gwarchae* 'siege'; *gorthrwm* 'oppress'.

tra-, dra-:

    s.c.: *trachefn* 'again'; *trachul* 'thin'.
    l.c.: *tra chryf* 'very strong'; *tra charedig* 'very kind'; *tra phwysig* 'very important'; see **124**.

140 Nasal Mutation

an-, a(m)-, a(ng)-: negative prefix

> s.c.: *amrwd* 'raw, crude'; *annoeth* 'unwise'; *amarch* 'dishonour'.
> l.c.: *annheilwng* 'unworthy'; *amhriodol* 'inappropriate'; *amher-ffaith* 'imperfect'.

cym-, cyn-, cy(ng)-:

> s.c.: *cymod* 'concord'; *cymorth* 'aid'.

Vowel and Diphthong Changes

141 Affection

Affection occurs when a vowel in a final syllable causes a change in a vowel in a preceding syllable by assimilating its sound to that of its own, as when *-i* is added to a syllable containing *-a-* such as *gardd* 'garden', *gerddi* 'gardens'. (The vowel that caused affection may later have disappeared but its effects remain.)

142 Affection is realized in feminine forms of adjectives (table 5: see also **190**).

Table 5

Original sound	Affection	Examples
y	e	*gwyn, gwen* 'white'
		byr, ber 'short'
		cryf, cref 'strong'
		melyn, melen 'yellow'
		llym, llem 'sharp'
		syml, seml 'easy'
w	o	*llwm, llom* 'poor'
		crwn, cron 'circular'
		dwfn, dofn 'deep'
		tlws, tlos 'pretty'
		trwm, trom 'heavy'
		cwta, cota 'short'
i	ai	*brith, braith* 'speckled'

143   The affection formerly caused by *i* (see table 6) is realized in the plural form of nouns (see **160–170**) and adjectives (see **182–188**) and in the 3 sing. present indicative of verbs (see **263** (ii)).

Table 6

Original sound	Affection	Examples
a	ai	*sant* 'saint', pl. *saint* *brân* 'crow', pl. *brain* *cyfan* 'whole', pl. *cyfain* *safaf* 'I stand', 3 sing. *saif* When affection occurs in the final syllable, *a* in the penult changes to *e*: *dafad* 'sheep', pl. *defaid*
a	ei	*bardd* 'bard', pl. *beirdd* *gafr* 'goat', pl. *geifr* *hardd* 'beautiful', pl. *heirdd* *galwaf* 'I call', 3 sing. *geilw* *cadwaf* 'I keep', 3 sing. *ceidw*
a	y (clear)	*bustach* 'steer', pl. *bustych* *bwytâf* 'I eat', 3 sing. *bwyty* When affection occurs in the final syllable, *a* in the penult changes to *e*: *aradr* 'plough', pl. *erydr* *alarch* 'swan', pl. *elyrch* *paladr* 'ray', pl. *pelydr* *cadarn* 'firm', pl. *cedyrn* *gwasgaraf* 'I scatter' 3 sing. *gwesgyr* *parhaf* 'I last', 3 sing. *pery*
ae	ai	*draen* 'thorn', pl. *drain*
e	y (clear)	*Gwyddel* 'Irishman', pl. *Gwyddyl* *cyllell* 'knife', pl. *cyllyll* When the change occurs in the final syllable, *a* in the penult changes to *e*: *castell* 'castle', pl. *cestyll* *padell* 'pan', pl. *pedyll* *bachgen* 'boy', pl. *bechgyn* *caled* 'hard', pl. *celyd* *atebaf* 'I answer', 3 sing. *etyb*

Table 6 *(cont.)*

Original sound	Affection	Examples
		In *maharen* 'ram' pl. *meheryn*, affection changes *a* in the penult and in the pre-penultima to *e*.
o	y (clear)	*porth* 'gate', pl. *pyrth* *ffon* 'stick', pl. *ffyn* *corff* 'body', pl. *cyrff* *Cymro* 'Welshman', pl. *Cymry* *collaf* 'I lose', 3 sing. *cyll* *torraf* 'I break', 3 sing. *tyr*
		When the change occurs in the final syllable, *o* in the penult changes to *e*; *a* in the penult also changes to *e*: *ymosodaf* 'I attack', 3 sing. *ymesyd* *gosodaf* 'I place', 3 sing. *gesyd* *agoraf* 'I open', 3 sing. *egyr* *dangosaf* 'I show', 3 sing. *dengys* *adroddaf* 'I report', 3 sing. *edrydd*
w	y (clear)	*asgwrn* 'bone', pl. *esgyrn*
oe	wy	*oen* 'lamb', pl. *ŵyn* 'lambs' *croen* 'skin', pl. *crwyn* 'skins'
aw	y (clear)	*gwrandawaf* 'I listen', 3 sing. *gwrendy* *gadawaf* 'I leave', 3 sing. *gedy*
		In these two examples affection has occurred in the final syllable and *a* in the penult has changed to *e*.

144 A sound in the final syllable can affect the vowel in the penult (see table 7).

Notes

(1) -*a*- frequently resists affection in the penult before *i* or *ia*:

(i) in nouns ending in -*iad*, -*iaid*: *hynafiad* 'ancestor', pl. *hynaf-iaid*; *anwariad* 'savage', pl. *anwariaid*; *Americaniad* 'American', pl. *Americaniaid*; *cariad* 'lover'; *casgliad* 'collection'; *caniad* 'song'; *llafariad* 'vowel'. In *galwad* (<*galw* + *ad*) 'call' and

Table 7

Original sound	Sound in final syllable	Affection	Examples
a	i	e	*gwlad* 'country', adj. *gwledig* *gardd* 'garden', pl. *gerddi* *canaf* 'I sing', 2 sing. pres. indic. *ceni* *distaw* 'quiet', v.n. *distewi* *gwahardd* 'prohibit', pres. impers. *gwaherddir*
a	i	ei	*gwas* 'servant', pl. *gweision* *mab* 'son', pl. *meibion* *sant* 'saint', pl. *seintiau* *cymar* 'mate', pl. *cymheiriaid*
a	y	e	*nant* 'brook', pl. *nentydd* *gwlad* 'country', pl. *gwledydd* *plant* 'children', sing. *plentyn*
e	i	ei	*capten* 'captain', pl. *capteiniaid* *gefell* 'twin', pl. *gefeilliaid* *niwed* 'harm', adj. *niweidiol* *toreth* 'abundance', adj. *toreithiog*
ae	i	ei	*gwaedd* 'shout', v.n. *gweiddi* *paent* 'paint', vn. *peintio* *saer* 'carpenter', pl. *seiri* *maer* 'mayor', pl. *meiri*
ae	y	ey	*maes* 'field', pl. *meysydd* *caer* 'fort', pl. *ceyrydd*
ae	u	eu	*aeth* 'he went', 1 sing. pret. *euthum* *daeth* 'he came', 1 sing. pret. *deuthum* *gwnaeth* 'he made', 1 sing. pret. *gwneuthum*
aw	i or y (clear)	ew	*cawr* 'giant', pl. *cewri* *cawell* 'cage', pl. *cewyll* *tawaf* 'I am silent', v.n. *tewi*

lladdiad 'slaughter' the vowel in the penult remains unaffected, but in *geilwad* (<*galw* + *iad*) 'caller' and *lleiddiad* 'killer' affection occurs.

(ii) in some plural nouns ending in -*ion*: *carthion* 'excrement'; *manion* 'trifles'; *eithafion* 'extremities'; *amcanion* 'aims'.

(iii) in the impersonal forms of pluperfect verbs (see **261**): *canu* 'sing', *canasid* (also *canesid*); *caru* 'love', *carasid* (also *caresid*); *prynu* 'buy', *prynasid* (also *prynesid*).

(iv) in the 2 sing. imperf. and pluperf. of verbs (see **265**): *canu* 'sing', *canit*, *canasit*; *dysgu* 'teach, learn', *dysgit*, *dysgasit*.

(v) in compounds (see **332–333**): *caswir* 'unpalatable truth'; *canrif* 'century'; *gwanddyn* 'weakling'; *talgryf* 'sturdy'; *candryll* 'shattered'.

(vi) in prefixed bound morphemes: *athrist* 'sorrowful'; *afiach* 'sick'; *amgylch* 'circumference'; *canlyn* 'follow'; *datrys* 'solve'.

(vii) in final syllables that do not have morphemic status: *anian* 'temperament'; *arian* 'money'; *arial* 'vigour'; *anial;* 'desolate'.
    When *y* in a verbal ending is an affected form of *o*, it affects the *a* or *o* of the penult:

datod	'undo'	3 sing. pres. indic.	*detyd*
aros	'stay'	3 sing. pres. indic.	*erys*
gosod	'place'	3 sing. pres. indic.	*gesyd*
agor	'open'	3 sing. pres. indic.	*egyr*
adrodd	'recite'	3 sing. pres. indic.	*edrydd*
ymosod	'attack'	3 sing. pres. indic.	*ymesyd*
datgloi	'unlock'	3 sing. pres. indic.	*detgly*
datro	'untwine'	3 sing. pres. indic.	*detry*

(2) In the 2 pl. pres. indic. and 2 pl. imper., *a* is affected to *e*, although the sound which originally triggered the affection has been lost (see D. Simon Evans, 1964: 119–20): *caru* 'love', *cerwch*; *canu* 'sing', *cenwch*; *parchu* 'honour', *perchwch*; *archaf* 'I request', *erchwch*; *gadael* 'leave', *gedwch*; *talu* 'pay', *telwch*; *galw* 'call', *gelwch*; *gallu* 'able', *gellwch*; *barnu* 'judge', *bernwch*.
    This change is often ignored in contemporary Welsh (e.g. *carwch*, *canwch*, *parchwch*, *gadwch*, *talwch*, *gallwch*) and is not realized in the 1988 translation of the Welsh Bible:

Perchwch bawb. Cerwch y brawdoliaeth. Ofnwch Dduw.
Anrhydeddwch y brenin (1955)
Rhowch barch i bawb, carwch y frawdoliaeth, ofnwch Dduw,
parchwch yr ymerawdwr (1988)
'Give due honour to everyone: love the brotherhood, fear God,
honour the sovereign'
   (1 Pet. 2: 17)

Cenwch i'r Arglwydd ganiad newydd (1955)
Canwch i'r Arglwydd gân newydd (1988)
'Sing unto the Lord a new song'
   (Ps. 98: 1)

Na fernwch, fel na'ch barner (1955)
'Pass no judgement, and you will not be judged'
   (Matt. 7: 1)

Mae'r lle'n siandifang pryd bynnag y galwch chi heibio
'The place is upside down whenever you call by'
   (Irma Chilton, 1989: 37)

Mi ellwch farnu trosoch eich hunain
'You can judge for yourselves'
   (J. Elwyn Hughes, 1989: 22)

Gellwch godi unrhyw un o'r llyfrau hyn
'You can pick up any one of these books'
   (*Barddas*, Gorff./Awst 1992: 7)

Reversion

145 When the affection occurs in the suffixless form of the word
and the original vowel remains unchanged when a suffix is added, the
change is called reversion (see table 8).

Note
The following examples are irregular: *chwaer* 'sister', pl. *chwiorydd*;
blwyddyn 'year', pl. *blynedd*; *pared* 'wall', pl. *parwydydd*; *morwyn*
'maid', pl. *morynion*.

Table 8

Affection	Original sound	Examples
ai	a	*gwraig* 'wife', pl. *gwragedd* *rhiain* 'maiden', pl. *rhianedd* *cainc* 'branch', pl. *cangau* *adain* 'wing', now *aden*, pl. *adanedd*, now *adenydd*
ei	a	*lleidr* 'thief', pl. *lladron* *neidr* 'snake', pl. *nadredd*
au	aw or af	*cenau* 'whelp', pl. *cenawon* or *cenafon* *edau* 'thread', pl. *edafedd*
ai	ae	*Sais* 'Englishman' pl. *Saeson* *Saesneg* 'English Language'

Vowel Mutation

146 Certain vowels and diphthongs change when they move from the ultima (or a monosyllabic word) to the penult or to some other syllable. The change is called Vowel Mutation (see table 9).

Table 9

In the ultima and monosyllables	Mutation	Examples		
ai	ei	*sail* 'foundation',	pl.	*seiliau*
		gair 'word',	pl.	*geiriau*
		iaith 'language',	pl.	*ieithoedd*
		llai 'small',	sup.	*lleiaf*
		Aifft 'Egypt',	adj.	*Eifftaidd*
		rhaid 'need', *rheidrwydd* 'necessity'		
		craig 'rock', *creigle* 'rocky place'		
au	eu	*gwaun* 'moor',	pl.	*gweunydd*
		ffau 'den',	pl.	*ffeuau*
		genau 'mouth',	pl.	*geneuau*

In the ultima and monosyllables	Mutation	Examples		
		traul 'expense',	pl.	*treuliau*
			v.n.	*treulio*
		aur 'gold',	adj.	*euraidd*
			v.n.	*euro*
		brau 'brittle',	comp.	*breuach*
		dau 'two', *deuddeg* 'twelve'		
aw	o	*brawd* 'brother'	pl.	*brodyr*
		sawdl 'heel',	pl.	*sodlau*
		llawr 'floor',	pl.	*lloriau*
		traethawd 'essay',	pl.	*traethodau*
		llaw 'hand', *llofnod* 'signature'		
		ffawd 'fate',	adj.	*ffodus*
w	y (dark)	*bwrdd* 'table',	pl.	*byrddau*
		cwch 'boat',	pl.	*cychod*
		cwmwl 'cloud',	pl.	*cymylau*
		ffrwd 'stream',	pl.	*ffrydiau*
		twf 'growth',	v.n.	*tyfu*
		trwm 'heavy'	comp.	*trymach*
y (clear)	y (dark)	*dyn* 'man',	pl.	*dynion*
		llyn 'lake',	pl.	*llynnoedd*
		telyn 'harp',	pl.	*telynau*
		ych 'ox',	pl.	*ychen*
		dilyn 'follow', 1 pres. indic. *dilynaf*		
		terfyn 'end',	v.n.	*terfynu*
uw	u	*buwch* 'cow',	pl.	*buchod*
		uwch 'higher',	sup.	*uchaf*
			abs.	*uchel*
		cuwch 'scowl'	v.n.	*cuchio*
			pl.	*cuchiau*

Notes

(1) There is no mutation of *aw* to *o* in the following: *mawr* 'large', pl. *mawrion*; *llawn* 'full', pl. *llawnion*; *awdur* 'author', pl. *awduron*; *cawg* 'bowl', pl. *cawgiau*; *hawdd* 'easy', sup. *hawsaf*.

aw remains unmutated before a vowel in: *addawol* 'promising'; *gwrandawaf* 'I listen'; *trawaf* 'I strike'.

By analogy *aw* becomes *o* in the ultima of the verb-noun: *addo* 'promise', formerly *addaw*; *gwrando* 'listen', formerly *gwrandaw*; *taro* 'strike', formerly *taraw*.

The change *aw* to *o* in the ultima is common: (dwy-law) *dwylo* 'hands'; (an-hawdd) *anodd* 'difficult'; (fydd-lawn) *fyddlon* 'faithful'.

(2) Penultimate *w* resists mutation when followed by *w* in the ultima: *cwmwl* 'cloud'; *cwrcwd* 'crouching'; *cwmwd* 'commot, division of land'; *mwdwl* 'haycock'; *cwpwrdd* 'cupboard'; *cwcwll* 'cowl'; *bwgwth* (also *bygwth*) 'threat'.

When an affix is added, both vowels may select mutation: *cwmwl* pl. *cymylau*, v.n. *cymylu*; *cwmwd* pl. *cymydau*; *cwpwrdd* pl. *cypyrddau*; *mwdwl* pl. *mydylau*, v.n. *mydylu*; *cwrcwd* pl. *cyrcydau*, v.n. *cyrcydu*; *bwgwth* sing. noun *bygythiad*.

Mutation is resisted in many other forms where the final syllable also has morphemic status: *gwrol* 'brave'; *gwra* 'seek a husband'; *gwraidd* 'roots'; *bwthyn* 'cottage'; *bwriad* 'intention'; *gwthiaf* 'I shall push'; *swnllyd* 'noisy'; *wrthyf* 'to me'; *gwgu* 'frown'.

Vowel mutation does not occur in the prefix *gwrth-*: *gwrthblaid* 'opposition party'; *gwrthglawdd* 'rampart'; *gwrthod* 'refuse'; *gwrthgilio* 'backslide'.

W normally resists mutation in borrowings: *cwsmer* 'customer', pl. *cwsmeriaid*; *cwmni* 'company', pl. *cwmnïoedd*.

(3) Dark *y* normally realizes vowel mutation of clear *y* or *w*, but clear *y* resists mutation before another vowel in the penult: *gwestyau* 'hotels'; *gwestywr* 'host'; *lletya* 'lodge'; *lletywr* 'host'; *gwelyau* 'beds'; *distrywio* 'destroy'; *benywaidd* 'feminine'; *gwryaidd* 'masculine'.

The *y* is dark in the prefix *rhy-* in *rhywyr* 'high time', and in *-yw-* in: *bywyd* 'life'; *cywydd* 'metrical composition'; *llywydd* 'president'; *tywydd* 'weather'; *tywod* 'sand'; *tywyll* 'dark'.

In antepenultimate syllables *y* is dark: *cyfarfod* 'meeting'; *hysbysu* 'inform'; *cynhaeaf* 'harvest'; *mynyddoedd* 'mountains'; *cyhoeddiadau* 'publications'; *hynafiaethau* 'antiquities'.

In loose compounds (see **333**), however, the prefixes *cyd-* and *cyn-* have clear *y*: *cydgerdded* 'accompany'; *cyn-gadeirydd* 'former chairman'.

Normally, loose compounds have clear *y* in the first element: *Rhyddfrydwr* 'Liberal'; *synfyfrio* 'mediate'.

When the first element is polysyllabic, the quality of *y*

depends on its position in each element of the compound; *y* is always dark in the penult of each element: *llygadrythu* 'stare'; *prysur-gerdded* 'busily walking'; *ysgafn-droed* 'light-footed'; *amcan-gyfrif* 'estimate'.

   In the rising diphthong *wy* the *y* element may mutate in the penult: *gwyn* 'white', sup. *gwynnaf; gwynt* 'wind', pl. *gwyntoedd*.

(4) *uw* does not mutate in the following: *duwies* 'goddess'; *duwiol* 'devout'; *duwdod* 'deity'; *duwiesan* 'nymph'.

Provection

147 Provection occurs either when an ending is added to a word or when two words are joined to form a compound. The changes are tabulated below:

    b + b > p
    d + d > t
    g + g > c
    b + h > p
    d + h > t
    g + h > c
    f + h > ff
    dd + h > th

In other consonant couplings, provection normally affects only the first consonant:

    b + t > p + t
    d + b > t + b
    d + c > t + g
    g + t > c + t
    g + p > c + b
    g + ll > c + ll
    d + ch > t + ch
    g + ff > c + ff

Provection is triggered in the following contexts:

148 When the equative ending -(*h*)*ed* or the superlative -(*h*)*af* is added to the absolute adjective (see **192**); -*h*- disappeared from these terminations (see D. Simon Evans, 1964: 39) but final *b*, *d*, *g*, *dd* are subject to provection:

gwlyb	'wet'	+ *hed*	equ.	*gwlyped*
		+ *haf*	sup.	*gwlypaf*
tlawd	'poor'	+ *hed*	equ.	*tloted*
		+ *haf*	sup.	*tlotaf*
teg	'fair'	+ *hed*	equ.	*teced*
		+ *haf*	sup.	*tecaf*
diwedd	'end'	+ *haf*	sup.	*diwethaf* 'last'

Note
Examples of *dd* + *h* > *th* are rare.

The comparative ending -*ach* did not contain -*h*-, but by the process of analogy provection spread to the comparative form:

gwlypach	'wetter'
tlotach	'poorer'
tecach	'fairer'

149 In the pres. subjunctive. The endings in the pres. subjunctive (see **268**) had an initial -*h*-; this *h* coalesced with the preceding consonant causing provection (see D. Simon Evans, 1964: 128). In Modern Welsh *h* has disappeared but instances of provection occur in proverbs and stereotyped expressions:

Duw cato pawb!   *cato* < *cad*- + *ho*
'May God keep everyone!'

Cas gŵr na charo'r wlad a'i maco   *maco* < *mag*- + *ho*
'Hateful is the man who does not
love the country that has reared him'
     (Proverb)

Canmoled pawb y bont a'i dyco drosodd   *dyco* < *dwg*- + *ho*
'Let everyone praise the bridge that has
brought him over'
     (Proverb)

150 In verb-nouns formed by adding the suffix -(*h*)*a* to nouns and adjectives. Although -*h*- has disappeared it has caused provection of the preceding consonant:

pysgota	'fish'	< *pysgod* + *ha*
cardota	'beg'	< *cardod* + *ha*

bwyta	'eat'		< *bwyd* + *ha*
gwreica	'to seek a wife'		< *gwraig* + *ha*
cryffa	'become strong'		< *cryf* + *ha*

Note
Examples of *f* + *h* > *ff* are rare.

151 When *u* is added to the stem-ending -*ha*- to form the verb-noun, -*h*- triggers provection of the preceding consonant:

gwacáu 'empty' < *gwag* + *ha* + *u*
bywiocáu 'enliven' < *bywiog* + *ha* + *u*

152 In the diminutive double plural form of the following nouns: *merch* 'girl', pl. *merched*, diminutive double pl. *merchetos* (also *merchetach*); *pryf* 'insect', pl. *pryfed*, diminutive double pl. *pryfetach*.

153 In proper compounds (see **333** (ii)) in the following combinations:

-d + d-> t	*abad* + *dy*	*abaty*	'abbey'
-g + g-> c	*costawg* + *gi*	*costawci*	'mastiff'
-b + b-> p	*wyneb* + *bryd*	*wynepryd*	'countenance'

or when -*h*- follows one of these consonants:

dryg + *hin* > *drycin*   'storm'

T is selected instead of *d* following the fricatives *ll*, *ff*, *s*, in the few forms where these consonants come together:

hoffter	'liking'
maestref	'suburb'
llystad	'stepfather'
maestir	'plain'
alltud	'exile'
beiston	'beach'

154 (i) in the following abstract noun endings:

-*der* > -*ter*	*dicter* 'anger'
-*did* > -*tid*	*ieuenctid* 'youth'
-*dra* > -*tra*	*cyfleustra* 'convenience'
-*had* > -*cad*, -*tad*	*ymwacâd* 'kenosis', *caniatâd* 'permission'

(ii) Following the prefixes *all*-, *dis*- in *alltud* 'foreigner', *distaw* 'silent'.

155 (i) In strict compounds (see **333**) provection normally affects only the first consonant in the following combinations:

p t	(*pob* + *tŷ*)	> *popty*	'bakehouse'
t b	(*ŷd* + *bys*)	> *ytbys*	'vetch'
t g	(*gwrid* + *coch*)	> *gwritgoch*	'ruddy'
c t	(*brag* + *tŷ*)	> *bracty*	'brewery'
c b	(*crog* + *pris*)	> *crocbris*	'exorbitant prices'
c ll	(*dig* + *llon*)	> *dicllon*	'angry'
t ch	(*lled* + *chwith*)	> *lletchwith*	'awkward'
c ff	(*pig* + *fforch*)	> *picfforch*	'pitchfork'

(ii) In the improper compounds (see **333** (ii)):

popeth	'everything'	*pob* + *peth*
pompren	'foot-bridge'	*pont* + *pren*

The Noun Phrase

Introduction

156 The noun phrase most frequently serves as the subject or object of its clause, but may also serve as an adverbial element or as the complement of a preposition.

A noun phrase includes either:

(a) a noun which may be accompanied by a determiner whose function is to introduce the noun but which may also reflect the gender and number of the noun, and/or an adjective or adjectives which may reflect the gender and number of the noun, and/or a prepositional phrase or a relative clause, or

(b) a pronoun which may be accompanied by an adjective and/or a relative clause, or

(c) a noun clause, or

(d) a relative clause.

The Article

157 In Welsh there is only one article, the definite article. Where English selects the indefinite article, Welsh selects the noun only:

bachgen	'a boy'	*rhwyd*	'a net'
merch	'a girl'	*traeth*	'a beach'

| *cyfaill* | 'a friend' | *mab* | 'a son' |
| *cath* | 'a cat' | *haf* | 'a summer' |

158 The definite article is *yr, y, 'r.*

yr is selected:

(i) before a vowel

yr afal	'the apple'	*yr undeb*	'the union'
yr ochr	'the side'	*yr ŷd*	'the corn'
yr ysgol	'the school'	*yr epa*	'the ape'

(ii) before a diphthong, except one with an initial consonantal *w* (note that in *wythnos, ŵyn,* etc., *w* is a vowel)

yr aur	'the gold'	*yr eira*	'the snow'
yr wythnos	'the week'	*yr oerni*	'the cold'
yr iaith	'the language'	*yr ŵyn*	'the lambs'

(iii) before *h*

yr haf	'the summer'	*yr hwrdd*	'the ram'
yr hydref	'the autumn'	*yr hwyaden*	'the duck'
yr haul	'the sun'	*yr hyder*	'the confidence'

(iv) between a word ending in a consonant and a word beginning in a vowel or diphthong (except for words with an initial consonantal *w*)

dyfodol yr iaith	'the future of the language'
Cymdeithas yr Iaith Gymraeg	'the Welsh Language Society'
diwedd yr wythnos	'the end of the week'
cabinet yr wrthblaid	'the shadow cabinet'
troed yr ebol	'the colt's foot'

y is selected:

(i) before consonants (except for *h*)

y dyn	'the man'	*y rhaw*	'the shovel'
y chwaer	'the sister'	*y ddannoedd*	'the toothache'
y lle	'the place'	*y glo*	'the coal'
y cae	'the field'	*y pant*	'the valley'

(ii) before consonantal *w*

y wal	'the wall'	*y wladwriaeth*	'the state'
y weinidogaeth	'the ministry'	*y weledigaeth*	'the vision'
y wraig	'the wife'	*y wawr*	'the dawn'

(iii) between two consonants or between a consonant and consonantal *w*

ger y dref	'near the town'
dros y glwyd	'over the gate'
yn y wlad	'in the country'
ar y cae	'on the field'
dan y bwrdd	'under the table'
oddi wrth y plant	'from the children'

'r is selected after a vowel or diphthong

i'r anifail	'to the animal'
o'r tŷ	'from the house'
i'r llyfrgell	'to the library'
lliw'r afon	'the colour of the river'
mae'r dyn	'the man is'

Note
Y or *yr* may occur if a pause is required after the vowel: *Ni alwodd neb yma y dydd o'r blaen* 'No one called here the other day'; *Nid aethom yno yr haf diwethaf* 'We did not go there last year'.

159 The article must be selected with each noun in a noun phrase consisting of a series of definite nouns:

Yn y gaeaf byddai'n gan gwaith anos teithio oherwydd y dŵr a'r llaid a'r tyllau
'In the winter it would be far more difficult to travel because of the water and (the) mud and (the) holes'
(Gwyn Thomas, 1971: 73)

Y mae'r haul a'r ddaear a'r môr yn elynol i ddyn
'The sun and (the) earth and (the) sea are hostile to man'
(D. Tecwyn Lloyd, 1988: 68)

yr Annibynwyr, y Presbyteriaid a'r Bedyddwyr
'the Independents, (the) Presbyterians and (the) Baptists'
(Geraint H. Jenkins, 1983: 41)

The article occurs:

(i) before certain place-names

Y Barri	(Barry)
Y Borth	(Borth)

Y Felinheli	(Port Dinorwig)
Y Bala	(Bala)
Y Porth	(Porth)
Y Fenni	(Abergavenny)
Yr Wyddgrug	(Mold)
Y Caerau	(Caerau)
Yr As Fach	(Nash)

Note
Erroneous use of the article is common before *Amwythig* (Shrewsbury).

(ii) before the names of certain countries beginning with a vowel

Yr Alban	(Scotland)
Yr India	(India)
Yr Almaen	(Germany)
Yr Amerig	(America)
Yr Aifft	(Egypt)
Yr Eidal	(Italy)

Note
The article does not occur before *Iwerddon* (Ireland), *Ewrob* (Europe), *America* (America).

(iii) before the names of languages

y Gymraeg	(Welsh)
y Lladin	(Latin)
y Saesneg	(English)
y Ffrangeg	(French)
yr Wyddeleg	(Irish)
y Llydaweg	(Breton)

See also **180** B (iii).

(iv) before titles and appointments

yr Arglwydd Rhys	(Lord Rhys)
yr Athro John Morris-Jones	(Professor John Morris-Jones)
yr Arlywydd Clinton	(President Clinton)
yr Esgob William Morgan	(Bishop William Morgan)
Y Pab Ioan Paul II	(Pope John Paul II)
Y Parch. J. Puleston Jones	(Rev. J. Puleston Jones)

yr Ymerawdwr Akihito	(Emperor Akihito)
y Ficer Prichard	(Vicar Prichard)

Note

The article does not occur before *Syr* 'Sir': *Syr John Rhŷs* (Sir John Rhŷs). It is frequently omitted before *Dr, arglwydd* 'lord'.

(v)   before a noun denoting a group of people

y Cymry	'Welshmen'
yr Hwntws	'South Walians'
y Gogs	'North Walians'
y Saeson	'Englishmen'
y Crynwyr	'Quakers'
y Gwyddelod	'Irishmen'
y Bedyddwyr	'Baptists'
yr Undodiaid	'Unitarians'
y Mormoniaid	'Mormons'

(vi)   before the names of the seasons, certain festivals and days

y gwanwyn	'spring'
yr haf	'summer'
yr hydref	'autumn'
y gaeaf	'winter'
y Nadolig	'Christmas'
y Pasg	'Easter'
yr Ystwyll	'Epiphany'
y Grawys	'Lent'
y Calan	'New-Year's Day, first day of each month'
y Sadwrn	'Saturday'
y Sul	'Sunday'

(vii)   before the names of certain diseases, ailments and fevers

y frech goch	'measles'
y pas	'whooping cough'
y ddannoedd	'toothache'
yr annwyd	'cold'
y clefyd melyn	'yellow jaundice'
y felan	'melancholy'
y ferch wen	'smallpox'

(viii) before the names of two rivers

Menai   *Y Fenai*   *Iorddonen*   *Yr Iorddonen*   (Jordan)

Note
These names also occur without the article.

(ix) in certain phrases where there is no definite article in the corresponding English phrase or where English has an indefinite article

yn y funud	'in a minute'
yn y gwaith	'in work'
yn y golwg	'in sight'
yn y capel	'in chapel'
yn yr ysbyty	'in hospital'
yn yr eglwys	'in church'
o'r coleg	'from college'
i'r ysgol	'to school'
i'r dref	'to town'
i'r gwely	'to bed'
ar y tro	'at a time'
mynd ar/yn y trên	'going by train'
deg ceiniog yr un	'ten pence each/for one'
trigain milltir yr awr	'sixty miles an hour'
wythpunt y noson	'eight pounds a night'
heb yr un geiniog	'without a penny'

(x) occasionally with fractions

gwell o'r hanner	'better by half'
ni ddywedwyd mo'r hanner wrthyf!	'I was not told half of it!'

On mutation following the article see **48, 49, 51**.

The Noun

Number

160 The noun in Modern Welsh has two numbers, singular and plural. Traces of the dual number survive in a few compounds with *deu-* and *dwy-*; the initial consonant of the second element of the compound is subject to soft mutation:

deurudd	'cheeks' (*grudd*)	
deuddwrn	'fists' (*dwrn*)	
dwyfron	'breasts' (*bron*)	
deuddyn	'persons' (*dyn*)	
dwylaw	'hands' (*llaw*)	
dwyglust	'ears' (*clust*)	
dwyen	'jaws' (*gên*)	
dwyfraich	'arms' (*braich*)	
deulin	'knees' (*glin*)	

Mutation is resisted (see **59**) in:

deupen	'two ends'	*deutu*	'two sides'

The dual plural is also subject to soft mutation following the article (see **48**):
The plural can be formed from the singular in seven ways:

1 By change of internal vowel (see **161**)
2 By addition of a plural ending (see **162**)
3 By addition of a plural ending and internal vowel change (see **163**)
4 By losing a singular ending (see **164**)
5 By losing a singular ending and internal vowel change (see **165**)
6 By changing a singular ending for a plural ending (see **166**)
7 By changing a singular ending for a plural ending together with internal vowel change (see **167**).

161 By change of internal vowel

Affection by **-i**: see **141, 143**. Some additional examples are noted below:

a becomes ai

llygad 'eye'	pl. *llygaid*
arddodiad 'preposition'	pl. *arddodiaid*
gleisiad 'young salmon'	pl. *gleisiaid*
deiliad 'tenant'	pl. *deiliaid*
bytheiad 'hound'	pl. *bytheiaid*

a becomes ei

iâr 'hen'	pl. *ieir*
car 'car'	pl. *ceir*

sarff 'serpent'	pl. *seirff*
march 'steed'	pl. *meirch*
carw 'stag'	pl. *ceirw*

a becomes y (clear)

aradr 'plough'	pl. *erydr*

ae becomes ai

draen 'thorn'	pl. *drain*

e becomes y (clear)

cyllell 'knife'	pl. *cyllyll*
astell 'shelf'	pl. *estyll*
asgell 'wing'	pl. *esgyll*
llawes 'sleeve'	pl. *llewys*

o becomes y (clear)

ffon 'stick'	pl. *ffyn*
corff 'body'	pl. *cyrff*
ffordd 'way'	pl. *ffyrdd*

w becomes y (clear)

asgwrn 'bone'	pl. *esgyrn*

oe becomes wy

croen 'skin'	pl. *crwyn*

162   By addition of a plural ending:

-au	*adeilad* 'building'	pl. *adeiladau*
	cae 'field'	pl. *caeau*
	llong 'ship'	pl. *llongau*
	ffrwyth 'fruit'	pl. *ffrwythau*
-iau	*esgid* 'boot'	pl. *esgidiau*
	grudd 'cheek'	pl. *gruddiau*
	llun 'picture'	pl. *lluniau*
	llanc 'youth'	pl. *llanciau*
-on	*cysur* 'comfort'	pl. *cysuron*
	awel 'breeze'	pl. *awelon*
	gofal 'care'	pl. *gofalon*
	nwy 'gas'	pl. *nwyon*
-ion	*esgob* 'bishop'	pl. *esgobion*
	swyddog 'official'	pl. *swyddogion*

	ysgol 'school'	pl. *ysgolion*
	rhodd 'gift'	pl. *rhoddion*
-i	*bwced* 'bucket'	pl. *bwcedi*
	llwyn 'shrub'	pl. *llwyni*
	ffenestr 'window'	pl. *ffenestri*
	arglwydd 'lord'	pl. *arglwyddi*
-ydd	*afon* 'river'	pl. *afonydd*
	fferm 'farm'	pl. *ffermydd*
	pont 'bridge'	pl. *pontydd*
	ffos 'ditch'	pl. *ffosydd*

A few nouns may select either **-i** or **-ydd**:

	tref 'town'	pl. *trefi*, *trefydd*
	plwyf 'parish'	pl. *plwyfi*, *plwyfydd*
	eglwys 'church'	pl. *eglwysi*, *eglwysydd*
-edd	*ewythr* 'uncle'	pl. *ewythredd*
	ewin 'nail'	pl. *ewinedd*
	dant 'tooth'	pl. *dannedd*
-oedd	*môr* 'sea'	pl. *moroedd*
	lle 'place'	pl. *lleoedd*
	gwisg 'dress'	pl. *gwisgoedd*
-ed	*merch* 'girl'	pl. *merched*
	pryf 'worm, insect'	pl. *pryfed*
-aint	*gof* 'smith'	pl. *gofaint*
-od	*cath* 'cat'	pl. *cathod*
	geneth 'girl'	pl. *genethod*
	llyffant 'toad'	pl. *llyffantod*
	baban 'baby'	pl. *babanod*
-iaid	*estron* 'stranger'	pl. *estroniaid*
	person 'parson'	pl. *personiaid*
	pechadur 'sinner'	pl. *pechaduriaid*

-iaid is often selected in plural names of persons, peoples, nations, etc.:

	y Jonesiaid	'the Jones family'
	y Williamsiaid	'the Wlilliams family'
	Groegiaid	'Greeks'

Pwyliaid	'Poles'
Americaniaid	'Americans'
Eifftiaid	'Egyptians'
Rhufeiniaid	'Romans'
Arabiaid	'Arabs'
Llydawiaid	'Bretons'

Notes

(1) A stress shift caused by the addition of a syllable may change *-nn* and *-rr* in a stressed syllable to *-n* and *-r* in an unaccented syllable; an original *h* may also be restored to the stressed syllable (see **4, 33**): *corrach* 'dwarf', pl. *corachod*; *cennad* 'messenger', pl. *cenhadon*; *cannwyll* 'candle', pl. *canhwyllau*.

(2) In many monosyllables *-n* and *-r* are derived from the earlier forms *-nn* and *-rr*. When a syllable is added, the original double consonant remains: *llan* 'church', pl. *llannau*; *gwar* 'nape of neck', pl. *gwarrau*; *man* 'place', pl. *mannau*; *cwr* 'edge', pl. *cyrrau*.

(3) In a few forms *-nt* and *-nc* may mutate to *-nn* and *-ng* on adding a termination: *cant* 'hundred', pl. *cannoedd*; *punt* 'pound', pl. *punnoedd, punnau*; *tant* 'string of instrument', pl. *tannau*; *dant* 'tooth', pl. *dannedd*; *meddiant* 'possession', pl. *meddiannau*; *crafanc* 'claw', pl. *crafangau*; *cainc* 'branch', pl. *cangau, ceinciau*; *amrant* 'eyelid', pl. *amrannau, amrantau*.

(4) The most productive plural ending is *-au*, which in varieties of spoken Welsh is realized as *-a* (south-east and north-west) and *-e* (south-west and north-east).

(5) In loan-words from English such as *bocs* 'box' and *bws* 'bus', the English pluralizing morpheme is well established: *bocsys* (also *bocsiau*) 'boxes', *bysys* (also *bysiau*) 'buses'. See also **2**.

163 By addition of a plural ending and internal vowel change. On vowel mutation see **146**. Some additional examples are noted below:

ai becomes ei

caib 'mattock'	pl. *ceibiau*
haint 'pestilence'	pl. *heintiau*
nai 'nephew'	pl. *neiaint*
ffair 'fair'	pl. *ffeiriau*

au becomes eu

haul 'sun'	pl. *heuliau*

aroglau 'smell'   pl. *arogleuon*
ffau 'den'   pl. *ffeuau*

aw becomes o

awr 'hour'   pl. *oriau*
traethawd 'essay'   pl. *traethodau*
bawd 'thumb'   pl. *bodiau*

w becomes y (dark)

cwch 'boat'   pl. *cychod*
sibrwd 'whisper'   pl. *sibrydion*
cwm 'valley'   pl. *cymoedd*
cwrdd 'meeting'   pl. *cyrddau*

y (clear) becomes y (dark)

bryn 'hill'   pl. *bryniau*
dyffryn 'valley'   pl. *dyffrynnoedd*
terfyn 'limit'   pl. *terfynau*

uw becomes u

buwch 'cow'   pl. *buchod*

On vowel affection in the penult see **144**. Some additional examples are noted below:

a becomes ei

mab 'son'   pl. *meibion*
sant 'saint'   pl. *seintiau*

e becomes ei

pencerdd 'chief in song' pl. *penceirddiaid*
gefell 'twin'   pl. *gefeilliaid*

a becomes e

nant 'brook'   pl. *nentydd*

ae becomes ei

caer 'fort'   pl. *ceiri, ceyrydd*
maen 'stone'   pl. *meini*

ae becomes ey

maes 'field'   pl. *meysydd*

aw becomes ew

cawr 'giant'   pl. *cewri*

On reversion see **145**. Some additional examples are noted below:

ai becomes **a**

celain 'corpse'	pl. *celanedd*
gwraig 'wife'	pl. *gwragedd*

ei becomes **a**

deigr 'tear'	pl. *dagrau*

ai becomes **ae**

Sais 'Englishman'	pl. *Saeson*

au becomes **aw** or **af**

cenau 'whelp'	pl. *cenawon, cenafon*

164 By losing a singular ending (**-yn** or **-en**):

mochyn 'pig'	pl. *moch*
blewyn 'hair'	pl. *blew*
gwelltyn 'straw'	pl. *gwellt*
pysgodyn 'fish'	pl. *pysgod*
rhosyn 'rose'	pl. *rhos* (also *rhosynnau*)
plufyn 'feather'	pl. *pluf*
pluen 'feather'	pl. *plu*
pysen 'pea'	pl. *pys*
mwyaren 'blackberry'	pl. *mwyar*
coeden 'tree'	pl. *coed*
mesen 'acorn'	pl. *mes*
seren 'star'	pl. *sêr*
ffäen 'bean'	pl. *ffa*
derwen 'oak'	pl. *derw*

165 By losing a singular ending and internal vowel change. On vowel mutation see **146**. Some additional examples are noted below:

ei becomes **ai**

meipen 'turnip'	pl. *maip*
deilen 'leaf'	pl. *dail*
eisen 'rib'	pl. *ais*

eu becomes **au**

cneuen 'nut'	pl. *cnau*
lleuen 'louse'	pl. *llau*
blodeuyn 'flower'	pl. *blodau*

$$o \text{ becomes } aw$$

conyn 'stalk'	pl. *cawn*

$$y \text{ (dark) becomes } w$$

cacynen 'hornet'	pl. *cacwn*

$$y \text{ (dark) becomes } y \text{ (clear)}$$

gellygen 'pear'	pl. *gellyg*
gwenynen 'bee'	pl. *gwenyn*

On affection by **-i**. See **141, 143**. Some additional examples are noted below:

$$a \text{ becomes } ai$$

dalen 'leaf of a book'	pl. *dail* (also *dalennau*)
chwannen 'flea'	pl. *chwain*
hwyaden 'duck'	pl. *hwyaid*
gwialen 'rod'	pl. *gwiail*
asen 'rib'	pl. *ais* (also *asennau*)

$$o \text{ becomes } y \text{ (clear)}$$

collen 'hazel'	pl. *cyll*
onnen 'ash-tree'	pl. *ynn*
corcyn 'cork'	pl. *cyrc*

$$a \text{ becomes } ei \text{ or } y \text{ (clear)}$$

tywarchen 'turf'	pl. *tyweirch, tywyrch*

On reversion see **145**. Some additional examples are noted below:

plentyn 'child'	pl. *plant*
aderyn 'bird'	pl. *adar*
dilledyn 'garment'	pl. *dillad*
rhecsyn 'rag'	pl. *rhacs*

Affection in the penult (for example *ew* > *aw*) may, following the loss of the singular ending, occur in the final syllable (*aw* > *au*):

gewyn, giewyn 'sinew'	pl. *giau*
llysewyn 'herb'	pl. *llysau, llysiau*

166 By changing a singular ending for a plural ending:

blodyn 'flower'	pl. *blodau*
brigyn 'twig'	pl. *brigau*
cwningen 'rabbit'	pl. *cwningod*
planhigyn 'plant'	pl. *planhigion*

diferyn 'drop'	pl. *diferion*
rholyn 'roll'	pl. *rholiau, rholion*
meddwyn 'drunkard'	pl. *meddwon*
dieithryn 'stranger'	pl. *dieithriaid*
unigolyn 'individual'	pl. *unigolion*

167 By changing a singular ending for a plural ending together with internal vowel change:

On affection by **-i** see **141, 144**. Additional example:

a becomes **e**

miaren 'bramble'	pl. *mieri*

On reversion see **145**. Some additional examples are noted below:

e becomes **a**

teclyn 'tool'	pl. *taclau*
cerdyn 'card'	pl. *cardiau*
cerpyn 'rag'	pl. *carpiau*

168 The nouns listed below have irregularly formed plurals:

blwyddyn 'year'	pl. *blynyddoedd, blynedd* (after numerals)
caseg 'mare'	pl. *cesig*
ci 'dog'	pl. *cŵn*
cragen 'shell'	pl. *cregyn*
credadun 'believer'	pl. *credinwyr*
cydymaith 'companion'	pl. *cymdeithion*
chwaer 'sister'	pl. *chwiorydd*
dydd 'day'	pl. *diau* (only in *tridiau* 'three days') (see **204**, n. 2)
dyniawed 'yearling'	pl. *dyniewaid*
gweithiwr 'worker'	pl. *gweithwyr*
gŵr 'man'	pl. *gwŷr*
haearn 'iron'	pl. *heyrn*
llo 'calf'	pl. *lloi, lloe*
maneg 'glove'	pl. *menig*
morwyn 'maid'	pl. *morynion, morwynion*
pared 'partition'	pl. *parwydydd*
pennog, penwag 'herring'	pl. *penwaig*

rhaeadr 'waterfall'	pl. *rhaeadrau*, also *rhëydr*, *rhyeidr*
troed 'foot'	pl. *traed*
tŷ 'house'	pl. *tai*

An unaccented syllable is dropped from the prepenult of the following plurals:

llysywen 'eel'	pl. *llyswennod*
cystadleuaeth 'competition'	pl. *cystadlaethau*
perchennog 'owner'	pl. *perchnogion*
cymydog 'neighbour'	pl. *cymdogion*

Compounds ending in **-dy**, (**-ty**):

beudy 'cowshed'	pl. *beudyau, beudai, beudái*
bwyty 'restaurant'	pl. *bwytyau, bwytai*
elusendy 'almshouse'	pl. *elusendai*
gweithdy 'workshop'	pl. *gweithdai, gweithdái*
gwallgofdy 'madhouse'	pl. *gwallgofdai*
llety 'lodging'	pl. *lletyau*
ysbyty 'hospital'	pl. *ysbytyau, ysbytai*
gwesty 'hotel'	pl. *gwestyau, gwestai*

Note
Gwestai also occurs as a sing. noun, 'guest'.

169 The plural may be formed from a derivative of the singular form:

Cristion 'Christian'	pl. *Cristionogion, Cristnogion*
glaw 'rain'	pl. *glawogydd*
llif 'flood'	pl. *llifogydd*
addurn 'adornment'	pl. *addurniadau*
crwydr 'wandering'	pl. *crwydriadau*
rheg 'curse'	pl. *rhegfeydd*
diwedd 'end'	pl. *diweddiadau*
dechrau 'beginning'	pl. *dechreuadau*
gwich 'squeak'	pl. *gwichiadau*
serch 'love, affection'	pl. *serchiadau*
gwaith 'work(s)'	pl. *gweithfeydd, gweithiau*
gras 'grace'	pl. *grasusau, grasau*

170 Double plural. Certain nouns have double plural forms.

(i) The diminutive endings -*ach*, -*os* are added to the plural. Vowel changes may occur:

Singular	Plural	Diminutive double plural
ci 'dog'	*cŵn*	*cynos*
crydd 'shoemaker'	*cryddion*	*cryddionach*
dilledyn 'garment'	*dillad*	*dilladach, dillados*
gwraig 'wife, woman'	*gwragedd*	*gwrageddos*
merch 'girl'	*merched*	*merchetos, merchetach*
bachgen 'boy'	*bechgyn*	*bechgynnos, bechgynnach*
plentyn 'child'	*plant*	*plantos, plantach*
pryf 'insect'	*pryfed*	*pryfetach*
tŷ 'house'	*tai*	*teios*
lleidr 'thief'	*lladron*	*lladronach*
dyn 'man'	*dynion*	*dynionach*
oen 'lamb'	*ŵyn*	*wynos*
crwt(yn) 'lad'	*cryts*	*crytsach* (dial.)
crotyn 'lad'	*crots*	*crotsach* (dial.)

The ending may be added to the singular:

carreg 'stone'	*cerrig*	*caregos*
gwerin 'folk'	*gwerinoedd*	*gwerinach, gwerinos*
dŵr 'water'	*dyfroedd*	*dwrach* (dial.)
bwyd 'food'	*bwydau, bwydydd*	*bwydach* (dial)
gêr 'gear'	*ger(i)au, gêrs*	*geriach* (dial.)

-**os** normally suggests endearment, and -**ach** derision.

(ii) Other double plurals are formed by adding a plural ending to a form already plural (see **2**):

Singular	Plural	Double plural
celain 'corpse'	*celanedd*	*celaneddau*
cloch 'bell'	*clych*	*clychau*
neges 'errand'	*negesau*	*negeseuau, negeseuon*
paladr 'ray'	*pelydr*	*pelydrau*
peth 'thing'	*pethau*	*petheuau*
sant 'saint'	*saint*	*seintiau*
tŷ 'house'	*tai*	*teiau*
llo 'calf'	*lloi, lloe*	*lloeau, lloeon*
mach 'surety'	*meichiau*	*meichiafon*

171 Nouns with more than one plural form:

(i) Where the plural forms have the same meaning

Singular	Plural
eglwys 'church'	*eglwysi, eglwysydd*
tref 'town'	*trefi, trefydd*
plwyf 'parish'	*plwyfi, plwyfydd*
pêl 'ball'	*pelau, peli*
pibell 'pipe'	*pibellau, pibelli*
canhwyllbren 'candlestick'	*canwyllbrenni, canwyllbrennau*
cell 'cell'	*cellau, celloedd*
oes 'age'	*oesoedd, oesau*
llythyr 'letter'	*llythyron, llythyrau*
glan 'bank'	*glannau, glennydd*
caer 'fort'	*caerau, ceyrydd*
gwal/wal 'wall'	*gwaliau, gwelydd/waliau, welydd*
gwinllan 'vineyard'	*gwinllannau, gwinllannoedd*
cefnder 'first cousin'	*cefnderoedd, cefndyr*
cyfyrder 'male 2nd cousin'	*cyfyrderoedd, cyfyrdyr*
llyn 'lake'	*llynnoedd, llynnau*
amser 'time'	*amserau, amseroedd*
porfa 'pasture'	*porfaoedd, porfeydd*
preswylfa 'dwelling place'	*preswylfeydd, preswylfâu*
cath 'cat'	*cathod, cathau*
padell 'pan'	*pedyll, padellau, padelli*
chwarel 'quarry'	*chwareli, chwarelau, chwarelydd*
alarch 'swan'	*elyrch, eleirch*
mynach 'monk'	*mynaich, mynachod*
gwely 'bed'	*gwelyau, gwelâu*
gwersyll 'camp'	*gwersylloedd, gwersyllau*
mynydd 'mountain'	*mynyddoedd, mynyddau*
Groegwr 'Greek'	*Groegwyr, Groegiaid*
Gwyddel 'Irishman'	*Gwyddyl, Gwyddelod*
Llydawr 'Breton'	*Llydawyr, Llydawiaid*

(ii) Where a singular noun has two meanings the difference of meaning is sometimes shown in different plural forms:

Singular	Plural	Plural
bron	*bronnau* 'breasts'	*bronnydd* 'hillside'
brawd	*brodyr* 'brothers'	*brodiau* 'judgements'
canon	*canonau* 'rules'	*canoniaid* 'church canons'

llwyth	*llwythau* 'tribes'	*llwythi* 'loads'
person	*personau* 'persons'	*personiaid* 'parsons'
cyngor	*cynghorau* 'councils'	*cynghorion* 'counsels'
pwys	*pwysau* 'weights'	*pwysi* 'lbs'
pryd	*prydiau* 'times'	*prydau* 'meals'
helm	*helmydd* 'ricks'	*helmau* 'helmets, ship helms'
asen	*asennau* 'ribs'	*asennod* 'she-asses'
llif	*llifogydd* 'floods'	*llifiau* 'saws'
mil	*miloedd* 'thousands'	*milod* 'animals'
llwyn, lwyn	*llwynau, lwynau* 'loins'	*llwyni, llwynau* 'shrubs, bushes'
ysbryd	*ysbrydion* 'ghosts'	*ysbrydoedd* 'spirits'
anrhaith	*anrheithiau* 'plunder'	*anrheithi* 'darlings'

172 A few nouns have two or more singular forms:

Singular	Plural
cleddyf, cleddau 'sword'	*cleddyfau*
dant, daint 'tooth'	*dannedd*
dwfr, dŵr 'water'	*dyfroedd*
neddyf, neddau 'adze'	*neddyfau*
cofl, côl 'bosom, lap'	*coflau*
edau, edefyn 'thread'	*edafedd*
gwyry, gwyrf, gwyryf,	
gwyrydd 'virgin, bachelor'	*gweryddon*
pared, parwyd 'partition'	*parwydydd*
gwarthafl, gwrthafl, gwarthol 'stirrup'	*gwarthaflau*
arf, erfyn 'weapon'	*arfau*
mil, milyn 'animal'	*milod*
ysgallen, ysgellyn 'thistle'	*ysgall*
cawnen, conyn 'stalk, rush'	*cawn*
hoel, hoelen 'nail'	*hoelion*

173 Some nouns have no singular form:

plwyfolion	'parishioners'
trigolion	'inhabitants'
gwehilion	'dregs'
ysgarthion	'refuse'
ysgubion	'sweepings'
pigion	'selections'
bawcoed	'tinder'
gwartheg	'cattle'
aeron	'fruits'

teithi	'qualities'
creifion	'scrapings'
ymysgaroedd	'bowels'
llodrau	'trousers'

Note
Formerly *rhieni* 'parents' belonged to this class, but the artificial singular form *rhiant* is now in general use.

174 Nouns with no plural:

(i) Many abstract nouns, e.g.

newyn	'famine'
syched	'thirst'
ffydd	'faith'
tywydd	'weather'
gwres	'heat'
caredigrwydd	'kindness'
tegwch	'beauty'
glendid	'cleanness'
ffyddlondeb	'faithfulness'
tristwch	'sadness'

(ii) Nouns denoting substances, e.g.

mêl	'honey'
olew	'oil'
glo	'coal'
uwd	'porridge'
caws	'cheese'
siwgr	'sugar'
te	'tea'
ymenyn	'butter'
eira	'snow'
medd	'mead'
iâ	'ice'

(iii) Some diminutive nouns in **-ig**, **-an**, **-cyn**, **-cen**, e.g.

afonig	'brook'
dynan	'a small person'
ffwlcyn	'fool' (masc.)
ffolcen	'fool' (fem.)

Other diminutives with these terminations have plural forms, e.g.

llecyn 'place'	pl. *llecynnau*
bryncyn 'hillock'	pl. *bryncynnau*

(iv) Proper nouns, e.g.

Brynaich	'(tribe of the) Bernicians'
Cymru	'Wales'
Dafydd	'David'
Dyfed	'Dyfed'
Y Pasg	'Easter'
Chwefror	'February'
Yr Wyddfa	'Snowdon'

Note

The plural forms *Gwenerau* 'Fridays', *Sadyrnau* 'Saturdays', *Suliau* 'Sundays' occur, but *dyddiau Llun* 'Mondays'; *boreau Mawrth* 'Tuesday mornings'; *prynhawniau Mercher* 'Wednesday afternoons'; *nosau Iau* 'Thursday nights', etc.

175 The following diminutive endings are added to the singular. Vowel changes may occur:

-ach	*cor* 'dwarf'	*corrach*
	pobl 'people'	*poblach*
-an	*dyn* 'man'	*dynan*
	gwraig 'wife, woman'	*gwreigan*
	mab 'son'	*maban*
	llyfr 'book'	*llyfran*
-ig	*oen* 'lamb'	*oenig*
	hoel 'nail'	*hoelig*
	afon 'river'	*afonig*
	cân 'song'	*canig*
	geneth 'girl'	*genethig*
-ell	*traeth* 'beach'	*traethell*
	hun 'slumber'	*hunell*
-yn	*pamffled* 'pamphlet'	*pamffledyn*
	cwpan 'cup'	*cwpenyn*
	bachgen 'boy'	*bachgennyn*
	gwerin 'folk'	*gwerinyn*
	llanc 'youth'	*llencyn*

Note

In *crafionyn* the diminutive termination is added to the plural *crafion* 'peelings'.

-cyn (masc.)	*bryn* 'hill'	*bryncyn*
	lle 'place'	*llecyn*
	ffŵl 'fool'	*ffwlcyn*
-cen (fem.)	*ffŵl* 'fool'	*ffolcen*

For double plurals with a diminutive value see **170** (i).

Gender

176 All nouns are either masculine or feminine in gender. Certain nouns vary in gender:

(i) according to the sex of the individual referred to, e.g.

priod	'spouse'
tyst	'witness'
mudan	'deaf-mute'
perthynas	'relation'
ymwelydd	'visitor'
cariad	'loved one'
gefell	'twin'

(ii) according to the local usage, e.g.

angladd	'funeral'
breuddwyd	'dream'
troed	'foot'
tafarn	'pub'
clust	'ear'
cwpan	'cup'
munud	'minute'
delfryd	'ideal'
rhyfel	'war'
nifer	'number'
cinio	'dinner'
penbleth	'doubt'
cyflog	'salary'
clorian	'scales'
emyn	'hymn'

(iii) according to meaning, e.g.

golwg masc. 'sight':
> *yn y golwg*   'in sight'

golwg fem. 'appearance':
> *gwael yr olwg*   'looking ill'
> *mae golwg dda arno*   'he looks well'

coes masc. 'stem, handle':
> *y coes hwn*   'this handle'

coes fem. 'leg':
> *y goes hon*   'this leg'

man masc. 'place':
> *yn y man hwn*   'in this place'
> *yn y man*   'on the spot, presently'

man fem. in the expression:
> *yn y fan*   'immediately'

math masc. 'kind' in:
> *dau fath*   'two kinds'
> *y math hwn*   'this kind'

math fem. in:
> *y fath beth*   'such a thing'

The nouns paired below are similar in form but different in origin, meaning, gender:

llith 'mash, bait', masc.	*llith* 'lesson', fem.
mil 'animal', masc.	*mil* 'thousand', fem.
brawd 'brother', masc.	*brawd* 'judgement', fem.
gwaith 'work', masc.	*gwaith* 'occasion', fem.

(iv) due to uncertainty as regards gender in recent borrowings, e.g.

blows	'blouse'
record	'record'
coler	'collar'

177 Nouns denoting animate objects normally agree in gender with the sex of the object:

Masculine

bachgen   'boy'

brawd	'brother'
cigydd	'butcher'
march	'stallion'
ci	'dog'
gŵr	'man, husband'
gwas	'manservant'

Feminine

merch	'girl'
chwaer	'sister'
caseg	'mare'
gast	'bitch'
gwraig	'woman, wife'
morwyn	'maid'

Some epicene nouns have their own gender regardless of the sex of the object they denote:

Masculine

plentyn	'child'
baban	'baby'
barcud	'kite'
ehedydd	'lark'
bardd	'bard'
deiliad	'tenant'
dryw	'wren'
giach	'snipe'

Feminine

cath	'cat'
tylluan	'owl'
mwyalchen	'blackbird'
ysgyfarnog	'hare'
cennad	'messenger'

Note

When the adjectives *gwryw* 'male' and *benyw* 'female' modify an epicene noun, the gender of that noun is not normally affected; the adjectives select soft mutation following fem. sing. nouns (see **50**) but normally no mutation occurs following masc. nouns: *oen* n.m. 'lamb', *oen benyw*; *gafr* n.f. 'goat', *gafr fenyw*. A common exception is *llo* n.m. 'calf': *llo gwryw, llo fenyw*.

178 The feminine forms of some nouns are formed by:

(i) adding **-es** to the masculine noun, e.g.

Masculine	Feminine
arglwydd 'lord'	*arglwyddes*
brenin 'king'	*brenhines*
cyfyrder 'male 2nd cousin'	*cyfyrderes*
llew 'lion'	*llewes*
tywysog 'prince'	*tywysoges*
cawr 'giant'	*cawres*
ebol 'foal'	*eboles*
organydd 'organist'	*organyddes*
ardalydd 'marquis'	*ardalyddes*
dyn 'man'	*dynes*
ŵyr 'grandson'	*wyres*
plismon 'policeman'	*plismones*
sant 'saint'	*santes*
marchog 'rider'	*marchoges*
llanc 'youth'	*llances*
meistr 'master'	*meistres*
maer 'mayor'	*maeres*
iarll 'earl'	*iarlles*

Occasionally **-es** is added to a stem which differs from the masculine:

Masculine	Feminine
athro 'male teacher'	*athrawes*
Sais 'Englishman'	*Saesnes*
Cymro 'Welshman'	*Cymraes*
cenau 'whelp'	*cenawes*
lleidr 'thief'	*lladrones*

Note
The feminine noun *bachgennes* 'maiden', formed from *bachgen* 'boy', is obsolete in contemporary written Welsh, but occurs in varieties of spoken Welsh and in earlier editions of the Bible: *a gwerthasant fachgennes er gwin* (1955); *a gwerthu geneth am win* (1988) 'and sold a girl for wine' (Joel 3: 3).

(ii) by changing the ending **-yn** *to* **-en**

Masculine	Feminine
asyn 'ass'	*asen*
crwtyn 'boy'	*croten*
hogyn 'boy'	*hogen*
ffwlcyn 'fool'	*ffolcen*
ffrwmpyn 'prig'	*ffrwmpen*
coegyn 'fop'	*coegen*
merlyn 'pony'	*merlen*
clobyn 'strapping fellow'	*cloben*
clampyn 'big person'	*clampen*
hwlcyn 'lout'	*hwlcen*

(iii) by changing the ending **-wr** to **-es**

Masculine	Feminine
cenhadwr 'missionary'	*cenhades*
Almaenwr 'German'	*Almaenes*
Albanwr 'Scot'	*Albanes*
Groegwr 'Greek'	*Groeges*

(iv) by changing the ending **-(i)wr** to **-wraig** or, as an alternative in some cases, **-reg**

Masculine	Feminine
pysgotwr 'fisherman'	*pysgotwraig*
myfyriwr 'student'	*myfyrwraig*
gweithiwr 'workman'	*gweithwraig, gweithreg*
adroddwr 'reciter'	*adroddwraig, adroddreg*
cantwr 'singer'	*cantwraig, cantreg*
ffermwr 'farmer'	*ffermwraig, ffermreg*

179 The masculine and feminine of a few nouns denoting animals and close family relationships are unrelated or highly differentiated:

Masculine	Feminine
tad 'father'	*mam* 'mother'
brawd 'brother'	*chwaer* 'sister'
ewythr 'uncle'	*modryb* 'aunt'
tad-cu, taid 'grandfather'	*mam-gu, nain* 'grandmother'
nai 'nephew'	*nith* 'niece'
cefnder 'male 1st cousin'	*cyfnither* 'female 1st cousin'
ceffyl, march 'horse, stallion'	*caseg* 'mare'

hwrdd, maharen 'ram'	*dafad, mamog* 'ewe'
ceiliog 'cock'	*iâr* 'hen'
ci 'dog'	*gast* 'bitch'
bustach, eidion, ych 'steer, ox'	*anner, treisiad* 'heifer'
tarw 'bull'	*buwch* 'cow'
marlat 'drake'	*hwyad* 'duck'

Notes

(1) *Chwegrwn* 'father-in-law', *chwegr* 'mother-in-law', *daw* 'son-in-law', *gwaudd* 'daughter-in-law' occur mostly in older Biblical prose. The 1988 translation of the Welsh Bible selects *tad-yng-nghyfraith* 'father-in-law' (John 18: 13), *mam-yng-nghyfraith* 'mother-in-law' (Luke 4: 38), *meibion-yng-nghyfraith* 'sons-in-law' (Gen. 19: 14) and *merch-yng-nghyfraith* 'daughter-in-law' (Luke 12: 53).

(2) The nouns *bwch* 'buck' and *ceiliog* 'cock' may be selected with the feminine to form a masculine: *gafr* 'goat', *bwch gafr*; *cwningen* 'rabbit', *bwch cwningen*; *danas* 'deer', *bwch danas*; *bronfraith* 'thrush', *ceiliog bronfraith*; *ffesant* 'pheasant', *ceiliog ffesant*; *mwyalch(en)* 'blackbird', *ceiliog mwyalch*; *hwyad* 'duck', *ceiliog hwyad* 'drake'.

The Gender of Inanimate Objects and Abstractions

180 (A) The following nouns are masculine:

(i) *tymor* 'season' and the names of the seasons: *gwanwyn* 'spring'; *haf* 'summer'; *hydref* 'autumn'; *gaeaf* 'winter'.

(ii) *mis* 'month' and the names of the months: (*Mis*) *Ionawr, Ionor* 'January'; *Medi* 'September'.

(iii) *dydd, diwrnod* 'day' and the names of days: *Dydd Sul* 'Sunday'; *Dydd Gwener* 'Friday'.

Note

Gŵyl 'feast' is fem. sing. and the names of festivals and feast days are feminine: *Gŵyl Fair* (see **50**).

(iv) *gwynt* 'wind' and the names of points of the compass: *gogledd* 'north'; *dwyrain* 'east'; *de, deau* 'south'; *gorllewin* 'west'; etc.

(v) names of substances or materials: *arian* 'silver'; *aur* 'gold'; *haearn* 'iron'; *cig* 'meat'; *medd* 'mead'; *calch* 'lime'; *te* 'tea'; *cwrw* 'beer'; *cotwm* 'cotton'; *gwlân* 'wool'; *dur* 'steel'; *iâ* 'ice'; *eira* 'snow'; *gwydr* 'glass' etc.

Notes
(1) The following nouns are feminine: *torth* 'loaf'; *teisen* 'cake'; *pastai* 'tart'; *gwledd* 'feast'; *saig* 'feast'; *diod* 'drink'; *tablen* 'ale'.
(2) Names of fruit ending in **-en** are feminine: *gellygen* 'pear'; *eirinen* 'plum'.

(vi) verb-nouns: *cyfarch* 'greet'; *chwarae* 'play'; *gweithio* 'work'; *canu* 'sing'; *cysgu* 'sleep'; *yfed* 'drink' etc.

Note
Gafael 'grasp', *cyfeddach* 'carouse' vacillate between masc. and fem. gender.

(B) The following nouns are feminine:

(i) *tywysogaeth* 'principality'; *cymdogaeth* 'neighbourhood'; *ardal* 'area'; *bro* 'region'; *daear* 'land'; *gwlad* 'country'; *teyrnas* 'kingdom'; *ynys* 'island' and the names of countries and regions, e.g. *Cymru* 'Wales'; *Lloegr* 'England'; *Yr Aifft* 'Egypt'; *Môn* 'Anglesey'; *Morgannwg* 'Glamorgan'.

Note
Tir 'land', *rhandir* 'region', *cyfandir* 'continent', *rhanbarth* 'area', *parth* 'district' *cylch* 'area' are masculine.

(ii) *tref* 'town'; *llan* 'church'; *dinas* 'city'; *caer* 'fort' and the names of towns and parishes, e.g. *Llanelli, Bangor, Llanbadarn Fawr, Hengynwydd Fach, Llanbadarn Ddiffaith*. Place names beginning in *Tre(f)-, Llan-, Caer-, Ynys-, Ystrad-* e.g. *Trefranwen, Llanfair, Caerfyrddin, Ynys-ddu, Ystradgynlais*.

(iii) *iaith* 'language'; *tafodiaith* 'dialect' and the names of languages and dialects, e.g. *Y Gymraeg* 'Welsh'; *yr Wyddeleg* 'Irish'; *y Ddyfedeg* 'Demetian'; *y Wenhwyseg* 'Gwentian'. See also **159** (iii).

Note
When the reference points to quality of usage, or to a particular period in the history of the language, it is masculine: *Cymraeg Canol* 'Middle Welsh'; *Llydaweg Diweddar* 'Modern Breton'; *Cymraeg cywir* 'correct Welsh'; *Ffrangeg graenus* 'elegant French'.

(iv) *llythyren* 'letter'; *cytsain* 'consonant'; *llafariad* 'vowel' and the names of the letters of the alphabet: e.g. *A fawr* 'capital A'; *n ddwbl* 'double n'.

(v) *afon* 'river'; *nant* 'stream' and the names of rivers and streams: *Teifi, Dyfrdwy, Tywi, Conwy, Hafren.*

Note
Old names with *Nant-* are sometimes masculine, e.g. *Nant-mawr, Nantlleidiog, Nantgarw.*

(vi) names of mountains: *Y Fan*; *Yr Wyddfa* 'Snowdon'; *Y Garn*; *Y Foel*; *Y Glydair Fawr*; *Carnedd Ddafydd.*

Note
If *mynydd* 'mountain' or *bryn* 'hill' is part of the name, then that name is masculine, e.g. *Y Mynydd Du* 'The Black Mountain'; *Mynyddmelyn*; *Bryn-gwyn*; *Bryn-glas.*

(vii) *coeden* 'tree' and the names of trees, e.g. *derwen* 'oak'; *onnen* 'ash'; *collen* 'hazel'; *ywen* 'yew'; *olewydden* 'olive'.

Note
In compounds whose second element is *pren* (*-bren*) the noun is masculine: *ffigysbren* 'fig-tree'; *cambren* 'cambrel'; *esgynbren* 'perch'. *Croesbren* 'cross' and *crocbren* 'gibbet' vacillate between masc. and fem. gender.

(viii) collective nouns: *cenedl* 'nation'; *ciwed* 'rabble'; *ach, llinach, hil* 'lineage'; *cymanfa* 'assembly'; *cynhadledd* 'conference'; *cymdeithas* 'society'; *diadell* 'flock'; *buches* 'herd'; *haid* 'swarm'; *mintai* 'company'; *byddin* 'army'; *catrawd* 'regiment'; *tyrfa* 'crowd'; *pobl* 'people'; *cynulleidfa* 'congregation'; *corfforaeth* 'corporation'; *cwt* 'queue'; *ysgol* 'school'; *prifysgol* 'university'; *athrofa* 'academy'; *urdd* 'order'; *cyngres* 'congress'; *cyfeillach* 'fellowship'; *llynges* 'navy'.

Note
The following collective nouns are masculine: *llu* 'host'; *teulu* 'family'; *tylwyth* 'relatives'; *llwyth* 'tribe'; *côr* 'choir'; *cyngor* 'council'; *pwyllgor* 'committee'; *bwrdd* 'board'; *undeb* 'union'; *cwmni* 'company'; *coleg* 'college'; *cynulliad* 'assembly'; *cyfarfod* 'meeting'; *enwad* 'denomination'; *gweithgor* 'working party'.

·181   The gender of derivative nouns may be classified according to endings.

(i) Derivative nouns with the following endings are normally masculine:

-ad: *cyflenwad* 'supply'; *enwad* 'denomination'; *troad* 'turning'.
Note
Galwad 'call' vacillates between masc. and fem. gender.
-aint: *henaint* 'old age'.
-deb: *cywirdeb* 'correctness'; *uniondeb* 'rightness'; *duwioldeb* 'godliness'.
-der: *poethder* 'heat'; *blinder* 'weariness'; *dicter* 'anger'. On *dicter* see **147, 155**.
-did: *glendid* 'cleanness'; *gwendid* 'weakness'; *ieuenctid* 'youth'. On *ieuenctid* see **147, 155**.
-dra: *glanweithdra* 'cleanliness'; *ffieidd-dra* 'loathing'; *cyfleustra* 'convenience'. On *cyfleustra* see **147, 155**.
-dwr: *cryfdwr* 'strength'; *sychdwr* 'drought'.
-edd: *amynedd* 'patience'; *cydbwysedd* 'balance'; *gwirionedd* 'truth'.
Note
Buchedd 'life', *cynghanedd* 'metre', *trugaredd* 'mercy' are feminine.
-had: *mwynhad* 'joy'; *eglurhad* 'explanation'; *caniatâd* 'permission'. On *caniatâd* see **147, 155**.
Note
Ordinhad 'sacrament' is feminine.
-i: *tlodi* 'poverty'; *diogi* 'idleness'; *cwrteisi* 'courtesy'.
-iad: *cariad* 'love'; *cysylltiad* 'connection'; *tarddiad* 'source'.
-iant: *mwyniant* 'enjoyment'; *ffyniant* 'prosperity'.
-id: *cadernid* 'strength'; *rhyddid* 'freedom'.
Note
Addewid 'promise' vacillates between masc. and fem. gender.
-ineb: *ffolineb* 'folly'; *taerineb* 'earnestness'.
Note
Doethineb 'wisdom' vacillates between masc. and fem. gender, masc. in *y doethineb hwn* (1955) 'this wisdom' (Matt. 13: 54; Jas. 3: 15), fem. in Mark 6: 2; Jas. 3: 17. The 1988 translation of the Bible selects feminine gender.
-ioni: *daioni* 'goodness'; *haelioni* 'generosity'.
-ni: *noethni* 'nakedness'; *bryntni* 'filth'; *glesni* 'blueness'.
-awd, -od: *traethawd* 'essay'; *unawd* 'solo'; *cryndod* 'shivering'.

Note
Trindod 'trinity' is feminine.
-rwydd: *caredigrwydd* 'kindness'; *addasrwydd* 'suitability'.
-wch: *heddwch* 'peace'; *tywyllwch* 'darkness'; *dedwyddwch* 'bliss'.
-yd: *iechyd* 'health'; *seguryd* 'idleness'; *esmwythyd* 'ease'.

(ii) Derivative nouns with the following endings are normally feminine:

-aeth, -iaeth: *gwybodaeth* 'knowledge'; *brawdoliaeth* 'brotherhood'; *gwyddoniaeth* 'science'; *athroniaeth* 'philosophy'; *dirnadaeth* 'comprehension'; *swyddogaeth* 'function'; *amheuaeth* 'doubt'; *diwinyddiaeth* 'theology'; *barddoniaeth* 'poetry'; *rhagluniaeth* 'providence'; *rhagoriaeth* 'superiority'.
Note
The following are masculine: *gwasanaeth* 'service'; *darfodedigaeth* 'consumption'; *hiraeth* 'longing'; *gwahaniaeth* 'difference'. *Claddedigaeth* 'burial' vacillates between masc. and fem. gender.
-as: *priodas* 'wedding'; *teyrnas* 'kingdom'; *perthynas* 'relationship'.
-en, -cen: *hogen* 'girl'; *seren* 'star'; *ffolcen* 'fool' (see **174** (iii)).
Note
Maharen 'ram' is masc.
-es: *llewes* 'lioness'.
-ell: *llinell* 'line'; *pothell* 'blister'; *tarddell* 'source'.
Note
In the masc. nouns *hanes* 'history', *castell* 'castle', *cawell* 'cage', *-es*, *-ell* are not suffixes.
-fa: *noddfa* 'refuge'; *graddfa* 'scale'; *porfa* 'pasture'; *amddiffynfa* 'protection'.

(iii) Derivative nouns ending in **-aid** ('-ful') and **-od** ('blow') have the same gender as the nouns to which the suffix is added:

Masculine	Feminine
tŷ 'house', *tyaid* 'houseful'	*casgen* 'cask', *casgenaid* 'caskful'
crochan 'pot', *crochanaid* 'potful'	*padell* 'pan', *padellaid* 'panful'
bocs 'box', *bocsaid* 'boxful'	*basged* 'basket', *basgedaid* 'basketful'

cleddyf 'sword', *cleddyfod*   *ffon* 'stick', *ffonnod*
    'sword-stroke'   'blow with a stick'
                                     cern 'cheek', *cernod* 'clout'

Note
Cwpan 'cup', *cwpanaid* 'cupful' and *nyth* 'nest', *nythaid* 'nestful' vary
in gender according to area and dialect.

(iv) Gender of compound nouns.

Normally the gender of a proper compound (see **333** (i)) is that of its
chief (final) element. *Tŷ* 'house' is masc. and likewise *gweithdy*
'workshop', *bracdy* 'brewery', *ffermdy* 'farmhouse', *stordy* 'store-
house' etc.; *llan* 'enclosure' is fem. and likewise *gwinllan* 'vineyard',
perllan 'orchard' etc.

Note
There are many exceptions: *canrif* 'century' and *pendro* 'giddyness',
for example, are fem. though *rhif* 'number' and *tro* 'turn' are masc.

The gender of an improper compound (see **333** (ii)) is that of its
initial element:

masculine: *gwrda* (*gŵr* + *da*) 'worthy man'; *pentir* (*pen* + *tir*)
'headland'; *brawdmaeth* (*brawd* + *maeth*) 'foster-brother'.

feminine: *treflan* (*tref* + *llan*) 'townlet'; *pontbren* (*pont* + *pren*)
'wooden bridge'; *chwaerfaeth* (*chwaer* + *maeth*) 'foster-sister'.

The Adjective

Number

182 Most adjectives have no plural form, and the singular form of
those adjectives which have plurals is frequently used with plural
nouns. The plural is formed from the masculine singular in three
ways:

  1 By change of internal vowel (see **183**)
  2 By addition of a plural ending (see **184**)
  3 By addition of a plural ending and change of internal vowel (see
       185).

183 By change of internal vowel

Affection by **-i**, see **141**, **143**. Some examples are noted below:

a becomes **ai**

bychan 'small'	pl. *bychain*
cyfan 'complete'	pl. *cyfain*
llydan 'wide'	pl. *llydain*
buan 'quick'	pl. *buain*
truan 'wretched'	pl. *truain*
ieuanc, ifanc 'young'	pl. *ieuainc, ifainc*
byddar 'deaf'	pl. *byddair*

a becomes **ei**

ysgafn 'light'	pl. *ysgeifn*
marw 'dead'	pl. *meirw*
garw 'rough'	pl. *geirw*
balch 'proud'	pl. *beilch*
hardd 'beautiful'	pl. *heirdd*

a–a become **e–y** (clear)

cadarn 'firm'	pl. *cedyrn*

a–e become **e–y** (clear)

caled 'hard'	pl. *celyd*

184 By addition of a plural ending

-on is selected following **-u**, **-eu**; following a consonant **+ r**; following **-oyw**; following a consonant **+** consonantal **w**:

du 'black'	pl. *duon*
tenau 'thin'	pl. *teneuon*
budr 'dirty'	pl. *budron*
gloyw 'bright'	pl. *gloywon*
croyw 'clear'	pl. *croywon*
gwelw 'pale'	pl. *gwelwon*
chwerw 'bitter'	pl. *chwerwon*
gweddw 'widowed'	pl. *gweddwon*

-ion is selected elsewhere:

mud 'dumb'	pl. *mudion*
cul 'narrow'	pl. *culion*
coch 'red'	pl. *cochion*
llwyd 'grey'	pl. *llwydion*

sur 'sour'	pl. *surion*
tew 'fat'	pl. *tewion*
brith 'speckled'	pl. *brithion*
mawr 'big'	pl. *mawrion*
dewr 'brave'	pl. *dewrion*
hir 'long'	pl. *hirion*
blith 'milch'	pl. *blithion*

185 By addition of a plural ending and change of internal vowel. On vowel mutation in the ultima see **146**. Some additional examples are noted below:

ai becomes **ei**

main 'slim'	pl. *meinion*
cain 'elegant'	pl. *ceinion*

aw becomes **o**

tlawd 'poor'	pl. *tlodion*

clear **y** becomes **y**

melyn 'yellow'	pl. *melynion*
gwyn 'white'	pl. *gwynion*
hyll 'ugly'	pl. *hyllion*
byr 'short'	pl. *byrion*
llyfn 'smooth'	pl. *llyfnion*
gwyrdd 'green'	pl. *gwyrddion*

w becomes **y** (dark)

llwm 'poor'	pl. *llymion*
dwfn 'deep'	pl. *dyfnion*
pwdr 'rotten'	pl. *pydron*
trwm 'heavy'	pl. *trymion*

au becomes **eu**

brau 'brittle'	pl. *breuon*
tenau 'thin'	pl. *teneuon*

Affection by **-i-**, see **141**, **143**. Some additional examples are noted below:

a becomes **ei**

glas 'blue'	pl. *gleision*
hallt 'salty'	pl. *heilltion*
gwag 'empty'	pl. *gweigion*
praff 'thick'	pl. *preiffion*

dall 'blind'   pl. *deillion*
bras 'large'   pl. *breision*

186 Adjectives with more than one plural form

Some adjectives have two plural forms, one plural realizing affection (see **143**) and the other formed by addition of the plural ending **-(i)on**:

hardd 'beautiful'   pl. *heirdd, heirddion*
garw 'rough'   pl. *geirw, geirwon*
marw 'dead'   pl. *meirw, meirwon*
caled 'hard'   pl. *celyd, caledion*
balch 'proud'   pl. *beilch, beilchion*

187 The following adjectives have no distinctive plural forms:

(i) Simple adjectives: *aeddfed* 'mature'; *aml* 'frequent'; *araf* 'slow'; *bach* 'small'; *ban* 'loud'; *blwng* 'surly'; *briw* 'broken'; *byw* 'alive'; *call* 'wise'; *cas* 'nasty'; *cau* 'hollow'; *certh* 'awful'; *craff* 'observant'; *chwim* 'nimble'; *chwith* 'strange'; *da* 'good'; *dig* 'angry'; *drwg* 'bad'; *dwys* 'grave'; *ffiaidd* 'foul'; *gau* 'false'; *glân* 'clean'; *gwâr* 'civilized'; *gwir* 'true'; *hafal* 'similar'; *hagr* 'ugly'; *hawdd* 'easy'; *hen* 'old'; *hoff* 'fond'; *hy* 'bold'; *iach* 'healthy'; *llawen* 'happy'; *llesg* 'feeble'; *llwyr* 'complete'; *llosg* 'burning'; *mân* 'small'; *mwll* 'close'; *pur* 'pure'; *rhad* 'cheap'; *rhwydd* 'easy'; *rhwth* 'gaping'; *sâl* 'ill'; *serth* 'steep'; *sobr* 'sober'; *swrth* 'sullen'; *sicr* 'sure'; *tal* 'tall'; *teg* 'fair'; *tywyll* 'dark' etc.

(ii) Adjectives ending in **-adwy, -aid, -aidd, -gar, -in, -lyd, -llyd**: *gweladwy* 'visible'; *credadwy* 'credible'; *euraid* 'golden'; *cannaid* 'bright'; *prennaidd* 'stiff'; *tlodaidd* 'sparse'; *beiddgar* 'daring'; *hawddgar* 'amiable'; *gerwin* 'rough'; *cysefin* 'original'; *gwaedlyd* 'bloody'; *llychlyd* 'dusty'; *oerllyd* 'chilly'; *tanllyd* 'fiery' etc.

Note
-ion can be added to some adjectives ending in **-ig, -og, -ol, -us**: *caredig* 'kind', *caredigion*; *daearol* 'earthly', *daearolion*; *cyfoethog* 'rich', *cyfoethogion*; *anffodus* 'unfortunate', *anffodusion*. These plural forms normally occur as nouns: *caredigion yr eisteddfod* 'friends of the eisteddfod'; *anffodusion y trydydd byd* 'unfortunates of the Third World'. Many adjectives ending in **-ig, -ol, -us** cannot select **-ion** to form the plural: *deheuig* 'skilful'; *lloerig* 'lunatic'; *gwledig* 'rural'; *hudol* 'enchanting'; *estronol* 'foreign'; *swynol* 'charming'; *hapus* 'happy'; *costus* 'expensive'; *llafurus* 'laborious'.

(iii) Adjectives in the equative and comparative degree, see **192**: *cryfed* 'as strong as', *cryfach* 'stronger than'; *byrred* 'as short as', *byrrach* 'shorter than'; *teced* 'as fair as', *tecach* 'fairer than'.

(iv) Compound adjectives: *hyglyw* 'audible'; *hyglod* 'famous'; *ffrwythlon* 'fertile'; *hirben* 'shrewd'; *melyslais* 'sweet-voiced'; *melynwallt* 'yellow-haired' etc.

Note
If the second element of the compound is an adjective which may select **-ion**, the compound may also do so: *claer* + *gwynion* > *claerwynion* 'brilliant white'; *tal* + *cryfion* > *talgryfion* 'of a hard forehead'; *pen* + *crynion* > *pengrynion* 'round-headed'.

188 Some plural adjectives are used as abstract nouns:

Singular adjective	Plural adjective	Plural abstract noun
uchel 'high'	*uchelion*	*uchelion*
dirgel 'secret'	*dirgelion*	*dirgelion*
cyfrin 'mystic'	*cyfrinion*	*cyfrinion*
eithaf 'furthest'		*eithafion*

Normally, however, these nouns denote classes of persons or kinds of animals:

Singular adjective	Plural adjective	Plural abstract noun
tlawd 'poor'	*tlodion*	*tlodion*
cyfoethog 'rich'	*cyfoethogion*	*cyfoethogion*
caeth 'not free'	*caethion*	*caethion*
doeth 'wise'	*doethion*	*doethion*
dall 'blind'	*deillion*	*deillion*
gwan 'weak'	*gweinion, gweiniaid*	*gweinion, gweiniaid*
truan 'wretched'	*truain*	*trueiniaid, truain*
ffyddlon 'faithful'		*ffyddloniaid*
prydferth 'beautiful'		*prydferthion*
enwog 'famous'		*enwogion*
rheidus 'needy'		*rheidusion*
gorau sup. 'best'		*goreuon*
hynaf sup. 'oldest'		*hynafiaid* 'ancestors'
pellaf sup. 'furthest'		*pellafion*
anwar 'wild'		*anwariaid*
cyfoed 'of the same age'		*cyfoedion*
cain 'fine'		*ceinion*

Concord

189 A plural or singular form of the adjective may be selected with a plural noun.

Plural:

ffyrdd culion 'narrow roads'
(Jane Edwards, 1976: 68)

byrddau crynion 'round tables'
(Robat Gruffudd, 1986: 109)

camau breision 'great strides'
(Geraint H. Jenkins, 1983: 77)

sanau gwynion ac esgidiau duon 'white stockings and black shoes'
(Rhiannon Davies Jones, 1985: 103)

dyddiau celyd 'hard days'
(Rhiannon Davies Jones, 1987: 102)

dramâu cyfain 'complete plays'
(Geraint Bowen, 1976: 211)

sgidiau ysgeifn 'light shoes'
(*Taliesin*, Tachwedd 1989: 21)

dynion bychain 'small men'
(*Taliesin*, Tachwedd 1989: 9)

rhyfeddodau mawrion 'great wonders'
(Ps. 136: 18)

blaenwyr cryfion 'strong forwards'
(R. Gerallt Jones, 1977: 42)

dagrau heilltion 'bitter tears'
(Rhiannon Davies Jones, 1977: 161)

esgyrn sychion 'dry bones'
(Gerhart Hauptman and Heinrich Böll, 1974: 4)

slediau trymion 'heavy sleighs'
(*ibid.*: 7)

dillad llaesion 'long clothes'
(*Taliesin*, Gorffennaf 1992: 68)

ysgwyddau llydain 'broad shoulders'
(Rhiannon Davies Jones, 1989: 28)

chwaraewyr geirwon 'rough players'
(*Y Faner*, 10 Ionawr 1992: 22)

Singular:

llygaid mawr 'big eyes'
(Jane Edwards 1976: 15)

rhosynnau coch 'red roses'
(Gerhart Hauptman and Heinrich Böll, 1974: 9)

swyddi bras 'prosperous positions'
(Urien Williams, 1974: 21)

dynion caled 'tough men'
(*ibid.*: 19)

llwyni tew 'dense bushes'
(*Barn*, Awst/Medi 1992: 19)

hancesi coch 'red handkerchiefs'
(*Taliesin*, Gorffennaf 1992: 46)

Note
Pobl 'people' is a singular noun but collective in meaning and may select a plural adjective as modifier: *pobl ifainc* 'young people' (Rhiannon Thomas, 1988: 40); *pobl dduon* 'black people'.

Gender

190 Most adjectives have no distinctive feminine form. Some adjectives (mostly monosyllabic) containing **y** or **w** have feminine forms. In the feminine **y** and **w** are affected to **e** and **o** respectively (see **142**):

w becomes **o**	
Masculine	Feminine
brwnt 'dirty'	*bront*
crwm 'bent'	*crom*
crwn 'round'	*cron*
cwta 'brief'	*cota*

dwfn 'deep'	*dofn*
llwm 'poor'	*llom*
tlws 'pretty'	*tlos*
trwm 'heavy'	*trom*
trwsgl 'clumsy'	*trosgl*

y becomes e

bychan 'small'	*bechan*
byr 'short'	*ber*
cryf 'strong'	*cref*
gwyn 'white'	*gwen*
gwyrdd 'green'	*gwerdd*
hysb 'barren'	*hesb*
llym 'sharp'	*llem*
syml 'simple'	*seml*
tywyll 'dark'	*tywell*
melyn 'yellow'	*melen*
llyfn 'smooth'	*llefn*

i becomes ai

brith 'speckled'	*braith*

Examples:

cadair drom 'a heavy chair'
(Alan Llwyd, 1991: 21)

chwarel ddofn 'a deep quarry'
(Aneirin Talfan Davies, 1976: 3)

lawnt lefn 'an even lawn'
(Rhiannon Davies Jones, 1989: 156)

carfan gref 'a strong group'
(Rhiannon Davies Jones, 1989: 75)

taith fer 'a short journey'
(Emyr Hywel, 1989: 44)

disgyblaeth lem 'a stern discipline'
(*Taliesin*, Rhagfyr 1988: 7)

ardal lom, ddiffrwyth, hesb ac oer
'a poor, infertile barren and cold area'
(*Y Faner*, 3 Chwefror 1989: 12)

merch fer 'a short girl'
(Rhiannon Davies Jones, 1977: 20)

cornel dywell 'a dark corner'
(Rhiannon Davies Jones, 1987: 212)

Notes

(1) Masculine forms of the adjective are frequently selected with fem. sing. nouns: *merch gryf* 'a strong girl'; *cornel dywyll* 'a dark corner'; *wythnos drwm* 'a heavy (busy) week'; *daear wlyb* 'wet soil'; *llaw drwm* 'a heavy hand'.

(2) The feminine forms listed below are not used in speech or in contemporary prose but occur occasionally in verse:

Masculine	Feminine
blwng 'surly'	*blong*
mwll 'sultry'	*moll*
hyll 'ugly'	*hell*
syth 'straight'	*seth*
llwfr 'cowardly'	*llofr*
swrth 'sullen'	*sorth*
twn 'broken'	*ton*
cryg 'hoarse'	*creg*

(3) The masculine form of the adjective is normally selected in the predicate: *y mae'r gaseg yn gryf* 'the mare is strong'; *yr oedd y ferch yn wyn* 'the girl was white'. In older prose, however, the adjective agreed with the noun in gender: *ni bydd fy llaw yn drom arnat* (1955), *ni fyddaf yn llawdrwm arnat* (1988) 'my hand shall not be heavy upon thee' (Job 33: 7); *A'r afon hefyd a â'n hesb ac yn sech* (1955), *bydd yr afon yn hesb a sych* (1988): 'the river shall be wasted and dried up' (Isa. 19: 5).

Position

191 The normal position of adjectives modifying the head of the Noun Phrase in Welsh is after the head they modify:

pentref bach prydferth, diarffordd Llanfihangel-y-pwll
'the small pretty, remote village of Llanfihangel-y-pwll'
(Aneirin Talfan Davies, 1972: 30)

edrychiad hir, ceryddol, du
'a long, chastening black look'
  (T. Glynne Davies, 1974: 375)

merch fer dywyll 'a short dark girl'
  (Rhiannon Davies Jones, 1977: 20)

On mutation of the initial consonant of the adjective in this position see **50**.

The following adjectives normally precede the noun and form a proper compound (see **333**) with it:

(i) *hen* 'old'; *prif* 'chief'; *gwir* 'true, genuine'; *unig* 'lonely'; *gau* 'false'; *cam* 'wrong, unjust'; *cryn* 'a good, a considerable':

ei brif bwrpas 'his main purpose'
  (R. Cyril Hughes, 1975: 48)

yr hen dŷ mawr digalon 'the big old sad house'
  (R. Cyril Hughes, 1976: 207)

On mutation of the noun in this position see **51**.

(ii) the pronominalia, *y naill* 'the one'; *rhyw* 'some'; *amryw* 'many'; *cyfryw* 'such'; *unrhyw* 'any'; *holl* 'every'; *ychydig* 'few'; *ambell* 'some'; *aml* 'many'.

ambell ddafad ddu 'an occasional black sheep'
  (Geraint H. Jenkins, 1983: 150)

amryw resymau 'many reasons'
  (David Roberts, 1978: 7)

rhyw greadur clyfar clyfar 'some clever, clever, creature'
  (John Rowlands, 1978: 14)

On mutation of the noun in this position see **51**.

Notes
(1) *Pob* 'every' does not cause mutation of the following noun: *pob cyfeiriad* 'every direction'.
(2) *ambell, aml, llawer* 'many' may be followed by *i* and the following noun is subject to mutation: *llawer i brynhawn* 'many an afternoon' (Aneirin Talfan Davies, 1972: 237); *aml i noson* 'many a night' (Rhiannon Thomas, 1988: 60); *ambell i rwystr* 'an occasional hindrance' (Friedrich Dürrenmatt, 1958: 22).

(3) *llawer* does not cause mutation of the following noun: *llawer brawddeg gwbl nodweddiadol o Kate Roberts* 'many a sentence wholly characteristic of Kate Roberts' (*Y Faner*, 19 Ionawr 1978: 13).

(4) *nemor* 'few' is followed by mutation of the following noun: *nemor air* 'hardly a word'.

(iii) The plural adjectives *uchelion* 'high', *dirgelion* 'secret', *cyfrinion* 'mystic' precede the noun:

uchelion fannau	'high places'
dirgelion leoedd	'secret places'
cyfrinion bethau	'mystic things'

(iv) The following adjectives vary in meaning according to their position:

unig	(a)	'only'	*yr unig dŷ* 'the only house'
	(b)	'lonely'	*y tŷ unig* 'the lonely house'
gwir	(a)	'genuine'	*gwir bartneriaeth* 'a genuine partnership'
	(b)	'true'	*stori wir* 'a true story'
cam	(a)	'unjust'	*cam farn* 'wrong judgement'
	(b)	'crooked'	*coes gam* 'a crooked leg'
priod	(a)	'proper'	*ei briod waith* 'his proper work'
	(b)	'married'	*gŵr priod* 'a married man'
union	(a)	'exact'	*yr union beth* 'the exact thing'
	(b)	'straight'	*y llwybr union* 'the straight path'
hen	(a)	'old'	*hen ddyn* 'an old man'
	(b)	'ancient'	*cenedl hen* 'an ancient nation'

Notes

(1) When *hen* precedes the noun it may express either disgust or endearment: *yr un hen thema* 'the same old theme'; *hen ddyn digri yw ef* 'he is an amusing old fellow'.

(2) When *pur* is an adjective meaning 'pure' it normally follows the noun: *dŵr pur* 'pure water'; *aur pur* 'pure gold'. When it is an adverb, meaning 'very, fairly', it precedes the adjective: *pur dda* 'very good'; *pur llwyddiannus* 'very successful'. On soft mutation following *pur* see **90**.

(3) In poetry, and to a lesser extent in prose, most adjectives may occur before the noun they modify, but this is a literary device:

Daw arall ddydd ac arall ddwylo ... 'Another day and other hands will come ...' (Rhiannon Davies Jones, 1977: 172); *Mi fydd y sychedig rai yma yn y munud* 'The thirsty ones will be here in a minute' (T. Glynne Davies, 1974: 47); *yr ystyfnig rai* 'the stubborn ones' (J. G. Williams, 1978: 176).

Comparison

192 There are four degrees of comparison of the adjective in Welsh. They are:

1 absolute
2 equative
3 comparative
4 superlative

The derived degrees are formed from the absolute by the addition of *-ed*, *-ach*, *-af* respectively. Before these affixes the voiced plosives *b*, *d*, *g* are replaced by the voiceless plosives *p*, *t*, *c*. The change also occurs when these consonants are followed by a sonant. Vowel mutation may occur, see **146**. After a short vowel in the penult, *n* and *r* are doubled. In speech and also in poetry *-f* is frequently omitted (see **45** (iv)).

193 Regular adjectives

Absolute	Equative	Comparative	Superlative
cas 'hateful'	*cased*	*casach*	*casaf*
cryf 'strong'	*cryfed*	*cryfach*	*cryfaf*
dewr 'brave'	*dewred*	*dewrach*	*dewraf*
glân 'clean'	*glaned*	*glanach*	*glanaf*
llawn 'full'	*llawned*	*llawnach*	*llawnaf*
pur 'pure'	*pured*	*purach*	*puraf*
ysgafn 'light'	*ysgafned*	*ysgafnach*	*ysgafnaf*
grymus 'powerful'	*grymused*	*grymusach*	*grymusaf*
hyfryd 'pleasant'	*hyfryted*	*hyfrytach*	*hyfrytaf*
gwlyb 'wet'	*gwlyped*	*gwlypach*	*gwlypaf*
tlawd 'poor'	*tloted*	*tlotach*	*tlotaf*
teg 'fair'	*teced*	*tecach*	*tecaf*
caredig 'kind'	*carediced*	*caredicach*	*caredicaf*
budr 'dirty'	*butred*	*butrach*	*butraf*
gwydn 'tough'	*gwytned*	*gwytnach*	*gwytnaf*

hagr 'ugly'	*hacred*	*hacrach*	*hacraf*
huawdl 'eloquent'	*huotled*	*huotlach*	*huotlaf*
brau 'brittle'	*breued*	*breuach*	*breuaf*
main 'slim'	*meined*	*meinach*	*meinaf*
tlws 'pretty'	*tlysed*	*tlysach*	*tlysaf*
trwm 'heavy'	*trymed*	*trymach*	*trymaf*
byr 'short'	*byrred*	*byrrach*	*byrraf*
llon 'cheerful'	*llonned*	*llonnach*	*llonnaf*
gwyn 'white'	*gwynned*	*gwynnach*	*gwynnaf*

Notes

(1) The derived degrees are the same for masc. and fem., but at an earlier period in the history of the language a few feminine forms occur (see D. Simon Evans, 1964: 39).

(2) Adjectives with the absolute ending in -*aidd* select -*ied*, -*iach*, -*iaf*, in other degrees: *peraidd* 'fragrant', *pereiddied*, *pereiddiach*, *pereiddiaf*; *mwynaidd* 'gentle', *mwyneiddied*, *mwyneiddiach*, *mwyneiddiaf*.

(3) The few adjectives ending in -*aid* change *d* to *t* before -*ied*, -*iach*, -*iaf*: *rhaid* 'necessary', *rheitied*, *rheitiach*, *rheitiaf*; *telaid* 'graceful', *teleitied*, *teleitiach*, *teleitiaf*.

194 Irregular adjectives

Absolute	Equative	Comparative	Superlative
agos 'near'	*nesed*	*nes*	*nesaf*
bychan 'small'	*lleied*	*llai*	*lleiaf*
⎰ *cynnar* 'early'	*cynted*	*cynt*	*cyntaf*
⎱ *buan* 'quick'			
da 'good'	*cystal*	*gwell*	*gorau*
drwg 'bad'	*cynddrwg*	*gwaeth*	*gwaethaf*
hawdd 'easy'	*hawsed*	*haws*	*hawsaf*
anodd 'difficult'	*anhawsed*	*anos*	*anhawsaf*
hen 'old'	*hyned*	*hŷn*	*hynaf*
hir 'long'	*cyhyd*	*hwy*	*hwyaf*
ieuanc, ifanc 'young'	*ieuanged, ifanged, ifanced*	*iau, ifangach, ifancach,*	*ieuaf, ieuangaf, ifancaf*
isel 'low'	*ised*	*is*	*isaf*
uchel 'high'	*uched, cyfuwch*	*uwch*	*uchaf*
mawr 'big'	*cymaint*	*mwy*	*mwyaf*
llydan 'wide'	*cyfled, lleted*	*lletach*	*lletaf*

The following may be compared regularly in varieties of informal Welsh:

agos	*agosed*	*agosach*	*agosaf*
cynnar	*cynhared*	*cynharach*	*cynharaf*
hawdd	*hawdded*	*hawddach*	*hawddaf*
llydan	*llydaned*	*llydanach*	*llydanaf*
hen	*hened*	*henach*	*henaf*
hir	*hired*	*hirach*	*hiraf*
isel	*iseled*	*iselach*	*iselaf*
uchel	*ucheled*	*uchelach*	*uchelaf*

195 The following adjectives have defective comparison, i.e. only the following forms exist:

(i)   superlative   *eithaf* 'uttermost'
(ii) comparative   *trech* 'stronger', superlative *trechaf* 'strongest'
(iii) comparative   *amgen, amgenach* 'other, better'.

196 A few nouns may select affixes of comparison, thereby changing their word class and becoming adjectives of comparison:

pen 'head'	sup. *pennaf* 'chief'
rhaid 'need'	equ. *rheitied*, comp. *rheitiach*, sup. *rheitiaf*
elw 'profit'	comp. *elwach* 'better off'
blaen 'point front'	sup. *blaenaf* 'foremost'
ôl 'rear'	sup. *olaf* 'last'
diwedd 'end'	sup. *diwethaf* 'last'
lles 'benefit'	comp. *llesach* 'more advantageous'
amser 'time'	comp. *amserach* 'more timely'
rhagor 'difference'	comp. *rhagorach* 'superior'

197 Equative adjectives may be formed from the following nouns by prefixing *cyf-*:

lliw 'colour'	*cyfliw* 'of the same colour'
lled 'breadth, width'	*cyfled* 'of the same breadth or width'
urdd 'order'	*cyfurdd* 'of the same order'
gwerth 'value'	*cyfwerth* 'of the same value'
oed 'age'	*cyfoed* 'of the same age'
rhyw 'kind'	*cyfryw* 'of the same kind, such'
gradd 'rank'	*cyfradd* 'of equal rank'
gwedd 'appearance'	*cyfwedd* 'similar in appearance'

Un may be used in the same way: *unlliw* 'of the same colour'; *unwedd* 'similar in appearance'. *Trilliw* 'of three colours' also occurs.

On mutation following *cyf-* see **137–138**.

On mutation following *un* see **57**.

198 Adjectives containing more than two syllables are mostly compared periphrastically, i.e. by placing *mor, mwy, mwyaf* before the absolute. *Mor* is followed by soft mutation (see **52**) except that *ll-* and *rh-* are not subject to mutation:

Absolute	Equative	Comparative	Superlative
dymunol 'desirable'	*mor ddymunol*	*mwy dymunol*	*mwyaf dymunol*
gwyntog 'windy'	*mor wyntog*	*mwy gwyntog*	*mwyaf gwyntog*
swynol 'charming'	*mor swynol*	*mwy swynol*	*mwyaf swynol*
diog 'lazy'	*mor ddiog*	*mwy diog*	*mwyaf diog*
llwfr 'cowardly'	*mor llwfr*	*mwy llwfr*	*mwyaf llwfr*
rhydlyd 'rusty'	*mor rhydlyd*	*mwy rhydlyd*	*mwyaf rhydlyd*

Most adjectives may be compared regularly, including many derivative adjectives in *-aidd, -ig, -in, -og, -us*: *peraidd* 'sweet'; *pwysig* 'important'; *gerwin* 'rough'; *grymus* 'powerful'; *ardderchog* 'splendid'; *cyfoethog* 'wealthy'.

Compound adjectives are mostly compared periphrastically but *gwerthfawr* 'valuable' may be compared thus:

gwerthfawroced   *gwerthfawrocach*   *gwerthfawrocaf*

Every adjective may be compared periphrastically apart from the irregular adjectives (see **194**).

Mor can be selected with the absolute of all adjectives: *mor fawr* 'so big'; *mor dda* 'so good'; *mor llydan* 'so wide'.

Notes

(1) The initial in *mor* is never mutated: *merch mor hardd* 'such a beautiful girl'.

(2) In varieties of spoken Welsh the equative may follow *mor*: *mor laned â phìn* 'as clean as a pin'; *mor goched â'r tân* 'as red as the fire'. On mutation following *mor* see **52**.

The Syntax of Compared Forms
199 Equative

(i) In a simple comparison the normal pattern is:

copula + noun/pronoun + *cyn* + equative + *â/ag* + noun/pronoun

After the equative, *â* is used before a consonant and *ag* before a vowel:

Y mae'r dillad cyn wynned â'r eira
'The clothes are as white as snow'

Yr oedd hi cyn llonned â'r gog
'She was as cheerful as the cuckoo'

Yr oedd cyn wynned ag ewyn
'She was as white as foam'

Mae'r bachgen cyn gryfed â cheffyl
'The boy is as strong as a horse'

On mutation following *â*, see **119**.
On mutation following *cyn*, see **52**.

The following adjectives are equative in form and, therefore, are not preceded by *cyn*:

cynddrwg 'as bad'	*cymaint* 'as much'
cystal 'as good'	*cyfled* 'as wide'
cyfuwch 'as high'	*cyhyd* 'as long'

For the periphrastic construction see **198**.

The equative frequently functions adverbially:

Rhedodd cyn gyflymed â'r gwynt
'He ran as fast as the wind'

Siaradai mor gyflym â'i frawd
'He spoke as rapidly as his brother'

Cyn + equative/*mor* + absolute + *â* may be followed by a clause (see **405**):

(a) a relative clause introduced by either *y* or *a*:

Nid yw ef cystal ag y bu
'He is not as good as he has been'

Ewch mor gyflym ag y galloch
'Go as fast as you can'

Nid wyf mor ddigalon ag a fûm
'I am not so sad as I have been'
(*Y Faner*, 19 Ionawr 1991: 21)

(b) an adverbial clause with *pe* or *pan*:

Mae pris y llyfr cymaint â phe bai'n newydd
'The book costs as much as if it were new'

Roedd hi mor ddeniadol â phan welais i hi ddiwethaf
'She was as attractive as when I last saw her'

(c) a clause denoting consequence:

Yr oedd y tywydd cynddrwg fel y caewyd yr ysgol
'The weather was so bad that the school was closed'

Yr oedd cystal graen ar y tŷ fel na chafwyd trafferth i'w werthu
'The house was in such good condition that it was not difficult to sell'

A verb-noun also occurs in the same construction:

Bu mor ffôl â phrynu car newydd
'He had been so foolish as to buy a new car'

Byddwch cystal â chau'r drws
'Be good enough to close the door'

Note
The initial of *cyn* is not subject to mutation following a fem. sing. noun: *merch cyn deced â Mair* 'a girl as fair as Mair'.

(ii) The equative (without *cyn*, except in the case of irregular adjectives, see **194**) or *mor* and the positive may follow a preposition:

er cystal 'however good'   *er cynddrwg* 'however bad'
rhag gwlyped 'though so wet'   *er mor arw* 'however rough'
gan gyflymed 'so rapid'   *er teced* 'however fair'

The equative may function as an abstract noun:

rhag cryfed y gwynt
'because of the might of the wind'

A pronoun may precede the equative:

rhag ei theced
'because of her beauty'

gan eu hanwoced
'because of their fame'

Clauses containing the equative are frequently causal or concessive:

Aeth i hwylio er gwaethed oedd y tywydd
'He went sailing though the weather was so bad'

Safodd gydol y gêm er mor boenus oedd ei goesau
'He stood throughout the game though his legs were so painful'

The verb *bod* 'to be' may be understood:

Af i hwylio er gwaethed y tywydd
'I shall go sailing though the weather is so bad'

(iii) The equative (without *cyn*) may be used to express astonishment or wonder: see **53**.

(iv) The equative occurs in certain idiomatic expressions:

cymaint a chymaint 'not so much, not a large measure'
(*y*) *dau cymaint* 'twice as much' (see **59**)
y cymaint arall 'as much again, as many again'
llawn cymaint 'quite as much'
hanner cystal 'half as good'

(v) The equative is followed by the radical of the noun:

cystal person 'as good a person'
cymaint tlodi 'so much poverty'

200 Comparative

(i) The comparative adjective is followed by *na(g)* 'than' + the noun or pronoun that is compared. *Na* occurs before consonants, *nag* before vowels:

Y mae'n gweithio'n galetach na'i ragflaenydd
'He works harder than his predecessor'

Gwell dysg na golud
'Better learning than wealth'
(Proverb)

Gwell pwyll nag aur
'Prudence is better than gold'
(Proverb)

On mutation following *na*, see **116**.

(ii) The comparative adjective may be used as a noun:

> *Ni welais erioed ei well*
> 'I never saw his better'

(iii) The comparative is followed by the radical of the noun:

> *gwell lle* 'a better place'
> *glanach traeth* 'a cleaner beach'
> *sicrach gafael* 'a firmer grip'

(iv) *Mwy*, *mwyach*, *bellach*, *gynt* may be used adverbially:

> *Ni chofiaf am y pethau hynny mwy*
> 'I do not remember those things any more'

> *Ni all symud o'r gadair bellach*
> 'He is not able to move from the chair now'

> *Ni welaf ef mwyach*
> 'I shall not see him any longer'

> *Yr oedd dau deulu'n byw yma gynt*
> 'There were two families living here formerly'

Notes
(1) The noun *rhagor* can have a comparative meaning (see **253** (i)) and may function adverbially: *Nid ydynt yn dod yma rhagor* 'They do not come here any more'.
(2) *Amgen* is used adverbially, 'other(wise), differently, (any) better': *Ni wyddwn amgen* 'I did not know any better'. A comparative, *amgenach*, also occurs, meaning 'better', see **195**: *Cytunwyd fod yn rhaid wrth rhywbeth amgenach na miri byrhoedlog* 'It was agreed that something better than shortlived merriment was necessary' (Hywel Teifi Edwards, 1989: 240); *Fe fyddant yn dod i le llawer amgenach na'r dinasoedd hynny* 'They will be coming to a far better place than those cities' (*Y Faner*, 28 Gorffennaf 1989: 5).

(v) A numeral may precede the comparative adjective:

> *canmil gwell* 'a hundred thousand (times) better'
> *saith gwaeth* 'seven times worse'
> *deuwell* 'twice better'
> *deufwy* 'twice as much'

*Swydd anodd ydy gwarchod gwlad ond mae'n fil anos gwarchod
fy mhlant fy hun*
'Protecting a country is a difficult task but it is a thousand
(times) more difficult to protect my own children'
    (Rhiannon Davies Jones, 1977: 191)

(vi) The comparative adjective may follow a noun or adjective
denoting extent or degree:

llawer gwaeth 'much worse'
ychydig gwell 'a little better'
llawn cystal 'quite as good'
rhywfaint brafiach 'somewhat more pleasant'

(vii) In comparing two objects the superlative must be selected if the
article is used, rather than the comparative as in English:

Ef yw'r gorau o'r ddau
'He is the better of the two'

Hi yw'r talaf o'r ddwy
'She is the taller of the two'

If the article is not selected, however, either the comparative or the
superlative may occur:

Pa un o'r ddwy fyddai orau gennych?
'Which of the two would you prefer?'

Hwn fyddai orau gennyf
'I would prefer this one'

Byddai'n well gennyf hwn
'I would prefer this one'

*Prun sydd hawsaf, ai dweud wrth y claf, 'Maddeuwyd dy
bechodau', ai ynteu dweud, 'Cod, a chymer dy fatras a cherdda?'*
'Which of these is easier to say to the sick person, "Your sins are
forgiven", or to say, "Get up, pick up your stretcher and walk"?'
    (Mark 2: 9)

If *na(g)* is selected before the noun or pronoun to be compared only
the comparative may occur:

Mae hi'n llawer gwannach nag ef
'She is far weaker than him'

(viii) The comparative occurs in certain idiomatic expressions:

mwy na mwy 'a great deal'
mwy na mesur 'beyond measure'

201 Superlative

(i) The superlative may emphasize the quality denoted by the adjective rather than suggest comparison; in this usage soft mutation may be selected following the superlative, see **55**.

(ii) Proportionate equality is expressed by *po* + 'superlative ... superlative':

Po dynnaf fo'r llinyn, cyntaf y tyr
'The tighter the rope, the sooner it breaks'
     (Proverb)

Po fwyaf y caent eu gorthrymu, mwyaf yn y byd yr oeddent yn amlhau ac yn cynyddu
'The more harshly they were treated, the more their number increased beyond all bounds'
     (Exod. 1: 12)

Po fwyaf yr oedd ef yn gorchymyn iddynt, mwyaf yn y byd yr oeddent hwy'n cyhoeddi'r peth
'The more he forbade them, the more they published it'
     (Mark 7: 36)

In the expressions *gorau po fwyaf* 'the more the better', *gorau po gyntaf* 'the sooner the better', *gorau* precedes *po*:

Gorau po gyntaf yr wynebwn y sefyllfa'n onest
'The sooner we face the situation honestly, the better'
     (John Jenkins, 1978: 24)

(iii) In addition to the expressions *yn gyntaf* 'firstly', *yn olaf* 'lastly', *yn bennaf* 'chiefly', the superlative may be used adverbially:

(a) without *yn* when followed by a relative clause:

Gwna orau y gelli
'Do your best'

Cer gyntaf y medri
'Go as quickly as you can'

Soft mutation occurs in the initial of the adjective, see **83**.

(b) with or without *yn* where no relative clause follows:

Ef a gyrhaeddodd adref gyntaf/yn gyntaf
'He arrived home first, most quickly'

Dyma'r côr a ganodd orau/yn orau
'This is the choir that sang best'

Note
In the following proverbial saying the superlative stands for a noun, without the article: *Gwannaf gwaedded, trechaf treisied* 'Let the weakest cry out, let the mightiest oppress'.

(iv) The superlative is selected following a preposition in idiomatic expressions:

am y cyntaf	'for the first'
ar ei orau	'at his best'
o'r gorau	'very well'
er/ar fy ngwaethaf	'in spite of me'
gyda'r rhataf	'about the cheapest'
ar y cochaf	'a little too red/lean'

Numerals

Cardinals

202 Cardinal numbers note the number of items in question.

0	dim
1	un
2	dau (masc.)
	dwy (fem.)
3	tri (masc.)
	tair (fem.)
4	pedwar (masc.)
	pedair (fem.)
5	pump, pum
6	chwech, chwe
7	saith
8	wyth
9	naw
10	deg, deng

On mutation following *un* see **57, 110.**
On mutation following *dau, dwy* see **58, 59, 160.**
On mutation following *tri* see **112.**
On mutation following *pum* see **109.**
On mutation following *chwe* see **112.**
On mutation following *saith* see **86, 109.**
On mutation following *wyth* see **86, 109.**
On mutation following *naw* see **109.**
On numerals preceding the comparative see **200** (v).

Notes

(1) The forms *pum, chwe* are used before nouns: *pum dyn* 'five men'; *pum cath* 'five cats'; *chwe bachgen* 'six boys'; *chwe merch* 'six girls'. If the noun is not selected the forms *pump, chwech* are used: *Roedd y pump wedi cyrraedd* 'The five had arrived'.

(2) The form *deng* (see **109**) occurs before *blynedd* 'year'; *blwydd* 'a year old'; *diwrnod* 'day'; and nouns with an initial nasal: *deng mlynedd* 'ten years'; *deng mlwydd oed* 'ten years old'; *deng milltir* 'ten miles'; *deng mil* '10,000'. Both *deng niwrnod* and *deg diwrnod* 'ten days' occur; both forms may also occur before vowels: *deng awr, deg awr* 'ten hours'.

203

11	*un ar ddeg*	*un deg un*
12	*deuddeg, deuddeng*	*un deg dau/dwy*
13	*tri/tair ar ddeg*	*un deg tri/tair*
14	*pedwar/pedair ar ddeg*	*un deg pedwar/pedair*
15	*pymtheg/pymtheng*	*un deg pump*
16	*un ar bymtheg*	*un deg chwech*
17	*dau/dwy ar bymtheg*	*un deg saith*
18	*deunaw*	*un deg wyth*
19	*pedwar/pedair ar bymtheg*	*un deg naw*
20	*ugain*	*dau ddeg*
21	*un ar hugain*	*dau ddeg un*
22	*dau/dwy ar hugain*	*dau ddeg dau/dwy*
30	*deg ar hugain*	*tri deg*
31	*un ar ddeg ar hugain*	*tri deg un*
32	*deuddeg ar hugain*	*tri deg dau/dwy*
40	*deugain*	*pedwar deg*
50	*hanner cant*	*pum deg*

60	*trigain*	*chwe deg*
80	*pedwar ugain*	*wyth deg*
100	*cant, can*	
300	*tri chant, trichant*	
1,000	*mil*	
1,000,000	*miliwn*	

On mutation following *deuddeng, pymtheng, deunaw, ugain* see **109**.

On mutation following *un* in composite numerals see **110**.

On *h-* following *ar* before *ugain* see **125** (ix).

Notes

(1) The forms *deuddeng, pymtheng* are selected in the same circumstances as *deng*: see **202** n. 2.

(2) The forms *un deg un, wyth deg, wyth deg tri* '83', *cant tri deg wyth* '138' etc. are frequently used when giving the numbers of pages and hymns, to indicate the scores of games, in teaching mathematics, and increasingly in other contexts.

(3) The form *can* occurs before a noun: *can cyfer* '100 acres'; *can milltir* '100 miles'; *canpunt, can punt* '£100'.

(4) The vigesimal system of numeration (reckoning in multiples of 20) may make limited use of subtraction. In earlier editions of the Bible the interpretation of a numeral by subtraction is indicated by the forms *onid* and *namyn*, which are in free variation and expressed initially: *onid pedwar trigain* (1955) Ezra 2: 22 (−4 ... 3 × 20) (= 56); *namyn tri pedwar ugain* (1955) Ezra 8: 35 (−3 ... 4 × 20) (= 77); *onid dwy flynedd deugain* (1955) Deut. 2: 14 (−2 ... 2 × 20) (= 38). Subtraction has been abandoned in the 1988 translation of the Bible and is rare in contemporary formal texts; the interpretation of subtraction in contemporary Welsh is signalled by *namyn* and expressed finally: *deugain mlynedd namyn tair* (2 × 20 ... −3) (= 37) (R. Geraint Gruffyd, 1988: 27), *deugain cerdd namyn un* (2 × 20 ... −1) (= 39) (Dafydd Johnson, 1989: 31). See **402**.

(5) In the 1988 translation of the Bible the conj. *a* 'and' (see **399**) is used to link the decimal and unitary elements in forms like *un deg a naw* '19' (Gen. 11: 25), *chwe deg a phump* '65' (Gen. 5: 21), *naw deg a naw* '99' (Gen. 17: 1).

204 The numerals may be used as substantives or as adjectives.

(i) As a substantive a numeral may be followed either by a plural noun or pronoun governed by the preposition *o*, or by a personal form of the preposition *o*:

saith o blant	'seven children'
cannoedd ohonom	'hundreds of us'
naw o ddynion	'nine men'
ugain o bethau	'twenty things'
chwech ohonynt	'six of them'

On mutation following the preposition *o* see **69**.

In the examples quoted above the noun is indefinite and normally there is no semantic difference between *saith o blant* and *saith plentyn*: see **202**.

(ii) A definite plural noun may also be selected following the preposition in partitive constructions:

naw o'r merched	'nine of the girls'
dau o'r plant	'two of the children'
ugain o'r pryfed	'twenty of the insects'
pump o'r rhain	'five of these'

A plural form of the numeral may be selected:

degau o ddynion	'tens of men'
cannoedd o'r pryfed	'hundreds of the insects'
miloedd o ddynion	'thousands of men'

An indefinite plural noun is selected to denote the individual component units of the numeral:

Oes gennyt ti bump o geiniogau?
'Do you have five (individual) pennies?'

Note
Mil and *miliwn* are nouns and are normally followed by the preposition *o*: *mil o ddynion* 'a thousand men'; *miliynau o blant* 'millions of children'; *mil ohonom* 'a thousand of us'; *miloedd ohonynt* 'thousands of them'.

(iii) When a cardinal numeral is followed directly by a noun, the noun is in the singular:

dau afal	'two apples'

deg ceiniog	'ten pence'
ugain munud	'twenty minutes'

In composite numbers the noun occurs after the first element:

pum munud ar hugain	'twenty-five minutes'
pedair awr ar hugain	'twenty-four hours'
un gŵr ar bymtheg	'sixteen men'
un mlynedd ar ddeg ar hugain	'thirty-one years'

The same word order may be adopted in phrases expressing alternatives when two numerals are connected by the conjunction *neu* 'or':

wyth gwaith neu naw	'eight or nine times'
pum punt neu chwech	'£5 or £6'

In such expressions *un* 'one' is only included for emphasis:

blwyddyn neu ddwy	'a year or two'
un funud neu ddwy	'(only) one or two minutes'

The noun may occur following the second numeral:

dwy neu dair gwaith	'two or three times'
tri neu bedwar peth	'three or four things'

A numeral may be compounded with a noun:

dwybunt	'£2'
canllath	'100 yards'
decpunt	'£10'

Pymtheg 'fifteen' + *nos* 'night' yield *pythefnos*, *pythewnos* 'a fortnight'.

On numerals following plural nouns see **60**.

Notes

(1) In earlier versions of the Welsh Bible examples occur of plural nouns following the numeral: *dau frodyr* 'two brothers' (1955) (Matt. 4: 18).

(2) The old plural forms *blynedd* 'years' and *diau* 'days' are still selected following numerals: *tridiau* 'three days'; *chwe blynedd* 'six years'. *Diau* occurs only with *tri*. *Blynedd* is selected following all numerals except for *un* and *mil*. *Un* is followed by the singular noun *blwyddyn* 'year'; *un flwyddyn* 'one year'. *Mil* is

followed by the plural noun *blynyddoedd*: *mil blynyddoedd*, *mil o flynyddoedd* 'thousand years'.

(3) The feminine form of the numeral (when it occurs) is always selected with *blynedd*: *tair blynedd* 'three years'; *pedair blynedd ar ddeg* 'fourteen years'.

Ordinals

205 Ordinal numbers note the place of each item in numerical order.

1st	*cyntaf*
2nd	*ail*
3rd	*trydydd* (masc.)
	trydedd (fem.)
4th	*pedwerydd* (masc.)
	pedwaredd (fem.)
5th	*pumed*
6th	*chweched*
7th	*seithfed*
8th	*wythfed*
9th	*nawfed*
10th	*degfed*
11th	*unfed ar ddeg*
12th	*deuddegfed*
13th	*trydydd/trydedd ar ddeg*
14th	*pedwerydd/pedwaredd ar ddeg*
15th	*pymthegfed*
16th	*unfed ar bymtheg*
17th	*ail ar bymtheg*
18th	*deunawfed*
19th	*pedwerydd/pedwaredd ar bymtheg*
20th	*ugeinfed*
21st	*unfed ar hugain*
22nd	*ail ar hugain*
30th	*degfed ar hugain*
32nd	*deuddegfed ar hugain*
40th	*deugeinfed*
50th	*hanner canfed*
60th	*trigeinfed*
80th	*pedwar ugeinfed*

100th	*canfed*
300th	*tri chanfed*
1,000th	*milfed*
1,000,000th	*miliynfed*

On *h-* following *ar* before *ugain* see **125** (ix).
On mutation following ordinals see **62**.

206 Simple ordinals are followed by the noun:

ail blentyn	'a second child'
y bumed ferch	'the fifth girl'
y seithfed bennod	'the seventh chapter'

In composite ordinals the noun occurs after the first element:

yr unfed waith ar ddeg	'the eleventh time'

If the noun is feminine, the feminine ordinal (when it occurs) is selected:

y drydedd salm ar hugain	'the twenty-third psalm'

Cyntaf normally follows the noun, but it may also occur (without the article) before the noun:

y peth cyntaf	'the first thing'
ein cartref cyntaf	'our first home'
y tro cyntaf	'the first time'
cyntaf peth	'first thing'

It can be adverbial following *yn*:

yn gyntaf dim	'first of all'

Ordinals are placed after the names of monarchs, popes, etc.:

Edward y seithfed	'Edward VII'
Elizabeth yr ail	'Elizabeth II'
Siarl y cyntaf	'Charles I'
Pius y trydydd ar ddeg	'Pius XIII'

Days of the month follow the same pattern and always select the masculine ordinal since the noun *dydd* 'day' is masculine:

Ionawr y pumed	'January 5th'
Medi'r trydydd	'September 3rd'
Tachwedd y pedwerydd ar hugain	'November 24th'

Multiplicatives

207 The numeral is combined with the fem. sing. noun *gwaith* 'time':

'once'	*unwaith*
'twice'	*dwywaith*
'three times'	*teirgwaith*
'four times'	*pedair gwaith*
'five times'	*pum gwaith/waith*
'six times'	*chwe gwaith*
'seven times'	*seithwaith, saith gwaith*
'eight times'	*wythwaith, wyth gwaith*
'nine times'	*naw gwaith*
'ten times'	*dengwaith, deg gwaith*
'eleven times'	*un waith ar ddeg*
'twelve times'	*deuddeng waith, deuddeg gwaith*
'thirteen times'	*teirgwaith ar ddeg*
'fourteen times'	*pedair gwaith ar ddeg*
'fifteen times'	*pymthengwaith, pymtheg gwaith*
'sixteen times'	*unwaith ar bymtheg*
'seventeen times'	*dwywaith ar bymtheg*
'eighteen times'	*deunaw gwaith*
'nineteen times'	*pedair gwaith ar bymtheg*
'twenty times'	*ugeinwaith, ugain gwaith*
'thirty times'	*dengwaith ar hugain*
'fifty times'	*hanner canwaith*
'hundred times'	*canwaith*
'three hundred times'	*tri chanwaith*
'a thousand times'	*milwaith*
'a million times'	*miliwn gwaith*

Note

An old nasal of *g-* is preserved in *dengwaith*.

208 Distributives are formed by placing *bob yn* before the numeral; the initial of the numeral is subject to soft mutation:

bob yn un	'one by one'
bob yn ddau	'two by two'
bob yn bedwar	'four by four'
bob yn ddeg	'ten by ten'

The ordinal *ail* 'second' is used in *bob yn ail, ar yn ail, bob eilwers* 'alternately'.

Fractions

209

$\frac{1}{2}$	=	*hanner*
$\frac{1}{3}$	=	*traean*
$\frac{2}{3}$	=	*deuparth*
$\frac{1}{4}$	=	*chwarter, pedwaran*
$\frac{3}{8}$	=	*tri wyth*
$\frac{7}{8}$	=	*saith wyth*
$\frac{1}{5}$	=	*pumed* (*rhan*)
$\frac{1}{10}$	=	*degfed, degwm*
$\frac{1}{100}$	=	*canfed, canran* = 'percentage'.

The article may occur with fractions: see **159** (x).

Pronouns

Personal Pronouns

210 Personal pronouns may be either Independent or Dependent. The Independent Personal Pronouns are so called because they are not dependent upon nouns or finite verbs or inflected forms of prepositions: they function as heads in a noun phrase.

211 Independent pronouns are either simple, reduplicated or conjunctive:

(a) Simple

Singular	Plural
1 *mi, fi*	1 *ni*
2 *ti, di*	2 *chwi, chi*
3 *ef, fe, fo* (masc.) *hi* (fem.)	3 *hwy, hwynt, nhw*

Notes
(1) The colloquial forms *fe* (South Wales), *fo* (North Wales), *chi*, *nhw* are permissible in the literary language except in the most formal of texts: *Chi fydd y ddwy smartia yn y briodas* 'You will be the smartest two in the wedding' (Kate Roberts, 1976: 27); *Tyrd*

â nhw i mewn 'Bring them in' (Emyr Hywel, 1989: 9); *Fo ydy brenin y drwgweithredwyr i gyd!* 'He is the king of all the evil-doers!' (Idwal Jones, 1979: 5); *Fe yw e reit i wala* 'It is him right enough' (Emyr Humphreys, 1981: 260).

(2) *Hwynt* is not used in the accusative with verbs ending in *-nt*: *Dysgwch hwynt/nhw* 'Teach them'; *Saethwch hwynt/nhw* 'Shoot them'; *Gwelant hwy* 'They will see them'.

(b) Reduplicated

Singular	Plural
1 *myfi*	1 *nyni*
2 *tydi*	2 *chwychwi*
3 *efe, efô, fe, fo* (masc.)	3 *hwynt-hwy*
hyhi (fem.)	

Notes

(1) Stress normally occurs on the final syllable.
(2) The reduplicated pronouns are more emphatic than the simple.
(3) In informal texts and in varieties of spoken Welsh the reduplicated pronouns are realized thus: Sing. 1 *y fi*; 2 *y ti*; 3 *y fe, y fo* (masc.), *y hi* (fem.); Pl. 1 *y ni*; 2 *y chi*; 3 *y nhw*.

(c) Conjunctive

Singular	Plural
1 *minnau*	1 *ninnau*
2 *tithau*	2 *chwithau, chithau*
3 *yntau* (masc.)	3 *hwythau, nhwythau*
hithau (fem.)	

Notes

(1) The conjunctive forms are used in conjunction with other nouns or pronouns to imply contrast, qualification and shades of meaning, such as 'I also, I for my part, but I, while I', etc.
(2) *Chithau, nhwythau* are permissible in the literary language except in the most formal of texts.

212 The independent pronouns are used as follows.

(i) As object of the verb:

Tywysodd fi'n gyflym o gwmpas yr eglwys
'He led me quickly around the church'
(Aneirin Talfan Davies, 1972: 1)

Cusanodd rhai hi
'Some kissed her'
   (Kate Roberts, 1976: 77)

Gorfodai fy nhad fi i wisgo'n wahanol i bob plentyn arall
'My father made me dress differently from every other child'
   (Harri Williams, 1978: 11)

Oni ddewisais i chwychwi? (1955)
'Have not I chosen you?'
   (John 6: 70)

Glywi di o'n crio?
'Can you hear him crying?'
   (Rhiannon Davies Jones, 1989: 124)

(ii) As the complement before the form of *bod* 'to be':

Ti ydy ffefryn dy dad
'You are your father's favourite'
   (Rhiannon Davies Jones, 1977: 144)

Nhw yw'r dosbarth sy'n rheoli
'They are the class that govern'
   (Robat Gruffudd, 1986: 171)

Myfi yw'r winwydden, chwithau yw'r canghennau (1955)
Myfi yw'r winwydden; chwi yw'r canghennau (1988)
'I am the vine, you (for your part) are the branches'
   (John 15: 5)

Chi fydd y ddwy smartia yn y briodas
'You will be the smartest two in the wedding'
   (Kate Roberts, 1976: 27)

On mutation of *b*- forms of *bod* 'to be' following the complement see
75.

(iii) As antecedent of a relative clause:

Nid nhw sy'n talu am ei betrol o
'It is not they who pay for his petrol'
   (Idwal Jones, n.d.: 54)

Hi a fu'n swcwr iddo dros y blynyddoedd
'It was she who had succoured him over the years'
   (Rhiannon Davies Jones, 1987: 132)

Hi oedd yn eistedd â'i chefn at y ffenest
'It was she who was sitting with her back to the window'
 (Emyr Humphreys, 1986: 35)

Hwynt-hwy a ddarfyddant; ond tydi sydd yn parhau; a hwynt-
hwy oll fel dilledyn a heneiddiant (1955)
'It is they who shall perish; but it is you who shall remain, and it
is they all who shall become old as does a garment'
 (Heb. 1: 11)

(iv)   Before a verb or *a* + verb, with no emphasis on the pronoun:

. . . a phan ddaeth yn ôl, ef a archebodd ddiodydd ar gyfer y lleill
'. . . and when he returned, he ordered drinks for the rest'
 (John Rowlands, 1978: 13)

Mi a godaf ac a af at fy nhad (1955)
Fe godaf, ac fe af at fy nhad (1988)
'I will arise and go to my father'
 (Luke 15: 18)

Ac efe a gododd ac a aeth at ei dad (1955)
'And he arose and went to his father'
 (Luke 15: 20)

In the above examples, *ef a*, *mi a*, *efe a* are considered pre-verbal
particles rather than true pronouns. At one time *mi a*, *ti a* etc., were
selected with their corresponding form of the finite verb, but only *mi*
a and *fe a* in the forms *mi*, *fe*, have survived in the literary language
as pre-verbal particles (see **336**). On mutation following the pre-
verbal particles see **80**.

(v)   As vocatives:

Chwychwi benaethiaid y bobl (1955)
'You rulers of the people'
 (Acts 4: 8)

Er mor annheilwng ydwyt ti o'n serch
Di, butain fudr y stryd â'r taeog lais
'Although you are so unworthy of our affection
You, dirty whore of the streets with the churlish voice'
 (David James Jones, Gwenallt, 1899–1968)

(vi)   After conjunctions or after non-inflecting prepositions:

Nid oeddynt yn bwriadu mynd â Gustavchen gyda hwy
'They did not intend taking Gustavchen with them'
> (Gerhart Hauptman and Heinrich Böll, 1974: 7)

Byddwn yn cael llawer o hwyl efo hwynt hefyd
'I used to have a lot of fun with them also'
> (Kate Roberts, 1976: 24)

Cynigiodd aros yno efo hi
'She offered to stay there with her'
> (Kate Roberts, 1972: 26)

Mi ddelia i efo nhw
'I shall deal with them'
> (Rhiannon Davies Jones, 1989: 97)

Er bod y telynor yn hen bryd hynny a'r delyn hŷn nag yntau roedd y cwbl wrth fodd y plant
'Although the harpist was old at that time and the harp older than him the children were content with everything'
> (Rhiannon Davies Jones, 1989: 118)

Cerddodd Rhisiart a hithau i fyny drwy'r ardd
'She and Richard walked up through the garden'
> (R. Cyril Hughes, 1976: 115)

Mae Mati a minnau am fynd i'r dref ddydd Mercher
'Mati and I wish to go to town on Wednesday'
> (Kate Roberts, 1976: 27)

Notes
(1)   In varieties of northern Welsh *chdi* regularly occurs instead of *ti* in the 2 sing. following non-inflecting prepositions: *efo chdi* 'with you'; *heblaw chdi* 'apart from you'.
(2)   In varieties of northern Welsh *chditha(u)* regularly occurs instead of *tithau* in the 2 sing. following a conjunction: *a chdithau* 'and you'.

(vii)   Conjunctive personal pronouns occur in apposition to a noun:

Yr olwynion hwythau ni throent chwaith oddi wrthynt (1955)
'The wheels did not turn from beside them'
> (Ezek. 10: 16)

Sila hithau a esgorodd ar Tubal-Cain (1955)
'Zillah too bore Tubal-Cain'
    (Gen. 4: 22)

Dioddefodd Crist yntau
'Christ too suffered'
    (1 Pet. 2: 21)

Aeth Dafydd yntau i'r ffair
'Dafydd too went to the fair'

Caiff y plant hwythau gyfle i fwynhau
'The children too shall have an opportunity to enjoy themselves'

(viii) As the subject of an independent phrase (absolute construction) (see **359**):

Nid oeddent hwy am symud cam o'r fan, a hwythau mor gysurus eu byd
'They did not wish to move a step from the place, and they so comfortable with their circumstances'
    (John Bunyan, 1962: 12)

Ac yntau'n ddeunaw mlwydd oed, mudodd Thomas Jones i Lundain oddeutu 1666
'And he being eighteen years old, Thomas Jones moved to London about 1666'
    (Geraint H. Jenkins, 1980: 1)

Yr oeddwn eisoes yn hen ŵr, a minnau'n blentyn
'I was already an old man, though I was a child'
    (Harri Williams, 1978: 12)

A mi wedi crybwyll enw John Stuart Corbett, mae'n werth sylwi bod y gŵr yma yn gyfreithiwr i ystâd yr Ardalydd Bute
'And I having mentioned John Stuart Corbett's name, it is worth noting that this man was a solicitor to the Marquis of Bute's estate'
    (Aneirin Talfan Davies, 1972: 37)

(ix) The pronoun alone is often used in replies:

Pwy a atebodd yn gyntaf? Fi
'Who answered first? I (did)'

Pwy oedd y cadeirydd? Fe
'Who was the chairman? He (was)'

213 Dependent pronouns are either prefixed, infixed or affixed, and function either as modifiers of the head of a noun phrase or as extensions of the head or modifier.

214 Prefixed

Singular		Plural	
1	*fy* 'my'	1	*ein* 'our'
2	*dy* 'your', 'thy'	2	*eich* 'your'
3	*ei* 'his/her'	3	*eu* 'their'

Notes

(1) The 1 sing. may be realized as *yn* [ən] in varieties of southern Welsh.

(2) The prefixed pronouns are atonic and therefore do not normally carry stress; stress occurs on the following word: *fy 'mhen* 'my head'. If the phrase, however, is marked by emphasis, stress is carried by the affixed pronoun: see **222** (i).

(3) *Ei, eu* are pronounced [i]; in colloquial Welsh *ein* may be pronounced [ən] and *eich* may be pronounced [əx].

215 Prefixed pronouns denote possession and are selected alone:

(i) before nouns and verb-nouns in unemphatic contexts:

eich rhieni	'your parents'
eu tad	'their father'
fy afal	'my apple'
ein canu	'our singing'

Before a vowel *fy, dy* often become *f', d'* (see **45, 108**):

f'anwylyd	'my darling'
d'enaid	'your soul'

An adjective or numeral may occur between the pronoun or verb-noun:

fy nhair merch	'my three girls'
ei lawen gyfeillion	'his happy friends'
eu swynol ganu	'their charming singing'

(ii) when the pronoun is in person-number concord with the predicator, i.e. when there is a reflexive reference:

Gwelodd ei dad ar waelod yr ardd
'He saw his father at the bottom of the garden'

Dodais yr het ar fy mhen
'I put the hat on my head'

216 Mutation following the prefixed pronouns:

fy, see **108**
dy, see **63**
ei (masc.), see **63**
ei (fem.), see **113**, **125** (i)
ein, see **125** (iv)
eu, see **125** (vii)
See also **222** (ii)

217 Infixed

These forms may be used either as possessives or as direct object
forms; the forms are the same for both, apart from the 3rd person:

Possessives

Singular		Plural	
1	*'m* 'my'	1	*'n* 'our'
2	*'th* 'your, thy'	2	*'ch* 'your'
3	*'i, 'w* 'his/her'	3	*'u, 'w* 'their'

Direct object forms

Singular		Plural	
1	*'m* 'me'	1	*'n* 'us'
2	*'th* 'thee'	2	*'ch* 'you'
3	*'i, -s* 'him/her'	3	*'u, -s* 'them'

218 The infixed pronouns are used as follows:

(a) As possessives:

Before nouns and verb-nouns and following words ending in a vowel
or diphthong:

fy mam a'm tad 'my mother and my father'
ein hafon a'n pysgota 'our river and our fishing'
o'i gorun i'w sawdl 'from his tip to his toe'
gyda'ch ffrindiau a'ch teuluoedd 'with your friends and your
   families'

In this type of linkage the possessive is used before each noun (see also **159**):

> *Ynddo pardduodd gymeriad y Cymry, eu bwyd, eu hanifeiliaid, eu cartrefi a'u harferion*
> 'In it he blackened the character of the Welsh, their food, their animals, their homes and their customs'
>   (Geraint H. Jenkins, 1980: 123)

'm, 'th may only be selected following *a* 'and', *â* 'with', *gyda* 'with, accompanying', *efo* 'with', *tua* 'towards, about', *na* 'than, neither, nor', *i* 'to', *o* 'from, of', *mo* (from *ddim o*: see **256** (iii)):

> *i'm tŷ* 'to my house'
> *o'm gardd* 'from my garden'
> *gyda'th dad* 'with your father'
> *Ni welais mo'th chwaer* 'I did not see your sister'

'w (sing. and pl.) can only be selected following the prep. *i* 'to':

> *i'w gar* 'to his car'
> *i'w cartrefi* 'to their homes'
> *i'w bwthyn* 'to her cottage; to their cottage'
> *i'w fwthyn* 'to his cottage'

Notes
(1) In varieties of southern Welsh *i'w* is realized as *iddi*: *iddi fam* 'to his mother'; *iddi mam* 'to her mother'; *iddi mamau* 'to their mothers' (see D. Simon Evans, 1964: 53, n. 2).
(2) In speech the prefixed pronoun is usually selected in place of the infixed, except in the 3 sing. and pl.: *gyda dy dad* 'with your father'; *fy nghi a fy nghath* 'my dog and my cat'; *gyda'i blant* 'with his children'.

(b) As direct object forms:

Before verbs:

(i) Following the pre-verbal particles:

> *Fe'm cyffrowyd ac fe'm synnwyd*
> 'I was excited and I was amazed'
>   (*Y Faner*, 19 Ionawr 1991: 21)

Fe'i claddwyd hi yn Llansamlet
'She was buried in Llansamlet'
    (Aneirin Talfan Davies, 1972: 241)

Fe'u cerais i nhw fel y bydd dyn yn caru blodau
'I loved them as a person loves flowers'
    (Rhiannon Davies Jones, 1977: 143)

(ii) following the relative pronoun:

Gwrin ap Rhydderch a Chadell Hir a'u gwelodd nhw gyntaf
'It was Gwrin ap Rhydderch and Cadell Hir who saw them first'
    (Rhiannon Davies Jones, 1977: 116)

(iii) following the negative pre-verbal particles *ni*, *na*:

Nis rhestraf yma
'I will not list them here'
    (Derec Llwyd Morgan, 1983: 38)

Ni'm symudir
'I shall not be shaken'
    (Ps. 10: 6)

Yr hyn nas dywedir ynddo a wnaeth yr argraff gryfaf arnaf
'It is what is not stated in it that made the strongest impression
on me'
    (*Y Faner*, 17 Chwefror 1989: 5)

Na'n twyller
'Let us not be fooled'
    (*Y Faner*, 4 Awst 1989: 8)

(iv) following the conjunctions *pe* 'if', *oni* 'unless, if not':

Chwaraewn pe'm dewisid
'I would play were I selected'

Buaswn wedi dweud wrthych pe'ch gwelswn
'I would have told you had I seen you'

Oni'ch gwelaf, fe ysgrifennaf
'Unless I see you, I will write'

Os felly, ti sy'n dysgu dy gyd-ddyn, oni'th ddysgi dy hun?
'If therefore, it is you who teach your fellow-man, do you not
teach yourself?'
    (Rom. 2: 21)

(v) following the relative particle *y* in expressions such as *lle y'm*, *lle y'th*, *yna y'm*, *yno y'th*, or their contracted forms *lle'm*, *lle'th*, *yna'm*, *yno'th*:

> *y wlad lle'u ganed*
> 'the country where they were born'
>   (*Y Faner*, 25 Ionawr 1991: 5)

> *y fferm lle y'i ganed*
> 'the farm where she was born'

> *y tŷ lle'm ganed*
> 'the house where I was born'

> *yno y'm ganed*
> 'it is there that I was born'

-s may only be suffixed to *ni*, *na*, *oni*, *pe*:

> *Dyma drefn naturiol pethau, ac er y breuid y llinyn, nis torrid*
> 'This was the natural order of things, and although the cord
> would become worn, it would not be broken'
>   (Jane Edwards, 1976: 147)

> *y pethau nis gwyddant* (1955)
> *y pethau nad ydynt yn eu deall* (1988)
> 'the things which they do not know'
>   (Jude 1: 10)

> *er nas cyhoeddwyd tan 1552*
> 'although it was not published until 1552'
>   (R. Geraint Gruffydd, 1988: 12)

> *hyd onis caffo ef* (1955)
> 'till she finds it'
>   (Luke 15: 8)

> *pes ysgrifennid heddiw*
> 'if it were written today'
>   (Geraint Bowen, 1976: 118)

-s only occurs in formal Welsh. See also n. 2 above.

219 Mutation following the infixed pronouns:

'th, see **64**
'i (masc.) as a possessive, see **64**
'w (masc.), see **64**
'i (fem.) as a possessive, see **114, 125** (ii)
'w (fem.), see **114, 125** (ii)
'i (masc. and fem.) as a direct object form, see **125** (iii)
'n, see **125** (v)
'm, see **125** (vi)
'u, see **125** (viii)

220 1 and 2 pl. prefixed and infixed pronouns occur with numerals in apposition after personal pronuns or 1 and 2 pl. personal endings:

ni ein dau/ni'n dau 'we two'
chi eich pedwar/chi'ch pedwar 'you four'

Dyna yw ein barn ni'n tri o Graig y Bedol
'That is the opinion of the three of us from Craig y Bedol'
    (Bryan Martin Davies, 1988: 32)

Bydd y peth yn gyfrinach rhyngoch eich dau ac efallai'n eich clymu'n dynnach wrth eich gilydd
'The thing will be a secret between you two and will perhaps tie you closer together'
    (Harri Williams, 1978: 49)

Ydach chi'n iach, eich dau?
'Are you well, you two?'
    (Rhiannon Davies Jones, 1989: 74)

With the 3 pl. *ill* is selected (see **249**):

Fe losgant ill dau ynghyd
'They shall both burn together'
    (Isa. 1: 31)

Edrychent ill dau tua'r llawr
'Both of them looked towards the floor'
    (Ioan Kidd, 1977: 88)

The auxiliary pronoun (see **221**) does not occur after numerals in the constructions described in this section.

221 Affixed or Auxiliary

These have simple and conjunctive forms:

Simple

Singular	Plural
1 *i, fi*	1 *ni*
2 *ti, di*	2 *chwi, chi*
3 *ef, fe, fo* (masc.)	3 *hwy, hwynt, nhw*
hi (fem.)	

Conjunctive

Singular	Plural
1 *finnau, innau*	1 *ninnau*
2 *tithau, dithau*	2 *chwithau*
3 *yntau* (masc.)	3 *hwythau, nhwythau*
hithau (fem.)	

Notes

(1) The 1 sing. present tense of most verbs and the 1 sing. of inflected prepositions end in *-f*, and either *i, fi* or *innau, finnau* may be selected: *gwelaf* (*f*)*i*/(*f*)*innau* 'I see'; *yr wyf* (*f*)*i*/ (*f*)*innau* 'I am'; *arnaf* (*f*)*i*/(*f*)*innau* 'on me'; *drosof* (*f*)*i*/ (*f*)*innau* 'over me'. In other contexts *i* or *innau* are selected: *bûm i*/*innau* 'I have been'; *euthum i*/*innau* 'I went'.

(2) When the verb or preposition (2 sing.) ends in *-t*, the form *ti*/ *tithau* is selected: *aethost ti*/*tithau* 'you went'; *arnat ti*/*tithau* 'on you'.

(3) *Hwynt* is not selected with verbs and prepositions ending in *-nt*: *y maent hwy* 'they are'; *aethant hwy* 'they went'; *lladdwyd hwy*/ *hwynt* 'they were killed'.

(4) On *fe, fo, chi, nhw* see **211** (a) n. 1. On *nhwythau* see **211** (c) n. 2.

222 The affixed or auxiliary pronouns are used as follows.

(i) To emphasize a prefixed or infixed pronoun (see **214** n. 2):

*fy mhen **i** 'my* head'
*i'w chartref **hi** 'to her* home'
*nis gwelais **ef** 'I did not see him'*
*fe'm saethwyd **i** 'I* was shot'

The conjunctive forms are selected either with or instead of *hefyd* 'also', with the implication that there is a recurrent reference:

Roeddwn innau hefyd wedi glân flino
'I also was very tired'
(Rhiannon Davies Jones, 1977: 40)

Roedd bywyd yn garedig wrth Mr Williams, ac roedd yntau'n garedig wrtho'i hun
'Life was kind to Mr Williams, and he was kind to himself as well'
(Urien William, 1974: 20)

Contrast or emphasis may be implied:

Os oedd hi'n dewis yr wylo, dewiswn innau'r boen
'If she chose the crying, I would choose the pain'
(Harri Williams, 1978: 65)

Yr oedd wedi sgwennu ati hithau, debyg iawn, i ddweud ei fod yn dod adref
'He had written to her, most probably, to say that he was coming home'
(T. Glynne Davies, 1974: 343–4)

A serial nominal phrase will often select a conjunctive pronoun for the last of the series:

fy nhad i, dy dad di a'i dad yntau
'my father, your father and his father'

Normally a sentence is syntactically complete without an auxiliary pronoun, but in the following examples it clarifies the gender of the subject or object:

Canodd (ef/hi) yn y gyngerdd
'He/she sang in the concert'

Fe'i cipiwyd (ef/hi) neithiwr
'He/she was abducted last night'

Mae (ef/hi)'n cerdded yn gyflym
'He/she walks quickly'

(ii) When the possessive pronoun is not in person-number concord with the predicator, i.e. where there is no reflexive reference (see **215** (ii)):

> *Gwelais ei dad ef ar waelod yr ardd*
> 'I saw his father at the bottom of the garden'

> *Dodais yr het ar ei phen hi*
> 'I put the hat on her head'

A sentence like:

> *Gwelodd ei dad ef ar waelod yr ardd*

can have two structures:

(a)

Gwelodd	*ei dad*	*ef*	*ar waelod yr ardd*
P(redicator)	S(ubject)	C(omplement)	A(dverb)

'His father saw him at the bottom of the garden'

(b)

Gwelodd	*ei dad ef*	*ar waelod yr ardd*
P + S	C	A

'He saw his father at the bottom of the garden'
(i.e. someone else's father)

(iii) When a numeral/ordinal occurs as head of the noun phrase with a prefixed or infixed pronoun as modifier, the auxiliary pronoun must also be selected:

> *Fy nhri i a'th ail di*
> 'My three and your second'

> *Byddai eu un hwy yn gweithredu o dan aden y Teledu Annibynnol*
> 'Theirs would function under the wing of Independent Television'
> (*Y Faner*, 21 Medi 1979: 2)

> *Mi gymera i feic mam, a chei di fy un i*
> 'I will take mother's bike, and you shall have mine'
> (Anwen P. Williams, 1976: 24)

The auxiliary pronoun, however, never occurs after the numeral when the prefixed pronoun and the numeral occur in an appositional construction.

aethom (ni) ein pedwar
'the four of us went'

See **220**.

Possessive Pronouns

223

Singular	Plural
1 *eiddof*	1 *eiddom*
2 *eiddot*	2 *eiddoch*
3 *eiddo* (masc.)	3 *eiddynt*
eiddi (fem.)	

Notes

(1) In an earlier period these forms were used to modify nouns and were called Possessive Adjectives (see J. J. Evans, 1946, 107).

(2) The older forms of the pronouns were *mau, tau, eiddo, eiddi, einym, einwch, eiddynt*, but by the modern period a new inflection based on the 3rd person had developed.

(3) The possessive pronouns, as pronouns, do not occur in colloquial Welsh but survive in the highly literary register.

(4) The older forms *mau, tau* occur in twentieth-century poetry and prose: *A llyma llun y fun fau* 'And this is a picture of my love' (R. Williams Parry (1884–1956), 'Yr Haf'); *y geiriau mau fi nid ânt heibio ddim* (1955), *fy ngeiriau i nid ânt heibio ddim* (1988) 'my words shall not pass away' (Mark 13: 31); *i'r tir tau* 'to your land' (T. Gwynn Jones (1871–1949), 'Gwlad y Bryniau'); *y Fun fau* 'my Love' (J. Elwyn Hughes, 1991: 52).

The possessive pronouns are used:

(i) following the article:

'Rwyn hoffi ei wasanaeth, ei gyflog, ei weision, ei lywodraeth, ei gwmni a'i wlad yn well na'r eiddot ti
'I enjoy his services, his wages, his servants, his government, his company and his country better than yours'
(John Bunyan, 1962: 35)

Pwy a rydd i chwi yr eiddoch eich hun? (1955)
'Who will give you what is your own?'
(Luke 16: 12)

A phan glybu'r eiddo ef, hwy a aethant i'w ddal ef (1955)
A phan glywodd ei deulu, aethant allan i'w atal ef (1988)
'And when his family heard, they set out to restrain him'
(Mark 3: 21)

Yr eiddoch yn gywir
'Yours sincerely' (at the end of a letter)

(ii) without the article:

nid eiddof ei roddi (1955)
nid gennyf fi y mae'r hawl i roi hynny (1988)
'it is not mine to give'
(Matt. 20: 23)

Caled yw hi wrth ei chywion, fel pe na byddent eiddi hi (1955)
Y mae'n esgeulus o'i chywion, ac yn eu trin fel pe na baent yn perthyn iddi (1988)
'She is hardened against her young ones, as though they were not hers'
(Job 39: 16)

Eiddof fi yw'r tir
'The land is mine'
(Lev. 25: 23)

224 *Eiddo* is also used as a noun meaning 'property, belongings':

Canys eiddo'r Arglwydd y ddaear, a'i chyflawnder (1955)
Oherwydd eiddo'r Arglwydd yw'r ddaear, a'i llawnder (1988)
'For the earth is the Lord's and everything in it'
(1 Cor. 10: 26)

Faint o eiddo'ch gwraig gafodd ei ddwyn?
'How much of your wife's property was stolen?'
(Wil Roberts, 1985: 56)

eiddo'r bobl fawr
'the property of the important people'
(Urien Williams, 1974: 21)

Yr oedd yn fwy ffiaidd nag unrhyw weithred ddiraddiol arall o eiddo'r Siapaneaid
'It was more abominable than any other degrading action by the Japanese'
(David Roberts, 1978: 167)

Dydy peri difrod i eiddo ddim yn fy mhoeni'n ormodol
'Causing damage to property does not worry me too much'
(*Y Faner*, 23 Chwefror 1989: 4)

Ei heiddo hi oedd y castell y nos hon
'The castle was her property this night'
(Rhiannon Davies Jones, 1987: 47)

Mae'n cyfeirio hefyd at nifer o gerddi o'm heiddo
'He refers also to a number of poems of mine'
(*Barddas*, Gorff./Awst 1992: 9)

The Relative Pronoun

225 The relative pronoun *a* functions as either the subject or object in a relative clause. It is followed directly by the verb, except when an infixed personal pronoun is selected:

(i) Subject

Uwchben y pentref fe welwch gapel bach a saif ar ymyl chwarel ddofn
'Above the village you see a small chapel that stands near a deep quarry'
(Aneirin Talfan Davies, 1976: 3)

Cododd y bibell a oedd wedi disgyn o'i enau
'He picked up the pipe that had fallen from his mouth'
(Gerhart Hauptmann and Heinrich Böll, 1974: 4) .

. . . cadnawes ifanc, gref a'm llygadai yn awchus yng ngwyll y ffau
'. . . a young strong vixen which eyed me eagerly in the darkness of the lair'
(Bryan Martin Davies, 1988: 109)

(ii) Object

Beth yw'r pethau olaf a gofiaf cyn dod yma?
'What are the last things that I remember before coming here?'
(Harri Williams, 1978: 7)

Gwerthodd y cyfan a feddai er mwyn ei brynu
'He sold all that he possessed in order to buy it'
(John Bunyan, 1962: 12)

yr her a'n hwyneba ni yng Nghymru
'the challenge that faces us in Wales'
(*Y Faner*, 21 Ebrill 1989: 6)

The relative pronoun is often omitted, especially before *oedd* (see **73**):

Tynnodd y sach oedd ar ei ysgwyddau
'He removed the sack that was over his shoulders'
(Emyr Humphreys, 1986: 97)

yr ychydig ddefnyddiau prin oedd ar gael
'the few scant materials that were available'
(Rhiannon Davies Jones, 1989: 5)

Negative. The verb in the relative clause is preceded by *na(d)*, *ni(d)*; *na*, *ni*, occur before consonants, *nad*, *nid* before vowels. Examples of *nis*, *ni(d)* as negative relative markers are usually found only in the most formal of texts:

Gwyn ei fyd y gŵr ni rodia yng nghyngor yr annuwiolion, ac ni saif yn ffordd pechaduriaid, ac nid eistedd yn eisteddfa gwat- warwyr (1955)
Gwyn ei fyd y gŵr nad yw'n dilyn cyngor y drygionus nac yn ymdroi hyd ffordd pechaduriaid nac yn eistedd ar sedd gwat- warwyr (1988)
'Blessed is the man that walketh not in the counsel of the ungodly, nor standeth in the way of sinners, nor sitteth in the seat of the scornful'
(Ps. 1: 1)

Ti yw'r plentyn na chaf
'You are the child that I shall not have'
(Marion Eames, 1982: 97)

y pethau ni welir (1955)
y pethau na welir (1988)
'the things which are not seen'
(2 Cor. 4: 18)

*Byddi'n edrych ar genedl nid adweini a bydd cenedl nad yw'n dy
adnabod yn rhedeg atat*
'You will look at a nation that you do not know, and a nation
that does not know you will run to you'
(Isa. 55: 5)

The infixed object forms (see **217**, **218** (b)) may be suffixed to *ni, na*:

y pethau nis gwyddant (1955)
y pethau nad ydynt yn eu deall (1988)
'the things which they know not'
(Jude 1: 10)

Yr hyn nas dywedir ynddo a wnaeth yr argraff gryfaf arnaf
'It is what is not stated in it that made the strongest impression
on me'
(*Y Faner*, 17 Chwefror 1989: 5)

On mutation following the relative pronoun *a* see **73**.
On mutation following *ni(d)*, *na(d)* see **87**, **115**.
Mutation following the infixed pronoun depends on the person
and the gender of the pronoun (see **64**, **125**).
In informal texts and in varieties of spoken Welsh *ddim* may occur
after the verb to convey negation:

Maen nhw'n gofnod o fywyd oedd ddim yn ddrwg i gyd
'They are a record of a life that was not wholly bad'
(Alun Jones, 1989: 14)

226 When the relative pronoun represents the subject, the verb in
the relative clause following the rel. pron. is 3rd person sing. even
when the antecedent is plural:

Trodd y dyn du mawr a oedd yn cerdded wrth ei ochr
'The big black man who was walking at his side turned'
(Harri Prichard Jones, 1978: 105)

Canmolent eu meddygon a roddai iddynt eu valium a'u librium
'They would praise their doctors who would give them their
valium and their librium'
(Jane Edwards, 1976: 87)

*Yr oedd ef wedi dod i adnabod llwyth arall o gadnoid a drigai yn
nhueddau dwyreiniol y Mynydd Du*

'He had got to know another tribe of foxes that lived on the
eastern side of Mynydd Du'
   (Bryan Martin Davies, 1988: 105)

In a negative construction the verb normally agrees with the
antecedent:

bysedd nad oeddynt ond megis esgyrn sychion, melyn
'fingers that were merely like dry, yellow bones'
   (Gerhart Hauptman and Heinrich Böll, 1974: 4)

*Yr unig ddau greadur yn y gegin nad oedden nhw'n tisian oedd y
cwc a chath fawr a eisteddai ar y aelwyd yn gwenu o glust i glust*
'The only two creatures in the kitchen who were not sneezing
were the cook and a large cat who was sitting on the hearth smil-
ing broadly'
   (Lewis Carroll, 1982: 53)

*Dau farchog gosgeiddig cryf eu gewynnau oedd Cawl a Chlud na
fyddent byth yn gwahanu oddi wrth eu harglwydd*
'Cawl and Clud were two handsome muscular knights who
would never be separated from their lord'
   (Rhiannon Davies Jones, 1989: 74)

*Mae rhai miloedd o Sosialwyr na pherthynant i unrhyw undeb
nac i'r Blaid Lafur*
'There are several thousand Socialists that do not belong to any
union or to the Labour Party'
   (*Y Faner*, 26 Mai 1989: 7)

Notes

(1) Examples occur in older prose of the verb following *a* in person-
   number concord with the antecedent: *bendithiwch y rhai a'ch
   melltithiant* (1955) 'bless them that curse you' (Matt. 5: 44).

(2) Examples occur of a plural antecedent followed by a verb in the
   3rd person sing. in a negative construction: *y llygaid na all agor*
   'the eyes that cannot open' (R. Williams Parry (1884–1956),
   'Hedd Wyn'); *y pethau nid oedd weddaidd* (1955) 'the things
   which were not decent' (Rom. 1: 28).

When the relative is either subject or object the relative clause is
called a Proper Relative Clause.

227 *Bod* 'to be' has a relative form in the 3 sing. pres. indic., namely
sydd, sy.

Its antecedent may be either singular or plural:

Mae'r hogan yma sy'n priodi reit glyfar
'This girl who is getting married is quite clever'
(Kate Roberts, 1976: 26)

Peth hawdd yw twyllo dyn sy wedi ymgladdu yn ei waith
'It's an easy thing to deceive a man who has buried himself in his work'
(Emyr Humphreys, 1981: 74)

Mae pob un o'r bechgyn hyn sydd yn nhîm y coleg yn fabol-gampwyr cymesur, cyflym, cryf
'Every one of these boys who are in the college team are fit, fast, strong athletes'
(R. Gerallt Jones, 1977: 27)

Mae'r ysgrifen ar y mur i'r rhai sy'n medru darllen arwyddion yr amserau!
'The writing is on the wall for those that can read the signs of the times!'
(*Y Faner*, 14 Ebrill 1989: 5)

The relative pronoun is not selected before *sydd, sy*.

Negative. *Sydd* is replaced by *nad yw* (*ydyw*)/*ydynt*, the verb agreeing with the antecedent in number:

Mae dail y goeden ffigys, nad yw byth yn aeddfedu, yn cau allan llawer o'r golau
'The leaves of the fig tree, that never matures, shut out much of the light'
(Emyr Humphreys, 1981: 71)

stryd fawr nad yw'n llawer mwy nag ychydig gannoedd o lathenni o hyd
'a main street that is not much more than a few hundred yards in length'
(Aneirin Talfan Davies, 1976: 58)

Mae ffurfiau ar wrth-Iddewiaeth nad ydynt mor amrwd ac annynol
'There are forms of anti-Semitism that are not so crude and inhuman'
(*Taliesin*, Tachwedd 1989: 39)

gweithiau nad ydynt ar gael yn awr
'works that are not available at present'
    (*Llais Llyfrau*, Gaeaf 1989: 6)

In informal texts and in varieties of spoken Welsh *sy*(*dd*) *ddim* occurs:

Oes 'na rwbeth sydd ddim fel y dyla fo fod?
'Is there something that isn't as it should be?'
    (Alun Jones, 1989: 190)

Nid oes unrhyw gyfundrefn arall ... sydd ddim yn gwneud camgymeriadau sylfaenol yn yr un modd
'There isn't any other system ... that doesn't make basic mistakes in the same way'
    (*Y Faner*, 25 Ionawr 1991: 4)

It also occurs in the 1988 translation of the Bible:

Gwyliwch y rhai sy ddim yn gwaedu'r cnawd
'Beware of those who do not circumcise'
    (Phil. 3: 2)

Nid yw/ydynt is usually found only in the most formal of texts.

228 *Piau* is another relative form which does not require the relative pronoun before it, except when it is the object of an infixed pronoun. The initial of *piau* may mutate (see **95**).

Ni biau Eryri
'It is we who own Snowdonia'
    (Rhiannon Davies Jones, 1977: 107)

Hon piau'r wobr gynta'
'The first prize is hers'
    (J. Elwyn Hughes, 1991: 73)

Safodd yn fy ymyl angel y Duw a'm piau
'There stood by me an angel of the God whose I am'
    (Acts 27: 23)

Myfi piau dial, myfi a dalaf yn ôl
'Revenge is mine, I will repay'
    (Heb. 10: 30)

In tenses other than the present tense the 3 sing. forms of *bod* 'to be' are used with *piau* to denote tense meaning:

Ni oedd biau'r byd
'It was we who owned the world'
  (Rhiannon Davies Jones, 1977: 13)

Chi fydd piau'r dyfodol
'The future will be yours'
(It is you who will own the future)
  (Rhiannon Davies Jones, 1987: 204)

Notes
(1) In varieties of spoken Welsh *sy(dd) piau* occurs: *Pwy sy bia'*
    hwn? 'Who owns this?'
(2) The 3 sing. imperf. *pioedd* is confined to a highly literary
    register.

229 When the relative is governed by a possessive pronoun, or is
governed by a preposition, or is adverbial, the relative clause is
called an Oblique Relative Clause or an Improper Relative Clause.
In contemporary writing, the verb in an affirmative clause is usually
preceded by the particle *y(r)*; *y* occurs before consonants, *yr* before
vowels and *h*. The relative particle is frequently omitted in varieties
of spoken Welsh and in informal texts.

230 Governed by a possessive pronoun. The relative clause has a
discontinuous construction, with the shape

y(r)	[Verb]	*ei/'i/'w*	'his'
		ei/'i/'w	'her'
		eu/'u/'w	'their'

Y(r) occurs at clause initial and is followed by a verb + a possessive
pronoun (see **214, 217**) + a noun or verb-noun which the relative
clause qualifies in number and gender. *Y* occurs before consonants,
yr before vowels:

y dyn y chwythodd ei het i ffwrdd
'the man whose hat blew away'

y wraig y prynasoch chi ei defaid
'the woman whose sheep you bought'

y ffermwyr y gwelsoch chi eu caeau
'the farmers whose fields you saw'

Credaf imi gyflawni'r gwaith y'm galwyd i'w gyflawni
'I believe that I accomplished the work that I was called to accomplish'
(Harri Williams, 1978: 7)

Hon oedd y stori y mynnai T. Llew Jones . . . ei chlywed dro ar ôl tro
'This was the story that T. Llew Jones ... insisted on hearing time after time'
(*Golwg*, 20 Ebrill 1989: 20)

yr asennod yr aethost i'w ceisio
'the asses which you went to seek'
(1 Sam. 10: 2)

Examples of the relative clause introduced by *a* also occur in contemporary writing, especially when the relative is dependent on a verb-noun:

Mawr obeithio y bydd y deunaw clwb yn gwneud popeth a allant ei wneud i sicrhau y sefydlir Cynghrair cenedlaethol yn 1990
'I sincerely hope that the eighteen clubs will do all that they can to ensure that a national League is established in 1990'
(*Y Faner*, 2 Mehefin 1989: 21)

Mae'n amheus gen i a ydy athrawon yn sylweddoli'r cam a allant ei wneud â'r pwnc y maent yn ei ddysgu
'I doubt whether teachers realize the wrong that they can do to the subject that they teach'
(Geraint Bowen, 1972: 67)

On mutation following *a* see **73**.

Where the relative clause begins with a form of the verb *bod* 'to be' only *y(r)* may occur

Dy fraint di yw prynu'r pethau y mae arna i eu hangen
'It is your privilege to buy the things that I need'
(Roy Lewis, 1978: 132)

Pwysleisiai Ned bob un gair bob amser dan fawr bwysau'r gwirionedd yr oedd yn hollol siwr ei fod yno, y tu ôl i'w eiriau doeth
'Ned would invariably emphasize every single word under the great pressure of the truth that he was certain was there, behind his wise words'
(T. Glynne Davies, 1974: 47)

Negative. The verb in the relative clause is usually preceded by *na* before consonants, *nad* before vowels:

> *Yr oedd nifer o blant bach newydd-anedig na wyddai neb eu henwau wedi marw yn Nhrefri a Threberfedd*
> 'A number of new-born babies whose names no one knew had died in Trefri and Treberfedd'
> (Rhiannon Davies Jones, 1977: 65)

On mutation following *na* see **87, 115**.

Examples of *ni(d)* are usually confined to the most formal of texts:

> *y pethau nid ydys yn eu gweld* (1955)
> *pethau na ellir eu gweld* (1988)
> 'things we cannot see'
> (Heb. 11: 1)

In informal varieties of spoken Welsh *ddim* may occur after the verb to convey negation:

> *y merched buodd e ddim yn 'u gweld nhw*
> 'the girls that he had not been to see'

231 Governed by a preposition. The relative clause has a discontinuous construction, with the shape

> *y(r)* [Verb] (a) personal inflection of a preposition
> (see **363–366**)
> (b) independent personal pronoun (see **211**)
> (c) dependent possessive pronoun (see **214, 217**)

Y(r) occurs at clause initial and (a) and (b) occur at clause final; (c) occurs with compound prepositions (see **368**): (a), (b) and (c) agree in person and number with the noun which the relative clause qualifies. *Y* occurs before consonants, *yr* before vowels:

(a) *y gwely y gorweddais arno*
'the bed I lay on' (lit. 'on it' [masc.])

y ceir yr eisteddodd hi ynddynt
'the cars she sat in' (lit. 'in them')

Nid i ddawnsiau'r pentref yn unig yr aent, ond i bob dawns y medrent fynd iddi yn yr ardal
'It was not only to the village dances they would go, but to every dance that they could go to (lit. 'to them') in the area'
(Gerhart Hauptman and Heinrich Böll, 1974: 2)

Gwyn ei byd y genedl y mae'r Arglwydd yn Dduw iddi
'Blessed is the nation whose God is the Lord'
(lit. 'the Lord is God to it' [fem.])
    (Ps. 33: 12)

Gwyddai fod yr esgus y bu'n aros amdano wedi cyrraedd
'She knew that the excuse that she had been waiting for (lit.
'for it' [masc.]) had arrived'
    (Jane Edwards, 1976: 157)

(b) *y plant y teithiais gyda hwy*
'the children I travelled with' (lit. 'with them')

y siswrn y torrodd ei ewinedd ag ef
'the scissors he cut his nails with' (lit. 'with it' [masc.])

*Weithiau awn drwy'r pentref a heibio i'r hen felin, y byddai fy
ngwraig yn ymweld â hi yn blentyn*
'Sometimes I would go through the village and past the old
mill, that my wife used to visit as a child' (lit. 'visit with it'
[fem.])
    (Aneirin Talfan Davies, 1972: 29–30)

*Gwyddwn fod hyn yn rhywbeth y byddai'n rhaid imi fyw
gydag ef weddill fy oes*
'I knew that this was something I would have to live with (lit.
'with it' [masc.]) for the rest of my life'
    (Emyr Humphreys, 1981: 222)

(c) *y cricedwr oedd y dyn y sefais yn ei ymyl*
'the cricketer was the man I stood by' (lit. 'by his side')

y llwyni y chwaraeai'r plentyn o'u blaen
'the shrubs that the child played in front of' (lit. 'their front')

Gwelais y dyn y dygwyd achos yn ei erbyn
'I saw the man a lawsuit was brought against' (lit. 'his
against')

Examples of *a* introducing the relative occur in biblical prose:

Hysbysa iddynt y ffordd a rodiant ynddi
'Show them the way in which they shall walk'
    (Exod. 18: 20)

On mutation following *a* see **73**.

Where the relative clause begins with a form of the verb *bod* 'to be', only *y(r)* may occur:

tai Sioraidd y mae'n werth bwrw golwg arnynt
'Georgian houses that it is worth looking at' (lit. 'at them')
    (Aneirin Talfan Davies, 1976: 15)

yr Adroddiad yr oedd yn gyfrifol amdano
'the Report he was responsible for' (lit. 'for it')
    (*Y Faner*, 28 Ebrill 1989: 17)

y cardiau y bu'n cofnodi cynifer o fân ffeithiau arnynt
'the cards he had noted so many detailed facts on' (lit. 'on them')
    (John Rowlands, 1978: 7)

Negative. The verb in the relative clause is preceded by *na* before consonants, *nad* before vowels.

y siopau hynny nad âi Harri byth i mewn iddyn nhw
'those shops that Harry never went into' (lit. 'into them')
    (John Rowlands, 1978: 86)

un o'r tafarnau nad oedd erioed wedi ymweld â nhw
'one of the pubs that he had never visited' (lit. 'visited with them')

On mutation following *na* see **87, 115**.

Examples of *ni(d)* are usually confined to the most formal of texts:

yr hwn nid oes iachawdwriaeth ynddo (1955)
'the one in whom there is no salvation' (lit. 'there is no salvation in him')
    (Ps. 146: 3)

In informal varieties of spoken Welsh *ddim* may occur after the verb to convey negation:

y ferch oedd e ddim wedi sôn amdani
'the girl that he had not mentioned'

232 Adverbial. When the relative is adverbial the relative clause follows a noun denoting time, place, manner or cause:

y dydd y cymerwyd ef i fyny
'the day when he was taken up'
    (Acts 1: 2)

'Roedd y munud neu ddau y bu'n gorwedd yno yn ddychrynllyd
'The minute or two that he had been lying there were terrible'
(Alun Jones, 1989: 189)

Dyna'r pryd y sylweddolodd nad oedd hi gydag ef yn y llyfrgell
'That was when he realized that she was not with him in the library'
(Alun Jones, 1989: 110)

Yr ydych wedi gwrthryfela yn erbyn yr Arglwydd o'r dydd y deuthum i'ch adnabod
'You have rebelled against the Lord from the day that I came to know you'
(Deut. 9: 24)

Negative. The verb in the adverbial relative is preceded by *na* before consonants, *nad* before vowels:

Dyna'r unig reswm nad aethom ni
'That is the only reason we did not go'

Dyma'r man na welsoch chi
'This is the place that you didn't see'

Adverbial clauses introduced by conjunctions and prepositions (e.g. *lle*, *pryd*, *fel*, *felly*, *megis*, *modd*: see **410**) are constructed on the same model as adverbial relative clauses introduced by *y*, *na(d)*.

In informal varieties of spoken Welsh *ddim* may occur after the verb to convey negation:

Dyna'r dydd aeth e ddim
'That is the day he did not go'

233 Many nouns and pronouns may be selected as antecedents of a relative pronoun or particle: *yr hwn* 'he who'; *yr hon* 'she who'; *yr un*, *y neb*, *y sawl* 'the one who'; *y rhai* 'those who'; *peth* 'that which'; *(pa) beth bynnag* 'whatsoever'; *pryd bynnag* 'whenever'; *pa le bynnag* 'wherever'; *pwy bynnag* 'whosoever', etc.

(i) The antecedent may be an integral part of the sentence:

Byddai raid i'r sawl a aned dan 'blaned flin' ddioddef pob math o helbulon
'Whosoever was born under "an evil planet" would have to suffer all sorts of adversities'
(Geraint H. Jenkins, 1983: 16)

Y neb a ymgymerer â thrais a dreisir, y neb a rydd bwys ar gystadlu a drechir yn y diwedd
'The one who engages in violence will be oppressed, the one who favours competition will be defeated in the end'
(*Y Faner*, 28 Ebrill 1989: 6)

Byddai'n rhaid iddo gael ffôn ble bynnag y byddai
'He would have to have a phone wherever he would be'
(Jane Edwards, 1976: 100)

Cydsyniodd Cristion am y gwyddai yn ei galon fod yr hyn a ddywedai ei gyfaill yn wir
'Christian agreed because he knew in his heart that what his friend said was true'
(John Bunyan, 1962: 61)

Beth bynnag a wna, fe lwydda
'Whatsoever he does, it prospers'
(Ps. 1: 3)

Pwy bynnag a wna hyn, nis symudir byth
'Whosoever does this, shall never be moved'
(Ps. 15: 5)

Gwnaed deddf fod pwy bynnag na syrthiai ac addoli ei ddelw aur i gael ei daflu i ffwrn o dân poeth
'A law was made that whosoever did not fall down and worship his golden image was to be thrown into a fiery furnace'
(John Bunyan, 1962: 49)

dawns fwgwd arall – un well a mwy arswydus na'r un a gynhaliwyd erioed
'another masked ball – a better one and more frightening one that had ever been held'
(Gerhart Hauptman and Heinrich Böll, 1974: 11)

Newidodd y rhai a oedd gynt yn erbyn mynd i'r dafarn eu meddwl
'The ones who had previously been against going to the pub changed their minds'
(Gerhart Hauptman and Heinrich Böll, 1974: 13)

Mae'r lle'n siangdifang pryd bynnag y galwch chi heibio
'The place is upside down whenever you call by'
(Irma Chilton, 1989: 37)

(ii) The antecedent may be in apposition to a form in the matrix clause:

Yn yr Alban roech chi'n delio ag Albanwyr, rhai a oedd yn un â dyheadau'r Alban
'In Scotland you were dealing with Scots, ones in step with Scotland's aspirations'
    (*Y Faner*, 28 Ebrill 1989: 5)

fel mân us yr hwn a chwâl y gwynt ymaith (1955)
'like chaff which the wind driveth away'
    (Ps 1: 4)

Doedd tŷ Jeroboam fab Nebat yr hwn a wnaeth i Israel bechu ddim yni hi
'The house of Jeroboam son of Nebat who made Israel sin wasn't in it'
    (Jane Edwards, 1977: 97)

A noun phrase can be repeated to make it an antecedent of a relative clause:

Roedd yn rhyfedd fel yr oedd y bobl niwtral – y bobl a safai yn y canol heb wneud dim byd – yn dod allan ohoni yn iach eu crwyn o hyd
'It was strange how the neutral people – the people who stood in the middle doing nothing – always came out of it well'
    (John Rowlands, 1965: 25)

Nid sôn am griw o wylanod yr ydw i, ond am un wylan, fy ngwylan i, sy'n dwad i'r lawnt bob bore
'I am not speaking about a host of seagulls, but about one seagull, my seagull, that comes to the lawn every morning'
    (Kate Roberts, 1976: 76)

Troes hithau ei phen ac edrych i gyfeiriad y ffenestr, y ffenestr y gwelodd gymaint o gysur trwyddi a daeth dagrau i'w llygaid
'She turned her head and looked in the direction of the window through which she saw so much comfort and tears came to her eyes'
    (Kate Roberts, 1976: 77)

234 In proverbs and fossilized expressions the antecedent is often assumed:

A ystyrio, cofied
'He who reflects, let him remember'
> (Proverb)

A aned yn daeog, taeog fydd o
'He who was born a serf, a serf he will be'
> (Rhiannon Davies Jones, 1977: 35)

Lladdwyd y carw, costied a gostio, yn Fforestydd yr Wyddfa
'The stag was killed, cost what it may cost, in the forests of Snowdonia'
> (Rhiannon Davies Jones, 1985: 102)

Gallai ei lladd am a wyddai
'It could kill her for all she knew'
> (Rhiannon Davies Jones, 1989: 73)

Prif atyniad yr ystafell fel y mae hi heddiw yw'r lle tân Tuduraidd, na welwch mo'i debyg trwy'r Fro achlân, am a wn i
'The room's main attraction as it is today is the Tudor fireplace, that you will not see its like throughout the entire Vale, for all that I know'
> (Aneirin Talfan Davies, 1976: 191)

Er a ddywedwyd am eu Cymreictod yn y ganrif ddiwethaf nid oes gymaint ag un garreg fedd Gymraeg ym mynwent eglwys y plwyf
'Despite what has been said about their Welshness in the last century there is not so much as one Welsh grave stone in the parish cemetery'
> (Aneirin Talfan Davies, 1976: 173)

Nid a ddigwyddodd ac a ddywedwyd yn Llundain a Berlin sy'n fyw i mi
'It is not that which happened and that which was said in London and Berlin that I remember'
> (Robin Lewis, 1980: 42)

Bid a fo am hynny, fe'i dienyddiwyd ar 4 Rhagfyr 1531
'Be that as it may, he was executed on 4 December 1531'
> (Geraint H. Jenkins, 1983: 92)

Rhaid gwisgo'r goeden, doed a ddelo, a threulio dyddiau yn coginio . . .
'(We) must decorate the tree, come what may, and spend days cooking . . .'
> (*Y Faner*, 23/30 Rhagfyr 1988: 5)

yn ôl a glywsom ar ôl hyn
'according to what we heard after this'
(Beti Rhys, 1988: 18)

Following *dyma, dyna, ond, ag, nag,* the antecedent is often omitted:

Dyna a wneuthum ymhen blynyddoedd
'That is what I did years later'
(Beti Rhys, 1988: 16)

Does ond a hedo a ddaw yma
'It is only that which flies that comes here'
(Idwal Jones, 1978: 21)

*Daliai'r ddau i gael cymaint o bleser mewn dawnsio a rhialtwch
ag a gawsent cyn iddynt briodi*
'The two continued to have as much pleasure in dancing and
merriment as they had had before they married'
(Gerhart Hauptman and Heinrich Böll, 1974: 1)

*Gwelwyd gornestau da lle profwyd yn ddiau fod safon rhai o'n
prif glybiau'n uwch o gryn dipyn nag a fuont*
'Good matches were seen where it was proven without doubt
that the standard of some of our premier clubs was quite a bit
higher than it had been'
(*Y Faner*, 12 Ionawr 1990: 21)

*Gallent brynu amgenach dodrefn a defnyddiau ar gyfer y plasty
nag a werthid yn Ninbych*
'They could buy better furniture and materials for the mansion
than were sold in Denbigh'
(R. Cyril Hughes, 1976: 158)

Interrogative Pronouns

235 The interrogative pronouns are *pwy* and *pa*. *Pwy?* 'who?'
refers only to persons; *pa?* 'what?' is followed by a noun or the
pronominalia *un* (see **240**), *rhyw* (see **241**), *rhai* (see **243**), *maint*
(see **244**), *peth* (see **245**), *sawl* (see **254**):

Pwy sydd yn galw i'n gweld-ni y dyddiau yma?
'Who calls to see us these days?'
(T. Glynne Davies, 1974: 246)

Pa effaith gafodd dy bregeth di?
'What effect did your sermon have?'
   (Emyr Humphreys, 1981: 297)

On mutation following *pa* see **66**.

(i) *Pa* combines with nouns and adjectives to form interrogative phrases:

pa beth?	contracted to *beth?*	'what?, what thing?'
pa bryd?	contracted to *pryd?*	'when?, what time?'
pa le?	contracted to *p'le?*, *ble?*	'where?'
pa un?	contracted to *p'un?*	'which?'
pa ryw un?	contracted to *p'run?*	'which?'
pa rai?		'which ones?'
pa fodd?		'how?, what manner?'
pa sut?	contracted to *sut?*	'how?, what sort of?'
pa sawl?	contracted to *sawl?*	'how many?'
pa fath?		'what sort of?'
pa faint?	contracted to *faint?*	'how many?, how much?'
pa waeth?		'what does it matter?'
pa ryw?		'what manner of?'

Note
In an earlier period (see D. Simon Evans, 1964: 77) the interrogative *pa* 'what' was followed by the preposition *am*. The construction has survived as *paham*, *pam* 'why?' (see (vi) below).

(ii) *Pa* may be followed by the equative:

Pa mor bell yn ôl y digwyddodd yr helynt?
'How long ago did the incident happen?'
   (Emyr Humphreys, 1986: 10)

Pa mor fawr garech chi fod?
'How big would you like to be?'
   (Lewis Carroll, 1982: 45)

(iii) The interrogative may be followed by a form of the verb *bod* 'to be':

Pwy wyt ti i ateb Duw yn ôl?
'Who are you to answer God back?'
   (Rom. 9: 20)

Pwy ydi'r carcharor pwysicaf sy'n Lloegr?
'Who is the most important prisoner that is in England?'
(R. Cyril Hughes, 1976: 181)

Faint yw dy oed?
'How old are you?'
(Gen. 47: 8)

Beth ydy fy ngwaith?
'What is my work?'
(Rhiannon Davies Jones, 1985: 8)

Beth fydd yr arwydd pan fydd hyn yn digwydd?
'What will be the sign when this will happen?'
(Luke 21: 7)

When *pwy* occurs after a noun at the beginning of a question it means 'whose?':

Cwpled pwy oedd hwnna?
'Whose couplet was that?'
(R. Cyril Hughes, 1976: 149)

(iv) The interrogative is frequently followed by a relative clause:

Pwy sy'n mynd i olchi'r llestri?
'Who is going to wash the dishes?'
(*Y Faner*, 23/30 Rhagfyr 1988: 5)

Beth sydd o'i le efo distawrwydd?
'What is wrong with silence?'
(Angharad Tomos, 1991: 15)

Beth a barodd iddo greu'r fath effaith?
'What caused it to create such an effect?'
(R. Gerallt Jones, 1977: 38)

The relative pronoun is often omitted; see **73**.

(v) The interrogative is followed by the particle *y(r)* when governed by a preposition:

I ble'r awn ni?
'To where shall we go?'
(Harri Williams, 1978: 15)

Ym mhwy yr ymddiriedaf?
'In whom shall I confide?'
   (Emyr Humphreys, 1986: 8)

I bwy yr oeddit yn traethu geiriau?
'To whom were you speaking words?'
   (Job 26: 4)

Ar bwy yr ydych yn gwneud ystumiau ac yn tynnu tafod?
'Against whom do you make gestures and wag tongues?'
   (Isa. 57: 4)

The particle is often omitted:

Am beth wyt ti'n sôn yn hollol?
'About what are you talking exactly?'
   (Emyr Humphreys, 1986: 35/36)

O ble doist ti heno?
'From where have you come tonight?'
   (Rhiannon Davies Jones, 1977: 99)

(vi) Adverbial interrogative expressions such as *pa fodd*, *pa ffordd*, *paham* (*pam*), *pa le* (*ble*), *pa sawl*, *pa bryd*, *sut* etc., are also followed by *y(r)*:

Paham y sefi di fan yma?
'Why do you stand here?'
   (John Bunyan, 1962: 13)

Pam y dylai ef boeni?
'Why should he worry?'
   (Emyr Humphreys, 1981: 74)

Sut y gwyddoch chi hynny?
'How do you know that?'
   (Rhiannon Davies Jones, 1985: 42)

Pa le yr wyt ti? (1955)
Ble'r wyt ti? (1988)
'Where are you?'
   (Gen. 3: 9)

Pa fodd y cwympodd y cedyrn! (1955)
'How have the mighty fallen!'
   (2 Sam. 1: 19)

Pa sawl gwaith y mae fy mrawd i bechu yn fy erbyn a minnau i faddau iddo?
'How often is my brother to sin against me and I to forgive him?'
   (Matt. 18: 21)

The particle may be omitted:

Sut cest ti wybod am yr hogan?
'How did you get to know about the girl?'
   (Alun Jones, 1989: 40)

Sut aeth hi?
'How did it go?'
   (John Rowlands, 1978: 9)

Sut wyt ti'n gallu gweithio i'r diawl?
'How are you able to work for the devil?'
   (Robat Gruffudd, 1986: 27)

Negative. The verb is preceded by *na* before consonants, *nad* before vowels:

Pam na chysyllti di â'r doctor lleol?
'Why don't you get in touch with the local doctor?'
   (Emyr Humphreys, 1981: 171)

Sut na fuasech chwi wedi digalonni?
'How did you not lose heart?'
   (John Bunyan, 1962: 31)

Pam na wnaethoch chi'n ffonio ni neithiwr?
'Why did you not phone us last night?'
   (Wil Roberts, 1985: 55)

Pam nad aethoch chi allan?
'Why didn't you go out?'
   (*Taliesin*, Hydref 1991; 36)

On mutation following *na* see **87, 115**.

(vii) In varieties of spoken Welsh and in informal texts the verb-noun *bod* 'to be' may follow *pam*:

Pam bod cynifer o bobl am ffoi?
'Why do so many people wish to flee?'
   (*Y Faner*, 14 Ebrill 1989: 8)

On the use of interrogative pronouns in indirect questions see **356**.

Demonstrative Pronouns

236 In the singular, masculine, feminine and neuter forms occur:

Singular	Masculine	Feminine	Neuter
	hwn 'this'	*hon* 'this'	*hyn* 'this'
	hwnnw 'that'	*honno* 'that'	*hynny* 'that'

In the plural there is no distinction of gender and *hyn* 'these', *hynny* 'those' occur. *Hwn*, *hon* and pl. *hyn* are used of persons and things close at hand or imminent. *Hwnnw*, *honno* and pl. *hynny* are used of persons and things further removed or more remote or previously referred to. The sing. neut. forms *hyn*, *hynny* refer to an abstraction such as circumstance, event, thought, statement, question, number, reason, manner or time. Masculine forms are selected with masculine nouns or refer to masculine nouns; feminine forms are used with feminine nouns or refer to feminine nouns. Neuter forms may be selected with masculine and feminine nouns especially in a register low on the formality cline. Plural forms are selected with plural nouns or refer to plural nouns.

These pronouns are used as substantives and adjectives:

(i) Substantival:

Yf hwn
'Drink this'
(Emyr Humphreys, 1981: 212)

Hon oedd ei hoff foment
'This was his favourite moment'
(Urien William, 1974: 20)

Rhoes hyn bleser diderfyn iddo
'This gave him infinite pleasure'
(Gerhart Hauptman and Heinrich Böll, 1974: 10)

Ef a anfonwyd at y Pab gan Harri'r Wythfed pan oedd hwnnw'n chwilio am ysgariad
'It was he who was sent to the Pope by Henry VIII when that (one) was seeking a divorce'
(Aneirin Talfan Davies, 1972: 55)

Roedd honno wastad yn dod ar ei warthaf
'That (one) was always coming upon him'
(Ioan Kidd, 1977: 45/46)

Fe wyddai ei fod yn haeddu hynny gan iddo ymddwyn mor fwystfilaidd
'He knew that he deserved that because he had behaved in such a beastly manner'
(T. Glynne Davies, 1974: 74)

Adverbs may be added to these demonstrative pronouns: *hwn yma, hwn yna, hon yna, hon yma, hyn yna, hyn yma, hwn acw*: *y tŷ hwn yna* 'that house there, that house near to you'; *y dyn hwn yma* 'this man here'; *y car hwn acw* 'that car there/yonder'. In speech and informal texts one finds the contractions *honna* (*hon yna*), *hwncw* (*hwn acw*), *hwnna* (*hwn yna*), *hynna* (*hyn yna*) etc.

Doedd dim rhaid mai hwnna oedd e
'It did not have to be that'
(Urien William, 1974: 22)

Nid i hynna maen nhw'n cael eu danfon i garchar
'It is not for that [reason] that they are sent to jail'
(Urien William, 1974: 22)

In varieties of southern Welsh *hwnco* (*hwn acw*), *honco* (*hon acw*) occur; in varieties of northern Welsh *nacw* (*hon acw*) occurs. The plural forms *hyn*, *hynny* are never used as substantives in contemporary Welsh but frequently occur with the pronominal *rhai* (see **243**): *y rhai hyn* 'these', *y rhai hynny* 'those', or the contracted forms *y rhain* 'these', *y rheini/y rheiny* 'those':

I wneuthur pa beth y daw y rhai hyn? (1955)
Beth y mae'r rhain am ei wneud? (1988)
'What do these wish to do?'
(Zech. 1: 21)

y rhai hynny hefyd a alwodd efe (1955)
'those also he called'
(Rom. 8: 30)

Nid oes cyfraith yn erbyn rhinweddau fel y rhain
'There is no law against virtues such as these'
(Gal. 5: 23)

Byddai'r rhain yn ei reoli ef a'r sioe i gyd
'These would control him and the whole show'
(Jane Edwards, 1976: 131)

Mi fedrai'r rheini arogli wenci led cae i ffwrdd!
'Those could scent a weasel a field's length away!'
(Rhiannon Davies Jones, 1977: 116)

Safai'r rheiny yn gil-agored fel rheol yr amser hwn o'r dydd
'Those stood ajar usually at this time of the day'
(Urien William, 1974: 20)

Adverbs may be added to *rhai*: *y rhai yna* (*y rheina*) 'those (fairly close)', *y rhai acw* 'those (further away)'.

Note
In varieties of spoken Welsh *rhain*, *rheini/rheiny* occur adjectivally: *y dyddiau rhain* 'these days'; *y merched rheini* 'those girls'.

(ii) Adjectivally

The article always precedes a noun followed by an adjectival pronoun:

y briodas anghymarus hon
'this ill-matched wedding'
(R. Cyril Hughes, 1976: 120)

Treuliais innau'r noson honno'n wylo
'I spent that night weeping'
(Harri Williams, 1978: 67)

Roedd yr achos hwnnw wedi hen orffen
'That case had long finished'
(Robat Gruffudd, 1986: 22)

Beth tybed oedd neges Cellan Ddu y tro hwn?
'I wonder what Cellan Ddu's message was this time?'
(Rhiannon Davies Jones, 1987: 115/116)

ei waith ar y pethau hyn
'his work on these things'
(Urien Williams, 1974: 21)

Nid oedd Galio yn gofalu am ddim o'r pethau hynny (1955)
'Gallio cared for none of those things'
(Acts 18: 17)

The adverbs *acw*, *yna*, *yma*, may be selected as demonstratives directly with nouns:

> *y brawd peniog uffernol acw sydd gen i*
> 'that devilishly able brother that I have'
>   (R. Cyril Hughes, 1976: 182)

> *Mae'r lle yma'n glustiau i gyd!*
> 'This place is all ears'
>   (Rhiannon Davies Jones, 1977: 26)

> *yr hen anghenfil hyll yna*
> 'that ugly old monster'
>   (Gerhart Hauptman and Heinrich Böll, 1974: 9)

> *yr holl buteiniaid sy'n y byd 'ma*
> 'all the whores that are in this world'
>   (John Rowlands, 1965: 23)

The neuter forms *hyn*, *hynny* are rarely found as adjectives in standard literary Welsh apart from common expressions such as: *y pryd hyn* 'this time'; *y pryd hynny* 'that time'; *y peth hyn* 'this thing'; *y modd hyn* 'this manner'; *y ffordd hyn* 'this way'. In varieties of spoken Welsh, however, *hyn* and *hynny* are frequently selected instead of the masculine *hwn*, *hwnnw* or the feminine *hon*, *honno*: *y dyn hyn* 'this man', *y wraig hyn* 'this woman', *yr wythnos hynny* 'that week'.

On mutation following the article see **48**.

Some temporal adverbs or adverbial expressions are derived from a noun + demonstrative, see **333** (ii):

> *yr awron*   (<*yr*+ *awr*   + *hon*) 'now'
> *weithion*   (<*y* + *gwaith*+ *hon*) 'now'
> *y dwthwn*   (<*y* + *dydd*   + *hwn*) 'day'

On *yr hwn*, *yr hon*, *y rhai*, *yr hyn* as antecedents in a relative clause, see **233**.

237 (i) The demonstrative pronouns *hyn*, *hynny* attach to prepositions to form adverbial expressions:

ar hynny	'thereupon'
wedi hynny	'thereafter'
hyd hynny	'until then'
wedi hyn, *wedyn*	'after this'
er hynny	'nevertheless'

am hynny	⎫	
gan hynny	⎪	
oblegid hynny	⎬	'therefore'
oherwydd hynny	⎪	
o achos hynny	⎭	
ers hynny		'since then'
erbyn hyn		'by now'
erbyn hynny		'by then'

Examples:

Am hynny ni fyddai'n dangos i'w gynorthwywyr fwy nag oedd rhaid o waith y swyddfa
'Therefore he would not show his assistants more than was necessary of the office work'
    (Urien William, 1974: 21)

Er hynny, aeth cryn dair blynedd heibio cyn i Jane fedru torri'r garw a siarad am Rolant
'Nevertheless, a good three years passed before Jane could break the ice and talk about Rolant'
    (Kate Roberts, 1972: 25)

Ar hynny torrodd y merched allan i feichio crio ac yn eu plith yr oedd Lowri, cariad y llanc
'Thereupon the girls began to sob and amongst them was Lowri, the youth's girlfriend'
    (Rhiannon Davies Jones, 1977: 35)

Yn yr argyfwng hwnnw, a oedd yn bell iawn erbyn hyn, cafodd hi gydymdeimlad ardal
'In that crisis, that was a long time ago by now, she had a district's sympathy'
    (Kate Roberts, 1972: 20)

Dadrithiasid hi'n llwyr ynghylch ei phlant erbyn hynny
'She had been completely disillusioned about her children by then'
    (Kate Roberts, 1972: 22)

Aethai'r gaeaf heibio yn hynod o ddifyr hyd hynny
'The winter had passed extremely well until then'
    (Gerhart Hauptman and Heinrich Böll, 1974: 7)

Yr oedd y tri yn byw o fewn agosrwydd ymweld â hi bob dydd a manteisient ar hynny i'w phluo . . . Hithau, oblegid hynny, wedi gorfod gofyn i'w chwsmeriaid chwilio am fenyn yn rhywle arall
'The three lived within daily visiting distance of her and they took advantage of that to profit . . . Therefore she had to ask her customers to seek butter elsewhere'
(Kate Roberts, 1972: 21)

Parhaodd y ffarwelio am gryn amser wedyn
'The farewells continued for quite a time afterwards'
(Gerhart Hauptman and Heinrich Böll, 1974: 17)

(ii) The demonstratives also occur in idiomatic expressions:

hwn-a-hwn	'so-and-so, this (man) and that'
hon-a-hon	'so-and-so, this (woman) and that'
hyn-a-hyn	'so much'
ar hyn o bryd	'at the present time'
hyn o daith	'this present journey'
hyn o lythyr	'this letter'
hyn o fyd	'this present world, the world such as it is'
ar hyn o dro	'on this occasion'
gymaint â hyn	'this much'
gymaint â hynny	'that much'
hwn a'r llall	'one person and another'
hyn a'r llall	'this and that'
yn hynny o beth	'in such a matter'
o ran hynny	'as far as that is concerned'
o hyn allan	'from now on'

Pronominalia

238 Pronominalia expressing alternatives may be either substantival or adjectival and either definite or indefinite:

(i) Substantival and definite: *y naill . . . y llall*

Disgwyliai y naill i'r llall dorri'r garw
'The one expected the other to break the ice'
(Wil Roberts, 1985: 15)

Plural: *y naill . . . y lleill*

Disgwyliai y naill i'r lleill dorri'r garw
'The one (group) expected the others to break the ice'

Substantival and indefinite: *un . . . arall*

> *Disgwyliai un i arall dorri'r garw*
> 'One expected another to break the ice'

Plural: *rhai . . . eraill*

> *Disgwyliai rhai i eraill dorri'r garw*
> 'Some expected others to break the ice'

(ii) Adjectival and definite: *y naill* + noun . . . + noun + *arall*

> *'Rwyn derbyn mai dyna drefn natur – y naill rywogaeth yn byw ar rwyogaeth arall*
> 'I agree that that is nature's way – one species living on another species'
> (*Y Faner*, 23 Chwefror 1990: 16)

Adjectival and indefinite: *un/rhyw* + noun . . . + noun + *arall*

> *'Rwy'n derbyn mai dyna drefn natur – un rywogaeth yn byw ar rywogaeth arall*
> 'I agree that that is nature's way – one species living on another species'

On mutation following *naill* see **67**.
On mutation following *un* see **57**.

(iii) *Naill* may occur without *y llall/arall*:

> *Rhoddaf y naill hanner o'r afal iddo*
> 'I shall give him one half of the apple'

> *Aeth o'r neilltu*
> 'He went to one side'

(iv) *Naill ai . . . neu* (*ynteu*) occur as conjunctions:

> *Fe ddaru Thomas Charles broffwydo y byddai un o ddau beth yn digwydd i Ann – y byddai hi naill ai'n marw'n ifanc neu'n colli'r weledigaeth oedd ganddi*
> 'Thomas Charles prophesied that one of two things would happen to Anne – she would either die young or lose her vision'
> (*Golwg*, 6 Gorffennaf 1989: 22)

(v) Before a noun *naill* can mean 'one': see **44** (vi), **67**:

> *plentyn naill-lygad*
> 'a one-eyed child'

239 Fy hun/hunan etc. Reflexive Pronouns. The forms *hun/hunan* (sing.) and *hun/hunain* (pl.) are used with either prefixed or infixed pronouns. Auxiliary pronouns are not selected following *hun/hunan* etc.

The reflexive pronouns may follow:

(i) a prefixed or infixed pronoun:

Pe bai ei thad ei hun yn ei gweld hi allan yn awr . . .
'If her own father were to see her out now . . .'
     (T. Glynne Davies, 1974: 61)

Fe'u caent eu hunain yn gweld ei gilydd ryw ben i bob diwrnod
'They found themselves seeing each other at some end of every day'
     (Kate Roberts, 1972: 23)

Fe'm hysgwydais fy hun . . .
'I shook myself . . .'
     (Bryan Martin Davies, 1988: 71)

i'w tai eu hunain
'to their own houses'

(ii) the personal form of a preposition:

Gallaf ofalu amdanaf fy hun
'I can take care of myself'
     (John Bunyan, 1962: 54)

Penderfynais wneud paned o de i mi fy hun
'I decided to make myself a cup of tea'
     (Wil Roberts, 1985: 46)

Roedd hynny ynddo'i hun yn ddigon i'w diflasu
'That in itself was enough to make her miserable'
     (Ioan Kidd, 1977: 89)

(iii) an independent or an affixed pronoun:

Ofnai mai efe ei hun oedd y pry yn y caws
'He feared that he himself was the fly in the ointment'
     (Idwal Jones, 1977: 35)

Yr oedd bai mawr arni hi ei hun
'She herself was at great fault'
     (T. Glynne Davies, 1974: 252)

(iv) a noun or verb-noun:

Nid oedd yr ustusiaid yng Ngogledd Cymru mor danbaid grefyddol â'r Frenhines ei hun
'The justices in North Wales were not so fervently religious as the Queen herself'
(R. Cyril Hughes, 1975: 12)

I mi'n bersonol doedd sŵn y dorf ddim yn bwysig iawn yn ystod y gêm ei hunan
'To me personally the noise of the crowd wasn't very important during the game itself'
(R. Gerallt Jones, 1977: 41)

The meaning may be adverbial: 'alone, by myself, by yourself etc.':

Pam nad ei di lawr yno dy hunan?
'Why will you not go down there alone?'
(Emyr Humphreys, 1981: 171)

Reflexive pronouns may also be selected:

(i) as object of an imperative verb:

Sobra dy hun, Angharad
'Sober yourself, Angharad'
(R. Cyril Hughes, 1976: 206)

(ii) as object of verbs in other moods and verb-nouns:

Gelwais fy hun yn fardd, er nad ysgrifennais linell o farddoniaeth
'I called myself a poet, although I had not written a line of poetry'
(Harri Williams, 1978: 75)

Daliai ei hun yn syth
'She held herself straight'
(Jane Edwards, 1976: 8)

When selected as objects of a verb-noun the reflexive pronouns are normally preceded by a prefixed or infixed pronoun:

Roeddwn yn fy ngwylio fy hun yn ofalus
'I was watching myself carefully'
(Robat Gruffudd, 1986: 33)

'Dwy ddim yn fy nhwyllo fy hun
'I am not deceiving myself'
    (Friedrich Dürrenmatt, 1958: 21)

Yr ydych i'ch disgyblu eich hunain
'You are to discipline yourselves'
    (Lev. 16: 31)

The pronoun may be omitted, especially in informal texts and in varieties of spoken Welsh:

Yr wyf wedi rhoi fy hun bellach i un arall
'I have given myself now to another'
    (John Bunyan, 1962: 35)

Sut fedraist ti dynnu dy hun oddi wrth y moch?
'How did you manage to drag yourself away from the pigs?'
    (Jane Edwards, 1976: 78)

Gallwn gicio fy hun
'I could kick myself'
    (Wil Roberts, 1985: 51)

240 Un occurs:

(i) as antecedent of a relative clause: see **233**.

(ii) as an 'alternative' pronoun: see **238**.

(iii) *un* is selected instead of a noun on which another noun or adjective depends:

Mae'r ffordd yn un syth a llydan
'The road is a straight one and wide'
    (*Y Faner*, 6 Mehefin 1989: 11)

Mae Traeth Cefnsidan, gerllaw Pembre, yn un mawr iawn
'Cefnsidan Beach, near Pembre, is a very extensive one'
    (T. Llew Jones, 1977: 7)

(iv) synonymous with *rhywun* 'someone':

Ac wele un gwahanglwyfus a ddaeth (1955)
A dyma ddyn gwahanglwyfus yn dod (1988)
'And behold a leper came'
    (Matt. 8: 2)

(v) synonymous with *unrhyw* 'any' in negative or interrogative sentences:

> *Gwyddem na ddeuai yr un gelyn i'r Berffro yr adeg honno*
> 'We knew that no enemy would come to Berffro at that time'
>> (Rhiannon Davies Jones, 1977: 147)

> *Ni allwn ddweud yr un gair*
> 'I could not utter one word'
>> (Harri Williams, 1978: 21)

(vi) expressing the meaning 'same' preceded by the article:

> *Aethom i'r un ysgolion, i'r un coleg, i'r un neuadd breswyl, i'r un capel ac ysgol Sul a Band of Hope*
> 'We went to the same schools, to the same college, to the same hostel, to the same chapel and Sunday school and Band of Hope'
>> (*Y Faner*, 2 Mehefin 1989: 12)

> *Sut y gwyddoch chi mai'r un un ydi hi?*
> 'How do you know that it is the same one?'
>> (Kate Roberts, 1976: 75)

(vii) expressing the meaning 'similar' (see **57**) preceded by the article:

> *Yr oedd tyrfa o Siapaneaid o'r un feddwl â mi*
> 'There was a party of Japanese of similar mind to me'
>> (*Y Faner*, 15 Chwefror 1990: 9)

(viii) with the preposition *o* + a definite noun or with the personal form of the preposition:

> *Anelodd ei boeriad brown at un o'r llestri*
> 'He aimed his brown spittle at one of the vessels'
>> (T. Glynne Davies, 1974: 48)

> *Anelodd ei boeriad brown at un ohonynt*
> 'He aimed his brown spittle at one of them'

(ix) meaning 'very' (followed by a demonstrative pron.):

> *ar yr un awr honno*   'in that very hour'

(x) in expressions signifying price, measurement etc. (see **159** (ix)).

(xi) in distributives (see **208**).

(xii)   *un* occurs in proper and improper compounds (see **333**):

(a)   proper: *unfryd, unllais, unfryd, unfarn*.
(b)   improper: *unwaith, unrhyw, unman, untro, undyn, unlle*.

(xiii)   in adverbial expressions such as:

un prynhawn	'one afternoon'
un noson	'one evening'
un diwrnod	'one day'

(xiv)   with *pa* in an interrogative phrase (see **235** (i)).

241   Rhyw 'some, (a) certain, one' occurs as a pronominal adjective:

Llifai rhyw ysfaon tywyll trwy'i holl gorff
'Some dark cravings flowed through his entire body'
(John Rowlands, 1965: 113)

It forms a strict or loose compound (see **333**) with a following noun:
rhywbeth, rhywbryd, rhywfaint, rhywle, rhywdro, rhyw eiriau, rhyw ddiwrnod, rhyw brynhawn, rhyw flwyddyn.

The second element may be a pronoun or numeral: *rhywrai, rhywun, rhyw ddau berson*.
On mutation following *rhyw* see **51**.

Rhyw is also used to express vagueness, contempt or compassion:

Cyhuddwyd a chondemniwyd ef ar air rhyw druanes o wraig
'He was accused and condemned on the word of some wretched woman'
(Aneirin Talfan Davies, 1972: 238)

Mi fyddwn yn hel rhyw hen frwgaish fel hyn
'We collect some old brushwood of this sort'
(Kate Roberts, 1976: 25)

Nid yw'r gŵr hwn yn cyfrif rhyw lawer yng nghanon y traddodiad llenyddol Cymraeg
'This man does not count for very much in the canon of Welsh literary tradition'
(Aneirin Talfan Davies, 1972: 28)

Preceding a verb-noun, *rhyw* implies that the action is imprecise or vague (see **51**). It may also precede *ychydig* (see **257**), and *llawer* (see **246**). The interrogative phrase *pa ryw un* may be contracted to *p'run* (see **235**).

242 **Amryw**, **Cyfryw**, **Unrhyw**: Compounds of *rhyw*

Amryw 'various, several', is selected with plural nouns:

amryw fudiadau	'various organizations'
amryw bethau	'several things'
amryw glefydau	'various diseases'

Amryw can also be substantive:

> *Mae amryw fel pe baent wedi cael gafael ar un linell weddol dda*
> 'Many seem to have got hold of one fairly good line'
>> (J. Elwyn Hughes, 1991: 47)

Amryw also occurs as a pronoun followed by the preposition *o* + definite or indefinite noun, or the personal form of the preposition *o*:

> *Mae amryw o'n diddordebau yn ddigon tebyg*
> 'Several of our interests are similar enough'
>> (*Y Faner*, 9 Mehefin 1989: 12)

> *Mae amryw ohonynt yn ddigon tebyg*
> 'Several of them are similar enough'

Cyfryw 'such' is used:

(i) as an adjective:

> *Ymaith â'r cyfryw un oddi ar y ddaear* (1955)
> 'Away with such a fellow from the earth'
>> (Acts 22: 22)

(ii) as a substantive:

> *Roeddwn yn mwynhau'r diodydd – y gwinoedd a'r cyfryw*
> 'I was enjoying the drinks –the wines and the like'

Cyfryw may be followed by *â*, *ag* 'as':

> *Bu rai ohonynt hwy gyfryw ag a adawsant enw ar eu hôl, fel y mynegid eu clod hwynt* (1959)
> 'Some there are who have left a name behind them, so that their praise be stated'
>> (Sirach 44: 8)

Unrhyw 'any, the same (kind, nature)' is adjectival:

> *Ni chai unrhyw Gymro Cymraeg ddal unrhyw swydd yn ei wlad ei hun oni allai ddefnyddio'r Saesneg*

'No Welsh-speaking Welshman was allowed to hold any office in his own country unless he could use English'
(Geraint H. Jenkins, 1983: 98)

It is a loose compound in *o'r un rhyw* 'of the same kind'.
It expresses the meaning 'selfsame, identical' in:

A'r holl bethau hyn y mae'r un a'r unrhyw Ysbryd yn eu gweithredu . . . (1955)
A'r holl bethau hyn, yr un a'r unrhyw Ysbryd sydd yn eu gweithredu . . . (1988)
'All these things are the work of one and the same spirit . . .'
(1 Cor. 12: 11)

243   Rhai 'some' occurs as:

(i)   a substantive pronoun:

Fe ddoi rhai yn ôl o'r rhyfel
'Some would return from the war'
(Rhiannon Davies Jones, 1977: 174)

(ii)   antecedent of a relative clause (see **233**).

(iii)   an 'alternative' pronoun (see **238**).

(iv)   *rhai* may be followed by the preposition *o* + the definite article + a plural noun, or the personal form of the preposition *o*:

rhai o'r myfyrwyr	'some of the students'
rhai ohonom	'some of us'

(v)   *rhai* serves as the plural of *un*, and like *un* is selected instead of a noun on which another noun or adjective depends:

Dylid chwilio am fathau melysach megis y rhai coch
'Sweeter varieties like the red ones should be sought'
(*Y Faner*, 2 Mawrth 1990: 16)

Gwna fy nhraed fel rhai ewig
'He makes my feet like those of a hind'
(Ps. 18: 33)

(vi)   as an adjective before a plural noun:

Gallai rhai pladurwyr da ennill cymaint â phymtheg swllt
'Some good scythesmen could earn as much as fifteen shillings'
(T. Glynne Davies, 1974: 86)

244 Maint 'size, stature' occurs:

(i) as a masc. sing. common noun:

*Roeddwn i'n gwybod yn iawn beth oedd maint y cynddaredd a'r
dryswch y tu mewn iddi*
'I knew well what was the magnitude of the anger and the
dilemma inside her'
> (R. Gerallt Jones, 1977: 36)

(ii) in interrogative sentences (see **235**):

Pa faint o gamweddau ac o bechodau sydd ynof? (1955)
'How many iniquities and sins are in me?'
> (Job 13: 23)

Wn i ddim faint a ymatebodd i'r apêl
'I do not know how many responded to the appeal'
> (*Llais Llyfrau*, Haf 1989: 7)

A comparative adjective may follow (*pa*) *faint*:

Faint gwaeth fyddi di?
'How much worse will you be?'

Pa faint mwy fydd y cyfoethogi pan ddônt yn eu cyflawn rif?
'How much more the enrichment when they come in full
strength?'
> (Rom. 11: 12)

(iii) to express the equative of *mawr* 'large', *llawer* 'much' following
the prep. *er*:

Aeth allan er maint y storm
'He went out although the storm was so great'

Er cymaint may be selected in this construction:

Aeth allan er cymaint y storm

(iv) as a fem. sing. noun. The article is not denoted in contemporary
Welsh, but soft mutation is retained:

Bydd faint a fynni o bopeth
'There will be as much as you wish of everything'

(v) following a prep.:

Llewygais gan faint y gwres
'I fainted because the heat was so great'

(vi) in idioms:

maint yn y byd	'the least bit'
yn ei (etc.) *lawn faint*	'fully grown'

245 Peth: As well as functioning as an interrogative pronoun (see **235**) and antecedent of a relative clause (see **233**), *peth* is used:

(i) to express 'a little, some, a certain quantity':

Ceir peth manylion gan Edward Matthews yn 'Y Drysorfa'
'Some details by Edward Matthews are to be found in *Y Drysorfa*'
(Aneirin Talfan Davies, 1976: 15)

Ces beth gwaith i'w berswadio
'I had some work to persuade him'
(Robat Gruffudd, 1986: 241)

It may be used without the noun:

A gawsoch chi waith i'w berswadio? Do, ces i beth
'Did you have work to persuade him? Yes, I had a little'

(ii) to express 'some of, a part of':

Ymddangosai peth o'r hanes yn ddigrif erbyn hyn
'Part of the tale appeared amusing by now'
(Kate Roberts, 1972: 25)

(iii) adverbially:

Oedodd Goronwy beth yn y castell yn Nolwyddelan
'Goronwy loitered a little in the castle in Dolwyddelan'
(Rhiannon Davies Jones, 1989: 140)

(iv) in idioms:

o dipyn i beth	'little by little'
truan o beth	'a sad thing'
da o beth	'a good thing'

246 Llawer 'many, much' is used:

(i) with the preposition *o* + an indefinite noun:

Aeth llawer o amser heibio
'Much time passed'
(J. G. Williams, 1978: 11)

(ii) with the preposition *o* + a definite noun:

Mae llawer o'r papurau wedi diflannu
'Many of the papers have disappeared'

A personal form of the preposition *o* may replace the noun:

Mae llawer ohonynt wedi diflannu
'Many of them have disappeared'

(iii) with no noun following:

Gwelodd lawer yn y rhyfel
'He saw much in the war'

Bydd llawer ganddo i'w adrodd
'He will have much to tell'

(iv) followed by a singular noun:

Llawer gwir, gwell ei gelu
'Many a truth is best hidden'
    (Proverb)

Mae llawer garddwr yn hoffi impio'i goed ffrwythau ei hun
'Many a gardener enjoys grafting his own fruit trees'
    (*Y Faner*, 23 Chwefror 1989: 4)

(v) adverbially (with soft mutation):

Nid arhosodd lawer gyda'i chwaer
'He did not stay long with his sister'

It may express degree or measure with a comparative adj.:

llawer gwell/gwell lawer	'much better'
llawer llai/llai lawer	'much smaller'
llawer tecach/tecach lawer	'much fairer'

(vi) The plural *llaweroedd* may replace *llawer* in (i), (ii), (iii) above.

(vii) *Llawer* is often followed by *iawn* 'very':

Bydd yr agwedd hon ar arddio'n rhoi llawer iawn o bleser i chi
'This aspect of gardening will give you very much pleasure'
    (*Y Faner*, 2 Mehefin 1989: 13)

(viii) *Rhyw* may precede *llawer* except when it is followed immediately by a noun; it expresses indistinctness or imprecision:

Nid oes rhyw lawer ohonom
'There aren't very many of us'

Nid yw ef yn rhyw lawer gwaeth
'He is not very much worse'

247 Pawb, Pob

(i) *Pawb* 'everybody' is substantival and in contemporary Welsh is normally plural in meaning:

Yr oedd ef, a phawb oedd gydag ef, wedi eu syfrdanu
'He, and everybody who was with him, were amazed'
  (Luke 5: 9)

In proverbs and fossilized expressions, however, it is regarded as singular:

Rhydd i bawb ei farn
'Every one to his opinion'

Pawb drosto'i hun
'Every one for himself'

Following a verb-noun or pl. verb *pawb* is appositional:

Yr oeddent yn mynd bawb i'w ffordd ei hun
'They were going every man his own way'

a chymerasant bawb eu gwŷr (1955)
'and they took every man their men'
  (2 Kgs. 11: 9)

(ii) *Pob* 'every, all' is adjectival and is followed by a noun or pronoun:

pob cyfrifydd
'every accountant'

pob enaid byw
'every living soul'

pob un
'every one'

It occurs in the improper compounds (see **333** (ii)) *popeth* 'everything', *pobman* 'everywhere', (*o*) *boptu* 'from all sides'.

Rhyw 'some' and *cyfryw* 'such' often follow *pob*:

pob rhyw beth
'every kind of thing'

pob cyfryw beth
'every such thing'

The mutated form *bob* is frequently selected in adverbial phrases and idioms:

bob nos	'every night'
bob dydd	'every day'
bob blwyddyn	'every year'
bob yn un	'one by one'
bob ail/bob yn ail	'every other'
bob yn eilddydd	'every other day'
bob yn awr ac eilwaith	'every now and then'
bob yn awr	'constantly'
bob yn dipyn	'bit by bit'

Pob + noun can be adjectival, qualifying a preceding noun:

esgidiau pob-dydd	'everyday shoes'
dillad pob-dydd	'everyday clothes'
Siôn pob-gwaith	'Jack-of-all-trades'

In *cot bob tywydd* 'all-weather coat', the mutation of *pob* reflects the fem. gender of the preceding noun.

248 Holl, oll 'all'

(i) *Holl* is an adjective and precedes the noun:

Bellach roedd o'n Dywysog holl Gymru
'Henceforth he was Prince of all Wales'
(Rhiannon Davies Jones, 1989: 105)

Casglwch holl Israel i Mispa
'Gather all Israel to Mizpeh'
(1 Sam. 7: 5)

holl drigolion Jerwsalem
'all the inhabitants of Jerusalem'
(Acts 1: 19)

Holl occurs as the first element of a compound adjective:

hollalluog	'almighty'
holliach	'completely healthy'
hollgyfoethog	'all powerful'
holl-bwysig	'all-important'

Followed by a noun *holl* may form a compound noun:

hollfyd	'the whole world'
hollallu	'omnipotence'
hollbresenoldeb	'omnipresence'

On mutation following *holl* see **51**.

Yn hollol 'altogether, entirely, wholly, thoroughly' is an adverbial phrase:

> *Na ad fi yn hollol* (1955)
> 'Do not forsake me altogether'
> > (Ps. 119: 8)

> *Mi a ymwneuthum yn bob peth i bawb, fel y gallwn yn hollol gadw rhai* (1955)
> 'I have become all things to all men, so that I might by all means save some'
> > (1 Cor. 9: 22)

> *Yr ydych yn hollol gywir*
> 'You are entirely correct'

> *Maen nhw'n hollol lwgr*
> 'They are wholly corrupt'

(ii) *Oll* is used adverbially following a singular or plural noun, a personal pronoun, personal form of a preposition, the neuter form of the demonstrative pronoun or the inflected verb:

> *yr Aifft oll* (1955)
> *yr Aifft gyfan* (1988)
> 'all Egypt'
> > (Ezek. 29: 2)

> *Nynni oll a grwydrasom fel defaid* (1955)
> *Rydym ni i gyd wedi crwydro fel defaid* (1988)
> 'We have all like sheep gone astray'
> > (Isa. 53: 6)

Maent oll yn gymharol gydradd
'They are all fairly equal'
>   (W. Rhys Nicholas, 1988: 120)

Dylem oll ystyried yn ofalus oblygiadau darlith Salman Rushdie
'We should all consider carefully the implications of Salman Rushdie's lecture'
>   (*Taliesin*, Mawrth 1990: 5)

Eich ateb i'ch problemau oll
'Your answer to all your problems'
>   (Alun Jones, 1989: 31)

Serch hyn oll, dangoswyd mwy a mwy o ddiddordeb yn ystod y blynyddoedd diweddaraf yma yn y dull organig
'Despite all this, more and more interest has been shown during the last year or two in the organic method'
>   (*Y Faner*, 5 Ionawr 1990: 19)

Mae ganddynt oll afael ar arddull
'All of them have a grasp of style'
>   (J. Elwyn Hughes, 1989: 69)

In negative clauses *oll* occurs in expressions such as *dim oll* 'nothing at all', *neb oll* 'nobody at all':

Ni wyddai hi ddim oll am fannau fel Buellt a Dinbych-y-pysgod
'She knew nothing at all about places like Buellt and Dinbych-y-pysgod'
>   (Rhiannon Davies Jones, 1989: 85)

Ni ddaeth neb oll i'w amddiffyn
'Nobody at all came to protect him'

Oll occurs in adjectival or adverbial phrases:

Gwerthodd gymaint oll ag a feddai (1955)
'He sold everything that he had'
>   (Matt. 13: 46)

It is also used to modify a superlative adjective:

Os ydych yn talu treth incwm ar y cyfradd uchaf oll . . .
'If you pay income tax on the highest rate of all . . .'
>   (*Y Faner*, 24 Chwefror 1978: 9)

y dylanwad grymusaf oll ar gyfieithwyr y Beibl
'the most powerful influence of all on the translators of the
Bible'
  (*Llên Cymru*, 1990: 10)

y cymhelliad cryfaf oll
'the strongest motivation of all'
  (David Roberts, 1978: 11)

Note
Yr holl ddynion and *y dynion oll* 'all the men' occur.

249 Ill 'the (two, etc.) of them' is selected with numerals in
apposition (see **220**) following 3 pl. personal pronouns or 3 pl. endings:

Anfonai yntau ei gofion atynt ill dau
'He also sent his regards to both of them'
  (R. Cyril Hughes, 1976: 140)

A hwy a'i cymerasant hi ill saith, ac ni adawsant had
'And they seven had her, and they left no seed'
  (Mark 12: 22)

Auxiliary pronouns do not occur following the numeral.

250 Digon 'enough, plenty' occurs:

(i) as a substantive:

Nid oeddit eto wedi cael digon
'You were still not content (lit. "had not had enough")'
  (Ezek. 16: 28)

It may be followed by the preposition *o* + a noun or a personal form
of the preposition *o*:

Rhoed digon o fwyd yn eu boliau
'Plenty of food was placed in their bellies'
  (Rhiannon Davies Jones, 1989: 189)

Rhoed digon ohono yn eu boliau
'Plenty of it was placed in their bellies'

*Ni chwaraeodd ddigon o weithiau mewn tymor i ennill cap y
clwb*

'He didn't play enough times in a season to win the club's cap'
(*Y Faner*, 14 Rhagfyr 1990: 21)

Digonedd, digonolrwydd, express 'abundance, sufficiency':

Ein digonedd ni sydd o Dduw (1955)
O Dduw y daw ein digonolrwydd ni (1988)
'Our sufficiency is of God'
(2 Cor. 3: 5)

Y mae yna ddigonedd o ewyllys da tuag at yr iaith
'There is plenty of good will towards the language'
(*Y Faner*, 14 Gorffennaf 1989: 4)

(ii) adjectival:

Nid yw hyn yn ddigon
'This is not enough'

Digonol expresses the same meaning:

Pwy sydd ddigonol i'r gwaith hwn?
'Who is sufficient for this work?'
(2 Cor. 2: 16)

(iii) as an adverb modifying an adjective:

Yr oedd y cig hallt a'r wyau yn ddigon prin
'The salted meat and the eggs were scarce enough'
(Rhiannon Davies Jones, 1977: 65)

Ffurflen ddigon syml yw hon
'This is a simple enough form'
(*Llais Llyfrau*, Haf 1989: 7)

251 Cwbl 'all, the whole' is used:

(i) as a substantive:

er mwyn ei brofi a gwybod y cwbl oedd yn ei galon
'in order to try him and know all that was in his heart'
(2 Chr. 32: 31)

(ii) as an adjective:

taliad cwbl	'complete payment'
cwbl werth	'whole value'

On mutation following *cwbl* see **51**.

(iii) adverbially:

> *Aeth y ddihangfa glyfar o Soke i Izmir yn gwbl ddi-rwystr*
> 'The clever escape from Soke to Izmir went wholly without problem'
>> (Elwyn A. Jones, 1978: 186)

> *Y maent hwy yn cwbl gredu fod Ioan yn broffwyd* (1955)
> 'They wholly believe that John is a prophet'
>> (Luke 20: 6)

In the above examples *cwbl* forms a compound with the adjective and verb-noun.

Yn gwbl 'wholly, completely', *o gwbl* 'at all' occur adverbially:

> *Ni chanodd o gwbl*
> 'He did not sing at all'

> *Gwadodd y carcharor y drosedd yn gwbl*
> 'The prisoner denied the offence completely'

O gwbl only occurs in negative, interrogative or 'potential' constructions:

> *A wyt ti'n gweld o gwbl?*
> 'Do you see at all?'

> *Bydd ef yn hwyr, os daw o gwbl*
> 'He will be late, if he comes at all'

On mutation when *cwbl* is used adverbially see **81**.

252 Gormod 'too much, too many' is used in the same way as *digon* (see **250**) except that *gormod* does not modify an adjective:

(i) as a substantive:

> *Yr oedd wedi siarad gormod*
> 'She had talked too much'
>> (R. Cyril Hughes, 1976: 119)

> *Fe ddygwyd rhagor o'r cargo a choed y llong gan fod gormod o ofn ar y cwnstabliaid*
> 'More of the ship's cargo and timber was stolen because the constables were too frightened'
>> (T. Llew Jones, 1977: 13)

Gormodedd expresses 'excess':

> *Na feddwer chwi gan win, yn yr hyn y mae gormodedd* (1955)
> 'Be not drunk with wine, wherein is excess'
>> (Eph. 5: 16)

(ii) adjectival:

> *Mae bywyd yn ormod iddo*
> 'Life is too much for him'

Gormodol expresses a similar meaning:

> *Roedd y pris yn ormodol*
> 'The price was excessive'

(iii) adverbial:

> *Na chwsg ormod!*
> 'Do not sleep too much'

> *Paid ag yfed yn ormodol*
> 'Do not drink too much'

Note
In varieties of southern Welsh *gormodd* occurs.

253 Rhagor 'difference, more' occurs:

(i) as a noun:

> *Y mae rhagor rhwng seren a seren mewn gogoniant*
> 'There is a difference between a star and a star in splendour'
>> (1 Cor. 15: 41)

> *Ni ddarllenodd ragor*
> 'He did not read more'
>> (Alun Jones, 1989: 178)

It may be followed by the preposition *o* + a noun or the personal form of the preposition *o*:

> *Yr oedd meithrin rhagor o bregethwyr yn ganolog bwysig*
> 'Nurturing more preachers was centrally important'
>> (*Llên Cymru*, 1989: 32)

> *Yr oedd meithrin rhagor ohonynt yn ganolog bwysig*
> 'Nurturing more of them was centrally important'

Rhagor + *na(g)* function as a comparative adjective:

Mae ganddo ragor nag un plentyn
'He has more than one child'

Bu'n byw gyda'i fam am ragor na blwyddyn
'He lived with his mother for more than a year'

(ii) as an adverb 'more than':

Roedd gwir angen hanes, rhagor barddoniaeth; ffeithiau rhagor chwedlau
'History was sorely needed, more than poetry; facts more than legends'
(Hywel Teifi Edwards, 1989: 188)

Geiriau y doethion a wrandewir mewn distawrwydd, rhagor bloedd yr hwn sydd yn llywodraethu ymysg ffyliaid (1955)
'The words of the wise men are heard in quiet more than the cry of him that ruleth among fools'
(Eccles. 9: 17)

Rhagorol (adj.), *rhagoriaeth* (noun), *rhagorach* (comp. adj.), *rhagori* (v.n.), *rhagoraf* (verb) are derivatives of *rhagor*.

254 Sawl 'such, as many' occurs:

(i) with the interrogative pronoun *pa* (see **235**):

Pa sawl gwaith y mae fy mrawd i bechu yn fy erbyn a minnau i faddau iddo?
'How many times is my brother to sin against me and I to forgive him?'
(Matt. 18: 21)

(ii) as antecedent of a relative clause (see **233**):

Y sawl a arweinir gan Ysbryd Duw, y rhai hyn sydd blant i Dduw
'Whosoever is led by the spirit of God, these are children of God'
(Rom. 8: 14)

Mae'r sawl a benodir i'r dosbarth is yn anhebyg iawn o godi i'r dosbarth uwch
'Whosoever is appointed to the lower class is very unlikely to advance to the higher class'
(*Y Faner*, 23 Chwefror 1990: 10)

(iii) as an alternative for *llawer* (see **246**) or *amryw* (see **242**):

Mae ganddynt sawl plentyn
'They have several children'

Cafodd ef sawl cyfle
'He had several opportunities'

Mae sawl arolwg wedi dangos fod amryw o bobl holliach efo colesterol uchel
'Several surveys have shown that many fit people have high cholesterol [levels]'
        (*Y Faner*, 2 Mehefin 1989: 16)

255 Cilydd. In an early period (see D. Simon Evans, 1964: 96–7) *cilydd* was used as a noun meaning 'partner, companion, fellow'. In contemporary writing, however, *cilydd* only occurs with the prefixed pronouns *ei, ein, eich* (see **214**) and the infixed pronouns *'i, 'w, 'n, 'ch* (see **217**) to express the meaning 'each, the other'. The singular form of the pronoun occurs in the 3rd person following a sing. and pl. verb. The auxiliary pronoun does not occur following *cilydd*.

Gwenodd y ddau ar ei gilydd
'The two smiled at each other'
        (R. Cyril Hughes, 1976: 198)

Gwenasant ar ei gilydd
'They smiled at each other'

Yr oedd rhai yn fwy gweithgar na'i gilydd
'Some were more industrious than others'
        (Geraint H. Jenkins, 1983: 149)

Rwy'n credu ein bod ni'n nes at ein gilydd nawr nag yr oeddem ni pan oedd hi'n blentyn
'I believe that we are closer to each other now than we were when she was a child'
        (R. Gerallt Jones, 1977: 9)

O bryd i'w gilydd, yn y gwaith, neu yn ei gartref, deuai eto i'w feddwl
'From time to time, at work, or at home, it would come once more to his mind'
        (Urien William, 1974: 22)

It occurs in the following idioms:

rhywbryd neu'i gilydd	'some time or other'
o ben bwygilydd	'from end to end'
mynd i'w gilydd	'to shrink, to shrivel'
at ei gilydd	'taken as a whole'

Note
The colloquial adverbial form *pentigili*, which occurs in south-west Wales, derives from *pen at ei gilydd* 'from end to end, altogether'.

256 Dim occurs:

(i) as a noun meaning 'anything' in negative sentences:

Heb Dduw, heb ddim
'Without God, without anything'

Nid oes gennyf ddim
'I do not have anything'

It expresses the meaning 'thing' in *pob dim* 'everything':

Y mae yn dioddef pob dim, yn credu pob dim, yn gobeithio pob dim
'It suffers everything, believes everything, hopes everything'
    (1 Cor. 13: 7)

It may follow the article:

Bu ond y dim iddi â throi'n ôl
'She had been on the verge of turning back'
    (Jane Edwards, 1977: 11)

Ni bu ond y dim rhyngddo â syrthio
'He almost fell'

It may be followed by an adjective:

Nid oes dim hyllach na dynion ifanc efo boliau cwrw mawr
'There is nothing more unsightly than young men with large beer bellies'
    (*Y Faner*, 14 Gorffennaf 1989: 16)

Nid wyf yn credu'r dim lleiaf a ddywedwch
'I do not believe the least thing that you say'

It may be predicative:

Nid wyf ddim
'I am nothing'
(1 Cor. 13: 2)

(ii) Because *dim* is used frequently in negative sentences (see **278** (vi), **337**) it has acquired the meaning 'nothing, none at all':

Gwneud rhywbeth o ddim
'To make something out of nothing'

This use of *dim* is common in replies in colloquial Welsh:

Beth sy'n bod? Dim
'What is the matter? Nothing'

Faint ddaliaist ti? Dim
'How many did you catch? None'

Dim ond/ddim ond may occur meaning 'nothing but, only' (see **81**).

(iii) An indefinite noun may follow *dim*:

Doedd gen i ddim syniad
'I had no idea'
(Wil Roberts, 1985: 41)

If the noun is definite *ddim o* occurs:

Ni chymerasant ddim o'm cyngor i (1955)
'They did not take my advice'
(Prov. 1: 30)

The personal form of the preposition *o* may occur:

Ni welodd ef ddim ohoni
'He saw nothing of her'

Dim o is frequently contracted to *mo*:

Ni fwriaf allan byth mo'r sawl sy'n dod ataf fi
'I will never turn away the person who comes to me'
(John 6: 37)

Ni chafodd mo'i wobr
'He did not receive his prize'
(Hywel Teifi Edwards, 1980: 4)

Chaiff e mo'r cyfle
'He will not have the opportunity'
  (*Y Faner*, 28 Ebrill 1989: 5)

The personal forms of the preposition may be appended to *mo*:

Chlyw neb mohonon ni o ben y tŵr
'Nobody will hear us from the top of the tower'
  (Rhiannon Davies Jones, 1987: 91)

Nid adnabûm erioed mohonoch
'I never knew you'
  (Matt. 7: 23)

Nid etholwyd mono'n aelod o'r Cyngor cyntaf
'He was not elected a member of the first Council'
  (Hywel Teifi Edwards, 1980: 62)

Mo also occurs in negative non-predicator clauses (see **337, 349**).

Nid breuddwyd mo hyn!
'This is not a dream'
  (Rhiannon Davies Jones, 1989: 105)

Nid Brenin mohono eithr Ymherawdr
'He is not a king but an Emperor'
  (*Y Faner*, 2 Rhagfyr 1988: 21)

(iv) *Ddim* is used adverbially (see **81**) to stress the negative element:

A'r hwn a ddêl ataf fi, nis bwriaf ef allan ddim (1955)
'He who comes to me, I will never turn away'
  (John 6: 37)

Beth a wna'r rhai a fedyddir dros y meirw, os y meirw ni chyfodir ddim? (1955)
'What shall they do which are baptized for the dead, if the dead are not raised at all?'
  (1 Cor. 15: 29)

A welaist ti'r ddamwain? Naddo ddim
'Did you see the accident? No'

In varieties of informal spoken Welsh *ni* (**337**) may occur in emphatic negative statements (**337** (i)), but is often elided; the mutation caused by the elided *ni* is retained in the written language and frequently in the spoken language, see **87, 115**:

Wyddwn i ddim p'run ai i roi coel ar hyn ai peidio
'I did not know whether to believe this or not'
    (Wil Roberts, 1985: 50)

Chafodd Eurwyn erioed mohono'i hun yn y fath sefyllfa
'Eurwyn had never had himself in such a situation'
    (Rhiannon Thomas, 1988: 7)

Wyddai Mam mo'r ffordd i'r llyfrgell
'Mother did not know the way to the library'
    (Irma Chilton, 1989: 24)

In varieties of spoken Welsh and informal texts where the mutation is not realized in the initial consonant of the verb, and in a simple verb where a vowel occurs initially, *ddim* has assumed the negative function without there being any emphasis whatsoever:

Wylais i ddim
'I did not cry'
    (Emyr Humphreys, 1981: 222)

Aeth hi ddim
'She did not go'

Canodd e ddim
'He did not sing'

Bydd hi ddim yn gyrru
'She will not be driving'

See also **278** (vi).

257 Ychydig 'a few, a little'

(i) *Ychydig* occurs as a noun:

Ychydig yn unig a welir ar y cae
'Only a few are seen on the field'
    (*Y Faner*, 26 Mai 1989: 21)

It may be followed by the prep. *o* + a noun or personal form of the prep.:

Ychydig o amser a dreuliodd y teulu ym Mhlas Teg
'Little time did the family spend in Plas Teg'
    (*Y Faner*, 16 Mehefin 1989: 10)

Ychydig ohono a dreuliodd y teulu ym Mhlas Teg
'Little of it did the family spend in Plas Teg'

Ychydig may be modified by an adjective:

> *ychydig bach*
> 'a small amount'

(ii) As an adj. *ychydig* occurs immediately before a sing. or pl. noun (see **78**).

(iii) *Ychydig* occurs adverbially:

> *Hoffai'r gaseg bori ychydig ar y ddôl*
> 'The mare would like to graze a little on the meadow'
>> (R. Cyril Hughes, 1975: 35)

It may modify a comparative adjective:

> *ychydig cyflymach*
> 'a little faster'

> *ychydig mwy blasus*
> 'a little more tasty'

Yn normally occurs between *ychydig* and the adjective:

> *ychydig yn gyflymach*
> *ychydig yn fwy blasus*

Rhyw may precede *ychydig* in all the above constructions and convey uncertainty, imprecision or indistinctness.

When *iawn* follows *ychydig* it expresses the meaning 'very':

> *Ychydig iawn o bobl sy'n barod i anwybyddu gwaith Peter Walker*
> 'It's very few people who are prepared to ignore Peter Walker's work'
>> (*Y Faner*, 4 Awst 1989: 2)

258 Neb occurs:

(i) as a noun meaning 'anyone' in affirmative and negative phrases. *Neb* may occur alone or may be followed by the prep. *o* + a pl. or collective noun (or its equivalent):

> *Mi wn i na wnaiff Mr Edwards ddweud wrth neb*
> 'I know that Mr Edwards will not tell anyone'
>> (Kate Roberts, 1976: 26)

Gwyddai ei bod yn rhy hwyr yrŵan i ychwanegu neb o bwys y munud olaf fel hyn
'She knew that it was too late now to add anyone of importance at the last minute like this'

    (R. Cyril Hughes, 1975: 56)

neb o'n teulu ni
'anyone of our family'

os daw neb o'r bechgyn
'if any (one) of the boys comes'

neb ohonynt
'anyone of them'

(ii) to express the meaning 'no one':

Pwy sydd yno? Neb
'Who is there? No one'

Pwy welaist ti? Neb
'Whom did you see? No one'

(iii) as antecedent of a relative clause (see **233**).

Note

In an earlier period *neb* was used adjectivally (see D. Simon Evans, 1964: 105) and in contemporary Welsh this usage is preserved in *nemor* < *neb* + *mawr* 'not much, not many, but little'; *nepell* < *neb* + *pell* 'not far'.

The Verb

Introduction

259 The verb in Welsh has a three-term mood system: the indicative, the subjunctive and the imperative. The indicative has four tenses: present, imperfect, preterite and pluperfect. The subjunctive has two tenses: present and imperfect. Each tense in the indicative and subjunctive has six persons and an impersonal form. The imperative mood has one tense, the present tense, and five persons (i.e. all except the first person sing.).

260 There are two classes of verb: simple concise inflected verb forms (see **261**), and periphrastic verb forms (see **286**). In a formal literary text the simple verb forms tend to be statistically more numerous than periphrastic forms, while the reverse is the case in an informal text. The functions of the simple verb are more extensive in standard literary Welsh than in other registers. In less formal registers the present simple verb often expresses only the future, whereas in the literary register it may express a universal present and an iterative present in addition to future:

Cofiaf ef yn dda
'I remember him well'

Gwelwn hwy bob wythnos
'We see them every week'

Gwyn y gwêl y frân ei chyw
'The crow sees its young faultless' (lit., 'white')

Af yno yfory
'I'll go there tomorrow'

The imperfect and pluperfect forms of the simple verb, in addition to their conditional and modal function, may express an uncompleted past time and pluperfect respectively:

Awn oddi yno petawn i chwi
'I would go from there if I were you'

Gwnaem ein gwaith gyda'n gilydd bob nos
'We used to do our work together every night'

Eisteddai wrth y tân yn myfyrio
'He sat by the fire meditating'

Priodasai fy rhieni ryw dair blynedd cyn iddo farw
'My parents had married some three years before his death'

Nid oes ond dyfalu sut gampwaith a gawsem petai wedi llunio nofel hir
'We can only conjecture what sort of masterpiece we would have had if he had written a long novel'

When the subject is a noun, the third person singular of the verb is selected even if the subject is a phrase:

(a) singular subject

Cynigiodd y llongwr wneud y gwaith ei hun
'The sailor offered to do the work himself'
(Gerhart Hauptman and Heinrich Böll, 1974: 14)

Yr oedd Ifan wedi cysgu yn hwyr y bore hwnnw
'Ifan had slept late that morning'
(T. Glynne Davies, 1974: 73)

Yr oedd ambell ddafad ddu ymhlith esgobion Elizabeth
'There was an occasional black sheep amongst Elizabeth's bishops'
(Geraint H. Jenkins, 1983: 15)

Canodd y teliffon
'The telephone rang'
(Urien William, 1974: 24)

(b) plural subject

Note that in the first example the plural subject is realized by a noun + pronoun.

Mae Mati a minnau am fynd i'r dref ddydd Mercher
'Mati and I wish to go to town on Wednesday'
    (Kate Roberts, 1976: 27)

Torrodd y merched allan i feichio crio
'The girls broke out sobbing'
    (Rhiannon Davies Jones, 1977: 35)

Mi fydd yr athrawon am fy ngwaed i
'The teachers will be after my blood'
    (Eigra Lewis Roberts, 1988: 61)

Y mae'r deillion yn cael eu golwg yn ôl
'The blind recover their sight'
    (Matt. 11: 5)

Where there is no noun subject the person and number are marked by the form of the verb:

Y maent i holi'r disgyblion
'They are to question the scholars'
    (R. Geraint Gruffydd, 1988: 123)

Gwagiais fy ngwydryn
'I emptied my glass'
    (Robat Gruffudd, 1986: 114)

Lleddais ŵr
'I killed a man'
    (Gen. 4: 23)

Wynebodd gynulleidfaoedd mawr a mân
'He faced large and small audiences'
    (Hywel Teifi Edwards, 1989: 120)

Bwytaodd stêc deirgwaith yr wythnos
'He ate steak three times a week'
    (Harri Prichard Jones, 1978: 39)

Credaf y gwerthfawrogwch gynnwys y gyfrol
'I believe that you will appreciate the contents of the volume'
    (J. Elwyn Hughes, 1989: v)

An affixed pronoun may be added to these forms (see **221**) but it functions as an accessory element whose presence is not necessary to mark the subject of the verb. This is also the case when a pronoun or particle occurs before the verb (see **212** (iv)).

The Regular Simple Verb

261 The verb *canu* 'sing' is conjugated as follows:

INDICATIVE MOOD

Present Tense			Imperfect Tense	
Sing.	Pl.		Sing.	Pl.
1 *canaf*	*canwn*	1	*canwn*	*canem*
2 *ceni*	*cenwch*	2	*canit*	*canech*
3 *cân*	*canant*	3	*canai*	*canent*
Impers. *cenir*			Impers. *cenid*	

Preterite Tense			Pluperfect Tense	
Sing.	Pl.		Sing.	Pl.
1 *cenais*	*canasom*	1	*canaswn*	*canasem*
2 *cenaist*	*canasoch*	2	*canasit*	*canasech*
3 *canodd*	*canasant*	3	*canasai*	*canasent*
Impers. *canwyd*			Impers. *canasid* (*canesid*)	

SUBJUNCTIVE MOOD

Present Tense			Imperfect Tense	
Sing.	Pl.		Sing.	Pl.
1 *canwyf*	*canom*	1	*canwn*	*canem*
2 *cenych*	*canoch*	2	*canit*	*canech*
3 *cano*	*canont*	3	*canai*	*canent*
Impers. *caner*			Impers. *cenid*	

IMPERATIVE MOOD

	Sing.	Pl.
1	—	*canwn*
2	*cân*	*cenwch*
3	*caned*	*canent*

Verb-noun: *canu*   Verbal adjectives: *canadwy, canedig*

Notes

(1) *a* in the last syllable of the stem changes to *e* by affection (see **141, 144** n. 2) following the endings:

-i	2 sing. pres. indic.
-wch	2 pl. pres. indic.; 2 pl. imper.
-ir	pres. impers.
-id	imperf. impers.
-ais	1 sing. pret.
-aist	2 sing. pret.
-ych	2 sing. pres. subj.

The change is often ignored in varieties of spoken Welsh and in informal texts (for example *cani* for *ceni* 'you will sing'; *canwch* for *cenwch* 'sing'; *canais* for *cenais* 'I sang'; *cadwch* for *cedwch* 'keep'). The affection of *aw* to *ew* and *ha* to *he* before these endings is, however, normally observed in writing:

Verb-noun	Stem	Affected form
gadael 'leave'	(*gadaw-*)	*gadewch*
addo 'promise'	(*addaw-*)	*addewais, addewir*
gwrando 'listen'	(*gwrandaw-*)	*gwrandewi, gwrandewch*
glanhau 'clean'	(*glanha-*)	*glanheais*

(2) In the 1 pl. of all tenses final *-m* may be realized as *-n*, in varieties of spoken Welsh and in informal texts.

(3) Final *-t* disappeared from the 3 pl. of all tenses and conjugated prepositions at an early date (see **362** n. 5) and the auxiliary pronouns *hwy, hwythau* (see **221**) developed as *nhw, nhwy-thau*. The final *-t* never occurs in natural speech; the inclusion of final *-t* is a characteristic of standard literary Welsh.

Indicative Present, 1 Sing.

262 In informal texts and in most varieties of spoken Welsh *-f* is omitted:

Ga' i fynd i brynu cacen fêl?
'May I go and buy a honey cake?'
(Gweneth Lilly, 1984: 40)

Mi ddyweda' i ragor wrthat ti
'I will tell you more'
(Rhiannon Davies Jones, 1987: 81)

Mi reda innau i roi f'un i amdanaf
'I will run to put mine on'
    (Kate Roberts, 1976: 27)

Indicative Present, 3 Sing.

263 The 3rd person forms in this section are mostly highly literary choices: see **264** n. 1.

(i) Many verbs select the stem of the verb in the 3 sing. pres. indic.

1 sing.	3 sing.
adferaf 'I restore'	*adfer*
arbedaf 'I save'	*arbed*
arferaf 'I use'	*arfer*
atebaf 'I answer'	*ateb* (also *etyb*)
barnaf 'I judge'	*barn*
brathaf 'I stab'	*brath*
canaf 'I sing'	*cân*
caraf 'I love'	*câr*
casglaf 'I collect'	*casgl*
claddaf 'I bury'	*cladd*
crafaf 'I scratch'	*craf*
credaf 'I believe'	*cred*
cyfaddefaf 'I admit'	*cyfaddef* (also *cyfeddyf*)
cymeraf 'I take'	*cymer*
cymhellaf 'I compel'	*cymell*
cynhaliaf 'I support'	*cynnal*
chwalaf 'I scatter'	*chwâl*
chwarddaf 'I laugh'	*chwardd*
darparaf 'I prepare'	*darpar*
deallaf 'I understand'	*deall*
dialaf 'I avenge'	*dial*
dihangaf 'I escape'	*dianc*
eisteddaf 'I sit'	*eistedd*
gadaf 'I allow'	*gad*
gallaf 'I am able'	*gall* (also *geill*)
goddefaf 'I bear'	*goddef*
goddiweddaf 'I overtake'	*goddiwedd*
gomeddaf 'I refuse'	*gomedd*
gorffennaf 'I complete'	*gorffen*
gwanaf 'I pierce'	*gwân*

gwaredaf 'I save'	*gwared* (formerly *gweryd*)
gwatwaraf 'I mock'	*gwatwar*
gwelaf 'I see'	*gwêl*
gwerthaf 'I sell'	*gwerth*
lladdaf 'I kill'	*lladd*
malaf 'I ground'	*mâl*
medaf 'I reap'	*med*
medraf 'I am able'	*medr*
meddaf 'I own'	*medd*
naddaf 'I chip'	*nadd*
rhannaf 'I share'	*rhan*
rhedaf 'I run'	*rhed*
sathraf 'I trample'	*sathr*
talaf 'I pay'	*tâl*
tarddaf 'I spring'	*tardd*
ymdrechaf 'I strive'	*ymdrech* (also *ymdrecha*)
ymddiriedaf 'I trust'	*ymddiried*
ymwelaf 'I visit'	*ymwêl*

(ii) Affection may cause changes to the vowel in the 3 pers. sing. (see **141**, **143**); some additional examples are noted below:

a becomes **ai**

1 sing.	3 sing.
caf (*caffaf*) 'I shall get'	*caiff*
dyrchafaf 'I raise'	*dyrchaif*
paraf 'I cause'	*pair*
safaf 'I stand'	*saif*

Note

(1) *caf, caffaf* is almost always future in meaning; the periphrastic construction *yr wyf yn cael* etc. is usually selected to denote the present, see **274**.

a becomes **ei**

1 sing.	3 sing.
archaf 'I request'	*eirch*
daliaf 'I catch'	*deil*
gallaf 'I am able'	*geill* (also *gall*)
llanwaf 'I fill'	*lleinw*
taflaf 'I throw'	*teifl*
ymaflaf 'I wrestle'	*ymeifl*

a becomes **y** (clear)

1 sing.	3 sing.
gwasgaraf 'I scatter'	*gwesgyr*
bwytâf 'I eat'	*bwyty*
parhaf 'I continue'	*pery* (with two changes)

e becomes **y** (clear)

1 sing.	3 sing.
atebaf 'I reply'	*etyb* (with two changes)

o becomes **y** (clear)

1 sing.	3 sing.
cloaf 'I lock'	*cly*
cyfodaf 'I arise'	*cyfyd*
cyffroaf 'I excite'	*cyffry*
deffroaf 'I awaken'	*deffry*
ffoaf 'I flee'	*ffy*
torraf 'I break'	*tyr*

a–o become **e–y**

1 sing.	3 sing.
adroddaf 'I recite'	*edrydd*
agoraf 'I open'	*egyr*
anfonaf 'I send'	*enfyn*
arhosaf 'I stay'	*erys*
ataliaf 'I restrain'	*etyl*
dangosaf 'I show'	*dengys*
datodaf 'I untie'	*detyd*

o–o become **e–y**

1 sing.	3 sing.
gosodaf 'I place'	*gesyd*
ymosodaf 'I attack'	*ymesyd*

aw becomes **y** (clear)

1 sing.	3 sing.
gadawaf 'I leave'	*gedy*
gwrandawaf 'I listen'	*gwrendy*

Note

(2) On the change in the penult of the 3 sing. see **143**.

(iii) Vowel mutation (see **146**) occurs in the following examples:

ei becomes ai

1 sing.	3 sing.
beiddiaf 'I dare'	*baidd*
ceisiaf 'I seek'	*cais*
meiddiaf 'I dare'	*maidd*
neidiaf 'I leap'	*naid*
peidiaf 'I desist'	*paid*
treiddiaf 'I penetrate'	*traidd*

o becomes aw

1 sing.	3 sing.
boddaf 'I drown'	*bawdd*
coddaf 'I offend'	*cawdd*
cronnaf 'I collect'	*crawn*
holaf 'I question'	*hawl*
molaf 'I praise'	*mawl*
nofiaf 'I swim'	*nawf*
poraf 'I graze'	*pawr*
profaf 'I test'	*prawf*
soddaf 'I sink'	*sawdd*
toddaf 'I melt'	*tawdd*
toliaf 'I reduce'	*tawl*

y (dark) becomes w

1 sing.	3 sing.
cysgaf 'I sleep'	*cwsg*
dygaf 'I bring'	*dwg*
tyngaf 'I swear'	*twng*
llyncaf 'I swallow'	*llwnc*

y (dark) becomes y (clear)

1 sing.	3 sing.
crynaf 'I shiver'	*crŷn, cryn*
cyrchaf 'I attack'	*cyrch*
chwenychaf 'I desire'	*chwennych*
dysgaf 'I learn, teach'	*dysg*
dilynaf 'I follow'	*dilyn*
derbyniaf 'I receive'	*derbyn*
disgynnaf 'I descend'	*disgyn*
esgynnaf 'I ascend'	*esgyn*

glynaf 'I adhere'	*glŷn*
gwlychaf 'I wet'	*gwlych*
gofynnaf 'I ask'	*gofyn*
mynnaf 'I insist'	*myn*
llyfaf 'I lick'	*llyf*
plygaf 'I fold'	*plyg*
prynaf 'I buy'	*prŷn, pryn*
syflaf 'I budge'	*syfl*
sychaf 'I dry'	*sych*
tynnaf 'I pull'	*tyn*
tybiaf 'I suppose'	*tyb, tybia*
yfaf 'I drink'	*yf*

264 When a noun or adjective has been made verbal by the addition of a verbal affix, *-a* is added to the stem:

Noun or adjective	1 sing.	3 sing.
bloedd 'yell'	*bloeddiaf*	*bloeddia*
coch 'red'	*cochaf*	*cocha*
cosb 'punishment'	*cosbaf*	*cosba*
dirmyg 'contempt'	*dirmygaf*	*dirmyga*
du 'black'	*duaf*	*dua*
gwasanaeth 'service'	*gwasanaethaf*	*gwasanaetha*
gwawd 'scorn'	*gwawdiaf*	*gwawdia*
gweddi 'prayer'	*gweddïaf*	*gweddïa*
gwyn 'white'	*gwynnaf*	*gwynna*
llyw 'helm, leader'	*llywiaf*	*llywia*
saeth 'arrow'	*saethaf*	*saetha*
tawel 'calm'	*tawelaf*	*tawela*
ysgrifen 'writing'	*ysgrifennaf*	*ysgrifenna*

By analogy *-a* as a 3 sing. ending has spread to other verbs not necessarily associated with a noun or adjective, for example:

cerdda 'he walks'
cilia 'he retreats'
cuddia 'he hides'
darpara 'he prepares'
dymuna 'he wishes'
eheda 'he flies'
fflamycha 'he inflames'
haera 'he asserts'
nodda 'he protects'

nofia 'he swims'
preswylia 'he lives'
traetha 'he relates'
tyrcha 'he burrows'
rhodia 'he walks'

When the endings in the 1 sing. and 3 sing. are *-haf* and *-ha* respectively, the verbal form is accented on the ultima:

1 sing.	3 sing.
byrhaf 'I shorten'	*byrha*
cryfhaf 'I strengthen'	*cryfha*
cwblhaf 'I complete'	*cwblha*
glanhaf 'I clean'	*glanha*
gwanhaf 'I weaken'	*gwanha*
llwfrhaf 'I lose heart'	*llwfrha*
mwynhaf 'I enjoy'	*mwynha*
pellhaf 'I move away'	*pellha*
rhyddhaf 'I free'	*rhyddha*
trugarhaf 'I show mercy'	*trugarha*
trymhaf 'I grow heavy'	*trymha*

In the above examples the *h* indicates the location of the accent; in other verbs, however, *-h-* has been assimilated to a preceding consonant and the stress is marked by a circumflex (see **37**):

1 sing.	3 sing.
agosâf 'I draw near'	*agosâ*
caniatâf 'I allow'	*caniatâ*
dwysâf 'I intensify'	*dwysâ*
gwacâf 'I empty'	*gwacâ*
iachâf 'I heal'	*iachâ*
nacâf 'I refuse'	*nacâ*
tecâf 'I beautify'	*tecâ*

In two forms the 3 pers. sing. is accented on the penult:

1 sing.	3 sing.
bwytâf 'I eat'	*bwyty*
parhaf 'I continue'	*pery, para* (*parha* also occurs)

Notes

(1) In varieties of spoken Welsh and informal texts, *-iff* and *-ith* occur in 3 pers. sing.: *gwnaiff/gwneith* for *gwna* 'he/she will

make'; *caniff/canith* for *cân* 'he/she will sing'; *cerddiff/cerddith* for *cerdd* 'he/she will walk'; *gwrandawiff/gwrandawith* for *gwrendy* 'he/she will listen'; *neidiff/neidith* for *naid* 'he/she will jump'; *yfiff/yfith* for *yf* 'he/she will drink'; *toriff/torrith* for *tyr* 'he/she will break'; *cysgiff/cysgith* for *cwsg* 'he/she will sleep'; *bwytiff/bwytith* for *bwyty* 'he/she will eat' etc. See **260**. A few of the stem affected and mutated forms such as *geill* (v.n. *gallu* 'be able'); *pery* (v.n. *parhau* 'last'); *rhydd* (v.n. *rhoi* 'give'); *gwêl* (v.n. *gweld* 'see'); *tyr* (v.n. *torri* 'break'); *cyfyd* (v.n. *codi* 'lift'); *myn* (v.n. *mynnu* 'insist') also occur in varieties of spoken Welsh as alternatives to the *-iff/-ith* forms *galliff/gallith*; *pariff/parith*; *gweliff/gwelith*; *torriff/torrith*; *codiff/codith*; *mynniff/mynnith*.

(2) An archaic ending, *-id*, is preserved in some proverbs: *Tyfid maban, ni thyf ei gadachan* 'An infant grows, his swaddling-clothes grow not'; *Trengid golud, ni threinc molud* 'Wealth perishes, fame perishes not'; *Chwaraeid mab noeth, ni chwarae mab newynog* 'A naked boy plays, a hungry boy plays not' (see D. Simon Evans, 1964: 118).

Imperfect

265 *-it* does not trigger affection in the 2 sing., see **144** n. 1 (iv).

In varieties of spoken Welsh (south-east and north-west) the following endings occur: *-at* (2 sing.); *-a* (3 sing.); *-an* (1 pl.); *-ach* (2 pl.); *-an* (3 pl.). In other areas (south-west and north-east) the following endings occur: *-et* (2 sing.); *-e* (3 sing.); *-en* (1 pl.); *-ech* (2 pl.); *-en* (3 pl.).

For example,

> *gwenan, gwenen* for *gwenem*
> *eisteddat, eisteddet* for *eisteddit*
> *agora, agore* for *agorai*

See also **307, 267**.

Preterite

266 (i) The most common ending in the 3 pers. sing. is *-odd*, but in an earlier period there were others (see D. Simon Evans, 1964: 122–4), one of which survives in the form *-ws* in the dialects of south-east Wales (*canws* for *canodd* 'he/she sang', *gwelws* for *gwelodd* 'he/she saw', *yfws* for *yfodd* 'he/she drank'). The same dialects preserve the form *cas*, a variant of *cafas* = *cafodd* 'he/she had'. Another ending, *-es*, is selected by verbs with stems in *-o-* or *-oe-*, for example *rhoes*, *rhoddes* = *rhoddodd* 'he/she gave'; *troes* = *trodd* 'he/she turned'; *ffoes* = *ffodd* 'he/she fled':

> *Efe a gymerodd fara, ac a'i bendithiodd, ac a'i torodd, ac a'i rhoddes iddynt* (1955)
> 'He took bread, and blessed it, and broke it, and gave it to them'
>> (Luke 24: 30)

> *Rhoes sylw i statws y beirdd yn y Gymru oedd ohoni*
> 'He attended to the status of the bards in Wales at the time'
>> (Hywel Teifi Edwards, 1989: 30)

> *Troes yn ffyrnig ar ei wrthwynebydd*
> 'He turned fiercely on his opponent'
>> (Rhiannon Davies Jones, 1989: 15)

The forms *cymerth* = *cymerodd* 'he took' and *cant* = *canodd* 'he sang, composed' preserve the old *-t* preterite:

> *yntau a gymerth arno ei fod yn myned ymhellach* (1955)
> 'and he made as if to continue his journey'
>> (Luke 24: 28)

> *Dafydd ap Gwilym a'i cant*
> 'Composed by Dafydd ap Gwilym'

Dialects of Welsh preserve the suffixless preterite *dwad* (*dywad*) = *dywedodd* 'he/she said'. *Dug* = *dygodd* 'he/she brought' also realizes the suffixless preterite and only occurs in formal texts:

> *Yr hwn ei hun a ddug ein pechodau yn ei gorff ar y pren* (1955)
> *Ef ei hun a ddygodd ein pechodau yn ei gorff ar y croesbren* (1988)
> 'In his own person he carried our sins in his body on the cross'
>> (1 Pet. 2: 24)

(ii) The plural endings *-asom*, *-asoch*, *-asant* are contracted to *-som*, *-soch*, *-sant* with stems ending in *-aw-*, *-ew-*, *-al-*, *-el-*, *-oe-*, *-yw-*:

Stem	Verb-noun	Pl. pret. endings
gadaw-	*gadael* 'leave'	*gadawsom, gadawsoch, gadawsant*
traw-	*taro* 'strike'	*trawsom, trawsoch, trawsant*

rhew-	*rhewi* 'freeze'	*rhewsom, rhewsoch, rhewsant*
tal-	*talu* 'pay'	*tal(a)som, tal(a)soch, tal(a)sant*
gwel-	*gweld, gweled* 'see'	*gwelsom, gwelsoch, gwelsant*
dychwel-	*dychwelyd* 'return'	*dychwel(a)som, dychwel(a)soch, dychwel(a)sant*
troe-	*troi* 'turn'	*troesom, troesoch, troesant*
clyw-	*clywed* 'hear'	*clywsom, clywsoch, clywsant*

In varieties of spoken Welsh the plural endings -(*s*)*on*, -(*s*)*och*, -(*s*)*on* occur:

rhewon, rhewson for *rhewsom* 'we froze', *rhewsant* 'they froze'
gadawon, gadawson for *gadawsom* 'we left', *gadawsant* 'they left'
taloch, talsoch for *tal(a)soch* 'you paid'

(iii) Both -*ed* and -*wyd* occur in the impersonal with the following verbs:

caed	*cafwyd* 'was had'
ganed	*ganwyd* 'was born'
rhoed, rhodded	*rhoddwyd* 'was given'

For example,

Ganed ef yn ôl ei dystiolaeth ef ei hun yng Nglan-yr-afon
'He was born according to his own evidence in Glan-yr-afon'
   (*Y Faner*, 22 Medi 1989: 5)

Ganwyd Moses
'Moses was born'
   (Acts 7: 20)

Philip a gaed yn Asotus
'Philip was found in Azotus'
   (Acts 8: 40)

Cafwyd dwy wers chwerw arall
'Two other bitter lessons were had'
   (*Y Faner*, 5 Ionawr 1990: 21)

Rhoed rhybudd i bawb
'Everybody was given a warning'
   (*Taliesin*, Tachwedd 1989: 15)

(iv)   A few irregular verbs select *-pwyd* in the impersonal:

aethpwyd	(also *aed*)	'there was a going'
daethpwyd	(also *deuwyd*)	'there was a coming'
ducpwyd	(also *dygwyd*)	'was brought'
gwnaethpwyd	(also *gwnaed*)	'was made'

For example,

Gwnaed y dyn yn iach (1955)
'The man was made whole'
(John 5: 9)

Gwnaethpwyd fel y gorchmynnaist (1955)
'It was done as you commanded'
(Luke 14: 25)

Daethpwyd â Paul gerbron (1988)
Ef a ddygwyd Paul gerbron (1955)
'Paul was brought forth'
(Acts 25: 23)

Ducpwyd ei ben ef mewn dysgl (1955)
Daethpwyd â'i ben ef ar ddysgl (1988)
'His head was brought on a dish'
(Matt. 14: 11)

Aethpwyd ati i lunio cynllun dosbarthu
'A distribution plan was formed'
(*Llais Llyfrau*, Gaeaf 1989: 5)

Aed ati mewn difrif i ddweud pethau mawr dwyieithog am haeddiannau'r Cymry
'Great bilingual things were seriously said about the merits of the Welsh people'
(Hywel Teifi Edwards, 1989: 6)

Fe ddaethpwyd â chorff yr arglwydd Gruffudd oddi yno i'w gladdu yn naear Aberconwy
'Lord Gruffudd's body was brought from there to be buried in the ground of Aberconwy'
(Rhiannon Davies Jones, 1989: 18)

Pluperfect

267 In varieties of spoken Welsh (south-east and north-west) the following endings occur: -*swn* (1 sing.); -*sat* (2 sing.); -*sa* (3 sing.); -*san* (1 pl.); -*sach* (2 pl.); -*san* (3 pl.). In other areas (south-west and north-east) the endings are: -*swn* (1 sing.); -*set* (2 sing.); -*se* (3 sing.); -*sen* (1 pl.); -*sech* (2 pl.); -*sen* (3 pl.). For example:

> *agorsa, agorse* for *agorsai*
> *cansach, cansech* for *canasech*
> *gwelsan, gwelsen* for *gwelasent*

See **309** n. 1, **261** n. 3, **265**.

In the pl. the endings -*asem*, -*asech*, -*asent* are contracted to -*sem*, -*sech*, -*sent* before stems ending in -*aw*-, -*ew*-, -*al*-, -*el*-, -*oe*-, -*yw*-, see **266** (ii):

Stem	Verb-noun	Pl. pluperf. endings
gadaw-	*gadael* 'leave'	*gadawsem, gadawsech, gadawsent*
rhew-	*rhewi* 'freeze'	*rhewsem, rhewsech, rhewsent*
gwel-	*gweld* 'see'	*gwelsem, gwelsech, gwelsent*
troe-	*troi* 'turn'	*troesem, troesech, troesent*
clyw-	*clywed* 'hear'	*clywsem, clywsech, clywsent*

Subjunctive Mood

268 (i) In an earlier period subjunctive endings were marked by -*h*- which caused provection (see **149**) when added to the stem; -*h*- has completely disappeared and provection only occurs in a few proverbs and stereotyped expressions:

> *Duw cato pawb!*
> 'God save everybody!'

> *Gwell y wialen a blyco na'r hon a dorro*
> 'Better the rod that bends than the one that breaks'
>   (Proverb)

> *Na ato Duw!*
> 'God forbid!'

Note
cato < *cad*(*w*) + *ho*; *plyco* < *plyg* + *ho*; *ato* < *gad* + *ho*.

(ii) In earlier editions of the Bible both -*ych* and -*ech* occur in the 2 sing. In the 1988 translation of the Bible the subjunctive has been abandoned in the following examples:

> *fel y llwyddych yn yr hyn a wnelych, ac i ba le bynnag y troëch* (1955)
> *fe lwyddi ym mhob peth a wnei ym mha le bynnag y byddi'n troi* (1988)
> 'that thou mayest prosper in all that thou doest, and whitherso-ever thou turnest'
> (1 Kgs. 2: 3)

> *Mi a'th ganlynaf i ba le bynnag yr elych* (1955)
> *Canlynaf di lle bynnag yr ei* (1988)
> 'I will follow you wherever you go'
> (Matt. 8: 19)

Imperative Mood

269 (i) Frequently the form of the 2 sing. imper. is identical to the form of the 3 sing. indic., for example:

Verb-noun	3 sing. indic.	2 sing. imper.
barnu 'judge'	*barn*	*barn!*
canu 'sing'	*cân*	*cân!*
credu 'believe'	*cred*	*cred!*
dychwelyd 'return'	*dychwel*	*dychwel!*
gwasanaethu 'serve'	*gwasanaetha*	*gwasanaetha!*
gweddïo 'pray'	*gweddïa*	*gweddïa!*
gweiddi 'shout'	*gwaedda*	*gwaedda!*
gweld, gweled 'see'	*gwêl*	*gwêl!*
mynegi 'state'	*mynega*	*mynega!*

The vowel in the 3 sing. indic. may be subject to affection (see **141**) but affection does not occur in the 2 sing. imper.:

Verb-noun	3 sing. indic.	2 sing. imper.
dal 'hold'	*deil*	*dal!*
sefyll 'stand'	*saif*	*saf!*
dangos 'show'	*dengys*	*dangos!*
torri 'break'	*tyr*	*tor!*
ateb 'reply'	*etyb*	*ateb!*

Note

tybio 'imagine' may select either *tyb* or *tybia* in the 3 sing. indic., but in the 2 sing. imper., only the latter may occur.

(ii) Verbs whose stems end in *-i-*, and verbs formed from nouns or adjectives (see **264**) add the affix *-a-* to the stem in the 2 sing., for example:

Verb-noun	Stem	2 sing. imper.
penlinio 'kneel'	*penlini-*	*penlinia!*
ysgrifennu 'write'	*ysgrifenn-*	*ysgrifenna!*
duo 'blacken'	*du-*	*dua!*

-i- occurs in the stem of *arwain* 'lead', *cynnal* 'support, hold', *dal* 'hold, catch', *meddwl* 'think', but the 2 sing. imper. is identical in form to the verb-noun:

Verb-noun	Stem	2 sing. imper.
arwain	*arweini-*	*arwain!*
cynnal	*cynhali-*	*cynnal!*
dal	*dali-*	*dal!*
meddwl	*meddyli-*	*meddwl!*

(iii) In varieties of spoken Welsh the ending *-a* is frequently added to the stem to form the 2 sing. imper.:

ateba! 'answer!'	*barna!* 'judge!'
cana! 'sing!'	*pryna!* 'buy!'
meddylia! 'think!'	*dalia!* 'hold!'
eistedda! 'sit!'	*cerdda!* 'walk!'
ysgrifenna! 'write!'	*darllena!* 'read!'

(iv) The normal ending in the 3 pl. imper. is *-ent*, but *-ant* occurs in earlier editions of the Bible:

Deuant hwy eu hunain (1955)
'Let them come themselves'
    (Acts 16: 27)

Deuant i fyny (1955)
'Let them come up'
    (Joel 3: 9)

Contracted Forms

270 Verbs with stems ending in *-o-* or *-a-* have contracted forms: for example, *trof* 'I turn' < stem *tro-* + 1 sing. ending *-af*, *mwynhaf* 'I enjoy' < stem *mwynha-* + 1 sing. ending *-af*. Stress falls on the final syllable in verbs like *mwynhaf* (see **35**).

Contraction, however, does not occur in every form of the verb *mwynhau*; the verbal affix may be appended to *-ha-* or *-he-* and a regular penultimate stressed verbal form results: *mwynhawyd*, *mwynheais*.

The verbs *trof* and *mwynhaf* are conjugated below:

INDICATIVE MOOD

Present Tense

	Sing.	Pl.	Sing.	Pl.
1	*trof, troaf*	*trown*	*mwynhaf*	*mwynhawn*
2	*troi*	*trowch*	*mwynhei*	*mwynhewch*
3	*try*	*trônt*	*mwynha*	*mwynhânt*
	Impers. *troir*		Impers. *mwynheir*	

Note
On final *-f* in 1 sing. see **262**.

Imperfect Tense

	Sing.	Pl.	Sing.	Pl.
1	*trown*	*troem*	*mwynhawn*	*mwynhaem*
2	*troit*	*troech*	*mwynhait*	*mwynhaech*
3	*trôi*	*troent*	*mwynhâi*	*mwynhaent*
	Impers. *troid*		Impers. *mwynheid*	

Preterite Tense

	Sing.	Pl.	Sing.	Pl.
1	*trois*	*troesom*	*mwynheais*	*mwynhasom*
2	*troist*	*troesoch*	*mwynheaist*	*mwynhasoch*
3	*troes, trodd*	*troesant*	*mwynhaodd*	*mwynhasant*
	Impers. *trowyd, troed*		Impers. *mwynhawd*	

Pluperfect Tense

Sing.	Pl.	Sing.	Pl.
1 *troeswn*	*troesem*	*mwynhaswn*	*mwynhasem*
2 *troesit*	*troesech*	*mwynhasit*	*mwynhasech*
3 *troesai*	*troesent*	*mwynhasai*	*mwynhasent*
Impers. *troesid*		Impers. *mwynhasid*	

SUBJUNCTIVE MOOD
Present Tense

Sing.	Pl.	Sing.	Pl.
1 *trowyf*	*trôm*	*mwynhawyf*	*mwynhaom*
2 *troech*	*troch*	*mwynheych*	*mwynhaoch*
3 *tro*	*trônt*	*mwynhao*	*mwynhaont*
Impers. *troer*		Impers. *mwynhaer*	

Imperfect Tense
(the same forms as in the indicative mood)

IMPERATIVE MOOD

Sing.	Pl.	Sing.	Pl.
1 —	*trown*	—	*mwynhawn*
2 *tro*	*trowch*	*mwynha*	*mwynhewch*
3 *troed*	*troent*	*mwynhaed*	*mwynhaent*
Impers. *troer*		Impers. *mwynhaer*	

Note
On final *-t* in 3 pl. see **261** n. 3.

VERB-NOUN

troi   *mwynhau*

VERBAL ADJECTIVES

troëdig, troadwy, tro   *mwynhaol*

271 The following verbs are conjugated like *troi*: *cloi* 'lock', *clof* (also *cloaf*); *cnoi* 'bite', *cnof* (also *cnoaf*); *crynhoi* 'gather', *crynhôf* (also *crynhoaf*); *cyffroi* 'provoke', *cyffroaf*; *datgloi* 'unlock', *datglôf* (also *datgloaf*); *ffoi* 'flee', *ffoaf*; *paratoi* 'prepare', *paratôf* (also *paratoaf*).

Although the ending -*oaf* may be selected by the 1 sing. pres. indic. of these verbs, the *trof* pattern occurs in the other persons and tenses.

Notes
(1) In the 2 sing. imper. of *rhoi* 'give', both *rho* and *dyro* occur; in the 3 sing. pres. indic. the forms *rhydd* or *rhy* or *dyry* occur.
(2) In *paratoi* 'prepare', *crynhoi* 'gather', the ending -*a* is added to the stem in the 3 sing. pres. indic. and 2 sing. imper.: *paratoa*, *crynhoa* (also *paratô*, *crynho*).
(3) The 3 sing. pres. indic. of *ffoi* 'flee' is *ffy*.
(4) In the 1 sing. pres. indic. of *rhoi* 'give', both *rhof* and *rhoddaf* occur.

272 The following verbs are conjugated like *mwynhau*. Where there is no *h* in the final syllable, a circumflex is required in the 1 sing. pres. indic. and in the 3 sing. pres. indic.; the acute accent is used to mark the stress on the final syllable of the verb-noun (see **35**):

Verb-noun	1 sing.	3 sing.
agosáu 'draw near'	*agosâf*	*agosâ*
byrhau 'shorten'	*byrhaf*	
cadarnhau 'confirm'	*cadarnhaf*	
caniatáu 'permit'	*caniatâf*	*caniatâ*
casáu 'hate'	*casâf*	*casâ*
cryfhau 'strengthen'	*cryfhaf*	
cwblhau 'complete'	*cwblhaf*	
glanhau 'clean'	*glanhaf*	
gwanhau 'weaken'	*gwanhaf*	
nesáu 'approach'	*nesâf*	*nesâ*
pellhau 'move away'	*pellhaf*	
tecáu 'beautify'	*tecâf*	*tecâ*
trugarhau 'take pity'	*trugarhaf*	

Notes
(1) The verbs *bwytâf* 'I eat' and *parhaf* 'I continue' belong to this class, but have irregular forms, *bwyty*, *pery* (also *para*), in the 3 sing. pres. indic.; see **263** (ii).
(2) Verbs in this class do not have verbal adjectives in -*edig*, -*adwy* except for *bwytedig*, *bwytadwy*, but adjectives in -*ol* or -*us* are

formed from several of them: *agosaol* 'approaching'; *boddhaol* 'satisfactory'; *boddhaus* 'pleasing'; *cadarnhaol* 'affirmative'; *caniataol* 'permitted'; *cryfhaol* 'invigorating'; *parhaol, parhaus* 'perpetual'; *iachaol* 'healing'; *nacaol* 'negative'.

(3) In some verbs the *-a-* or *-e-* (formed as a result of affection) of the stem combines with a following vowel to form a stressed diphthong: *agoseir, bwytaem, bwytei, casawn, nesewch.*

273 Contraction occurs where the endings *-wn, -wch* follow stems ending in *-aw, -ew, -yw*:

clywch (<*clyw* + *wch*) verb-noun *clywed* 'hear'
clywn (<*clyw* + *wn*)

gadewch (<*gadew* + *wch*) verb-noun *gadael* 'leave'
gadawn (<*gadaw* + *wn*)

gwrandewch (<*gwrandew* + *wch*) verb-noun *gwrando* 'listen'
gwrandawn (<*gwrandaw* + *wn*)

The verb-noun *cau* 'close' is a contraction of *cae-u* and the personal endings are added to the stem *cae-*: *caeaf, caei, caeir, caewyd, caeer* etc.

Due to contraction stress occurs on the final syllables of the verb nouns *dileu* 'delete', *dyheu* 'aspire'.

274 Cael 'have' is also a contracted verb. The conjugation in contemporary Welsh is based on two stems, *caff-* and *ca-*:

INDICATIVE MOOD

	Present Tense			Imperfect Tense	
	Sing.	Pl.		Sing.	Pl.
1	*caf*	*cawn*	1	*cawn*	*caem*
2	*cei*	*cewch*	2	*cait*	*caech*
3	*caiff*	*cânt*	3	*câi*	*caent*
	Impers. *ceir*			Impers. *ceid*	

See also **263** (ii) n. 1.

	Preterite Tense			Pluperfect Tense	
	Sing.	Pl.		Sing.	Pl.
1	*cefais, ces*	*cawsom*	1	*cawswn*	*cawsem*
2	*cefaist, cest*	*cawsoch*	2	*cawsit*	*cawsech*
3	*cafodd, cas*	*cawsant*	3	*cawsai*	*cawsent*
	Impers. *cafwyd, caed, cad*			Impers. *cawsid*	

SUBJUNCTIVE MOOD

Present Tense			Imperfect Tense	
Sing.	Pl.		Sing.	Pl.
1 *caffwyf*	*caffom*	1	*caffwn, cawn*	*caffem, caem*
2 *ceffych*	*caffoch*	2	*caffit, cait*	*caffech, caech*
3 *caffo*	*caffont*	3	*caffai, câi*	*caffent, caent*
Impers. *caffer*			Impers. *ceffid*	

IMPERATIVE MOOD

(Used only in the third person)

	Sing.	Pl.
3	*caffed, caed*	*caffent, caent*

Verb-noun: *cael, caffael, caffel*

There are no verbal adjectives.
On *cas* 3 sing. pret. see **266** (i).

Note
In varieties of spoken Welsh the stems *cel-*, *ces-*, *ceth-*, occur in the imperf. indic. and pret. indic.; for example, *cese, cethe, cele* 'câi'; *ceso, cesim, cetho, celo* 'cefais'.

275 Gadaw 'leave, leave behind' and **Gadael, Gado, Gadu** 'leave, allow, permit' were two separate verbs; they have largely merged with the *gadaw* forms gaining ascendancy.
   The conjugation of *gadaw* is regular: see **261** n. 1, **273**, and also **307**.

INDICATIVE MOOD

Present Tense			Imperfect Tense	
Sing.	Pl.		Sing.	Pl.
1 *gadawaf*	*gadawn*	1	*gadawn*	*gadawem*
2 *gadewi*	*gadewch*	2	*gadawit*	*gadawech*
3 *gedy*	*gadawant*	3	*gadawai*	*gadawent*
Impers. *gadewir*			Impers. *gadewid*	

Preterite Tense		Pluperfect Tense	
Sing.	Pl.	Sing.	Pl.
1 *gadewais*	*gadawsom*	1 *gadawswn*	*gadawsem*
2 *gadewaist*	*gadawsoch*	2 *gadawsit*	*gadawsech*
3 *gadawodd*	*gadawsant*	3 *gadawsai*	*gadawsent*
Impers. *gadawyd*		Impers. *gadawsid*	

SUBJUNCTIVE MOOD
Present Tense

Sing.	Pl.
1 *gadawyf*	*gadawom*
2 *gadawych, gadawech*	*gadawoch*
3 *gadawo*	*gadawont*
Impers. *gadawer*	

IMPERATIVE MOOD

Sing.	Pl.
1 —	*gadawn*
2 *gad*	*gadewch*
3 *gadawed*	*gadawent*
Impers. *gadawer*	

The conjugation of *gadael*, *gado* is also regular but verbal forms occur infrequently apart from the 2 sing. and 2 plur. imper. *gad*, *gedwch/gadwch*. The 3 sing. subj. *gato* is preserved in *Na ato Duw!* 'God forbid!' (see **268**).

Notes

(1) *ymadael*, *ymado* 'depart' is conjugated like *gadaw* except that *ymado* and *ymâd* occur in the 2 sing. imper.

(2) Normally *gadawaf* takes an object: *Gadawodd ef y wlad* 'He left the country'; *Nis gadawaf* 'I will not leave him'. With *ymadawaf*, however, the object is governed by the preposition *â*, *ag*: *Ymadawodd â'i deulu* 'He left his family'. *Ymadawaf* also occurs without an object governed by *â*, *ag*: *ymedy rhai yn yr amseroedd diwethaf oddi wrth y ffydd* (1955) 'some shall depart from the faith in the latter times' (1 Tim. 4: 1).

(3) On final *-t* in 3 pl. see **261** n. 3.

276 Codi, **cyfodi** 'raise'. The conjugation of *codi*, *cyfodi* is regular apart from the 3 sing. pres. indic. of *codaf* where *cyfyd* as well as *cwyd* may be selected.

The forms *codaf*, *codi*, *codir*, *codais* etc., are preferred to *cyfodaf*, *cyfodi*, *cyfodir*, *cyfodais* etc., in contemporary Welsh.

Irregular Verbs

277 *Bod* 'To Be'

INDICATIVE MOOD
Present Tense[1,2,3]

Sing.	Pl.
1 *wyf, ydwyf*	*ŷm, ydym, ydyn*
2 *wyt, ydwyt*	*ŷch, ydych*
3 *yw, ydyw, ydy, ydi, y mae,*	*ŷnt, ydynt, y maent,*
mae, oes	*maent*

Relatival form: *sydd, sy*
Impersonal form: *ys, ydys*
Conjunctive forms: *mai, taw*

Future and Consuetudinal Present Tense

Sing.	Pl.
1 *byddaf*	*byddwn*
2 *byddi*	*byddwch*
3 *bydd*	*byddant*

Impers. *byddir*

Imperfect Tense[4,5]

Sing.	Pl.
1 *oeddwn*	*oeddem*
2 *oeddit, oeddet*	*oeddech*
3 *oedd, ydoedd*	*oeddynt, oeddent*

Impers. *oeddid*

Consuetudinal Imperfect Tense

	Sing.	Pl.
1	*byddwn*	*byddem*
2	*byddit*	*byddech*
3	*byddai*	*byddent*

Impers. *byddid*

Preterite Tense[6]

	Sing.	Pl.
1	*bûm*	*buom*
2	*buost*	*buoch*
3	*bu*	*buant, buont*

Impers. *buwyd*

Pluperfect Tense[7]

	Sing.	Pl.
1	*buaswn*	*buasem*
2	*buasit*	*buasech*
3	*buasai*	*buasent*

Impers. *buasid*

SUBJUNCTIVE MOOD

Present Tense

	Sing.	Pl.
1	*bwyf, byddwyf*	*bôm, byddom*
2	*bych, byddych, -ech*	*boch, byddoch*
3	*bo, byddo*	*bônt, byddont*

Impers. *bydder*

Imperfect Tense

	Sing.	Pl.
1	*bawn, byddwn*	*baem, byddem*
2	*bait, byddit*	*baech, byddech*
3	*bai, byddai*	*baent, byddent*

Impers. *byddid*

IMPERATIVE MOOD

	Sing.	Pl.
1	—	*byddwn*
2	*bydd*	*byddwch*
3	*bydded, boed, bid*	*byddent*[8]

Impers. *bydder*

Notes

(1) *Y mae, y maent* occur in natural speech as *mae, maen* and this is permissible in all save very formal styles of language. See also **286**.

(2) In varieties of spoken Welsh the following contracted forms are common:

	Sing.	Pl.
1	*(yd)w*	*ŷn* (south); *ydyn*; *yden*; *ydan*
2	*w(y)t*	*ŷch* (south); *ydech*; *ydach*
3	*yw* (south); *(y)di*; *ma(e)*; *o(e)s*	*ŷn* (south); *ydyn*; *yden*

(3) On final *-f* in 1 sing. (present and future indic., present subj.) see **262**.

(4) In the 3 pl. both *oeddynt* and *oeddent* occur: *Nid oeddent hwy am symud cam* 'They did not wish to move a step' (John Bunyan, 1962: 12); *Nid oeddynt yn bwriadu mynd â Gustavchen gyda hwy* 'They did not intend taking Gustavchen with them' (Gerhart Hauptman and Heinrich Böll, 1974: 7).

(5) In varieties of spoken Welsh the following forms are common:

	Sing.	Pl.
1	*o(e)n; own*	*o(edde)n, oeddan*
2	*o(edde)t; oeddat*	*o(edde)ch, oeddach*
3	*o(e)dd*	*o(edde)n, oeddan*

(6) In varieties of spoken Welsh the following forms are common:

	Sing.	Pl.
1	*bues, bu(i)s, buo*	*buon*
2	*buest, buost*	*buoch*
3	*buo, buws, buodd*	*buon*

(7) In varieties of spoken Welsh the following forms are common:

	Sing.	Pl.
1	*busen*; *baswn*	*busen*; *basen*
2	*buset*; *basat*	*busech*; *basech*
3	*buse*; *basa*	*busen*; *basen*

(8) On final *-t* in 3 pl. throughout this conjugation see **261** n. 3.

Indicative Mood, Present Tense, 3 Sing.

278 (i) *Y mae*, *mae* occurs at the beginning of a simple affirmative sentence with either a definite or indefinite subject:

Mae hi'n nos Sul ac mae'r pentref yn hollol farw
'It's Sunday night and the village is completely dead'
      (R. Gerallt Jones, 1977: 50)

Y mae planhigyn a dyf yn dalach na'r lleill yn fwy tueddol o ddal y gwynt
'A plant which grows taller than the rest is more inclined to catch the wind'
      (Dic Jones, 1989: 244)

Mae'n well gen i farw allan na byw yn y fan yma efo'r rhain
'I prefer to die outside rather than live in this place with these'
      (John Idris Owen, 1984: 49)

Y mae'r deillion yn cael eu golwg yn ôl
'The blind recover their sight'
      (Matt. 11: 5)

Mae'r glaw yn dod
'The rain is coming'
      (Emyr Humphreys, 1986: 45)

The *yn/'n* preceding a noun or adjective as in *Mae hi'n nos Sul ac mae'r pentref yn hollol farw* is called the predicative *yn*, because it is related to the predicate; it projects soft mutation (see **54**).

In the periphrastic verbal construction as in *Mae'r glaw yn dod* the *yn* is referred to as a verbal adjunct (see **286**). In a phrase like *yn y fan yma*, *yn* is a preposition (see **364**).

(ii) *Yw/ydyw/ydy/ydi* occurs after *nid* in a negative sentence with a definite subject:

Nid yw yma
'He is not here'
> (Mark 16: 6)

Nid yw'r rhai sydd yng Nghrist dan gollfarn o unrhyw fath
'The ones who are in Christ are not under any sort of condemnation'
> (Rom. 8: 1)

See also (vi) below.

(iii) *Yw/ydyw/ydi/ydy* occurs after *nid* in a negative sentence with an indefinite subject followed by the predicative *yn* or by the verbal adjunct *yn* + a verb-noun:

Nid yw cwningod yn brin
'Rabbits are not scarce'

Nid yw pechod yn cael ei gyfrif
'Sin is not reckoned'
> (Rom. 5: 13)

(iv) *Yw/ydyw/ydy/ydi* occurs in questions introduced by the interrogative particles *a, onid* when the subject is definite:

A yw'r gweledydd yma?
'Is the seer here?'
> (1 Sam. 9: 11)

Onid yw'r Arglwydd yn Sion?
'Is the Lord not in Zion?'
> (Jer. 18: 19)

The particle *a* may be omitted (see **91**).

The affirmative response to these questions is *ydyw/ydy/ydi*; the negative reply is *nac ydyw/nac ydy/nac ydi*. The 3 sing. form of the verb is also selected before a plural subject; the affirmative response is *ydynt* and the negative reply is *nac ydynt*:

A ydy'r plant yn gwella?	*Ydynt* or	*Nac ydynt*
'Are the children improving?'	'Yes'	'No'
Onid yw'r recordiau hyn yn hen?	*Ydynt* or	*Nac ydynt*
'Aren't these records old?'	'Yes'	'No'

See **338**, **339**, **340**.

(v) *Yw/ydyw/ydy/ydi* occurs in questions introduced by the interrogative particles *a*, *onid* and followed either by the predicative *yn* or the verbal adjunct *yn* + a verb-noun:

A yw'n gyfreithlon gwneud da ar y Saboth . . .?
'Is it permitted to do good on the Sabbath . . .?'
(Mark 3: 4)

Ydy o'n dal i fynd yno?
'Does he continue to go there?'
(Idwal Jones, n.d.: 37)

Ydi'r nofel yn ateb ei diben?
'Does the novel serve its purpose?'
(*Y Faner*, 8 Rhagfyr 1989: 15)

Onid yw yn gyw i'r hen geiliog?
'Is he not a son of the old cock?'
(Gerhart Hauptman and Heinrich Böll, 1974: 2)

Onid yw'n gyfreithlon imi wneud fel 'rwyn dewis â'm heiddo fy hun?
'Is it not legal for me to do as I choose with my own property?'
(Matt. 20: 50)

The subject may be a verb-noun:

Ydi bridio'n anwyddonol?
'Is breeding unscientific?'
(Emyr Humphreys, 1981: 25)

Onid ydi bridio'n anwyddonol?
'Is not breeding unscientific?'

The interrogative introduced by *onid* may be rearranged and occur finally:

Onid yw yn gyw i'r hen geiliog?
'Is he not a son of the old cock?'

Mae yn gyw i'r hen geiliog, onid yw?
'He is a son of the old cock, isn't he?'

Onid yw bridio'n anwyddonol?
'Is not breeding unscientific?'

Mae bridio'n anwyddonol, onid yw?
'Breeding is unscientific, isn't it?'

(vi) *Oes* occurs after *nid* in a negative sentence with an indefinite subject:

Nid oes trosedd yn ei erbyn chwaith
'There is no breach (of law) against him either'
(Rom. 4: 15)

Nid oes dim yn guddiedig na ddaw'n amlwg
'There is nothing hidden that will not become public'
(Luke 8: 17)

In varieties of spoken Welsh the negative function is frequently assumed by *ddim* (see **256** (iv)) but the negative particle realized as *d* always occurs with the 3 sing. present tense of *bod*:

Dydy hi ddim yn perthyn i chi
'She does not belong to you'
(Kate Roberts, 1976: 76)

See **337** (i).

d . . . dim/neb expresses the negative with *oes*:

Does dim chwain mewn tas wair
'There are no fleas in a hay rick'
(Kate Roberts, 1976: 23)

Does neb am wneud dim i ti
'No one wishes to harm you'
(Gerhart Hauptman and Heinrich Böll, 1974: 8)

Note
Yr un may be preceded either by *nid oes* or by *nid yw*: *Nid oes yr un ohonom yn byw iddo'i hun, ac nid yw'r un yn marw iddo'i hun* (1955) 'No one of us lives for himself, and no one of us dies for himself' (Rom. 14: 7); *Nid oes yr un ohonynt, hyd y gwn i, wedi rhannu ei weledigaeth* 'Not one of them, as far as I know, has shared his vision' (*Y Faner*, 22/29 Rhagfyr 1989: 10).

(vii) *Oes* occurs in questions introduced by the interrogative particles *a*, *onid* when the subject is indefinite:

A oes rhywun yn glaf yn eich plith?
'Is someone ill in your midst?'
(Jas. 5: 14)

Onid oes deuddeg awr mewn diwrnod?
'Are there not twelve hours in a day?'
(John 11: 9)

The particle *a* may be omitted (see **339**).

The affirmative response is *oes* and the negative response is *nac oes*:

Oes yna deilyngdod? Nac oes meddai Nesta Wyn Jones.
Oes yn fy marn i
'Is there merit? No says Nesta Wyn Jones. Yes in my opinion'
(J. Elwyn Hughes, 1989: 27)

279 (i) In a copula clause that selects Complement + Predicate + Subject structure (see **349** (iv)) the copula is realized by *yw/ydyw/ ydy/ydi*:

Diawl ydy o!
'He is a devil!'
(Rhiannon Davies Jones, 1977: 68)

Prif atyniad y pentref yw Eglwys Sant Ioan Fedyddiwr
'The village's main attraction is the Church of Saint John the Baptist'
(Aneirin Talfan Davies, 1972: 232)

Dy air di yw'r gwirionedd
'Your word is the truth'
(John 17: 17)

Hogan neis gynddeiriog ydi Anna!
'Anna is an extremely nice girl!'
(T. Glynne Davies, 1974: 374)

Gwalch ydyw
'He is a rascal'
(John Bunyan, 1962: 50)

Lol ydyw
'It is nonsense'
(*Barn*, Ebrill 1990: 36)

Nid precedes the complement in a negative sentence:

Nid twpsan ydy Stella
'Stella is not a fool'
(John Rowlands, 1978: 15)

Nid hollti blew yw hyn
'This is not splitting hairs'
   (*Y Faner*, 29 Mehefin 1990: 11)

See also **81** (i).

The complement may be realized by *pwy*, *pa beth*, *beth* etc.:

Pwy ydi'r carcharor pwysicaf sy'n Lloegr?
'Who is the most important prisoner that is in England?'
   (R. Cyril Hughes, 1976: 181)

Pwy yw fy mam i a'm brodyr?
'Who are my mother and my brothers?'
   (Mark 3: 33)

Beth yw'r pethau olaf a gofiaf cyn dod yma?
'What are the last things that I remember before coming here?'
   (Harri Williams, 1978: 7)

Note
The corresponding forms in the other tenses are *fydd*, *fyddai*, *oedd/ ydoedd*, *fu*, *fuasai*, *fo/fyddo*: *Chi fydd y ddwy smartia yn y briodas* 'You will be the smartest two at the wedding' (Kate Roberts, 1976: 27); *Heno fyddai ei noson segur gyntaf ers rhai wythnosau* 'Tonight would be his first free night for some weeks' (Roy Lewis, 1978: 8); *Crwydryn fu Liam erioed* 'Liam had always been a wanderer' (Gweneth Lilly, 1981: 9): *Andros o storm fydd hi hefyd* 'It will be a terrible storm too' (Eigra Lewis Roberts, 1980: 103). On mutation of *b*- forms of *bod* see **75**.

(ii) If any emphasis is required, a verb-noun, adverb or adverbial expression may occur initially, but the copula is realized by *y mae/ mae*:

Mynd y mae'r hen betha i gyd o un i un
'All the old things are disappearing one by one'
   (Islwyn Ffowc Elis, 1970: 11)

Gofidio y mae Saunders Lewis nad oes meithrinfa debyg i lenorion ifanc Cymru
'Saunders Lewis is worried that there is not a similar nursery for young Welsh authors'
   (*Golwg*, 14 Rhagfyr 1988: 19)

Trwy bennaeth y cythreuliaid y mae'n bwrw allan cythreuliaid
'Through the prince of the devils he drives out devils'
(Mark 3: 22)

If the emphasized complement is a noun, pronoun or adjective, *yw* is selected (see **282** (iv)).

(iii) In adverbial clauses after *fel*, *megis*, *pryd*, *lle* etc., and in questions after *pa bryd*, *pa le*, *ble*, *paham*, *sut* etc., the copula is realized by *y mae*, *mae*:

Cawn ei weld ef fel y mae
'We shall see him as he is'
(1 John 3: 2)

Fe fydd Robert a Thomas Owen Plas Du yn cychwyn am y Creuddyn lle mae'r Puwiaid yn byw
'Robert Thomas Owen Plas Du will be starting for the Creuddyn where the Puws live'
(Rhiannon Davies Jones, 1985: 9)

megis y mae yn ysgrifenedig (1955)
fel y mae'n ysgrifenedig (1988)
'as it is written'
(Rom. 3: 10)

Ble mae Tudur ap Ednyfed?
'Where is Tudur ap Ednyfed?'
(Rhiannon Davies Jones, 1987: 161)

Sut mae Alys?
'How is Alys?'
(Robat Gruffudd, 1986: 143)

Paham mae pobl yn dal i fynd i garchar . . .?
'Why do people continue to go to prison . . .?'
(John Jenkins, 1978: 168)

Pam y mae arnoch ofn, chwi o ychydig ffydd?
'Why are you afraid, you of little faith?'
(Matt. 8: 26)

Pa bryd mae Dafydd Goch yn debyg o ddwad i Ddol'ddelan . . .?
'When is Dafydd Goch likely to come to Dol'ddelan . . .?'
(Rhiannon Davies Jones, 1989: 34)

These sentences are made negative (see **337** (vi)) by substituting *nad yw/nad oes* for *y mae*. *Nad yw* is normally selected when the subject is definite; *nad oes* is normally selected when the subject is indefinite:

> *Ni chyfrifir pechod pryd nad oes deddf* (1955)
> 'Sin is not reckoned when there is no law'
> >   (Rom. 5: 13)

> *Pam nad oedden nhw'n fodlon ateb ei chwestiynau?*
> 'Why weren't they willing to answer her questions?'
> >   (Marion Eames, 1992: 21–2)

> *Paham nad yw'r bobl yn dal i fynd i garchar?*
> 'Why don't the people continue to go to prison?'

But cf.

> *lle nid oes na gwyfyn na rhwd yn llygru* (1955)
> *lle nad yw gwyfyn na rhwd yn llygru* (1988)
> 'where there is no moth and no rust to spoil'
> >   (Matt. 6: 20)

Lle nid occurs in earlier writing.

In varieties of spoken Welsh and in informal texts *lle* may occur for *ble* in a question:

> *Lle yn y byd oedd Eleri wedi mynd?*
> 'Where in the world had Eleri gone?'
> >   (Angharad Tomos, 1991: 40)

> *Lle mae'r pils?*
> 'Where are the tablets?'
> >   (R. Gerallt Jones, 1977: 35)

280   The forms *sydd*, *sy* occur in a relative clause where the relative is subject (see **227**):

(i)   Qualifying a noun or nominal group in an affirmative clause:

> *Mae golwg flinedig a dryslyd a dychrynedig ar y rhai sydd o'n blaenau*
> 'There is a tired and confused and frightened look on these that are in front of us'
> >   (J. G. Williams, 1978: 170)

Gwyn eu byd y rhai sy'n newynu a sychedu am gyfiawnder
(1988)
'Blessed are those who hunger and thirst for justice'
(Matt. 5: 6)

Negative. *Sydd, sy* is replaced in a negative clause by *nad yw, nad ydynt*, the verb agreeing with the antecedent in number:

Gwyn eu byd y rhai nad ydynt yn newynu a sychedu am gyfiawnder
'Blessed are those who do not hunger and thirst for justice'

Paham y gweriwch eich arian am yr hyn nid ydyw'n fara . . . ?
(1955)
Pam y gwariwch arian am yr hyn nad yw'n fara . . . ? (1988)
'Why do you spend money for what is not bread . . . ?'
(Isa. 55: 2)

For additional examples see **227**.

(ii) In a mixed sentence (see **352**):

Llawer sydd wedi eu galw, ac ychydig wedi eu dewis (1955)
'(It's) many (that) were called, and few (that) were chosen'
(Matt. 22: 14)

Dy air sydd wirionedd (1955)
'(It's) thy word (that) is truth'
(John 17: 17)

Negative: see **337**.

(iii) When the prep. *â/ag* follows *sydd. Â* occurs before consonants and *ag* before vowels:

Pwy yw'r ferch sydd ag afal yn ei llaw?
'Who is the girl who has an apple in her hand?'

On mutation following *â* see **117**.

Negative. *Heb* is substituted for *â, ag* following *sydd*:

Pwy yw'r ferch sydd heb afal yn ei llaw?
'Who is the girl who does not have an apple in her hand?'

(iv) Other prepositions may also follow *sydd* but in such cases the relative is not a true subject:

Beth sydd arnoch ei eisiau?
'What do you need?' (lit. 'What is there lacking on you?')

Gwyn eu byd y rhai sydd arnynt newyn a syched am gyfiawnder (1955)
'Blessed are they that hunger and thirst for righteousness'
(Matt. 5: 6)

Gwasgar y bobl sydd dda ganddynt ryfel (1955)
Gwasgara'r bobl sy'n ymhyfrydu mewn rhyfel (1988)
'Scatter the people that delight in war'
(Ps. 68: 30)

Negative

(a) *sydd arno* is replaced by *nad oes arno*:

y rhai nad oes arnynt newyn

(b) *sydd* is replaced by *nad/nid yw*:

y bobl nad yw'n dda ganddynt ryfel

(v) with *rhaid i*:

y pethau sydd rhaid iddynt fod (1955)
'the things which must be'
(Rev. 22: 6)

Negative. *Sydd* is replaced by *nad oes*:

un nad oes raid iddo . . . offrymu aberthau
'one who has no need . . . to offer sacrifices'
(Heb. 7: 27)

y pethau nad oes rhaid iddynt fod

(vi) In an abnormal sentence (see **351**). The construction is rare in contemporary prose but occurs in earlier versions of the Bible:

Duw sydd noddfa a nerth i ni (1955)
Y mae Duw yn noddfa a nerth i ni (1988)
'God is our refuge and strength'
(Ps. 46: 1)

Ei drugaredd sydd yn dragywydd (1955)
'His mercy is everlasting'
(Ps. 100: 5)

The complement of *sydd*, *sy* may be preceded by the particle *yn*, but the particle is frequently omitted (see **74**):

Y cynhaeaf yn ddiau sydd fawr (1955)
'The harvest truly is heavy'
(Matt. 9: 37)

Pwy sydd ddigonol i'r gwaith hwn?
'Who is sufficient for this work?'
(2 Cor. 2: 16)

281   *Y mae* is selected in a relative clause where the relative element is governed by a possessive pronoun, serves as an adverb, or is governed by a preposition (see **229**).

Dy fraint di yw prynu'r pethau y mae arna i eu hangen
'It is your privilege to buy the things that I need'
(Roy Lewis, 1978: 132)

Gwyn ei byd y genedl y mae'r Arglwydd yn Dduw iddi
'Blessed is the nation whose God is the Lord'
(Ps. 33: 12)

y pethau y mae'n rhaid iddynt ddigwydd (1988)
'the things which must be'
(Rev. 22: 6)

Na thrysorwch i chwi drysorau ar y ddaear, lle y mae gwyfyn a rhwd yn llygru, a lle y mae lladron yn cloddio trwodd ac yn lladrata (1955)
Peidiwch â chasglu i chwi drysorau ar y ddaear, lle mae gwyfyn a rhwd yn difa, a lle mae lladron yn torri trwodd ac yn lladrata (1988)
'Do not store up for yourselves treasures on earth, where it grows rusty and moth-eaten, and where thieves break through and steal'
(Matt. 6: 9)

Gwell yw pryd o lysiau lle mae cariad nag ych pasgedig a chenfigen gydag ef
'Better is a meal of herbs where there is love than a fatted ox and envy with it'
(Prov 15: 17)

Negative. *Nad yw/ydyw* is normally selected with a definite subject, *nad oes* with an indefinite subject, but cf.:

lle nid oes na gwyfyn na rhwd yn llygru (1955)
lle nad yw gwyfyn na rhwd yn llygru (1988)
'where there is no moth and no rust to spoil'
(Matt. 6: 20)

282 *Yw* occurs in a conditional sentence where the conjunction *os* precedes the verbal form:

(i) With a definite subject:

> *Os yw e'n golygu cymaint i chi, fe arhosa i dros nos*
> 'If it means so much to you, I will stay overnight'
> > (Emyr Humphreys, 1981: 287)

(ii) With an indefinite subject followed by *yn*:

> *Os yw dyn yn cystadlu mewn mabolgampau, ni all ennill y dorch heb gystadlu yn ôl y rheolau*
> 'If a man competes in games, he cannot win the garland without competing according to the rules'
> > (2 Tim. 2: 5)

(iii) *Oes* is selected with an indefinite subject:

> *Os oes coel ar dafodau pobl, nid oedd sôn o gwbl am dad*
> 'If people's tongues are trustworthy, there was no mention at all of a father'
> > (T. Glynne Davies, 1974: 11)

(iv) When the complement comes first for emphasis, *yw* is selected if the emphasized complement is a noun, pronoun or adjective:

> *Os coch yw'r car . . .* 'If red is the car . . .'
> *Os merch yw'r cyflymaf . . .* 'If a girl is the fastest'
> *Os hwnnw yw'r gorau . . .* 'If that is the best'

If the emphasized complement is a verb-noun or adverb, *y mae* is selected, see **279** (ii).

283 The conjunction *pan* is frequently followed by the subjunctive mood in an adverbial clause:

> *Paham y dylem ni aros yma pan fo gan ein Brenin rywbeth gwell ar ein cyfer, ond i ni fynd i chwilio amdano*
> 'Why should we stay here when our King has something better for us, if we only go and seek it'
> > (John Bunyan, 1962: 12)

> *Mae blwyddyn yn amser hir pan fo rhywun yn ysu, ysu, ysu am gael gwybod*
> 'A year is a long time when someone is yearning to know'
> > (Marion Eames, 1992: 10)

In the pres. indic., however, *pan* is followed by *yw*:

Pan yw'n dod â'i gyntaf anedig i mewn i'r byd y mae'n dweud . . .
'When he brings his first-born into the world he says . . .'
(Heb. 1: 6)

Pan yw'r ddau frawd ar fin ymladd cwyd drychiolaeth eu mam o'r bedd i'w ceryddu a'u siarsio i gymodi â'i gilydd
'When the two brothers are about to fight, their mother's apparition rises from the grave to admonish them and charge them to conciliate'
(Hywel Teifi Edwards, 1989: 231)

Pan yw'n agor ei lygaid, nid oes ganddo ddim
'When he opens his eyes, he has nothing'
(Job 27: 19)

In informal texts and varieties of spoken Welsh *pan mae* may occur:

Mae'r awdl yn darfod pan mae'r bardd yn dihuno o'i swyngwsg i wynebu realiaeth ei ddydd
'The ode finishes when the poet awakes from his hypnotic state to face the reality of his world'
(*Y Faner*, 4 Awst 1989: 10)

Does neb yn crio pan mae o mewn cariad
'No one cries when he is in love'
(Rhiannon Davies Jones, 1985: 85)

The Particle *Y(r)* before Forms of the Verb **Bod** 'To Be'

284 (i) In the present and imperfect indicative *yr* precedes the verbal form in every case where *y mae* is selected in the 3 sing.:

Yr oedd hi wedi bod yno am hir amser
'She had been there for a long time'
(T. Glynne Davies, 1974: 75)

Yr oedd rhai yn fwy gweithgar na'i gilydd
'Some were more ready to work than others'
(Geraint H. Jenkins, 1983: 149)

Pam yr ydach chi mor drist?
'Why are you so sad?'
(Rhiannon Davies Jones, 1977: 109)

Yr oedd am ysgrifennu at Lady Margaret
'He wished to write to Lady Margaret'
(R. Cyril Hughes, 1975: 55)

As *y mae, y maent* are frequently realized as *mae, maen(t)* (see **261** n. 3, **277** n. 1), so *yr wyf* > *'rwyf*; *yr wyt* > *'rwyt*; *yr ydym* > *'rydym*; *yr ydych* > *'rydych*; *yr oeddwn* > *'roeddwn*; *yr oeddit* > *'roeddit*; *yr oedd* > *'roedd*; *yr oeddem* > *'roeddem*; *yr oeddech* > *'roeddech*; *yr oeddent* > *'roedden(t)* in the same circumstances:

'Roedd yna dro cyntaf i bob dim
'There was a first time for everything'
(Eigra Lewis Roberts, 1988: 89)

'Rwyf o'r un farn ag yr oeddwn wedi'r darlleniad cyntaf
'I am of the same opinion as I was after the first reading'
(J. Elwyn Hughes, 1989: 67)

Ganddyn nhw 'roedd y gair olaf
'They had the last word'
(Emyr Humphreys, 1986: 7)

Pam 'rwyt ti'n ymyrryd â mi, gyfaill?
'Why are you interfering with me, friend?'
(Harri Williams, 1978: 17)

The apostrophe is frequently omitted:

Rydw i wedi blino
'I am tired'
(Emyr Humphreys, 1986: 94)

Pam roedden nhw'n byw ar waelod y ffynnon?
'Why did they live at the bottom of the well?'
(Lewis Carroll, 1982: 68)

(ii) Forms of *bod* with an initial *b-*:

(a) In a simple sentence the verb form is not preceded by *y*:

Bu'r llys yn drugarog wrth y llanc
'The court was merciful to the youth'
(T. Glynne Davies, 1974: 31)

Bu farw oeddeutu 1580
'He died around 1580'
(Geraint H. Jenkins, 1983: 123)

Byddai pawb yn sylwi
'Everyone would notice'
>   (Rhiannon Thomas, 1988: 9)

The pre-verbal particle may precede the verb and project soft mutation (see **80**):

Fe fyddai ei habsenoldeb yn destun sgwrs
'Her absence would be a subject for gossip'
>   (Rhiannon Thomas, 1988: 9)

Mi fydd y sychedig rai yma yn y munud
'The thirsty ones will be here in a minute'
>   (T. Glynne Davies, 1974: 47)

See also **336**.

(b)   in all other cases where *y mae* may be selected in the 3 sing. pres. indic., *y* precedes forms with initial *b-*:

Ddwywaith yr wythnos y byddai hi'n pobi
'Twice a week she would bake'
>   (T. Glynne Davies, 1974: 195)

Islaw'r fan honno mae Ceredigion lle y bu Hywel ab Owain yn arglwydd
'Below that place is Ceredigion where Hywel ab Owain had been ruler'
>   (Rhiannon Davies Jones, 1977: 15)

Note
Y is often omitted following *lle*: *Lle mae dy drysor yno hefyd y bydd dy galon* 'Where your wealth is, there will your heart be also' (Matt. 6: 21). See also **311** (ii) n.

The Relative Pronoun **A** with Forms of **Bod** 'To Be'

285 In the present tense *a* does not occur before *sydd* because *sydd* is itself a relatival form (see **227**). In all other tenses, however, *a* may be selected before the form of the verb *bod*:

Ef hefyd a fyddai'n dosbarthu'r gwaith
'He also would share out the work'
>   (Urien William, 1974: 20)

yr offeiriad Methodistaidd o Aberddawan a fu farw'n drychine-
bus o gynnar
'the Methodist priest from Aberddawan who died tragically
early'
    (Aneirin Talfan Davies, 1976: 40)

The relative pronoun may be omitted more especially before *oedd*,
see **225**:

gwrthryfel o blaid y brawd Owain oedd yng ngharchar Dol-
badarn
'a civil war in support of brother Owain who was in Dolbadarn
prison'
    (Rhiannon Davies Jones, 1989: 34)

ŵy oedd wedi'i ferwi'n ysgafn
'an egg that had been lightly boiled'
    (Emyr Humphreys, 1981: 289)

In negative clauses *na(d)* normally precedes the verb: *na* occurs
before consonants, *nad* before vowels:

Pa wleidydd (gwrywaidd) na fyddai'n ochri ag ef?
'What (male) politician would not side with him?'
    (*Golwg*, 20 Ebrill 1989: 19)

Teimlai'r teithiwr ei fod yn treiddio i mewn i wlad hud nad oedd
yn perthyn i weddill y ddaear
'The traveller felt that he was penetrating into a magical world
that did not belong to the rest of the earth'
    (R. Bryn Williams, 1973: 14)

Gyda bysedd nad oeddynt ond megis esgyrn sychion, melyn,
tynnai'r darn arian allan, a bwriai ef i mewn i'r gist
'With fingers that were but like dry, yellow bones, she would
take the coin out, and toss it into the chest'
    (Gerhart Hauptman and Heinrich Böll, 1974: 4)

Examples occur of *ni(d)* preceding the verb, see **225**.
On mutation following *a*, see **73**.
On mutation following *ni*, *na*, see **87**.

Bod 'To Be' as an Auxiliary Verb

286 The verb *bod* regularly functions as an auxiliary verb with the verb-noun in a periphrastic construction. In order of occurrence the usual pattern is:

a tense of *bod* + verbal adjunct + verb-noun

The verbal adjunct is realized by *yn* or *wedi*, depending upon whether durative or completed action is articulated. We will adopt *dysgu* 'learn' as our verb-noun and the present tense structure will pattern thus:

		bod	+ verbal adjunct +	verb-noun
Singular	1	Yr wyf fi	yn	dysgu
	2	Yr wyt ti	yn	dysgu
	3	Yr mae ef	yn	dysgu
		Y mae hi	yn	dysgu
Plural	1	Yr ydym ni	yn	dysgu
	2	Yr ydych chwi	yn	dysgu
	3	Y maent hwy	yn	dysgu

In formal texts and informal styles of speech the inflection of *bod* is sufficient to mark the subject element unambiguously. In non-formal speech and often in formal texts too, the subject may be further realized by a pronoun. The 3 sing. must be realized thus, as without the pronoun the form is impersonal (= 'there is, there are').

Whenever it is necessary to indicate gender in the 3 sing., the subject pronoun *ef* 'he' or *hi* 'she' must be selected.

See **221** for the colloquial forms of the pronouns.

After vowels *yn* is normally elided to *'n*:

Yr wyt ti'n dysgu 'You are learning'
Y mae hi'n dysgu 'She is learning'

The Past Perfect tense is produced by switching *wedi* for *yn* as verbal adjunct:

Yr wyf fi'n dysgu 'I am learning'
Yr wyf fi wedi dysgu 'I have learnt'

Pairs of tenses are formed in this fashion by keeping the tense of *bod* constant and substituting *yn* and *wedi* as verbal adjunct:

Past Continuous

Yr oeddwn i'n dysgu 'I was learning'

Completed Past

Yr oeddwn i wedi dysgu 'I had learnt'

Future

Byddaf i'n dysgu 'I shall be learning'

Future Perfect

Byddaf i wedi dysgu 'I shall have learnt'

The remaining tenses choose between *yn* and *wedi*:

Imperfect

Byddwn i'n dysgu 'I used to learn'

Pluperfect

Buaswn i wedi dysgu, *Byddwn i wedi dysgu* 'I would have learnt'

See **309** (iii) n.

The preterite takes only *yn*:

Preterite

Bûm i'n dysgu 'I have been learning'

The aspective adjuncts trigger soft mutation (see **69**):

Yr wyf am ddysgu 'I wish to learn', also 'I am going to learn' in varieties of northern Welsh

Y maent i ddysgu 'They are to learn'

Y mae ef ar ddysgu 'He is about to learn'

Ar fedr, *ar fin* also express the meaning 'about to'.

Examples:

Roeddwn i am weddïo
'I wished to pray'
    (Emyr Humphreys, 1981: 310)

'Roeddwn ar redeg yn ôl am y Garthau
'I was about to run back to the Garthau'
    (Rhiannon Davies Jones, 1977: 23)

Yr ydym ar fedr colli ein trysor pwysicaf
'We are about to lose our greatest treasure'
    (*Taliesin*, Gorffennaf 1992: 5)

Yr oedd ei garfan ef i gyd i fynd i Ffrainc
'All of his section were to go to France'
    (T. Glynne Davies, 1974: 340)

I ba le y mae hwn ar fedr myned? (1955)
I ble mae hwn ar fynd? (1988)
'Where is he about to go?'
    (John 7: 35)

Nid oedd am gerdded
'She did not wish to walk'
    (Alun Jones, 1989: 110)

Y maent i holi'r disgyblion
'They are to examine the pupils'
    (R. Geraint Gruffydd, 1988: 123)

Yr oedd Ifan wedi cysgu yn hwyr y bore hwnnw
'Ifan had slept late that morning'
    (T. Glynne Davies, 1974: 73)

Mae e'n canmol, ymhlith eraill, Fyrddin a Thaliesin am eu bod
yn brydyddion Cristnogol
'He praises, amongst others, Myrddin and Taliesin because they
are Christian poets'
    (Gwyn Thomas, 1971: 60)

Roedd y plentyn bach yn wylo
'The little child was crying'
    (Gerhart Hauptman and Heinrich Böll, 1974: 18)

Heb may be selected to form a negative perfect or pluperfect and is
followed by mutation (see **69**):

(a) negative perfect

Bydd Catrin Salsbri heb	(= *Ni bydd Catrin Salsbri wedi*
ddychwelyd i Leweni	*dychwelyd i Leweni*)
'Catrin Salsbri will not have	
returned to Lleweni'	
(R. Cyril Hughes, 1975: 48)	

Y mae'r ci heb ei glymu	(= *Nid yw'r ci wedi ei glymu*)
'The dog has not been tied'	

Yr wyf heb ddarllen y llyfr   (= *Nid wyf wedi darllen y llyfr*)
'I have not read the book'

(b) negative pluperfect

Yr oeddent heb eu darganfod   (= *Nid oeddent wedi eu darganfod*)
'They had not been discovered'

Yr oeddwn heb orffen y gwaith   (= *Nid oeddwn wedi gorffen y*
'I had not completed the work'   *gwaith*)

Yr oeddwn heb ysgrifennu   (= *Nid oeddwn wedi ysgrifennu*)
'I had not written'

See also **329, 337**.

Notes

(1) In varieties of spoken Welsh [bʊiti/dʒəsd] may be selected in place of *ar* and [vod i] may occur in place of *i*. [bʊiti], [vod i] are followed by soft mutation; [dʒəsd] is followed by the radical: [man nhu bʊiti ðod] 'they are about to come'; [on i dʒəsd marʊ] 'I was about to die'; [on i vod i vɪnd] 'I was (supposed) to go'.

(2) In informal texts *heb* may occur with a negative verb: *Dydi o heb daro deuddeg* 'It has not been successful (lit., struck twelve)' (*Barn*, Mehefin 1989: 6).

Compounds of *Bod*

287 These are compounded of a root + *bod*. They are inflected anomalously, the root functioning as stem and *b-* forms of *bod* as inflectional affixes. If the compound is of the *cyfarfod* type (see **288–292**), with mutated *fod*, the affixes also take soft mutation. If the compound is of the *gwybod* type (see **293**) with unmutated *bod*, the affixes do not take mutation.

288 Verbs that are conjugated like *bod* 'to be', with *-b-* > *-f-*:

Verb noun	1 sing. Pres. Indic.
canfod 'perceive'	*canfyddaf*
cyfarfod 'meet'	*cyfarfyddaf*
darfod 'end, happen'	*darfyddaf*
gorfod 'overcome, be obliged'	*gorfyddaf*
darganfod 'discover'	*darganfyddaf*
hanfod 'be descended from' (see **292**)	

Canfod

INDICATIVE MOOD

Present Tense

Sing.	Pl.
1 *canfyddaf*	*canfyddwn*
2 *canfyddi*	*canfyddwch*
3 *cenfydd*	*canfyddant*

Impers. *canfyddir*

Imperfect Tense

Sing.	Pl.
1 *canfyddwn*	*canfyddem*
2 *canfyddit*	*canfyddech*
3 *canfyddai*	*canfyddent*

Impers. *canfyddid*

Preterite Tense

Sing.	Pl.
1 *canfûm*	*canfuom*
2 *canfuost*	*canfuoch*
3 *canfu*	*canfuant*

Impers. *canfuwyd*

Pluperfect Tense

Sing.	Pl.
1 *canfuaswn*	*canfuasem*
2 *canfuasit*	*canfuasech*
3 *canfuasai*	*canfuasent*

Impers. *canfuasid*

SUBJUNCTIVE MOOD

Present Tense

Sing.	Pl.
1 *canfyddwyf*	*canfyddom*
2 *canfyddych*	*canfyddoch*
3 *canfyddo*	*canfyddont*

Impers. *canfydder*

IMPERATIVE MOOD

	Sing.	Pl.
1	—	*canfyddwn*
2	*cenfydd*	*canfyddwch*
3	*canfydded*	*canfyddent*

Impers. *canfydder*

See **293** (iii) n.

289 Cyfarfod occurs:

(i) As an intransitive verb followed by *â*, *ag*; *â* occurs before consonants, *ag* before vowels:

Cyfarfu â geneth ifanc yn y maes glanio
'He met a young girl at the airport'

Cyfarfu â hwy
'He met them'

Cyfarfûm ag ewythr fy ngwraig
'I met my wife's uncle'

An infixed pronoun (see **217**) may follow *â*:

Cyfarfu â'i blant
'He met his children'

(ii) As a transitive verb taking an object:

Daethant i'm cyfarfod
'They came to meet me'

Brysiodd i gyfarfod ei chwaer
'He hurried to meet his sister'

290 Darfod

The following forms frequently occur:

3 sing. future *derfydd*
3 pl. future *darfyddant*
3 sing. imperfect *darfyddai*
3 sing. preterite *darfu*
3 sing. pluperfect *darfuasai*
Verb-noun *darfod*

Darfod is used:

(i) To express the meaning 'die, end, finish':

> *Llafuriwch nid am y bwyd a dderfydd, eithr am y bwyd a bery i*
> *fywyd tragwyddol* (1955)
> *Gweithiwch, nid am y bwyd sy'n darfod, ond am y bwyd sy'n*
> *para i fywyd tragwyddol* (1988)
> 'Work, not for the food that perishes, but for the food that lasts
> to eternal life'
>> (John 6: 27)

> *Darfyddant oll gyda'i gilydd*
> 'They shall all die together'
>> (Isa. 31: 3)

> *Mewn noson y daeth ac mewn noson y darfu*
> 'It came in a night and it perished in a night'
>> (Jonah 4: 10)

The 3 sing. may be followed by the preposition *am*:

> *Argylwydd, cadw ni: darfu amdanom* (1955)
> 'Lord, save us: we are finished'
>> (Matt. 8: 25)

> *O'r saithdegau ymlaen darfu'r sôn am farddoniaeth goncrit*
> 'From the seventies onwards mention of concrete poetry
> ceased'
>> (*Barn*, Ebrill 1990: 36)

(ii) To express the meaning 'happen'; the verb is always 3 sing. and
in formal texts is followed by the preposition *i*:

> *Pa beth a ddarfu i'w gar?*
> 'What happened to his car?'

> *Os derfydd i chi glywed, anfonwch air*
> 'If it will happen that you will hear, send word'

Notes
(1) A sentence like *Darfu i'r fuwch farw* can mean either 'It
     happened that the cow died' or 'The cow died'. Thus *darfu* has
     developed an auxiliary role and in speech and informal texts the
     preposition *i* may be omitted.

(2) In varieties of northern Welsh *darfu* is realized as *ddaru*: *Ddaru chi ganu?* 'Did you sing?' (*Y Faner*, 22/29 Rhagfyr 1989: 18); *Chwerthin a chwerthin ddaru ni* 'We laughed and laughed' (Angharad Tomos, 1991: 58).

291 Gorfod occurs both as an intransitive and as a transitive verb. As an intransitive verb it is used:

(i) To express the meaning 'conquer, overcome' followed by the preposition *ar*:

> *Gorfu ar ei holl elynion*
> 'He overcame all his enemies'

The preposition and the object may be omitted:

> *Pa fyddin a orfu?*
> 'Which army won?'

(ii) To express the meaning 'be obliged, be compelled' in the construction *gorfod* + prep. *i* or *ar* + verb-noun:

> *Gorfu i bawb adael*
> 'Every one was obliged to leave'

> *Gorfu ar y ferch weithio*
> 'The girl was obliged to work'

The personal form of the preposition may be selected instead of the noun:

> *Gorfu iddynt godi*
> 'They were obliged to get up'

> *Gorfu arni symud*
> 'She was obliged to move'

The verb-noun may be selected instead of the personal form of the verb:

> *Gorfod imi fynd yn erbyn fy ewyllys*
> 'I had to go against my will'

Gorfod also occurs as a transitive verb with a verb-noun object in a periphrastic verbal sentence:

> *Mae'n gorfod ymarfer yn gyson*
> 'He has to train regularly'

292 Hanfod 'be from, be descended from, exist'. Apart from the verb-noun *hanfod* and the 2 sing. subj. *henffych* 'mayst thou prosper, hail', this verb is rarely used in contemporary Welsh:

> *o'r rhai yr hanoedd Crist* (1955)
> *oddi wrthynt hwy . . . y daeth y Meseia* (1988)
> 'of whom Christ descended'
> > (Rom. 9: 5)

> *o'r lle yr hanwyf* (1955)
> *un oddi yno wyf i* (1988)
> 'from thence I am'
> > (Judg. 19: 18)

> *Hanfu Watkyn Powel o deulu diwylliedig*
> 'Watkyn Powel came from a cultured family'
> > (*Studia Celtica*, 18/19, 1983/1984: 171)

> *Henffych, foneddiges*
> 'Hail, lady'
> > (R. Cyril Hughes, 1975: 35)

Note

The verb-noun also occurs in the form *hanu*: *pobl sy'n hanu o Ddyfed* 'people who are from Dyfed' (*Y Faner*, 23 Chwefror 1990: 19).

293 Verbs that are conjugated like *bod* 'to be' with *-b-* unmutated:

(i) **Gwybod** 'know things and facts'

INDICATIVE MOOD

Present Tense

Sing.	Pl.
1 *gwn*	*gwyddom*
2 *gwyddost*	*gwyddoch*
3 *gŵyr*	*gwyddant*

Impers. *gwŷs, gwyddys*

Future Tense

Sing.	Pl.
1 *gwybyddaf*	*gwybyddwn*
2 *gwybyddi*	*gwybyddwch*
3 *gwybydd*	*gwybyddant*

Impers. *gwybyddir*

Imperfect Tense

Sing.   Pl.

1 *gwyddwn*   *gwyddem*
2 *gwyddit*   *gwyddech*
3 *gwyddai, gwyddiad*   *gwyddent*
          Impers. *gwyddid*

Preterite Tense

Sing.   Pl.

1 *gwybûm*   *gwybuom*
2 *gwybuost*   *gwybuoch*
3 *gwybu*   *gwybuont, -ant*
          Impers. *gwybuwyd*

Pluperfect Tense

Sing.   Pl.

1 *gwybuaswn*   *gwybuasem*
2 *gwybuasit*   *gwybuasech*
3 *gwybuasai*   *gwybuasent*
          Impers. *gwybuasid*

SUBJUNCTIVE MOOD

Present Tense

Sing.   Pl.

1 *gwypwyf, gwybyddwyf*   *gwypom, gwybyddom*
2 *gwypych, gwybyddych*   *gwypoch, gwybyddoch*
3 *gwypo, gwybyddo*   *gwypont, gwybyddont*
        Impers. *gwyper, gwybydder*

Imperfect Tense

Sing.   Pl.

1 *gwypwn, gwybyddwn*   *gwypem, gwybyddem*
2 *gwypit, gwybyddit*   *gwypech, gwybyddech*
3 *gwypai, gwybyddai*   *gwypent, gwybyddent*
        Impers. *gwypid, gwybyddid*

IMPERATIVE MOOD

Sing.	Pl.
1 —	*gwybyddwn*
2 *gwybydd*	*gwybyddwch*
3 *gwyped, gwybydded*	*gwypent, gwybyddent*

Impers. *gwybydder*

Verb-noun *gwybod*   Verbal adjectives *gwybyddus, gwybodus*

(ii) **Adnabod** 'know people and places, recognize'

INDICATIVE MOOD

Present Tense

Sing.	Pl.
1 *adwaen, adwen*	*adwaenom, adwaenwn*
2 *adwaenost, adweini*	*adwaenoch, adwaenwch*
3 *adwaen, adwen, edwyn*	*adwaenant*

Impers. *adwaenir, adweinir*

Future Tense

Sing.	Pl.
1 *adnabyddaf*	*adnabyddwn*
2 *adnabyddi*	*adnabyddwch*
3 *adnebydd*	*adnabyddant*

Impers. *adnabyddir*

Imperfect Tense

Sing.	Pl.
1 *adwaenwn*	*adwaenem*
2 *adwaenit*	*adwaenech*
3 *adwaenai*	*adwaenent*

Impers. *adwaenid, adweinid*

Preterite Tense

Sing.	Pl.
1 *adnabûm*	*adnabuom*
2 *adnabuost*	*adnabuoch*
3 *adnabu*	*adnabuont, adnabuant*

Impers. *adnabuwyd*

Pluperfect Tense

Sing.	Pl.
1 *adnabuaswn*	*adnabuasem*
2 *adnabuasit*	*adnabuasech*
3 *adnabuasai*	*adnabuasent*

Impers. *adnabuasid*

SUBJUNCTIVE MOOD

Present Tense

Sing.	Pl.
1 *adnapwyf, adnabyddwyf*	*adnapom, adnabyddom*
2 *adnepych, adnabyddych*	*adnapoch, adnabyddoch*
3 *adnapo, adnabyddo*	*adnapont, adnabyddont*

Impers. *adnaper, adnabydder*

Imperfect Tense

Sing.	Pl.
1 *adnapwn, adnabyddwn*	*adnapem, adnabyddem*
2 *adnapit, adnabyddit*	*adnapech, adnabyddech*
3 *adnapai, adnabyddai*	*adnapent, adnabyddent*

Impers. *adnepid, adnabyddid*

IMPERATIVE MOOD

Sing.	Pl.
1 —	*adnabyddwn*
2 *adnebydd*	*adnabyddwch*
3 *adnabydded*	*adnabyddent*

Impers. *adnabydder*

Verb-noun *adnabod* Verbal adjectives *adnabyddus*, *adnabyddedig*

Notes
(1) Subjunctive forms in *-nap-*, *-nep-* are now considered obsolete.
(2) *Bod*, *gwybod* and *adnabod* are the only three verbs in Welsh that have distinct forms for Present and Future tenses.

(iii) **Cydnabod** 'acknowledge, show appreciation of'

INDICATIVE MOOD

Present Tense

Sing.	Pl.
1 *cydnabyddaf*	*cydnabyddwn*
2 *cydnabyddi*	*cydnabyddwch*
3 *cydnebydd*	*cydnabyddant*

Impers. *cydnabyddir*

Imperfect Tense

Sing.	Pl.
1 *cydnabyddwn*	*cydnabyddem*
2 *cydnabyddit*	*cydnabyddech*
3 *cydnabyddai*	*cydnabyddent*

Impers. *cydnabyddid*

Preterite Tense

Sing.	Pl.
1 *cydnabûm*	*cydnabuom*
2 *cydnabuost*	*cydnabuoch*
3 *cydnabu*	*cydnabuont*

Impers. *cydnabuwyd*

Pluperfect Tense

Sing.	Pl.
1 *cydnabuaswn*	*cydnabuasem*
2 *cydnabuasit*	*cydnabuasech*
3 *cydnabuasai*	*cydnabuasent*

Impers. *cydnabuasid*

SUBJUNCTIVE MOOD

Present Tense

Sing.	Pl.
1 *cydnabyddwyf*	*cydnabyddom*
2 *cydnabyddych*	*cydnabyddoch*
3 *cydnabyddo*	*cydnabyddont*

Impers. *cydnabydder*

Imperfect Tense = Imperfect Indic.

IMPERATIVE MOOD

	Sing.	Pl.
1	—	*cydnabyddwn*
2	*cydnebydd*	*cydnabyddwch*
3	*cydnabydded*	*cydnabyddent*

Impers. *cydnabydder*

Verb-noun: *cydnabod* Verbal adjectives: *cydnabyddus*, *cydnabyddedig*

Note

In varieties of spoken Welsh *adnabod* 'recognize', *darganfod* 'discover', *cyfarfod* 'meet', *cydnabod* 'acknowledge', which generally agree with *bod* and have a preterite tense, adopt regular verb endings (see **261**) with a *-bydd-* or *-fydd-* stem: *adnabyddais* for *adnabûm* 'I recognized', *adnabyddodd* for *adnabu* 'he/she recognized', *adnabyddon* for *adnabuont* 'they recognized', *darganfyddais* for *darganfûm* 'I discovered', *darganfyddoch* for *darganfuoch* 'you discovered', *cyfarfyddodd* for *cyfarfu* 'he/she met', *cydnabyddais* for *cydnabûm* 'I acknowledged', *cydnabyddodd* for *cydnabu* 'he/she acknowledged', *cydnabyddon* for *cydnabuont* 'they acknowledged' etc.

Examples:

Fel James Rhys Jones yr adweinid ef am gyfnod
'He was known as James Rhys Jones for a time'
    (*Barn*, Mehefin 1989: 8)

Cydnabyddir hyn yn gyffredinol gan D.T.L.
'This is generally acknowledged by D.T.L.'
    (*Taliesin*, Tachwedd 1989: 37)

Dyna'r unig fangre a adnabu mewn gwirionedd er dyddiau ei ieuenctid
'That is the only place that he had known in reality since the days of his youth'
    (Rhiannon Davies Jones, 1989: 22)

Cydnebydd Iolo hawliau'r Goron wrth iddo gyfarch Edward III a Syr Rhosier Mortimer
'Iolo recognizes the authority of the Crown as he greets Edward III and Sir Roger Mortimer'
    (*Llais Llyfrau*, Gaeaf 1989: 16)

Gwyddai'r naill fod y llall yn effro
'The one knew that the other was awake'
(Alun Jones, 1989: 27)

294 Mynd 'go'; **gwneud** 'do, make'; **dod** 'come'

Mynd

INDICATIVE MOOD

Present Tense

	Sing.	Pl.
1	*af*	*awn*
2	*ei*	*ewch*
3	*â*	*ânt*

Impers. *eir*

Note

In varieties of spoken Welsh and in informal texts *aiff*, *eith* occur in the 3 sing.

Gwneud forms its pres. tense exactly like *mynd* with the addition of *gwn-* initially:

	Sing.	Pl.
1	*gwnaf*	*gwnawn*
2	*gwnei*	*gwnewch*
3	*gwna*	*gwnânt*

Impers. *gwneir*

Note

In varieties of spoken Welsh, initial *gw-* may be omitted in *gwnaf*, *gwnawn*, *gwneuthum*, *gwnes*, *gwna*, *gwneud*, *gwneuthur* etc.: *nes*, *na*, *neud* etc. *-w-* may also be omitted: *gnes*, *gna*, *gneud* etc. The forms also occur in informal texts.

Dod differs from the others in this tense. The stem in the strict literary form is *deu-*:

	Sing.	Pl.
1	*deuaf*	*deuwn*
2	*deui*	*deuwch*
3	*daw*	*deuant*

Impers. *deuir*

An abbreviated, more colloquial form also occurs in writing evident mostly in varieties of northern Welsh:

	Sing.	Pl.
1	*dof*	*down*
2	*doi*	*dowch, dewch*
3	*daw*	*dônt*

Impers. *doir*

Mynd, *gwneud* go together:

Imperfect Tense

Mynd

	Sing.	Pl.
1	*awn*	*aem*
2	*ait*	*aech*
3	*âi*	*aent*

Impers. *eid*

Gwneud

	Sing.	Pl.
1	*gwnawn*	*gwnaem*
2	*gwnait*	*gwnaech*
3	*gwnâi*	*gwnaent*

Impers. *gwneid*

Dod selects the stem *deu-*:

	Sing.	Pl.
1	*deuwn*	*deuem*
2	*deuit*	*deuech*
3	*deuai*	*deuent*

Impers. *deuid*

An abbreviated form also occurs:

	Sing.	Pl.
1	*down*	*doem*
2	*doit*	*doech*
3	*dôi*	*doent*

Impers. *doed*

Note

In varieties of spoken Welsh stems in -*l*-, -*s*-, -*th*- occur in the imperf. indic. of *mynd, dod, gwneud,* for example:

elen, esen, ethen for *awn*
nelen, nesen, nethen for *gwnawn* (see also previous note)
delen, desen, dethen for *deuwn*

Preterite Tense

Mynd, gwneud, dod are conjugated in a similar fashion, *gwn-* or *d-* being added to the initial of *mynd*:

	Sing.	Pl.
1	*euthum*	*aethom*
2	*aethost*	*aethoch*
3	*aeth*	*aethont*
	Impers. *aethpwyd*	

Gwneud

1	*gwneuthum*	*gwnaethom*
2	*gwnaethost*	*gwnaethoch*
3	*gwnaeth*	*gwnaethont*
	Impers. *gwnaethpwyd*	

Dod

1	*deuthum*	*daethom*
2	*daethost*	*daethoch*
3	*daeth*	*daethont*
	Impers. *daethpwyd*	

Note

In varieties of spoken Welsh *es, gwnes, des* may occur in the 1 sing.; *est, gwnest, dest* may occur in the 2 sing.; *aed, gwnaed* in the Impers. These forms are permissible in all save very formal styles of the language. *Dois = des, doist = dest* are all permissible. In varieties of spoken Welsh stems in -*l*-, -*s*-, -*th*- occur, for example:

eloch, esoch, ethoch for *aethoch*
neloch, nesoch, nethoch for *gwnaethoch*
deloch, desoch, dethoch for *daethoch*

Pluperfect Tense

Mynd, *gwneud*, *dod* are conjugated in a similar fashion, *gwn-* or *d-* being added to the initial of *mynd*:

	Sing.	Pl.
1	*aethwn*	*aethem*
2	*aethit*	*aethech*
3	*aethai*	*aethent*

Impers. *aethid*

Gwneud

1	*gwnaethwn*	*gwnaethem*
2	*gwnaethit*	*gwnaethech*
3	*gwnaethai*	*gwnaethent*

Impers. *gwnaethid*

Dod

1	*daethwn*	*daethem*
2	*daethit*	*daethech*
3	*daethai*	*daethent*

Impers. *daethid*

SUBJUNCTIVE MOOD

Mynd, *gwneud*, *dod* are conjugated in a similar fashion:

Present Tense

Mynd

	Sing.	Pl.
1	*elwyf*	*elom*
2	*elych*	*eloch*
3	*êl, elo*	*elont*

Impers. *eler*

Gwneud

1	*gwnelwyf*	*gwnelom*
2	*gwnelych*	*gwneloch*
3	*gwnêl, gwnelo*	*gwnelont*

Impers. *gwneler*

Dod

	Sing.	Pl.
1	*delwyf*	*delom*
2	*delych*	*deloch*
3	*dêl, delo*	*delont*

Impers. *deler*

Imperfect Tense

Mynd

	Sing.	Pl.
1	*elwn*	*elem*
2	*elit*	*elech*
3	*elai*	*elent*

Impers. *elid*

Gwneud

1	*gwnelwn*	*gwnelem*
2	*gwnelit*	*gwnelech*
3	*gwnelai*	*gwnelent*

Impers. *gwnelid*

Dod

1	*delwn*	*delem*
2	*delit*	*delech*
3	*delai*	*delent*

Impers. *delid*

IMPERATIVE MOOD

Mynd

	Sing.	Pl.
1	—	*awn*
2	*dos*	*ewch*
3	*aed, eled*	*aent, elent*

Impers. *aer, eler*

Verb-noun *mynd*

Note

Varieties of southern Welsh select *cer, cera, cere* in the 2 sing.; *cerwch* in the 2 pl. is universal.

Gwneud

	Sing.	Pl.
1	—	*gwnawn*
2	*gwna*	*gwnewch*
3	*gwnaed, gwneled*	*gwnelent*

Impers. *gwnaer, gwneler*
Verb-noun *gwneud, gwneuthur*
Verbal adjectives *gwneuthuredig, gwneuthuradwy*

Dod

	Sing.	Pl.
1	—	*deuwn, down*
2	*tyr(e)d*	*deuwch, dowch, dewch*
3	*deued, doed, deled*	*deuent, doent, delent*

Impers. *deuer, doer, deler*
Verb-noun *dyfod, dod, dywad* (*dwad* – dial.)
Verbal adjective *dyfodol*

Note
Dere occurs in the 2 sing. in varieties of southern Welsh and in
literary texts.

Examples:

Uchaf yn y byd yr aent, oeraf yn y byd yr oedd yr hin
'The higher they went, the colder the weather'
(Rhiannon Davies Jones, 1989: 47)

*Pan eloch allan o'r ddinas honno, ysgwydwch hyd yn oed y llwch
oddi wrth eich traed* (1955)
*Ewch allan o'r dref honno ac ysgydwch ymaith y llwch oddi ar
eich traed* (1988)
'When you leave that town shake even the dust off your feet'
(Luke 9: 5)

Dos yn dy flaen
'Go on your way'
(Prov. 4: 15)

Cerwch i hôl torth i fi
'Go and fetch a loaf for me'
(Ray Evans, 1986: 19)

Dof gyda thi ar unwaith
'I will come with you at once'
    (Emyr Hywel, 1989: 28)

Wyt ti'n meddwl y down ni drwy hyn?
'Do you think that we will come through this?'
    (Alun Jones, 1989: 231)

Y mae'r Ysbryd a'r briodferch yn dweud, 'Tyrd'; a'r hwn sy'n clywed, dyweded yntau 'Tyrd'. A'r hwn sy'n sychedig deued ymlaen
'The Spirit and the bride say "Come"; and the one who hears, let him say "Come". And the one who is thirsty let him come forward'
    (Rev. 22: 17)

yr wybodaeth newydd y daethai ar ei thraws
'the fresh knowledge that he had come across'
    (R. Geraint Gruffydd, 1988: 31)

Yr un a ddylai wneuthur y penderfyniadau ynglŷn â'r corff yw'r ferch sydd yn feichiog
'The one who should make the decisions regarding the body is the girl who is pregnant'
    (*Llais Llyfrau*, Gaeaf 1989: 18)

Gwnaed ambell ddarganfyddiad diddorol
'Some interesting discoveries were made'
    (J. Elwyn Hughes, 1991: 120)

Gwna ganhwyllbren o aur pur
'Make a candlestick of pure gold'
    (Exod. 25: 31)

Chwi a'i gwnaethoch yn ogof lladron (1955)
Yr ydych chwi yn ei wneud yn ogof lladron (1988)
'You have made it a robbers' cave'
    (Matt. 21: 13)

Defective Verbs

295 Dichon occurs only in the 3 sing. pres. indic. It is used to express the meaning:

(i) 'Can, is able'. In other persons and tenses *gallu* and *medru* 'be able' occur; they may also replace *dichon*:

> *Ni ddichon neb wasanaethu dau arglwydd* (1955)
> *Ni all neb wasanaethu dau arglwydd* (1988)
> 'No man can serve two masters'
> > (Matt. 6: 24)

> *Pa fodd y dichon y pethau hyn fod* (1955)
> *Sut y gall hyn fod?* (1988)
> 'How can these things be?'
> > (John 3: 9)

(ii) 'It may be, perhaps':

> *Os yw'r clybiau mawr yn medru fforddio talu miliynau o bunnau am chwaraewyr pêldroed dichon na allent fforddio meysydd chwarae diogel*
> 'If the big clubs are able to afford to pay millions of pounds for soccer players it may be that they cannot afford safe playing grounds'
> > (*Y Faner*, 2 Chwefror 1990: 4)

> *Dichon bod polareiddio yn anochel mewn cymdeithas ddemocrataidd*
> 'Perhaps polarization is inevitable in a democratic society'
> > (*Barn*, Tachwedd 1989: 5)

Note
Dichon also occurs as a masc. sing. noun meaning 'possibility'. *Does dichon gwneud dim byd â nhw* 'There is no possibility of doing anything with them'.

296 Dylwn 'I ought'. In contemporary Welsh this verb occurs in the imperfect and pluperfect:

Imperfect Tense

	Sing.	Pl.
1	*dylwn*	*dylem*
2	*dylit*	*dylech*
3	*dylai*	*dylent*

Impers. *dylid*

Pluperfect Tense

	Sing.	Pl.
1	*dylaswn*	*dylasem*
2	*dylasit*	*dylasech*
3	*dylasai*	*dylasent*

Impers. *dylasid*

Although *dylwn* and *dylaswn* etc. are imperfect and pluperfect in form, both may express a general present. The difference between the imperfect and pluperfect has largely eroded in varieties of spoken Welsh and in recent literary texts.

Examples:

Efallai y dylwn fod wedi dwyn yr achos i'r llys
'Perhaps I ought to have taken the matter to the court'
(Emyr Humphreys, 1981: 105)

Mi ddylen edrych y tu draw i'n maes bach arbennig ni
'We ought to look beyond our small specialist field'
(John Rowlands, 1978: 69)

Fe ddylem ddiolch i Dduw
'We ought to thank God'
(2 Thess. 2: 13)

Mi ddylai rhywun ddweud wrthi
'Someone ought to tell her'
(Alun Jones, 1989: 17)

Dylaswn fod wedi hen ddysgu'r wers
'I ought to have learned the lesson of old'
(Robat Gruffudd, 1986: 248)

Ddynion, dylasech fod wedi gwrando arnaf i
'Gentlemen, you ought to have listened to me'
(Acts 27: 21)

Dylasai'r gweithiwr a'r taeog brofi ffrwyth yr artist ar ôl diwrnod caled o waith
'The worker and the man in the street ought to sample the artist's output after a hard day's work'
   (*Taliesin*, Tachwedd 1989: 6)

297 Ebe, eb 'says, said'. These are used in all persons and tenses when a speaker's actual words are reported; the verbal form is followed by the noun or pronoun subject:

Melltigwch Meros, eb angel yr Arglwydd (1955)
'Curse Meros, said the angel of the Lord'
   (Judg. 5: 23)

Gwypoch fod gan Fab y dyn awdurdod i faddau pechodau ar y ddaear, (*eb efe wrth y claf o'r parlys*) (1955)
'You know that the Son of man has authority to forgive sins on earth, (he said to the paralysed man)'
   (Mark 2: 10)

Note
In varieties of northern Welsh *ebra* occurs: *ebra fi* 'I said', *ebra nhw* 'they said'.

298 Meddaf 'I say'. The two tenses that occur are the present and imperfect:

Present Tense

	Sing.	Pl.
1	*meddaf*	*meddwn*
2	*meddi*	*meddwch*
3	*medd*	*meddant*

Impers. *meddir*

Imperfect Tense

	Sing.	Pl.
1	*meddwn*	*meddem*
2	*meddit*	*meddech*
3	*meddai*	*meddent*

Impers. *meddid*

Pwy meddwch ydwyf i?
'Who do you say I am?'
   (Matt. 16: 15)

Yr oedd yn boblogaidd iawn, meddir, gyda'r ymwelwyr
'He was very popular, it is said, with the visitors'
   (*Barn*, Mehefin 1989: 8)

The imperfect and present are often used like *eb*, *ebe*, to report a speaker's actual words:

Melltigwch Meros, medd angel yr Arglwydd
'Curse Meros, said the angel of the Lord'
   (Judg. 5: 23)

'Pen-blwydd hapus,' meddwn
'"Happy birthday," I said'
   (Irma Chilton, 1989: 83)

Note
In varieties of southern Welsh *myntwn*, *myntit*, *mynte*, *myntem*, *myntech*, *mynten* occur in the imperf.

299   Geni 'be born'. The following forms occur:

INDICATIVE MOOD

> Present Impersonal: *genir*
> Imperfect Impersonal: *genid*
> Preterite Impersonal: *ganwyd*, *ganed*
> Pluperfect Impersonal: *ganesid*, *ganasid*

SUBJUNCTIVE MOOD

> Present Impersonal: *ganer*
> Imperfect Impersonal: *genid*
> Verb-noun: *geni*
> Verbal adjective: *ganedig*

Examples:

Ganed iddynt ym Maldwyn fachgen a alwyd yn Robert
'A son was born to them in Maldwyn who was called Robert'
   (Hywel Teifi Edwards, 1989: 85)

Da fuasai i'r dyn hwnnw pe nas ganesid ef (1955)
Da fuasai i'r dyn hwnnw petai heb ei eni (1988)
'It would be better for that man if he had never been born'
   (Matt. 26: 24)

Yn Detroit y ganwyd Ray Robinson
'It was in Detroit that Ray Robinson was born'
(*Barn*, Mehefin 1989: 14)

300 Gweddu 'befit, suit, become'. The following forms occur:

3 sing. pres. indic.: *gwedda*
3 sing. imperf. indic.: *gweddai*
Verb-noun: *gweddu*

The verb is frequently followed by the preposition *i*:

Sancteiddrwydd sy'n gweddu i'th dŷ
'Holiness befits your house'
(Ps. 93: 5)

Gwialen a weddai i gefn yr angall (1955)
'A rod would suit the back of the fool'
(Prov. 10: 13)

301 Tycio 'avail'. The following forms occur:

INDICATIVE MOOD

3 sing. present: *tycia*
3 sing. imperfect: *tyciai*
3 sing. preterite: *tyciodd*
3 sing. pluperfect: *tyciasai*
Verb-noun: *tycio*

Tycio normally occurs with a negative:

Ni thycia iddynt (1955)
'It does not avail them'
(Jer. 12: 13)

If no person is mentioned the prep. *i* is omitted following the verb:

Pan welodd Pilat nad oedd dim yn tycio . . . cymerodd ddŵr, a golchodd ei ddwylo o flaen y dyrfa
'When Pilate saw that it was to no avail . . . he took water and washed his hands before the people'
(Matt. 27: 24)

Ni thyciai ddim
'It was of no avail'
(Alun Jones, 1989: 36)

Ni thyciodd fy nadlau ddim
'My argument was of no avail'
   (*Y Faner*, 2 Mawrth 1990)

302 Hwde 'take'; **Moes** 'give'. The following forms occur:

IMPERATIVE MOOD

2 sing.: *hwde*
2 pl.: *hwdwch*
2 sing.: *moes*
2 pl.: *moeswch*

Examples:

Hwde i ti a moes i minnau
'Take for yourself and give to me'
   (Proverb)

Moes i mi'r llyfr bychan (1955)
'Give me the little book'
   (Rev. 10: 9)

Moeswch i'r Arglwydd ogoniant a nerth (1955)
Rhowch i'r Arglwydd ogoniant a nerth (1988)
'Give to the Lord glory and strength'
   (Ps. 29: 1)

Hwda, dyma i chdi Woodbine
'Take (one), here is a Woodbine for you'
   (Jane Edwards, 1989: 53)

Note
In varieties of southern Welsh the forms *hwre*, *hwr(i)wch* occur for *hwde*, *hwdwch*.

303 Methu 'fail', **Synnu** 'be astonished', formerly only occurred in the 3 sing.

In contemporary Welsh, persons other than the 3 sing. occur and *methu* and *synnu* are inflected like other regular verbs; the preposition *â* may follow *methu* and the prepositions *wrth* and *at* may follow *synnu*:

Synnwn i ddim ei fod wedi dysgu ei grefft oddi wrth hen gyfarwyddiaid dilychwyn y Mabinogi
'I would not be surprised that he had learned his craft from the old unsullied story-tellers of the Mabinogi'
   (*Barn*, Mehefin 1989: 47)

Synnwn i fawr nad yw Geraint Howells yn tynnu pleidlais bersonol gref, yn debyg i Gwynfor Evans gynt
'I would not be surprised that Geraint Howells attracts a strong personal vote, similar to Gwynfor Evans in the past'
(*Y Faner*, 12 Ionawr 1990: 6)

Maen nhw wedi methu dod o hyd i'r babi
'They have failed to discover the baby'
(Alun Jones, 1989: 234)

Y mae heddlu Llundain yn methu'n lân â denu pobl dduon i'w rhengau
'The London police utterly fail to attract black people to their ranks'
(*Y Faner*, 23 Chwefror 1990: 3)

Synnais at y ddarpariaeth
'I was surprised at the provision'

Rwy'n synnu wrthych chi
'I'm astonished at you'

304 Digwydd, damwain 'happen', followed by the prep. *i* were used in a similar way to *methu, synnu* (see **303**) in the 3 sing.:

Yr un peth a ddamwain i'r cyfiawn ac i'r annuwiol (1955)
Yr un peth sy'n digwydd i bawb – i'r cyfiawn ac i'r drygionus (1988)
'The same thing happens to the just and to the ungodly'
(Eccles. 9: 2)

Digwyddodd iddo syrthio
'He happened to fall'

In contemporary Welsh, persons other than the 3 sing. occur and the prep. *i* is frequently omitted:

Digwyddais weld y cyfan
'I happened to see everything'

Digwyddodd syrthio
'He happened to fall'

305 It has been possible to give only generalized indications of localized variation in this discussion of the verb. No comprehensive study listing the literary paradigms and spoken variations exists.

Some indication of the variety is to be found in Thomas and Thomas, 1989: 60–81 and in Martin J. Ball, 1988: 144–7.

The Indicative Mood

306 The Present Indicative

The present indicative is used:

(i) To express the simple or true present:

Fedri di ddim twyllo Mali achos mi wn i fod Gwladus Twrcelyn
yn mynd at y Meini Hirion yn feunyddiol bron
'You can't deceive Mali because I know that Gwladus Twrcelyn goes to the Standing Stones almost daily'
(Rhiannon Davies Jones, 1977: 27)

Mae yno swm helaeth
'There is a substantial sum there'
(Gerhard Hauptman and Heinrich Böll, 1974: 5)

Gyda rhai menywod gallaf honni fy mod yn llwyddiant
'With some women I can declare that I am a success'
(Emyr Humphreys, 1981: 72)

Only verbs whose simple concise forms convey continuous action may express the true present, e.g.,

gweld 'see'	*credu* 'believe'	*clywed* 'hear'
sefyll 'stand'	*dymuno* 'wish'	*aros* 'remain'
tybied 'suppose'	*bod* 'to be'	*gwybod* 'know'
adnabod 'recognize'	*gallu* 'able'	*medru* 'able'

The periphrastic construction *bod* 'to be' + *yn* + verb-noun is generally used to convey this meaning:

Mae'n berwi drosodd
'It is boiling over'
(Emyr Humphreys, 1986: 81)

Mae'r diawl 'ma'n cnoi fy nhu mewn i a fedra i wneud dim ynglŷn â'r peth
'This fiend is tearing at my inside and I can't do a thing about it'
(R. Gerallt Jones, 1977: 35)

(ii) To express a universal or timeless present, without specific reference to time as in proverbs, epigrams or expressions of universal truth:

Gwyn y gwêl y frân ei chyw
'The crow sees its young white (faultless)'
(Proverb)

Adar o'r unlliw hedant i'r un lle
'Birds of a feather flock together'
(Proverb)

Ceir heddiw ddramâu heb iddynt na phlot na thema bositif
'There are plays to be had today without either a plot or a positive theme'
(Geraint Bowen, 1972: 133)

Ni ad efe i'th droed lithro: ac ni huna dy geidwad. Wele, ni huna ac ni chwsg ceidwad Israel (1955)
Nid yw'n gadael i'th droed lithro, ac nid yw dy geidwad yn cysgu. Nid yw ceidwad Israel yn cysgu nac yn huno (1988)
'He does not allow your foot to stumble and your guardian does not sleep. The guardian of Israel does not slumber nor sleep'
(Ps. 121: 3–4)

The time is general when certain verbs are used parenthetically (often with soft mutation (see **82**)) to convey opinion or feeling:

Ni hoffai gyfaddef, welwch chi, na allai wneud na rhwch na blewyn ohono
'He did not like to confess, you see, that he could not make head nor tail of it'
(Lewis Carroll, 1984: 23)

(iii) To express future time. This meaning is very common as verbs, with the exception of *bod* 'to be' and its compounds, have no future tense forms (see **277**, **288–293**):

Mi gei boen bol os bwyti di ormod o siwgr
'You will have stomach-ache if you eat too much sugar'
(Rhiannon Davies Jones, 1985: 52)

Mi rof fwled trwy dy ben
'I shall put a bullet through your head'
(Harri Williams, 1978: 67)

Mi wisgwn ni'r dillad yma i fynd i'r dre, wedyn mi gawn weld pa liw fydd yn gweddu orau
'We will wear these clothes to go to town, then we will see what colour will suit best'
    (Kate Roberts, 1976: 28)

(iv) To express the dramatic present in graphic narrative:

Mae'r drws yn agor a dyma ddyn â dryll yn ei law yn sleifio i mewn. Cerdda ar draws yr ystafell i gyfeiriad y ddesg. Gesyd y dryll ar y gadair. Dyma fe'n agor y drôr canol. Cydia mewn pentwr o ddogfennau a bwrw golwg frysiog drostynt. Gwthia'r papurau i'w boced. Egyr y drws yn sydyn ond mae'r lleidr yn diflannu drwy'r ffenestr agored
'The door opens and a man with a gun in his hand slips in. He walks across the room towards the desk. He places the gun on the chair. He opens the middle drawer and picks up a bundle of documents and takes a quick look at them. He pushes the papers into his pocket. The door opens suddenly but the thief disappears through the open window'

(v) To express an action or condition continuing up to the present:

'Rydw i yma ers wythnos . . .
'I have been here for a week . . .'
    (Rhiannon Davies Jones, 1985: 41)

Mae hi'n aros ers awr
'She has been waiting for an hour'

(vi) To express a habitual condition or action that continues up to the present. Generally this construction is formed by the con-suetudinal forms of *bod* 'to be' and the verb-noun:

Byddaf yn mynd i'r eisteddfod am wythnos bob mis Awst
'I go to the eisteddfod for a week every August'

Bydd yn aros mewn llety yn y pentref agosaf
'He stays in lodgings in the nearest village'

The forms *wyf* 'I am', *wyt* 'you are' etc., are also used in the same way:

Mi'r ydach chi'n drwsiadus bob amser
'You are well-dressed always'
    (Kate Roberts, 1976: 26)

Mae dy gyngor yn werthfawr bob amser
'Your advice is valuable always'
   (R. Cyril Hughes, 1976: 116)

The concise forms of other verbs are also used to express habitual
action:

Gallaf fwynhau cwmni plant bob amser
'I am able to enjoy children's company always'
   (Harri Williams, 1978: 9)

*Teflir ennyd o gysgod dros y modurwyr a brysura i lawr Adam St;
a phan gerddwch ar hyd Gaol Lane, fe deimlwch ias glyd wrth
gofio'r crogiadau gynt a'r dynion caled sy'n gaeth y tu ôl i'r
barrau*
'A momentary shadow is cast over the motorists who hurry
down Adam St; and when you walk along Gaol Lane, you feel a
warm thrill remembering the hangings of the past and the hard
men that are captive behind the bars'
   (Urien William, 1974: 19)

(vii) The present tense of *bod* 'to be' may be selected to express
future meaning when the context indicates that reference is being
made to the future:

Mae'n dod yfory
'He/she is coming tomorrow'

Mae ysgol yma yr wythnos nesaf
'There is school here next week'

307   The Imperfect Indicative

The imperfect indicative and the imperfect subjunctive are identical
in form except in the case of the following irregular verbs: *mynd* 'go';
dod, dyfod 'come'; *gwneud, gwneuthur* 'make' (see **294**); *bod* 'to be'
(see **277**).
   The imperfect indicative is used:

(i) To express a continuous action or state in the past:

Ni oedd yn breuddwydio breuddwydion
'It was we who were dreaming dreams'
   (Rhiannon Davies Jones, 1977: 13)

Yr oedd dwy ddynes aflêr a gweflog a diffurf yn cerdded tuag atynt
'There were two untidy and thick-lipped and shapeless women walking towards them'
(T. Glynne Davies, 1974: 78)

(ii) To express a habitual or iterative action in the past:

Bore a hwyr dôi cigfrain â bara a chig iddo, ac yfai o'r nant
'Morning and evening ravens used to bring him bread and meat, and he used to drink from the stream'
(1 Kgs. 17: 6)

Epiliai'r Kennedys cyn pob etholiad
'The Kennedys used to procreate before every election'
(Jane Edwards, 1976: 134)

Darllenai drosodd a throsodd hanes angel yr Arglwydd yn hysbysu genedigaeth Ioan Fedyddiwr a'r Iesu
'He used to read over and over again the account of the angel of the Lord, proclaiming the birth of John the Baptist and Jesus'
(*Taliesin*, Rhagfyr 1988: 11)

(iii) To express the subject's wish, desire or intention. The time referent is either general or indefinite:

Ni fynnai fynd at y meddyg
'He did not wish to go to the doctor'
(Urien Williams, 1974: 22)

(iv) In reported speech following a verb in the preterite or imperfect, where the future would occur in direct speech (i.e. as the equivalent of the English conditional):

Tyngais wrthynt y byddwn yn dod â hwy allan o wlad yr Aifft
'I swore to them that I would bring them out of the land of Egypt'
(Ezek. 20: 6)

Dywedodd y deallent y cyfan
'He said that they would understand everything'

Gwyddwn y cawn i bob chwarae têg
'I knew that I would be given every opportunity'

Credai y byddent yn dychwelyd
'He believed that they would return'

(v) To express possibility or ability, mainly with verbs like *gweld* 'see', *clywed* 'hear', *teimlo* 'feel', *medru*, *gallu* 'able':

Clywem ymchwydd y môr o'r traethau fel dyn yn anadlu'n drwm
'We could hear the swell of the sea from the beaches like a man breathing heavily'
(Rhiannon Davies Jones, 1977: 10)

Fe welai hi'r wylan yn dyfod o bell ar hyd y lawnt
'She could see the gull coming from afar across the lawn'
(Kate Roberts, 1976: 75)

Mi fedrai'r rheini arogli wenci led cae i ffwrdd!
'Those could scent a weasel a field's length away!'
(Rhiannon Davies Jones, 1977: 116)

Am bris rhesymol fe allai gael y toriad a'r lliwiau diweddaraf
'For a reasonable price she could have the latest style and colours'
(R. Cyril Hughes, 1975: 9)

(vi) In reported speech following a verb in the preterite where the simple present would occur in direct speech:

Pwy yw hi?	*Holodd pwy oedd hi*
'Who is she?'	'He/she asked who she was'
Ble maen nhw?	*Gofynnodd ble'r oedden nhw*
'Where are they?'	'He/she asked where they were'
Beth a weli di?	*Holais beth a welai ef*
'What do you see?'	'I asked what he could see'
Pwy wyt ti?	*Gofynasant pwy oeddet ti*
'Who are you?'	'They asked who you were'

(vii) In a main clause followed or preceded by a conditional clause or its equivalent:

Gallai fynd yn ôl i'w wely pe mynnai
'He could go back to his bed if he wished'
(John Rowlands, 1978: 130)

Ni allai neb wneud yr arwyddion hyn oni bai fod Duw gydag ef
'No one could perform these signs unless God were with him'
(John 3: 2)

Pe byddai ar y ddaear, ni byddai'n offeiriad o gwbl
'If he would be on earth, he would not be a priest at all'
(Heb. 8: 4)

308   The Preterite

The preterite is used:

(i) To express that a simple action has occurred in the past. This is the tense normally used in narrative.

Yna edrychodd ar y buarth dan ei orchudd gwyn o eira, a dechreuodd ddychmygu bwrdd wedi ei daenu â lliain main ac arno olwython o gig gwyddau a hwyaid, a'r ager yn codi yn gwmwl oddi arnynt. Llyfodd ei wefusau â blaen ei dafod a theimlodd y dŵr yn llifo o'i ddannedd
'Next he looked at the yard under its white cover of snow, and he began to imagine a table covered with a fine cloth and upon it portions of goose and duck meat and the steam rising off them like a cloud. He licked his lips with the tip of his tongue and felt the water flowing from his teeth'
(Gerhart Hauptman and Heinrich Böll, 1974: 6)

(ii) To express that an action has been completed by the time of speaking or writing:

Cyfieithodd William Salesbury lyfr rhetoreg o'r Lladin i'r Gymraeg
'William Salesbury translated a book of rhetoric from Latin into Welsh'
(Geraint H. Jenkins, 1983: 119)

Ni chyhoeddodd na llyfr na phamffled o unrhyw fath
'He did not publish a book or pamphlet of any sort'
(D. Tecwyn Lloyd, 1988: 35)

The periphrastic construction *bod* 'to be' + *wedi* + verb-noun is commonly used to express the perfect tense, especially in spoken Welsh and in informal texts:

Y mae fy ngwas wedi f'enllibio i wrth f'arglwydd frenin
'My servant has slandered me to my lord the king'
(2 Sam. 19: 27)

Rydw i wedi cytuno
'I have agreed'

Yr wyf wedi bod etc. may be selected for *bûm* etc.:

(a) with *bod* functioning as an auxiliary verb

Ydych chi wedi bod yn yfed?
'Have you been drinking?'
(Emyr Humphreys, 1986: 93)

Wyt ti wedi bod yn datgelu'n cyfrinache ni?
'Have you been disclosing our secrets?'
(Marcel Williams, 1990: 24)

(b) with *bod* functioning as a full verb

Y mae'r Toriaid wedi bod yn eithriadol o hael at yr iaith
'The Tories have been exceptionally generous towards the
language'
(*Y Faner*, 10 Tachwedd 1989: 4)

Mae rhestru brychau iaith wedi bod yn gêm
'Listing linguistic errors has been a game'
(J. Elwyn Hughes, 1991: 93)

Mae o wedi bod yn sâl
'He has been ill'
(Mair Wyn Hughes, 1989: 11)

Mae y ddarlith honno wedi bod yn drobwynt yn ein hanes
'That lecture has been a turning point in our history'
(*Y Faner*, 21 Chwefror 1992: 3)

309 The Pluperfect

The pluperfect tense is used:

(i) To express an action or state antecedent to a point of time in the
past:

Chwaraeasai gyntaf yn erbyn Lloegr yn 1934
'He had played for the first time against England in 1934'
(*Y Faner*, 14 Rhagfyr 1990: 21)

*Sgoriasai Pen-y-bont eu cais cyntaf yn gynnar iawn yn dilyn
sgrym yn 22 Abertawe*
'Bridgend had scored their first try very early following a scrum
in Swansea's 22'
(*Y Faner*, 20 Mawrth 1992: 21)

Jona a aethai i waered i ystlysau'r llong ac a orweddasai (1955)
Yr oedd Jona wedi mynd i grombil y llong i orwedd (1988)
'Jonah had gone down into holds of the ship and had lain down'
(Jonah 1: 5)

Yr oedd efe yn y man lle y cyfarfuasai Martha ag ef (1955)
Yr oedd yn dal yn y fan lle'r oedd Martha wedi ei gyfarfod (1988)
'He was in the place where Martha had met him'
(John 11: 30)

The periphrastic construction, formed from the imperfect of *bod* 'to be' + *wedi* + verb-noun, is common especially (but not only) in varieties of spoken Welsh and in informal texts:

'Roeddwn i wedi'ch gweld chi'n pasio, Mr Edwards, ac wedi dechrau hwylio te
'I had seen you passing, Mr Edwards, and had started preparing tea'
(Kate Roberts, 1976: 24)

Yr oedd y ferch wedi marw heb ddatgelu ei chyfrinach wrth neb
'The girl had died without revealing her secret to anyone'
(T. Glynne Davies, 1974: 11)

Yr oedd saith gythraul wedi dod allan ohoni
'Seven devils had come out from her'
(Luke 8: 2)

(ii) In a main clause followed or preceded by a conditional clause or its equivalent:

Pe buasit ti yma, syr, ni buasai fy mrawd wedi marw
'If you had been here, sir, my brother would not have died'
(John 11: 21)

Pe buasent wedi dal i feddwl am y wlad yr oeddent wedi mynd allan ohoni, buasent wedi cael cyfle i ddychwelyd iddi
'If they had continued to honour the country that they had left, they would have had an opportunity to return'
(Heb. 11: 15)

(iii) With interjections to express a regret or wish with regard to the past:

O na fuaswn farw drosot ti, Absalom, fy mab (1955)
'If only I had died instead of you, Absalom my son'
(2 Sam. 18: 33)

*O na buasem wedi marw yng ngwlad yr Aifft neu yn yr anialwch
hwn!*

'If only we had died in the land of Egypt or in this wilderness'
(Num. 14: 2)

Note

There is a tendency for the pluperfect and imperfect forms to merge
in contemporary Welsh:

*O na fyddwn (= fuaswn) wedi cael marw yn dy le, O Absalom fy
mab* (1988)

'If only I had been allowed to die instead of you, Absalom my
son'

(2 Sam. 18: 33)

*Yr wyf wedi dod i fwrw tân ar y ddaear, ac O na fyddai (= fuasai)
eisoes wedi ei gynnau!*

'I have come to set fire to the earth, and how I wish it had been
already kindled!'

(Luke 12: 49)

Ni buasai (= byddai) dadleuon diwinyddol Rhys Lewis *yn
gwneud y tro mewn stori fer*

'The theological arguments of *Rhys Lewis* would not do in a
short story'

(Geraint Bowen, 1972: 52)

Buasai wedi bod yn sialens cael cyflwyno rhaglen fel Heddiw *yn
hytrach na darllen y newyddion yn unig*

'It would have been a challenge to have presented a programme
like *Heddiw* rather than only reading the news'

(*Y Cymro*, 2 Awst 1989: 1)

*Byddai (= buasai) wedi bod o les i elynion gwleidyddol y Toriaid
pe bai Peter Walker wedi cael ei hel o'r Swyddfa Gymreig gan
Mrs Thatcher*

'It would have been of advantage to the Tories' political enemies
if Peter Walker had been sacked from the Welsh Office by Mrs
Thatcher'

(*Y Cymro*, 2 Awst 1989: 2)

*Fyddwn (= buaswn) i ddim wedi cymryd hynny pe na bai Mam
mor dynn gyda'i phres*

'I would not have taken that had not mother been so mean with
her money'

(Irma Chilton, 1989: 21)

The Subjunctive Mood

310 In contemporary Welsh the subjunctive is restricted to a few constructions, fossilized expressions and idioms. Its functions have been assumed by the indicative and imperative.

311 The Present Subjunctive

The present subjunctive is used:

(i) To express a wish or curse:

Duw a Mair a faddeuo i mi!
'May God and Mary pardon me!'
(Rhiannon Davies Jones, 1985: 36)

Duw â'n gwaredo rhag hynny
'May God deliver us from that'
(*Y Faner*, 15 Rhagfyr 1989: 8)

Duw a'r Forwyn a fo'n nodded i ni
'May God and the Virgin protect us'
(Rhiannon Davies Jones, 1989: 62)

Duw a'th fendithio
'May God bless you'
(*Golwg*, 22 Rhagfyr 1988: 27)

Duw gadwo'r brenin
'God save the king'

Pawb at y peth bo!
'Each one to what he may be!'
(Rhiannon Davies Jones, 1977: 27)

Hir y parhao pethau felly
'Long may things continue so'
(*Y Faner*, 8 Rhagfyr 1989: 19)

Fel hyn y gwnelo'r Arglwydd i mi
'The Lord do thus to me'
(Ruth 1: 17)
(1 Sam. 20: 13)

(ii) When the action of the verb is indefinite in time:

(a) in a relative clause:

> *Gobeithiaf y bydd cyfran o'r dystiolaeth yn y gyfrol hon o fudd i'r*
> *sawl a ymgymero â'r gwaith*
> 'I hope that some of the evidence in this volume will be of
> benefit to whosoever may undertake the work'
> > (Hywel Teifi Edwards, 1980: x)

> *Does ond a hedo a ddaw yma*
> 'It is only that which flies that comes here'
> > (Idwal Jones, 1978: 21)

This use is often found in idioms and proverbs:

> *Deued a ddelo, roedd yn rhaid bod yn ymwybodol o ymddygiad*
> *yng ngŵydd eraill*
> 'Come what may, it was necessary to be aware of actions in the
> presence of others'
> > (Wil Roberts, 1985: 21–2)

> *Y Nefoedd a'm helpo i!*
> 'Heaven help me!'
> > (*Y Faner*, 20/27 Rhagfyr 1991: 11)

> *Gadw yn graff a ddysgych*
> 'Keep securely what you learn'
> > (Proverb)

> *Canmoled pawb y bont a'i dyco drosodd*
> 'Let everyone praise the bridge that has brought him over'
> > (Proverb)

> *Boed a fo am hynny*
> 'Be that as it may'

> *Duw a'n helpo*
> 'God help us'

(b) in an adverbial clause after *lle y, pan, tra, oni, cyn y, wedi y, nes*
y, fel y (expressing purpose or comparison), *fel na, modd y, megis y,*
rhag na, am y:

> *Mae angen mwy a mwy o gopïau cyn yr elo'n rhy hwyr*
> 'More and more copies are needed before it may be too late'
> > (Rhiannon Davies Jones, 1985: 78)

Canaf i'r Arglwydd tra fyddwyf fyw: canaf i'm Duw tra fyddwyf
(1955)
Canaf i'r Arglwydd tra byddaf byw: rhof foliant i Dduw tra
byddaf (1988)
'I will sing to the Lord as long as I may live: I will sing to my God
as long as I have my being'
     (Ps 104: 33)

Y mae'r gwyddonwyr wrthi'n brysur yn ceisio ymestyn yr
adeiladweithiau presennol i'r trydydd dimensiwn fel y byddo'r
cyfanwaith terfynol yn fwy sylfaenol
'The scientists are busily engaged attempting to extend the
present structures into the third dimension so that the final
entity may be simpler'
     (*Y Faner*, 13 Rhagfyr 1991: 16)

Y pethau hyn yr wyf yn ysgrifennu atoch fel na phechoch (1955)
'These things I write to you so that you should not sin'
     (1 John 2: 1)

Pan edrychwyf ar y nefoedd, gwaith dy fysedd . . . (1955)
Pan edrychaf ar y nefoedd, gwaith dy fysedd . . . (1988)
'When I look at the heavens, the work of your fingers . . .'
     (Ps. 8: 3)

Pan fo'r galw'n codi mae'r safonau'n codi
'When the demand increases the standards rise'
     (Geraint Bowen, 1976: 95)

ofni yr wyf, rhag . . . na'ch caffwyf yn gyfryw rai (1955)
'I fear, I may find you different from what I will you to be'
     (2 Cor. 12: 20)

Un ciedd oedd Urien y Gwastrawd a chenfigennai wrth Brif
Wastrawd y Tywysog am y câi hwnnw eistedd yr ochr arall i'r
sgrin yn y neuadd gyferbyn â'r Tywysog
'Urien the Groom was a cruel person and was envious of the
prince's Chief Groom because he was allowed to sit on the other
side of the partition in the hall opposite the Prince'
     (Rhiannon Davies Jones, 1977: 25)

Y mae'r gwynt yn chwythu lle y mynno (1955)
Y mae'r gwynt yn chwythu lle y myn (1988)
'The wind blows where it wills'
     (John 3: 8)

Note

Y is often omitted following *lle*: *Lle bo dolur y bydd llaw* 'Wherever there is a wound there will be a hand' (Proverb). See **284** (ii) n.

(iii) In a negative noun clause following a main clause expressing a wish or command:

> *Edrychwch na thwyller chwi* (1955)
> *Gwyliwch na chewch eich twyllo* (1988)
> 'Take care that you are not misled'
> (Luke 21: 8)

> *Edrychwch, frodyr, na byddo un amser yn neb ohonoch galon ddrwg anghrediniaeth* (1955)
> *Gwyliwch, frodyr, na fydd yn neb ohonoch byth galon ddrwg anghrediniol* (1988)
> 'Take care, brothers, that no one of you ever has a wicked, faithless heart'
> (Heb. 3: 12)

In the examples quoted under (ii) (b) and (iii), the indicative rather than the subjunctive occurs in the 1988 translation of the Bible.

(iv) In the restricted register of bank cheques. The words 'Pay . . . or order' are rendered *Taler . . . neu a enwo*, *enwo* being 3 sing. pres. subjunctive. The subjunctive also features in modern poetry: *A phan ddelo'r adar yn ôl o'u deheudir* 'And when the birds return from their southern land' (Waldo Williams, 1904–71).

312 The Imperfect Subjunctive

The imperfect subjunctive is selected:

(i) In a conditional clause after *pe*(*d*) 'if'; *pe* occurs before consonants and *ped* before vowels:

> *Ni chysgwn i'n esmwyth pe dewisid yr un o'r rhain ar gyfer Tachwedd 4*
> 'I would not sleep soundly if one of these were selected for November 4'
> (*Y Faner*, 15 Medi 1989: 21)

> *Ped atelit fi, ni fwytawn o'th fara di* (1955)
> *Pe bait yn fy ngadw yma, ni fyddwn yn bwyta dy fwyd* (1988)
> 'If you were to keep me here, I would not eat your food'
> (Judg. 13: 16)

Cytunodd y merched, er eu bod yn gwybod y byddent yn cael eu cosbi'n drwm pe baent yn cael eu dal
'The girls agreed, although they knew that they would be severely punished if they were caught'
(T. Llew Jones, 1977: 58)

Pe peidiwn â charu Hywel, fe beidiai fy haul â chodi
'If I were to stop loving Hywel, my sun would stop rising'
(Rhiannon Davies Jones, 1977: 112)

Pe bai o'n gi bach fe fyddai wedi ysgwyd ei gynffon
'If he were a puppy he would have wagged his tail'
(Irma Chilton, 1989: 14)

In negative conditional clauses, either *pe na* or *oni* occur:

Pe na baem yn gwybod ond am y ddau air hyn, felly, byddai gennym raniad cymharol syml rhwng y rhan helaethaf o'r Gogledd a'r De
'If we knew only of these two words, then, we would have a fairly simple division between most of the North and the South'
(Thomas and Thomas, 1989: 13)

Byddent hwythau, yn ogystal â Parker, wedi trengi, pe na baent wedi lladd y llanc
'They, as well as Parker, would have died, had they not killed the youth'
(*Y Faner*, 15 Medi 1989: 9)

Oni bai am y briodas, byddent wedi dod gyda ni
'Were it not for the wedding, they would have come with us'

The accusative infixed pronoun *-s* may be affixed to *pe* (see **218** (b)).

(ii) With interjections to express a wish with regard to the present or future:

Byddi'n dweud yn y bore, 'O na fyddai'n hwyr!' ac yn yr hwyr, 'O na fyddai'n fore!'
'You will say in the morning, "Would it were evening!" and in the evening, "Would it were morning!"'
(Deut. 28: 67)

O na bawn i fel y nant!
'Would that I were like the stream!'

O na byddai'n haf o hyd!
'Would that it were summer all the time!'

313 The Imperative

The imperative is used to express:

(i)   An unequivocal command:

Deffro eneth!
'Wake up girl!'
(Emyr Humphreys, 1986: 81)

Llosgwch y dref a'i hysbail â thân, yn aberth llwyr i'r Arglwydd eich Duw
'Burn the city and its spoil with fire, as a complete sacrifice to the Lord your God'
(Deut. 13: 16)

Stopiwch o Owen, stopiwch o!
'Stop him Owen, stop him!'
(Emyr Humphreys, 1986: 94)

(ii)   Guidance, instruction, direction or advice:

Os yw dy law neu dy droed yn achos cwymp i ti, tor hi ymaith
'If your hand or your foot is your undoing, cut it off'
(Matt. 18: 8)

Ymddiried ynddo!
'Trust in him!'
(Emyr Humphreys, 1981: 211)

Llawenhewch a gorfoleddwch
'Rejoice and be glad'
(Matt. 5: 12)

(iii)   An invitation, request or wish:

Tyrd at y tân 'ngenath i
'Draw near to the fire my girl'
(Rhiannon Davies Jones, 1985: 136)

O Arglwydd, Duw fy meistr Abraham, rho lwyddiant i mi heddiw a gwna garedigrwydd â'm meistr Abraham
'O Lord, God of my master Abraham, give me good fortune today and be kind to my master Abraham'
(Gen. 24: 12)

Gorffen dy sieri
'Finish your sherry'
    (Emyr Humphrys, 1981: 21)

(iv) In a negative construction *na(c)* occurs before the verb; *na* is selected before consonants, *nac* before vowels:

Nac yf win na diod gadarn (1955)
'Do not drink wine or strong drink'
    (Judg. 13: 7)

Na feddylier na welsom chwarae llachar gan Bontypridd
'Don't think that we didn't see spectacular play by Pontypridd'
    (*Y Faner*, 3 Chwefror 1989: 21)

Na hidia
'Don't worry'
    (Rhiannon Davies Jones, 1977: 201)

Na cheisied neb awgrymu sen ar gydwybod dyn arall
'Let no one attempt to suggest censure on another person's conscience'
    (*Y Faner*, 13 Ionawr 1989: 9)

Na ladd
'Do not kill'
    (Matt. 5: 21)

On mutation following *na* see **87, 115**.

The *na(c)* + verb construction is rare in informal spoken Welsh apart from a few phrases such as *na phoener* 'not to worry', *na hidiwch* 'don't worry'.

It is possible to select the periphrastic construction consisting of the imperative form of *peidio* 'cease' + *â/ag* + verb-noun; *â* occurs before consonants and *ag* before vowels. This construction is common in varieties of spoken Welsh and is also widely used in literary texts:

Paid ag yfed na gwin na diod gadarn (1988)
'Do not drink wine or strong drink'
    (Judg. 13: 7)

Peidiwch â dwad dim pellach!
'Don't come any further!'
    (T. Glynne Davies, 1974: 238)

Peidiwch byth â gwrthod gwahoddiad i siarad
'Don't ever refuse an invitation to speak'
(Emyr Humphreys, 1986: 21)

Paid â mynd yn rhy aml i dŷ dy gymydog
'Do not go too often to your neighbour's house'
(Prov. 25: 17)

Peidiwch â phoeni, cariad
'Don't worry, darling'
(Emyr Humphreys, 1981: 27)

On mutation following *â* see **117**.

In informal texts and in varieties of spoken Welsh *â* is often omitted:

Peidiwch credu mod i'n galed, Idris
'Don't think that I am hard, Idris'
(Emyr Humphreys, 1981: 317)

See also **329**.

In varieties of southern spoken Welsh *paid â* is realized as *pida: pida dweud* 'don't say'.

314 The Impersonal

Impersonal forms vary for tense but not for person or number:

Teflir ennyd o gysgod dros y modurwyr a brysura i lawr Adam St . . .
'A momentary shadow is cast over the motorists who hurry down Adam St . . .'
(Urien William, 1974: 19)

Ni chyhoeddid nifer mawr o gopïau o lyfrau
'Large numbers of copies of books were not published'
(Gwyn Thomas, 1971: 92)

The impersonal is selected when no reference is made to any agent:

Cydnabuwyd fod swyddogaethau gwahanol i ryddiaith ac i farddoniaeth
'It was recognized that prose and poetry had different functions'
(Geraint Bowen, 1972: 24–5)

Gofelid bod yr efail yn ddigon pell o'r llys
'It was ensured that the smithy was far enough from the court'
(Rhiannon Davies Jones, 1977: 43)

The agent of an impersonal verb is indicated either by the use of the preposition *gan* followed by a noun or by the personal form of the preposition:

Blinid ef gan arfer y Piwritaniaid o bregethu mewn tai ac adeiladau heblaw eglwysi
'He was concerned by the Puritans' custom of preaching in houses and buildings other than churches'
(Gwyn Thomas, 1971: 43)

Cyfyngwyd y dramodydd o Roegwr gan ffurf y ddrama
'The Greek dramatist was confined by the form of the drama'
(Geraint Bowen, 1972: 132)

Cyfyngwyd y dramodydd o Roegwr ganddi
'The Greek dramatist was confined by it'

If the verb is transitive the impersonal form may select an object:

Fe'i hagorwyd ym mis Gorffennaf 1878
'It was opened in July 1878'
(D. Tecwyn Lloyd, 1988: 32)

Pan lansiwyd y llong-ofod yn 1977, nid oedd neb yn breu-ddwydio y byddai'r arbrawf mor llwyddiannus
'When the spaceship was launched in 1977, no one dreamed that the experiment would be so successful'
(*Y Faner*, 1 Medi 1989: 4)

Ataliwyd y wobr ar 19 o achlysuron
'The prize was withheld on 19 occasions'
(J. Elwyn Hughes, 1989: v)

Bore trannoeth fe'i cafwyd yn farw yn ei gwely
'The following morning she was found dead in her bed'
(Kate Roberts, 1972: 26)

Fe'i hurddwyd yn farchog gan Iago I
'He was knighted by James I'
(Geraint H. Jenkins, 1983: 35)

Fe'i hachubir gan Angel
'She is saved by an Angel'
(Gwyn Thomas, 1971: 253)

Dadrithasid hi'n llwyr ynghylch ei phlant erbyn hynny
'She had been completely disillusioned concerning her children by then'
(Kate Roberts, 1972: 22)

The impersonal forms that select an object are active grammatically, and since the verb in Welsh has no form corresponding exactly to the passive construction in English they are also used to express the passive voice in Welsh.

The verb *cael* 'have' together with the verb-noun may also express passive voice, both in speech and in the literary language:

Yr oedd Ysgol Sul yn cael ei chynnal gan y Methodistiaid yn nhŷ popty Robart Wilias y cariwr
'A Sunday school was held by the Methodists in Robart Wilias the carrier's bakehouse'
(T. Glynne Davies, 1974: 17)

Mae bachgen Huw Gors wedi cael ei ladd
'Huw Gors's son has been killed'
(T. Wilson Evans, 1983: 34)

Cefais fy nanfon o'r cae un prynhawn . . .
'I was sent from the field one afternoon . . .'
(Irma Chilton, 1989: 25)

Hwn yw fy nghorff, sy'n cael ei roi er eich mwyn chwi
'This is my body, which is given for you'
(Luke 22: 19)

Pan oedd yr holl bobl yn cael eu bedyddio
'When all the people were being baptized'
(Luke 3: 21)

The Verb-Noun

315 The verb-noun consists of either:

(i) the stem of the verb with no suffix (see **316**), or
(ii) the stem (or occasionally another form) together with a suffix (see **317**).

316 Verb-nouns consisting of a stem with no suffix, for example:

achub 'save'	*dianc* 'escape'
adrodd 'relate'	*dilyn* 'follow'
amau 'doubt'	*dioddef* 'suffer'
amgyffred 'comprehend'	*disgyn* 'fall'
anfon 'send'	*disgwyl* 'expect'
annog 'urge'	*edrych* 'look'
arbed 'save'	*eistedd* 'sit'
arfer 'use'	*ennill* 'win'
arllwys 'pour'	*erfyn* 'beg'
atal 'prevent'	*erlid* 'pursue'
ateb 'reply'	*erlyn* 'prosecute'
cadw 'keep'	*estyn* 'extend'
cyfaddef 'admit'	*ethol* 'elect'
cyfarch 'greet'	*gafael* 'grasp'
cyfarth 'bark'	*galw* 'call'
cyffwrdd 'touch'	*gorchymyn* 'command'
cymell 'compel'	*gorwedd* 'lie down'
cynnau 'light'	*gosod* 'place'
cynnig 'propose'	*gostwng* 'lower'
cynnull 'gather'	*gwarchod* 'guard'
cynnwys 'include'	*gwarchae* 'besiege'
cyrraedd 'arrive'	*gwrthod* 'refuse'
chwarae 'play'	*hel* 'gather'
dadlaith 'thaw'	*lladd* 'kill'
dangos 'show'	*ymddangos* 'appear'
dannod 'taunt'	*ymddeol* 'retire'
datod 'untie'	*ymladd* 'fight'
datrys 'solve'	*ymosod* 'attack'
deffro 'awake'	*ymwrthod* 'abstain'
dewis 'choose'	

If *-w-*, *-y-* (clear) or *-au-* occurs in the final syllable, vowel mutation (see **146**), occurs when a verbal ending is added:

	Verb-noun	1 sing. pres. indic.
au >eu	*amau* 'doubt'	*amheuaf*
	dechrau 'begin'	*dechreuaf*
	glanhau 'clean'	*glanheuaf*
w > y (dark)	*hebrwng* 'guide'	*hebryngaf*
	gollwng 'drop'	*gollyngaf*
	gostwng 'lower'	*gostyngaf*

y (clear) **> y** (dark)	*canlyn* 'follow'	*canlynaf*
	dilyn 'follow'	*dilynaf*
	derbyn 'receive'	*derbyniaf*

Adding a verbal ending moves the stress to a new penult and *-nn-* and *-rr-* in a stressed syllable become *-n-* or *-nh-* and *-rh-* (see **33**).

	Verb-noun	1 sing. pres. indic.
nn > n	*cynnau* 'light'	*cyneuaf*
	cynnull 'gather'	*cynullaf*
	annog 'urge'	*anogaf*
	chwennych 'desire'	*chwenychaf* (dark **y**)
	ennill 'earn'	*enillaf*
	cynnig 'propose'	*cynigiaf*

Note

In *ennyn* 'inflame', *enynnaf* a double change occurs as a result of the accent shift *y* (clear) *> y* (dark), *nn > n*.

nn > nh	*cynnal* 'support'	*cynhaliaf*
	cynnwys 'include'	*cynhwysaf*
rr > rh	*cyrraedd* 'arrive'	*cyrhaeddaf*

Note

In the following verbs, *-h-* precedes the stressed vowel in the penult of the verbal form: *aros* 'wait', *arhosaf*; *cymell* 'urge', *cymhellaf*; *amau* 'doubt', *amheuaf*; *dianc* 'flee', *dihangaf*.

317 Most verb-nouns are formed by adding a suffix (see **318**) to the verbal stem; vowel mutation (see **146**) may occur in the final syllable of the stem:

Stem	Verb-noun
golau	*goleuo* 'light'
tenau	*teneuo* 'become thin'

Before some verb-nouns ending in *-o*, *i* is added to a stem that is a noun or adjective:

Stem	Verb-noun
effaith	*effeithio* 'affect'
gwaith	*gweithio* 'work'
taith	*teithio* 'travel'
naid	*neidio* 'leap'

llais	*lleisio* 'voice'
plaid	*pleidio* 'favour'
sain	*seinio* 'sound'

When -*i* is added to a stem containing -*a*-, vowel affection (see **144**) occurs in a few verbs:

Stem	Verb-noun
par-	*peri* 'cause'
tranc-	*trengi* 'die'
sang-	*sengi* 'tread'
taw-	*tewi* 'be silent'
distaw	*distewi* 'be silent'

Endings of Verb-Nouns

318 Most verb-nouns are formed by adding either -*u*, -*o* or -*i* to the stem of the verb.

319 -u

(i) The ending -*u* is added to stems containing *a*, *ae*, *e*, *y* ((dark), mutated from *y* (clear) or from *w*: see **146**).

Examples:

caru 'love'	*canu* 'sing'
llamu 'leap'	*galaru* 'mourn'
naddu 'hew'	*meddiannu* 'possess'
glasu 'grow blue'	*bychanu* 'belittle'
dallu 'blind'	*diddanu* 'amuse'
tarfu 'scare'	*tarddu* 'spring'
baeddu 'soil'	*hiraethu* 'yearn'
ffaelu 'fail'	*taeru* 'insist'
gwaedu 'bleed'	*arfaethu* 'plan'
gwaelu 'sicken'	*saethu* 'shoot'
credu 'believe'	*rhyfeddu* 'wonder'
cefnu 'desert'	*anrhegu* 'present'
gweddu 'suit'	*trefnu* 'arrange'
caledu 'harden'	*darlledu* 'broadcast'
cysgu 'sleep'	*melysu* 'sweeten'
dyrnu 'thresh'	*synnu* 'wonder'
tynnu 'pull'	*tywyllu* 'darken'
gwylltu 'lose control of oneself'	*tyllu* 'bore'

(ii) *-u* is added to the following stem endings to form the verb-noun:

-ych	*bradychu* 'betray'	*chwenychu* 'desire' (also *chwennych*)
	clafychu 'sicken'	*tewychu* 'fatten'
-yg	*gwaethygu* 'make worse'	*mawrygu* 'glorify'
	dirmygu 'despise'	*ysgyrnygu* 'gnash the teeth'

-(h)a (with the contraction *-(h)a + u > -(h)au*: see **270, 272**)

> *cryfhau* 'strengthen'   *ufuddhau* 'obey'
> *glanhau* 'clean'   *rhyddhau* 'free'
> *parhau* 'continue'   *trugarhau* 'take pity'
> *gwacáu* 'empty' (< *gwag + ha + u*)
> *nesáu* 'approach' (< *nes + ha + u*)
> *cwpláu* 'complete' (< *cwbl + ha + u*)
> *casáu* 'hate' (< *cas + ha + u*)

(iii) *-u* occurs in the following verb-nouns where vowel mutation of *w* has not occurred:

gwgu 'frown'	*pwdu* 'sulk'
(dial.) *llwgu* 'famish'	(dial.) *rhwdu* 'rust'
(dial.) *mwgu* 'smoke'	(dial.) *cwnnu* 'rise'

Notes

(1) *-i* is added to a small number of stems containing *a* or *aw* (see **317**), and to a few other stems noted below (see **321**).

(2) *-u* occurs in *croesawu* 'welcome'.

320 -o

(i) When the verbal stem is a noun or adjective, *i* often occurs before the verb-noun ending (see **317**):

Stem	Verb-noun
gwaith	*gweithio* 'work'
glan	*glanio* 'land'
cof	*cofio* 'remember'
ffurf	*ffurfio* 'form'
coed	*coedio* 'timber'

araith	*areithio* 'make a speech'
gwawr	*gwawrio* 'dawn'
bawd	*bodio* 'thumb'
disglair	*disgleirio* 'shine'
caib	*ceibio* 'dig'
troed	*troedio* 'walk'
gweniaith	*gwenieithio* 'flatter'
rhaib	*rheibio* 'bewitch'

(ii) *i* also occurs before -*o* in borrowed forms:

smocio 'smoke'	*apelio* 'appeal'
teipio 'type'	*iwsio* 'use'
ffeindio 'find'	*cerfio* 'carve'
cracio 'crack'	*bildio* 'build'
peintio 'paint'	*potio* 'pot'

Note

i is often omitted in varieties of spoken Welsh: *smoco* for *smocio*, *iwso* for *iwsio*, *coedo* for *coedio*, *ceibo* for *ceibio* etc.

(iii) -*o* is added to stems with *i, u, eu, wy* in the final syllable:

blino 'tire'	*rhifo* 'count'
crino 'wither'	*cynefino* 'accustom'
cribo 'comb'	*britho* 'turn grey'
gweddïo 'pray'	*crio* 'cry'
curo 'knock'	*dymuno* 'wish'
hudo 'charm'	*addurno* 'adorn'
rhuo 'roar'	*llusgo* 'drag'
ceulo 'curdle'	*heulo* 'be sunny'
goleuo 'light'	*euro* 'gild'
teneuo 'become thin'	*breuo* 'become brittle'
bwydo 'feed'	*llwydo* 'turn grey'
rhwystro 'hinder'	*cwyro* 'polish'
cwyno 'complain'	*rhwyfo* 'row'
mwydo 'soak'	*rhwydo* 'net'
anwylo 'fondle'	*twyllo* 'deceive'
difwyno 'spoil'	*andwyo* 'harm'
tramwyo (also *tramwy*)	*arswydo* 'dread'
'traverse'	*mwytho* 'pamper'
mwydro 'bewilder'	

Notes

(1) The selection of *o* rather than *io* distinguishes between *llifo* 'flow' and *llifio* 'saw'.

(2) *Llifo* 'dye, colour' alternates with *lliwo* in varieties of spoken Welsh; the standard form is *lliwio*.

321 -i

(i) The ending *-i* is added to stems ending in consonantal *w*:

enwi 'name'	*chwerwi* 'embitter'
berwi 'boil'	*llenwi* 'fill'
meddwi 'get drunk'	*sylwi* 'observe'
gloywi 'brighten'	

Exceptions:

cadw 'keep'	*marw* 'die'
llanw 'fill'	*galw* 'call'

(ii) *-i* is added to stems ending in *-ew* (affected from *aw*; see **317**):

tewi 'become silent'	*distewi* 'be quiet'

(iii) *-i* is added to stems ending in *-awn, -enw*:

cyflawni 'fulfil' (< *cyflawn* + *i*)
cyflenwi 'supply' (< *cyflanw* + *i*)

(iv) *-i* is added to stems with *o* or *oe* in the final syllable:

rhoddi 'give'	*cyfodi* 'rise'
torri 'break'	*unioni* 'rectify'
llonni 'gladden'	*ffromi* 'fume'
sorri 'sulk'	*cronni* 'amass'
angori 'anchor'	*dogni* 'ration'
gori 'brood'	*arfogi* 'employ'
oeri 'cool'	*poeri* 'spit'
poethi 'heat'	*poeni* 'worry'
cyhoeddi 'publish'	*oedi* 'delay'

(v) *-i* occurs in contracted forms (see **270, 271**):

troi 'turn'	*ffoi* 'flee'
paratoi 'prepare'	*crynhoi* 'gather'
rhoi 'give'	*cloi* 'lock'
cnoi 'bite'	*datgloi* 'unlock'

(vi) -i is added to some stems where a in the final syllable is affected to e:

Verb-noun	1 sing. pres. indic.
erchi 'ask'	*archaf*
peri 'cause'	*paraf*
sengi (also *sangu*) 'tread'	*sangaf*

(vii) -i occurs in the forms

medi 'reap'	*rhegi* 'swear'
mynegi 'state'	*gweiddi* 'shout' (stem *gwaedd-*)

322 The endings listed below occur in a limited number of verb-nouns:

-ael, -el   *cael, caffael* 'have'; *gadael* 'leave'; *dyrchafael* (also *dyrchafu*) 'ascend'.

-ach   *clindarddach* 'crackle'; *cyfeddach* 'carouse'.

-aeth   *marchogaeth* (also *marchocáu*) 'ride'; *ymyrraeth* (also *ymyrryd, ymyrru*) 'interfere'.

-ain   *llefain* 'cry'; *ochain* (also *ochneidio*) 'groan'; *diasbedain* 'resound'; *ubain* 'howl'.

-ial   (variant of **-ian**) *tincial* 'tinkle'; *mwmial* 'mumble'; *sisial* 'whisper'.

-ed   *cerdded* 'walk'; *yfed* 'drink'; *clywed* 'hear'; *gweled* (*gweld*) 'see'; *myned* (*mynd*) 'go'.

-eg   *rhedeg* 'run'; *(e)hedeg* 'fly'.

-fan   *(e)hedfan* 'fly'.

-(h)a   (i) in verb-nouns formed from nouns:
pysgota 'fish'; *cardota* 'beg'; *lloffa* 'glean'; *gwledda* 'feast'; *cneua* 'nut'; *mwyara* 'gather blackberries'; *siopa* (also *siopio*) 'shop'; *gwreica* 'seek a wife'; *atgoffa* 'remind'.

(ii) in a few verb-nouns not formed from nouns:
chwilota 'pry'; *rhodianna* 'stroll'; *cryffa* (also *cryffáu, cryfhau*) 'strengthen'.

Note
Although *-h-* has disappeared it has caused provection of the preceding consonant (see **150**).

-yd   *cymryd* 'take' (1 sing. pres. indic. *cymeraf*); *edfryd* 'restore' (also *adferyd, adfer*; 1 sing. pres. indic. *adferaf*); *ymoglyd* 'avoid' (also *ymoglud, ymogel*; 1 sing. pres. indic. *ymogelaf*); *dychwelyd* 'return'; *ymyrryd* 'interfere' (also *ymyrru, ymyrraeth*).

-ian, -an (i) added to Welsh stems it forms a pejorative: *sefyllian* 'loaf'; *gorweddian* 'loaf'; *ymlwybran* 'plod one's way'; *clebran* 'prattle'.

(ii) it is added to borrowed stems: *hongian* 'hang'; *ystwrian* 'stir'; *trotian* 'trot'; *mwmian* 'mumble'; *tincian* 'tinkle'; *loetran* 'loiter'.

-wyn   *dwyn* 'bear' (also *dygyd, dygu*; 1 sing. pres. indic. *dygaf*); *ymddŵyn* 'bear children' (1 sing. pres. indic. *ymddygaf*).

-ad   *gwyliad* 'keep vigil' (also *gwylied, gwyl(i)o, gwyl(i)ad*); *nofiad* 'swim' (also *nofio*).

The following endings have survived only in one example each:

-yll   *sefyll* 'stand' (1 sing. pres. indic. *safaf*).

-as   *lluddias* 'hinder' (also *lluddio*; 1 sing. pres. indic. *lludd(i)af*).

-sach   *llamsach* 'leap' (also *llamsachu*).

-edd   *gwastrodedd* 'discipline' (also *gwastrodi, gwastradu*).

The following verb-nouns are irregular:

bod and its compounds (see **277, 284–293**).
mynd, gwneud, dod (see **294**).
aredig 'plough' (1 sing. pres. indic. *arddaf*).
chwerthin 'laugh' (1 sing. pres. indic. *chwarddaf*).
gweini 'serve' (also *gweinyddu*; 1 sing. pres. indic. *gweinyddaf*).
go(r)ddiweddyd 'overtake' (also *go(r)ddiwes, go(r)ddiweddu*, 1 sing. pres. indic. *go(r)ddiweddaf*).

In some verb-nouns the meaning varies depending upon which element is stressed.

Stress on the penult	Stress on the ultima
ymddwyn 'behave'	*ymddŵyn* 'bear child'
ymladd 'fight'	*ymlâdd* 'tire oneself'

Notes

(1) *Ymladdaf* can only mean 'I fight'.

(2) *Ymdrin* (stress on the penult) and *ymdrîn* (stress on the ultima) are synonymous = 'deal with'.

(3) The following verb-nouns do not have inflected forms: *clochdar* 'crackle'; *bugunad* 'bellow'; *mercheta* 'wench'; *adara* 'fowl'; *cardota* 'beg'; *wylofain* 'wail'. See also **331** n.

Syntax of the Verb-Noun

323 The verb-noun possesses the essential properties of both noun and verb. Basically its constructions are those of the noun, but it may also function instead of a finite verb and frequently occur with various prepositions and the verb *bod* 'to be', to form various tenses in a periphrastic verbal construction (see **286**).

324 The verb as a noun

(i) The article may precede the verb-noun:

Mi fydd diwedd ar yr hwylio cyn hir
'The sailing will cease before long'
  (Gerhart Hauptman and Heinrich Böll, 1974: 3)

Ynglyn â'r yfed, nid oedd gorfodaeth ar neb
'As regards the drinking, there was no compulsion on anyone'
  (Esther 1: 8)

(ii) An adjective may qualify the verb-noun:

Mae'r ymddadfeilio cyson a ddigwyddodd i'r capel yn y blynyddoedd diwethaf hyn wedi dwysáu y drych o dristwch a welodd W. J. Gruffydd
'The sustained dilapidation that has occurred to the chapel in recent years has intensified the mirror of sadness that W. J. Gruffydd saw'
  (Aneirin Talfan Davies, 1972: 13)

(iii) A pronoun may precede the verb-noun:

'Roedd ei hwylo'n ymbil am dynerwch
'Her sobbing solicited tenderness'
  (Alun Jones, 1989: 129)

Pa wrthdaro sy'n aros gliriaf yn fy nghof?
'Which clash remains clearest in my memory?'
  (J. Elwyn Hughes, 1989: 64)

(iv) The verb-noun may be governed by a preposition:

Bu gwelliant mawr yn chwarae'r tîm hwn
'There had been a great improvement in this team's playing'

Ac wedi dyfod dydd y Pentecost, yr oeddent hwy oll yn gytûn yn yr un lle (1955)
'And when the day of the Pentecost was come, they were all with one accord in the same place'
(Acts 2: 1)

Hwy a ddeuant i Seion â chanu (1955)
Dônt i Seion dan ganu (1988)
'They shall come to Zion singing'
(Isa. 51: 11)

The 1988 translation of the Welsh Bible has selected the sub-predicate or participle construction in the above example (see **325** (vi)).

(v) The verb-noun may function as subject or object in a sentence:

Meddyginiaeth dda ydy chwerthin
'Laughter is good medicine'
(Rhiannon Davies Jones, 1987: 144)

Ydi bridio'n anwyddonol?
'Is breeding unscientific?'
(Emyr Humphreys, 1981: 25)

Hir pob aros
'Every waiting (is) long'
(Proverb)

Fe hoffai fynd i newid ei grys
'He would like to go to change his shirt'
(R. Cyril Hughes, 1976: 201)

Ni allodd holl rym byddin fawr Harri'r Ail ddarostwng Gwynedd
'All the might of Henry II's large army could not conquer Gwynedd'
(Rhiannon Davies Jones, 1977: 187)

Ni allwn ddweud yr un gair
'I could not say one word'
(Harri Williams, 1978: 21)

See also **353** for examples of *bod*, *darfod* and other verb-nouns functioning as objects of verbs and verb-nouns in noun clauses.

(vi) The verb-noun may occur as the second element in a genitival construction:

esgidiau cerdded	*llestr yfed*
'walking boots'	'drinking vessel'
gwialen bysgota	*tir pori*
'fishing rod'	'grazing land'
bwrdd arholi	*dŵr ymolchi*
'examining board'	'washing water'
corn yfed	*cyngor datblygu*
'drinking horn'	'development council'
llyfr darllen	*offer cyfieithu*
'reading book'	'translation equipment'

Note
Dodi, *gosod* occur in this construction but convey the meaning 'false': *dannedd dodi*, *dannedd gosod* 'false teeth'; *gwallt gosod* 'false hair, wig'.

325 The verb-noun as a verb

(i) The verb-noun preceded by *yn*, *wedi* etc. occurs in the periphrastic verbal construction (see **286**):

Yr oedd Ifan wedi cysgu yn hwyr y bore hwnnw
'Ifan had slept late that morning'
(T. Glynne Davies, 1974: 73)

Byddai'n cyrraedd y lifft am ddeng munud i naw
'He would reach the lift at ten minutes to nine'
(Urien William, 1974: 20)

Yr oedd am ysgrifennu at Lady Margaret
'She wished to write to Lady Margaret'
(R. Cyril Hughes, 1975: 55)

'Roedd y darlun wedi mynd
'The picture had gone'
(Alun Jones, 1989: 82)

(ii) The verb-noun occurs as object of the verb *gwneuthur*, *gwneud* 'make, do' (see **294**) in an abnormal sentence (see **351**):

Sefyll wnaeth aelodau'r gynulleidfa drwy gydol yr awr a hanner o wasanaeth
'The members of the congregation stood throughout the service of an hour and a half'
(*Golwg*, 11 Ionawr 1990: 24)

Ofni yn ddirfawr a wnaethant (1955)
'They were terror-stricken'
(Luke 2: 9)

Mynd a wneuthum
'I went'
(Dic Jones, 1989: 14)

Hanner gwrando a wnâi Sioned
'Sioned was half-listening'
(Alun Jones, 1989: 45)

On mutation following the particle see **72**.

Note
With the exception of the example from Luke which is from the early modern period, these examples could also be explained as mixed sentences (see **352**) with the emphasis on the initial object element.

(iii) An adverb can modify a verb-noun:

blino'n gynnar 'tire early'   *cysgu'n hwyr* 'sleep late'
gyrru'n gyflym 'drive fast'   *paentio'n ofalus* 'paint carefully'

In the sentence

Mae ymarfer yn gyson yn llesol
'Regular exercise is beneficial'

the subject *ymarfer* 'exercise' is also a verb modified by the adverb *yn gyson*.

A compound verb-noun is formed when an adjective occurs before the verb-noun:

Buont yn mân siarad am ychydig
'They gossiped for a little while'
(Alun Jones, 1989: 113)

Yr oedd yn prysur gerdded y llwybr hwnnw
'She was rapidly going along that path'
    (Rhiannon Davies Jones, 1989: 37)

When *newydd* 'new' occurs in this construction the adjunct *yn* is not selected:

Roeddwn i newydd gael gwaith fel clarc bach
'I had just had work as a junior clerk'
    (*Golwg*, 19 Ionawr 1990)

The adjunct *wedi* may occur with *newydd*:

a'r gwylwyr wedi eu newydd osod (1955)
'and the watchmen had been newly set'
    (Judg. 7: 19)

A few compound verb-nouns serve as adjectives:

Fel rhai bychain newydd-eni, chwenychwch ddidwyll laeth y gair
(1955)
Fel babanod newydd eu geni, blysiwch am laeth ysbrydol pur
(1988)
'Like new-born infants, you crave for pure spiritual milk'
    (1 Pet. 2: 2)

(iv) The verb-noun occurs in a series of co-ordinate statements where the tense and person have already been identified by a finite verb. The sentence containing the verb-noun is considered to be a verbal sentence.

Daeth ei wraig yn ôl, a sefyll fel llewes uwch ei ben
'His wife returned, and stood like a lioness over him'
    (Alun Jones, 1989: 114)

Cyfarchodd Iesu ef a dweud, 'Beth yr wyt ti am i mi ei wneud iti?'
'Jesus greeted him and said, "What do you want me to do for you?"'
    (Mark 10: 51)

A phan ddaeth y newydd at frenin Ninefe, cododd yntau oddi ar ei orsedd, a diosg ei fantell a gwisgo sachliain ac eistedd mewn lludw
'And when word came to the king of Nineveh, he arose from his throne, and removed his robe and put on sackcloth and sat in ashes'
    (Jonah 3: 6)

Gwthiodd Margaret Rose y llyfr i'w bag a thynnu'r sip arno
'Margaret Rose pushed the book into her bag and closed the zip on it'
(Jane Edwards, 1976: 153)

(v)   The verb-noun occurs in absolute expressions (see **359**):

Yn 1960, a minnau'n paratoi ffilm ar y Fro ar gyfer y BBC, holais wraig ffermdy Gregory am unrhyw hanesion a glywsai am Iolo
'In 1960, while preparing a film on the Vale for the BBC, I asked the wife at Gregory farmhouse for any tales that she had heard about Iolo'
(Aneirin Talfan Davies, 1972: 64)

Daethant at y bedd a'r haul wedi codi (1955)
A'r haul newydd godi, dyma hwy'n dod at y bedd (1988)
'Just after sunrise, they came to the tomb'
(Mark 16: 2)

(vi) The verb-noun occurs with prepositions to form a sub-predicate or participle (see **376** (v)).

Aeth allan gan gau'r drws yn glep
'He went out slamming the door'
(T. Glynne Davies, 1974: 375)

Aeth yn ei flaen dan ganu
'He went on his way, singing'
(John Bunyan, 1962: 25)

Fe eisteddais yn y gornel yn yfed wisgi hefo'r ferch o'r BBC
'I sat in the corner drinking whisky with the girl from the BBC'
(R. Gerallt Jones, 1977: 32)

Gadawodd Hywel yr ystafell yn araf heb yngan gair
'Hywel left the room slowly without uttering a word'
(Emyr Hywel, 1989: 16)

326   The subject of the verb-noun

(i)   The subject of the verb-noun may occur before the verb-noun governed by the prep. *i*:

Na foed i mi dramgwyddo mewn gair na gweithred yn erbyn y dall hwn!
'Let me not transgress in word or deed against this blind person!'
(Rhiannon Davies Jones, 1989: 14)

Bu i gar heddlu o'r dref . . . roi stop ar y gêm fach honno
'A police car from the town . . . put a stop to that little game'
(Alun Jones, 1989: 62)

Ni fu i mi ddefnyddio'r un brwsh i bardduo'r Gymdeithas a'r Blaid Lafur
'I did not use the same brush to blacken the Society and the Labour Party'
(*Y Faner*, 2 Mawrth 1990: 17)

Gwyddai iddi gael ei siomi yn ei chariad
'She knew that she had been disappointed in love'
(Kate Roberts, 1972: 22)

On mutation of the verb-noun, see **106**.

(ii) In older texts the subject may follow the verb-noun governed by the prep. *o*:

Bûm droeon yn y fangre hon, cyn nesáu o'r anghyfanedd-dra hwn
'I visited this place several times, before the approach of this devastation'
(Aneirin Talfan Davies, 1972: 13)

Pan glybu hwn ddyfod o'r Iesu (1955)
Pan glywodd hwn fod Iesu wedi dod (1988)
'When he heard that Jesus had come'
(John 4: 47)

Yna y gwybu Noa dreio o'r dyfroedd oddi ar y ddaear (1955)
A deallodd Noa fod y dyfroedd wedi treio oddi ar y ddaear (1988)
'Then Noah knew that the waters had subsided from the earth'
(Gen. 8: 11)

In both of the biblical examples noted here the new translation of the Welsh Bible has abandoned the construction where the subject of the verb-noun is governed by the prep. *o* and selected instead a noun clause construction introduced by *bod* 'to be': see **353**.

Note
In older biblical prose the object of the verb-noun may be denoted by an independent pronoun which follows the verb-noun + *o* + subject: *Ond oherwydd caru o'r Arglwydd chwi* (1955) 'But because

the Lord loved you' (Deut. 7: 8). The dependent pronoun precedes the verb-noun: *Megis pe ffoai gŵr . . . a'i frathu o sarff* (1955) 'As if a man did flee and a serpent bit him' (Amos 5: 19).

(iii)   If the verb-noun is intransitive the subject may (a) occur after the verb-noun without a prep.:

> *Cofia yn awr dy Greawdwr yn nyddiau dy ieuenctid cyn dyfod y dyddiau blin* (1955)
> 'Remember now thy Creator in the days of thy youth before the evil days come'
> (Eccles. 12: 1)

> *Yfory, erbyn gwresogi yr haul, bydd i chwi ymwared* (1955)
> 'Tomorrow, by the time the sun be hot, ye shall have help'
> (1 Sam. 11: 9)

The pronominal subject is denoted by a prefixed or infixed pronoun:

> *Na thybiwch fy nyfod i dorri'r gyfraith* (1955)
> *Peidiwch â thybio i mi ddod i ddileu'r Gyfraith* (1988)
> 'Think not that I am come to destroy the Law'
> (Matt. 5: 17)

> *Rhaid yw i'r neb sydd yn dyfod at Dduw, gredu ei fod ef, a'i fod yn obrwywr i'r rhai sydd yn ei geisio ef* (1955)
> *Rhaid i'r sawl sy'n dod at Dduw gredu ei fod ef, a'i fod yn gwobrwyo'r rhai sy'n ei geisio* (1988)
> 'He that cometh to God must believe that he is, and that he is a rewarder of them that seek him'
> (Heb. 11: 6)

(b)   occur after the verb-noun with the prep. *o* as in (ii) above:

> *Na thybiwch ddyfod ohonof i dorri'r gyfraith*

> *Erbyn gwresogi o'r haul bydd i chwi ymwared*

The constructions in this section frequently occur in noun clauses (see **353**).

327   The object of the verb-noun

The object of the verb-noun is dependent on the verb-noun just as one noun may depend on another. Whereas the object of the simple verb mutates (see **70**), the object of the verb-noun retains the radical:

> *prynu llyfr* 'the buying of a book'
> *yfed te* 'the drinking of tea'

The object of the verb-noun always follows the verb-noun:

(i) noun:

Ni oedd yn breuddwydio breuddwydion
'It was we who were dreaming dreams'
    (Rhiannon Davies Jones, 1977: 13)

Doeddem ni ddim yn cario offer atal cenhedlu
'We weren't carrying contraceptives'
    (R. Gerallt Jones, 1977: 19)

(ii) verb-noun:

A oedd hi'n medru darogan y dyfodol?
'Was she able to foretell the future?'
    (Rhiannon Davies Jones, 1989: 106)

A allai fforddio cyflogi gwas arall Galan Mai?
'Could he afford to employ another manservant on Mayday?'
    (R. Cyril Hughes, 1976: 67)

(iii) sentence:

Wyt ti'n meddwl y bydd y brenin am ein lladd ni?
'Do you think that the king will wish to kill us?'
    (Rhiannon Davies Jones, 1987: 186)

See **353** (ii).

The pronominal object (prefixed or infixed) precedes the verb-noun:

Ni allai eu rhwystro
'She could not stop them'
    (Kate Roberts, 1972: 23)

Rydw i am dy adael di
'I wish to leave you'
    (Jane Edwards, 1976: 154)

Doeddwn i ddim am ei wynebu
'I did not wish to face him'
    (Harri Williams, 1978: 31)

Daethant yma i'n gweld
'They came here to see us'

328 The verb-noun and the passive voice

The impersonal forms of the verb are used in Welsh to signify the passive voice (see **314**). The verb-noun, however, has no impersonal form and other means are used to express the passive voice when the verb-noun is used:

(i) The verb-noun may be the object of an impersonal form:

Gellir rhoi chwistrelliad ysgafn o ddŵr i'r planhigion ifanc . . .
Gellir gwneud yr un peth gyda'r planhigion hŷn
'A light spray of water can be given to the young plants . . .
The same thing can be done with the mature plants'
    (*Y Faner*, 9 Chwefror 1990: 19)

Pa fodd y gellid disgwyl i werin dlawd eu prynu?
'How could a poor people be expected to buy them?'
    (Gwyn Thomas, 1971: 60)

Gallesid gwerthu'r ennaint hwn am fwy na thri chant o ddarnau arian
'This perfume might have been sold for more than three hundred pieces of silver'
    (Mark 14: 5)

(ii) The verb-noun may function as antecedent of a relative clause containing an impersonal form in a mixed sentence (see **352**):

Chwistrellu'r planhigion a wnaed
'The plants were sprayed'

Prynu'r llyfrau a wneir
'The books will be bought'

Gwerthu'r ennaint a wnaethpwyd
'The perfume was sold'

(iii) The verb-noun may be the object of a personal verb or of another verb-noun:

Gorchmynnodd ef roi iddi rywbeth i'w fwyta
'He told them to give her something to eat'
    (Luke 8: 55)

Cofiaf godi'r rhent
'I remember the rent being increased'

Byddem yn gweld saethu cwningod
'We used to see the shooting of rabbits'

In these examples the verb-noun has an object. If the verb-noun cannot take an object it cannot be passive.

(iv) Forms of the verb *cael* are frequently used to signify passive voice in a construction consisting of *cael* + prefixed pronoun + verb-noun:

Mi ges fy mrawychu gan agweddau pobl tuag at dramorwyr
'I was horrified by people's attitudes towards foreigners'
(*Golwg*, 21 Rhagfyr 1989: 15)

Ces fy magu gan gyfnither 'y nhad
'I was brought up by my father's cousin'
(Emyr Humphreys, 1981: 252)

Cydnabu Llew Llwyfo'r tebygolrwydd y cai'r gwaith ei gondem-nio gan amryw
'Llew Llwyfo acknowledged the probability that the work would be condemned by many'
(Hywel Teifi Edwards, 1989: 65)

Nid i hynna maen nhw'n cael eu danfon i garchar
'It is not for that that they are sent to prison'
(Urien William, 1974: 22)

Roedd o wedi cael ei ddewis yn ymgeisydd
'He had been selected as a candidate'
(Jane Edwards, 1976: 96)

Wedi and *heb* may occur with the verb-noun without *cael* to express the perfect, pluperfect or future perfect:

Roedd ef wedi ei ddewis
'He had been selected'

Roedd ef heb ei ddewis
'He had not been selected'

Bydd ef wedi ei ddewis
'He will have been selected'

It is considered good literary style to avoid excessive use of *cael* where possible:

Er mai yn Llundain y magwyd ef, yr oedd wedi ei drwytho cymaint gan ei frawd, y bardd Siôn Tudur, yn niwylliant ei genedl

'Although he had been brought up in London, he had been so steeped by his brother Siôn Tudur, the bard, in his nation's culture'
(R. Cyril Hughes, 1975: 9)

(v) An impersonal form of *bod* + a verbal adjunct + verb-noun + noun object can be selected to express passive voice:

yr ydys yn adeiladu tŵr	'a tower is being built'
yr oeddid yn adeiladu tŵr	'a tower was being built'
yr ydys wedi adeiladu tŵr	'a tower has been built'
yr oeddid wedi adeiladu tŵr	'a tower had been built'
yr oeddid heb adeiladu tŵr	'a tower had not been built'
yr oeddid ar adeiladu tŵr	'a tower was about to be built'

A prefixed or infixed pronoun may denote the object of the verb-noun:

yr oeddid yn ei adeiladu	'it was being built'
yr oeddid wedi'i adeiladu	'it had been built'

This is a highly literary construction, and the construction with *cael* (see (iv) above) occurs in less formal texts. In the following examples the highly literary construction has been abandoned in the 1988 translation of the Bible:

Yr ydys yn treisio teyrnas nefoedd (1955)
Y mae teyrnas nefoedd yn cael ei threisio (1988)
'The kingdom of heaven is being violated'
(Matt. 11: 12)

pan oeddid yn bedyddio'r holl bobl (1955)
pan oedd yr holl bobl yn cael eu bedyddio (1988)
'when all the people were being baptized'
(Luke 3: 21)

Chwe blynedd a deugain y buwyd yn adeiladu'r deml hon (1955)
Chwe blynedd a deugain y bu'r deml hon yn cael ei hadeiladu (1988)
'It has taken forty-six years to build this temple'
(John 2: 20)

Note
When a subject is denoted the 3rd person sing. of *bod* replaces the impersonal form: *Mae'r tŵr i'w adeiladu* 'The tower is to be built';

Roedd tŵr i'w adeiladu 'A tower was to be built'. An impersonal form, however, has no subject.

329 Negative constructions involving the verb-noun

The negative is expressed:

(i) By placing *peidio â/ag* before the verb-noun (see **313** (iv)):

Paid â gwneud cytundeb priodas â hwy
'Do not make a marriage treaty with them'
(Deut. 7: 3)

Paid â gwneud dim niwed i ti dy hun
'Do yourself no harm'
(Acts 16: 27)

Peidiodd â meddwl ac aeth yn ôl
'She stopped thinking and returned'
(Alun Jones, 1989: 177)

Peidied neb, ar sail hyn, â chadw draw
'Let no one, on this evidence, keep away'
(*Y Faner*, 9 Chwefror 1990: 15)

(ii) By selecting the prep. *heb* before the verb-noun to denote the perfect or pluperfect tense (see **286**):

yr wyf heb ei weld   = *nid wyf wedi ei weld*
'I have not seen him'

yr oeddwn heb ei weld   = *nid oeddwn wedi ei weld*
'I had not seen him'

The perfect tense is also implied in adjectival phrases:

plant heb weld pen draw'r ffwrn
'children without experience of life' (lit. 'who have not seen the far end of the oven')

Heb ei fai, heb ei eni
'He who is faultless has not been born'

(iii) Tense in the verb-noun phrase may depend on the context:

Present

Paid ag edrych arnynt heb wneud dim
'Don't look at them without doing anything'

Future

> *Bydd yn anodd imi adael heb gael caniatâd yr arweinydd*
> 'It will be difficult for me to leave without having the conductor's permission'

Preterite

> *Aeth i mewn i'r car heb edrych ar neb*
> 'He went into the car without looking at anybody'

Verbal Adjectives

330 Many verbal adjectives are formed by adding a suffix to the stem of the verb; in other cases the stem itself serves as a verbal adjective.

(i) Adding a suffix

-edig
The following verbal adjectives are the equivalent of the English past participle used adjectivally:

arferedig 'usual'	*planedig* 'planted'
lladdedig 'killed'	*bendigedig* 'blessed'
cuddiedig 'hidden'	*toredig* 'broken'
methedig 'infirm'	*melltigedig* 'accursed'

The following, however, have an active force:

caredig 'loved, kind'	*troëdig* 'turning'

-adwy
The following have a passive force, expressing that an action is possible or obligatory:

credadwy 'credible'	*moladwy* 'praiseworthy'
cyraeddadwy 'attainable'	*bwytadwy* 'edible'
gweladwy 'visible'	*ofnadwy* 'terrible'

The following have an active force:

safadwy 'stable'	*tyfadwy* 'growing well'
rhuadwy 'roaring'	

-ol

cadarnhaol 'affirmative'	*nacaol* 'negative'
arferol 'normal'	*gweithredol* 'active'
goddefol 'passive'	*dewisol* 'choice'
dymunol 'pleasant'	*boddhaol* 'satisfactory'
canlynol 'following'	*derbyniol* 'acceptable'
parhaol 'perpetual'	*andwyol* 'harmful'
diffygiol 'deficient'	*bygythiol* 'threatening'

-us

gwybodus 'knowledgeable'	*adnabyddus* 'well-known'
medrus 'capable'	*brawychus* 'terrifying'

Contraction occurs when the stem ends in a vowel; stress falls on the ultima:

chwareus 'playful'	*cyffrous* 'exciting'
ymarhous 'long-suffering'	*boddhaus* 'acceptable'

-ed, -ad

agored 'open'	*caead* 'closed'

-og
The suffix is added to the verb-noun in the following:

rhedegog 'flowing'	*galluog* 'able'
hedegog 'flying'	*chwerthinog* 'laughing'

The suffix is added to the stem in the following:

brathog 'biting'	*sefydlog* 'established'

-aidd
The suffix is added to the verb-noun:

caruaidd 'loved'

Note
A change of suffix may result in a change of meaning: *dealladwy* 'intelligible', *dealledig* 'understood'; *crogadwy* 'made to be hanged', *crogedig* 'hanging'; *arferol* 'usual', *arferedig* 'in use'; *boddhaol* 'pleasing, acceptable', *boddhaus* 'pleased, satisfied'; *parhaus* 'continual', *parhaol* 'continuing'.

(ii) The stem of the verb may operate as a verbal adjective:

Verb	Verbal adjective
anghofiaf 'I forget'	*angof* (also *anghofiedig*) 'forgotten'
bathaf 'I mint'	*bath* (also *bathedig*) 'minted'
berwaf 'I boil'	*berw* (also *berwedig*) 'boiling'
briwaf 'I smash'	*briw* (also *briwedig*) 'bruised'
canaf 'I sing'	*cân* 'sung'
cloaf 'I lock'	*clo* (also *cloëdig*) 'locked'
collaf 'I lose'	*coll* (also *colledig*) 'lost'
crogaf 'I hang'	*crog* (also *crogedig*) 'hanging'
cuddiaf 'I hide'	*cudd* (also *cuddedig*) 'hidden'
cysgaf 'I sleep'	*cwsg* 'sleeping'
chwalaf 'I scatter'	*chwâl* 'scattered'
gyrraf 'I drive'	*gyr* 'driven'
llosgaf 'I burn'	*llosg* 'burnt'
llusgaf 'I drag'	*llusg* 'dragged'
malaf 'I mince'	*mâl* 'ground'
naddaf 'I chip'	*nadd* 'carved'
pobaf 'I bake'	*pob* 'baked'
prynaf 'I buy'	*prŷn*, *pryn* 'bought'
rhostiaf 'I roast'	*rhost* 'roasted'
toddaf 'I melt'	*tawdd* 'molten'
troaf 'I turn'	*tro* (also *troëdig*, *troeog*) 'curved, turned'

Examples:

tir angof 'land of oblivion'   *arian bath* 'current money'
pwll tro 'whirlpool'   *maen clo* 'keystone'
mynydd llosg 'volcano'   *tatws pob* 'baked potatoes'
cerrig nadd 'carved stones'   *teisen brŷn* 'bought (shop) cake'
haearn tawdd 'molten iron'   *haearn gyr* 'wrought iron'
car llusg 'sled'

331 Byw, Marw. These may function as verb-nouns, nouns and adjectives.

(i) Verb-noun

Yr oedd y ferch wedi marw
'The girl had died'
(T. Glynne Davies, 1974: 11)

Yr wyf i'n byw
'I live'
    (John 6: 57)

(ii) Adjective

creaduriaid byw y môr
'the living creatures of the sea'
    (Rev. 8: 9)

draenog marw
'a dead hedgehog'

(iii) Noun

yn fy myw
'in my lifetime'

Cododd y marw ar ei eistedd
'The dead (man) sat up'
    (Luke 7: 15)

Dy fab di yw'r marw; fy mab i yw'r byw
'The dead is your son; the living is my son'
    (1 Kgs. 3: 22)

On mutation of *byw* and *marw* following initial *b-* in forms of *bod* 'to be' see **99**.

Note
In the literary language *byw* and *marw* do not have inflected forms but they may function as simple verbs in varieties of spoken Welsh: *mi fywith* 'he will live'; *fe farwodd* 'he died'.

Compounds

Introduction

332 Compounds occur in the following combinations:

(i) noun + noun
Examples:

gweithdy	(< *gwaith* + *tŷ*)	'workshop'
marchnerth	(< *march* + *nerth*)	'horsepower'
creigle	(< *craig* + *lle*)	'rocky place'
dwyreinwynt	(< *dwyrain* + *gwynt*)	'east wind'

(ii) adj. + noun
Examples:

glasfryn	(< *glas* + *bryn*)	'green hill'
glaslanc	(< *glas* + *llanc*)	'youth'
glanwedd	(< *glân* + *gwedd*)	'handsome'

(iii) adj. + adj.
Examples:

dugoch	(< *du* + *coch*)	'dark red'
llwydlas	(< *llwyd* + *glas*)	'greyish-blue'
glasddu	(< *glas* + *du*)	'bluish-black'
gwyrddlas	(< *gwyrdd* + *glas*)	'dark green'

(iv) noun + adj.
Examples:

troednoeth	(< *troed* + *noeth*)	'barefoot'
pendew	(< *pen* + *tew*)	'stupid'
blaenllym	(< *blaen* + *llym*)	'pointed'
hindda	(< *hin* + *da*)	'fair weather'

(v) noun + verb
Examples:

clustfeinio	(< *clust* + *meinio*)	'listen closely'
croesholi	(< *croes* + *holi*)	'cross-examine'
llygadrythu	(< *llygad* + *rhythu*)	'stare'

(vi) adj. + verb
Examples:

cyflym redeg	(< *cyflym* + *rhedeg*)	'run quickly'
prysur weithio	(< *prysur* + *gweithio*)	'busily working'

(vii) prefix + noun/adj./verb. See **137**.
Examples:

cyfran	(< *cyf-* + *rhan*)	'share'
addfwyn	(< *add-* + *mwyn*)	'pleasant'
ymladd	(< *ym-* + *lladd*)	'fight'

333 Proper and Improper Compounds

(i) Proper Compounds

A proper compound is formed when the first element of the compound qualifies the second; the second element in the compound, however, dictates what part of speech the compound is. For example, *glaslanc* 'youth' is a noun because *llanc* is a noun; *blaenllym* 'pointed' is an adjective because *llym* is an adjective. The initial of the second element is subject to soft mutation (see **47, 51**), except where radical *-ll-* or *-rh-* remain following *n* or *r*:

gwinllan	'vineyard'
perllan	'orchard'
penrhyn	'promontory'

Provection may occur: see **153**.

In strict compounds stress falls on the penult:

ffermdy	'farmhouse'
canhwyllbren	'candlestick'

Provection occurs in certain combinations: see **154**.

The following changes also occur:

f – ff > ff: prif + ffordd   *priffordd* 'highway'
th – dd > th: gwrth + ddrych   *gwrthrych* 'object'

Since stress falls on the initial element, in this type of compound an initial *h* is lost from the second element:

mor + hesg	*moresg* 'sea-sedges'

In loose compounds stress falls on both elements of the compound.
The loose compound may consist of

(a) two separate words, the first being an adjective:

hen ddyn	'old man'
hoff beth	'favourite thing'
ail waith	'second time'

See **51, 191, 206**.

A verb-noun or verb may occur as second element:

prysur baratoi	'busily prepare'
cyflym yrrodd	'he drove at speed'

(b) two words linked by a hyphen:

ôl-ysgrif	'postscript'
môr-forwyn	'mermaid'
cyn-olygydd	'former editor'
ail-greu	're-create'
llwyd-felyn	'beige'

See **44**.

(c) one word, but with secondary stress on the initial element of the compound:

camddefnydd	'misuse'
camarweiniol	'misleading'
prifysgol	'university'
prifathro	'head teacher, principal'

camargraff	'false impression'
camgymryd	'err'
camgyhuddiad	'false accusation'

A loose compound consisting of a noun and a verb or verb-noun is also written as one word:

llygadrythu	'stare'
croesholi	'cross-examine'
bolaheulo	'sunbathe'
ochrgamodd	'he side-stepped'
llofnodaf	'I sign'

(ii) Improper Compounds

In proper compounds the second element normally selects soft mutation: see **51**, and (i) above. In improper compounds mutation only occurs if the initial element of the compound regularly projects mutation. Stress normally occurs on the penult:

(a) adjectives following fem. sing. nouns (see **50**):

gwreigdda	(< *gwraig* + *da*)	'good woman'
gwrda	(< *gŵr* + *da*)	'good man'
hindda	(< *hin* + *da*)	'good weather'
heulwen	(< *haul* + *gwen*)	'sunshine'

Note
Haul 'sun' was formerly a fem. sing. noun.

(b) nouns following certain numerals (see **204** (iii)):

dwybunt	(< *dwy* + *punt*)	'£2'
deubwys	(< *dau* + *pwys*)	'2 lbs'
trichant	(< *tri* + *cant*)	'300'
chwephunt	(< *chwe* + *punt*)	'£6'
canpunt	(< *cant* + *punt*)	'£100'

(c) Many adverbs and prepositions are improper compounds:

weithion	(< *y* + *gwaith* + *hon*)	'now'
unwaith	(< *un* + *gwaith*)	'once'
rhywdro	(< *rhyw* + *tro*)	'sometime'
rhywbryd	(< *rhyw* + *pryd*)	'sometime'
gyda	(< *cyd* + *â*)	'with'
ichi	(< *i* + *chi*)	'for you'

(d) Place-names consisting of a noun + adj. or a noun + dependent noun are also improper compounds:

Drefach	(< *tre* + *bach*)
Llanfor	(< *llan* + *mor*)
Llanfair	(< *llan* + *Mair*)

Note
Penrhos with stress on the penult is an improper compound: *Penrhos* with stress on both elements is a proper compound.

(e) Stress occurs on the ultima in:

prynhawn	(*pryd* + *nawn*)	'afternoon'
heblaw	(*heb* + *llaw*)	'besides'
ymlaen	(*yn* + *blaen*)	'forward'
gerllaw	(*ger* + *llaw*)	'near'
gerbron	(*ger* + *bron*)	'before'
ynghlwm	(*yn* + *clwm*)	'tied'
drachefn	(*tra* + *cefn*)	'again'

Sentence and Clause Structure

Pre-Verbal Particles

Affirmative

334 Y(r). *Y* is selected before consonants, *yr* before vowels and *h-*.

(i) In affirmative simple statements before the pres. and imperf. indic. of *bod* 'to be' (see **284**):

> *Y mae'r dyfyniadau Saesneg cyn amled, os nad amlach na'r rhai Cymraeg*
> 'The English quotations are as numerous as, if not more numerous than the Welsh ones'
> > (Hywel Teifi Edwards, 1989: ix)

> *Yr oedd gofyn iddynt dyngu'r un llwon â'u cymrodyr Seisnig*
> 'They were required to swear the same oaths as their English colleagues'
> > (Geraint H. Jenkins, 1983: 97)

(ii) To introduce a noun clause (see **353** (ii)):

> *Ofnwn y byddai'n anodd cael enillydd clir*
> 'I feared that it would be difficult to have a clear winner'
> > (J. Elwyn Hughes, 1989: 78)

Gwyddwn y cawn groeso ganddynt
'I knew that I would be welcomed by them'
(Kate Roberts, 1976: 24)

(iii) In oblique relative clauses (see **229–232**):

Gwyddai fod yr esgus y bu'n aros amdano wedi cyrraedd
'She knew that the excuse that she had been waiting for had arrived'
(Jane Edwards, 1976: 157)

(iv) In an adverbial clause following *er*, *am*, *hyd nes*, *fel*, etc. (see **410**):

Ni fyddai hi byth yn mynd ar gyfyl na chapel na llan, er y byddai yn gweddïo bob nos a bore
'She never went near chapel or church, although she prayed every night and morning'
(T. Glynne Davies, 1974: 46)

Cydsyniodd Cristion am y gwyddai yn ei galon fod yr hyn a ddywedai ei gyfaill yn wir
'Christian agreed because he knew in his heart that what his friend was saying was true'
(John Bunyan, 1962: 61)

Aros yno hyd nes y clywi di Dewi a Cybi a Beuno yn siarad â thi
'Wait there until you hear Dewi and Cybi and Beuno speaking to you'
(J. G. Williams, 1978: 9)

Fel y nesaem at y cylch gwelwn y cerrig anferth fel cewri byw yn ymestyn tua'r ffurfafen
'As we approached the circle I could see the huge stones like living giants reaching towards the sky'
(Rhiannon Davies Jones, 1977: 21)

(v) Following an adverb or adverbial phrase in a mixed sentence or in an abnormal sentence:

(a) Mixed sentence (see **352**):

Yma yn y gwyll gwyrdd yr eisteddodd fy holl ragflaenwyr er pan sefydlwyd Bethania
'Here in the green twilight all my predecessors sat since Bethania was founded'
(Emyr Humphreys, 1981: 71)

Wrth eu ffrwythau yr adnabyddwch hwy
'By their fruits will you recognize them'
(Matt. 7: 16)

(b) Abnormal sentence (see **351**):

Am hynny y digiais wrth y genhedlaeth honno (1955)
'Because of that I was indignant with that generation'
(Heb. 3: 10)

A'r bore yr aeth Jonathan i'r maes (1955)
'And in the morning Jonathan went to the field'
(1 Sam. 20: 35)

Yn 1604 ymadawodd â Morgan er mwyn mynd yn Rheithor Mallwyd yn sir Feirionydd, ac yno y bu am y deugain mlynedd a oedd yn weddill o'i oes: yno y tyfodd yn bennaf ysgolhaig ieithyddol y Dadeni yng Nghymru
'In 1604 he left Morgan in order to become Rector of Mallwyd in Meirionethshire, and there he remained for the forty years which remained of his life: there he developed into the chief linguistic scholar of the Renaissance in Wales'
(R. Geraint Gruffydd, 1988: 35)

335 A. The particle *a* precedes the verb in an abnormal sentence:

A Duw a ddywedodd, Bydded goleuni, a goleuni a fu (1955)
'And God said, Let there be light, and there was light'
(Gen. 1: 3)

Jonathan a gyfododd oddi wrth y bwrdd mewn llid dicllon (1955)
'Jonathan left the table in a rage'
(1 Sam. 20: 34)

On mutation following the particle see **72**.

336 Fe, mi

Fe laddwyd fy nhad cyn imi gael fy ngeni
'My father was killed before I was born'
(Rhiannon Thomas, 1988: 35)

Mi gei boen bol os bwyti di ormod o siwgr
'You will have stomach-ache if you eat too much sugar'
(Rhiannon Davies Jones, 1985: 52)

On mutation following *mi, fe*, see **80**.

In formal texts *mi*, *fe* cannot replace *yr*, *y* before the pres. and imperf. indic. of *bod* 'to be'. In informal texts and in varieties of spoken Welsh *mi* may:

(i) be selected in place of *y(r)*:

> *Mi wyt ti wedi brifo dy fam*
> 'You have hurt your mother'
>> (Eigra Lewis Roberts, 1988: 57)

> *Mi oedd ei lais yn glir fel cloch*
> 'His voice was clear like a bell'
>> (*Y Faner*, 2 Rhagfyr 1988: 11)

(ii) be selected with *'r*:

> *Mi 'roedd Lewis yn casáu'r Saeson*
> 'Lewis hated the English'
>> (Rhiannon Davies Jones, 1985: 107)

> *Mi roeddwn i'n disgwyl babi*
> 'I was expecting a baby'
>> (Rhiannon Thomas, 1988: 117)

> *Mi rwyt ti'n uchelgeisiol a balch*
> 'You are ambitious and vain'
>> (Rhiannon Davies Jones, 1989: 61)

Note
Mi is never selected with *mae*, *maent*.

Negative

337 Ni(d), na(d). Before a verb with an initial vowel corresponding to a form with an initial *g-* that is lost as a result of soft mutation (see **47**), *ni*, *na* are used.

> *Ni allwn ddweud yr un gair*
> 'I could not utter one word'
>> (Harri Williams, 1978: 21)

> *Mi wn i na wnaiff Mr Edwards ddweud dim wrth neb*
> 'I know that Mr Edwards will not tell anyone'
>> (Kate Roberts, 1976: 26)

Examples also occur of *ni*, *na* preceding an initial vowel that is not the result of soft mutation (see T. J. Morgan, 1952: 361–3).

(i) In a main clause preceding a verb *ni* occurs before consonants, *nid* before vowels. *Nid* is selected before other parts of speech:

Ni chymerai honno unrhyw ddiddordeb
'That one took no notice'
(Kate Roberts, 1972: 25)

Ni hoffai acen estron eu Saesneg
'He did not like the foreign accent of their English'
(Emyr Humphreys, 1986: 16)

Nid oedd ei chwerwedd wedi pylu dim
'His bitterness had not subdued at all'
(Rhiannon Davies Jones, 1989: 78)

Nid dau frawd oeddynt
'They were not two brothers'
(*Taliesin*, Tachwedd 1989: 15)

Nid aur popeth melyn
'All that glitters (is) not gold'
(Proverb)

Nid Dafydd sydd yn y tŷ
'It isn't Dafydd who is in the house'

In varieties of spoken Welsh and informal texts the negative preceding *bod* 'to be', with an initial vowel, is realized by *d . . . ddim*:

Doeddem ni ddim yn cario offer atal cenhedlu
'We were not carrying contraceptives'
(R. Gerallt Jones, 1977: 19)

Dwy ddim am ei chondemnio am hynny
'I do not wish to condemn her for that'
(Robat Gruffudd, 1986: 16)

In informal spoken Welsh *ni* may occur in negative emphatic statements:

Ni fydda i yno
'I shall not be there'

Ni yfiff e
'He will not drink'

Ni chei di fynd
'You will not (be allowed to) go'

See also **256** (iv), **278** (vi).

(ii) At the beginning of a negative mixed sentence (see **352**) *nid* is selected:

Nid wrth ei big y prynir cyffylog
'It is not by its beak that a woodcock is bought'
(Proverb)

Nid nhw sy'n talu am ei betrol o
'It is not they who pay for his petrol'
(Idwal Jones, n.d.: 54)

Nid ar fara yn unig y bydd dyn fyw
'It is not on bread alone that man will live'
(Matt. 4: 4)

See also **81** (ii).

(iii) In a noun clause (see **353**) *na(d)* occurs:

Gwyddost nad hawdd yw'r dasg sy'n dy aros
'You know that the task that awaits you is not easy'
(John Bunyan, 1962: 21)

Darganfu ei gymdogion yn fuan iawn nad oedd y dieithryn yn ddyn croesawgar iawn
'His neighbours soon discovered that the stranger was not a very hospitable man'
(T. Llew Jones, 1977: 27)

(iv) In a relative clause both *ni(d)* and *na(d)* occur (see **225**, **231**):

Gwyn ei fyd y gŵr ni rodia yng nghyngor yr annuwiolion (1955)
Gwyn ei fyd y gŵr nad yw'n dilyn cyngor y drygionus (1988)
'Happy is the man who does not walk in the counsel of the ungodly'
(Ps. 1: 1)

Pa wleidydd (gwrywaidd) na fyddai'n ochri ag ef?
'What (male) politician would not support him?'
(*Golwg*, 20 Ebrill 1989: 19)

(v) In an adverbial clause following a prep. or conj. (see **410**) *na(d)* occurs:

Yr oeddwn i'n mwynhau'r te, er nad oedd dim ond arlliw o fenyn ar y frechdan
'I was enjoying the tea, although there was merely a hint of butter on the sandwich'
(Kate Roberts, 1976: 25)

Penliniais innau'n ufudd gan na feiddiwn groesi Gwladus
'I knelt obediently because I dared not cross Gwladus'
(Rhiannon Davies Jones, 1977: 22)

(vi) In questions following *paham, pa fodd, sut, na(d)* occurs:

Pam na ddylai dyn ddangos yn eglur ac yn gyhoeddus dros bwy yr oedd yn pleidleisio?
'Why should a man not show clearly and publicly for whom he was voting?'
(T. Glynne Davies, 1974: 27)

Pam nad ei di i Gaersalem efo'r Distain?
'Why don't you go to Jerusalem with the Principal Steward?'
(Rhiannon Davies Jones, 1987: 111)

Pa fodd nad ofnaist ti estyn dy law i ddifetha eneiniog yr Arglwydd? (1955)
Sut na fyddai arnat ofn estyn dy law i ddistrywio eneiniog yr Arglwydd? (1988)
'How was it that you were not afraid to stretch out your hand to destroy the Lord's anointed?'
(2 Sam. 1: 14)

For additional examples see **235**.

(vii) Following the conjunction *pe, na(d)* occurs (see **312**):

Yn nhŷ fy nhad y mae llawer o drigfannau; pe na byddai felly, a fyddwn i wedi dweud wrthych . . .?
'In my Father's house there are many dwelling-places; if it were not so, would I have told you . . .?'
(John 14: 2)

Fyddwn i ddim wedi cymryd hynny pe na bai mam mor dynn gyda'i phres
'I would not have taken that had not mother been so mean with her money'
(Irma Chilton, 1989: 21)

The infixed accusative pronoun -*s* may be affixed to *pe na*:

da fuasai i'r dyn hwnnw pe nas ganesid ef (1955)
'it would have been better for that man if he had never been born'
(Matt. 26: 24)

(viii)   With interjections (see **312** (ii)):

> *O na fyddai fy mhobl yn gwrando arnaf*
> 'O that my people would listen to me'
>   (Ps. 81: 13)

(ix)   The conjunction *o* is joined to *ni(d)* to form the conjunction *oni(d)*, 'if not, unless' (see **415** (iv)):

> *Ni allai neb wneud yr arwyddion hyn yr wyt ti'n eu gwneud oni bai fod Duw gydag ef*
> 'No one could perform these signs that you do unless God were with him'
>   (John 3: 2)

On mutation following *ni*, *na* see **87, 115**.

338   Na(c). *Nac* (pronounced [nag]) is selected before a vowel, *na* is selected before a consonant:

(i)   *Na(c)* precedes imperative verbs:

> *Na chuddia fy ngwaed*
> 'Do not cover my blood'
>   (Job 16: 18)

> *Nac anghofia'r anghenus*
> 'Do not forget the needy'
>   (Ps. 10: 12)

> *Nac italeiddier enwau llawysgrifau*
> 'Do not italicize names of manuscripts'
>   (*Llên Cymru*, 17: 185)

See **313** (iv).

(ii)   *Na(c)* occurs in negative replies (see **342**).

> *Oes yna deilyngdod? Nac oes meddai Nesta Wyn Jones.*
> *Oes yn fy marn i*
> 'Is there merit? No says Nesta Wyn Jones.
> Yes in my opinion'
>   (J. Elwyn Hughes, 1989: 27)

> *A ddihengi di yn ddigerydd? Na ddihengi* (1955)
> *A ddihengi di yn ddigerydd? Na wnei* (1988)
> 'Will you escape unpunished? No'
>   (Jer. 49: 12)

A fydd yno gwmni? Na fydd
'Will there be company there? No'

On mutation following *na* see **87, 115**.

Interrogative

339 A. *A* precedes the verb in direct and indirect questions:

A wyf yn euog o gamliwio?
'Am I guilty of misrepresentation?'
(*Y Faner*, Chwefror 1990: 12)

Gofynnais a oedd ganddynt ryw newydd
'I asked whether they had any news'
(Kate Roberts, 1976: 25)

The particle may be omitted:

Ydych chi wedi bod yn yfed?
'Have you been drinking?'
(Emyr Humphreys, 1986: 93)

Ysai Harri am ofyn iddo oedd o mor hapus ag yr ymddangosai
'Harri yearned to ask him whether he was as happy as he appeared to be'
(John Rowlands, 1978: 161)

On mutation following the interrogative particle *a* see **91**.

Note
In varieties of spoken Welsh *os* 'if' may occur instead of *a* in indirect questions: *Gofynnodd os oedd ganddo rywbeth i'w wneud* 'He asked whether (if) he had something to do'.

340 Oni(d). Preceding a verb *oni* is selected before consonants, *onid* before vowels. *Onid* occurs before other parts of speech. *Oni(d)* introduces a question which expects an affirmative answer:

On'd oedd yna sicrwydd cynnes yn y geiriau?
'Wasn't there a comforting assurance in the words?'
(Marion Eames, 1992: 9)

Oni thywelltaist fi fel llaeth a'm ceulo fel caws?
'Didst thou not pour me out like milk and curdle me like cheese?'
(Job 10: 10)

Oni wyddoch? Oni chlywsoch? Oni fynegwyd i chwi o'r dechreuad?
'Do you not know? Have you not heard? Have you not been told from the beginning?'
(Isa. 40: 21)

Onid Galileaid yw'r rhain oll sy'n llefaru?
'Are not all these who are speaking Galileans?'
(Acts 2: 7)

Onid er mwyn chwilio'r ddinas a'i hysbïo a'i goresgyn yr anfonodd Dafydd ei weision atat?
'Is it not to search the city and spy it out and overthrow it that David sent his servants to you?'
(2 Sam. 10: 3)

Onid hwn yw'r saer . . . ?
'Is not this the carpenter . . . ?'
(Mark 6: 3)

Onid o daith y daethost ti?
'Have you not come from a journey?'
(2 Sam. 11: 10)

On mutation following *oni* see **92, 121**.

Onid e? may follow a statement and make it interrogative:

Dyna i chwi gyd-ddigwyddiad onid e?
'That is a coincidence for you, is it not?'
(*Barn*, Awst/Medi 1991: 58)

Hwn yw'r saer, onid e?
'This is the carpenter, it is not?'

In varieties of spoken Welsh and informal texts *ynte?*, *yntefe?*, *ontefe?* occur instead of *onid e?*: *Dyna beth ydi o ynte?* 'That is what it is isn't it?' (*Y Faner*, 23 Chwefror 1990: 6).

341 Ai. In a direct or indirect question any part of speech other than a verb may follow *ai*:

Ai sumbol o waed y Cymry yw'r Môr Coch?
'Is the Red Sea a symbol of the blood of the Welsh?'
(*Y Faner*, 4 Hydref 1991: 8)

Ai ti yw Elias?
'Are you Elias?'
(John 1: 21)

Ai mewn heddwch yr wyt yn dod?
'Is it in peace that you come?'
(1 Kgs. 2: 13)

In a double question *ai . . . ai* occurs:

Arglwydd, ai i ni yr wyt yn adrodd y ddameg hon, ai i bawb yn ogystal?
'Lord, are you telling us this parable, or is it for everyone?'
(Luke 12: 41)

Nid may follow *ai* in a double question:

A yw'n gyfreithlon talu treth i Gesar, ai nid yw?
'Is it legal to pay tax to Caesar, or is it not?'
(Matt. 22: 17)

Pa un (or a contracted form) + *ai . . . ai/neu/(neu) ynteu* also occur:

Prun sydd orau, ai bod yn offeiriad i un teulu, ynteu'n offeiriad i lwyth a thylwyth yn Israel?
'Which is best, to be a priest to one family, or to be a priest to a tribe and a family in Israel?'
(Judg. 18: 19)

pa un ai yn y corff, ai allan o'r corff, ni wn i (1955)
'whether in the body, or out of the body, I do not know'
(2 Cor 12: 3)

For further examples see **84**.

Pa un bynnag may introduce the alternatives in indirect questions:

Pa un bynnag yr ydym ai byw ai marw, eiddo yr Arglwydd ydym (1955)
Prun bynnag ai byw ai marw ydym, eiddo'r Arglwydd ydym (1988)
'Whether we live or die, we belong to the Lord'
(Rom. 14: 8)

Ai e? may follow a statement and turn it interrogative:

Panel oedd gynnoch chi heno, ai e?
'It's a panel you had tonight, is it not?'
(*Barn*, Ebrill 1990: 14)

Ai e? as a question expresses amazement or doubt:

> *Dyma dy waith gorau. Ai e?*
> 'This is your best work. Is that so?'

For *naill ai . . . neu* see **238**.

Responses

342 In Welsh the choice of response is dependent on the clause structure of the interrogative clause. When the simple verb predicator is realized by a tense other than the preterite (see **344**), the response consists of a repetition, in phase, of the verbal form realizing the predicator in the interrogative clause, i.e. the verbal form of the response has the same tense as the verbal form in the interrogative clause, but makes relevant adjustments as regards person and number. The interrogative markers are *a* (see **339**) and *oni*(*d*) (see **340**); *a* causes soft mutation (see **91**), and *oni*(*d*) causes aspirate mutation of *c, p, t* (see **121**) and soft mutation of *g, b, d, m, ll, rh* (see **92**). The negative response marker is *na*(*c*) (see **338**); *na*(*c*) again causes aspirate mutation of *c, p, t* (see **115**) and soft mutation of *g, b, d, m, ll, rh* (see **87**).

Statement	*Gellwch chi ddarllen*	'You can read'
Interrogative	*A ellwch chi ddarllen?*	'Can you read?'
	Oni ellwch chi ddarllen?	'Can't you read?'
Responses	*Gallaf*	'Yes'
	Na allaf	'No'
Statement	*Gweithiant hwy*	'They will work'
Interrogative	*A weithiant hwy?*	'Will they work?'
	Oni weithiant hwy?	'Won't they work?'
Responses	*Gweithiant*	'Yes'
	Na weithiant	'No'
Statement	*Daw'r postmon heddiw*	'The postman will come today'
Interrogative	*A ddaw'r postmon heddiw?*	'Will the postman come today?'
	Oni ddaw'r postmon heddiw?	'Won't the postman come today?'
Responses	*Daw*	'Yes'
	Na ddaw	'No'

The person-number category of the response must exhibit concord with the noun realizing the subject:

Statement	*Yr oedd y plentyn*	'The child was'
Interrogative	*A oedd y plentyn?*	'Was the child?'
	Onid oedd y plentyn?	'Wasn't the child?'
Responses	*Oedd*	'Yes'
	Nac oedd	'No'

Statement	*Yr oedd y plant*	'The children were'
Interrogative	*A oedd y plant?*	'Were the children?'
	Onid oedd y plant?	'Weren't the children?'
Responses	*Oeddent*	'Yes'
	Nac oeddent	'No'

Statement	*Yr oedd hi*	'She was'
Interrogative	*A oedd hi?*	'Was she?'
	Onid oedd hi?	'Wasn't she?'
Responses	*Oedd*	'Yes'
	Nac oedd	'No'

Statement	*Yr oeddent hwy*	'They were'
Interrogative	*A oeddent hwy?*	'Were they?'
	Onid oeddent hwy?	'Weren't they?'
Responses	*Oeddent*	'Yes'
	Nac oeddent	'No'

Statement	*Caiff y dyn syndod*	'The man will have a surprise'
Interrogative	*A gaiff y dyn syndod?*	'Will the man have a surprise?'
	Oni chaiff y dyn syndod?	'Won't the man have a surprise?'
Responses	*Caiff*	'Yes'
	Na chaiff	'No'

Statement	*Caiff y dynion syndod*	'The men will have a surprise'
Interrogative	*A gaiff y dynion syndod?*	'Will the men have a surprise?'
	Oni chaiff y dynion syndod?	'Won't the men have a surprise?'

Responses	*Cânt*	'Yes'
	Na chânt	'No'
Statement	*Caiff ef syndod*	'He will have a surprise'
Interrogative	*A gaiff ef syndod?*	'Will he have a surprise?'
	Oni chaiff ef syndod?	'Won't he have a surprise?'
Responses	*Caiff*	'Yes'
	Na chaiff	'No'
Statement	*Cânt hwy syndod*	'They will have a surprise'
Interrogative	*A gânt hwy syndod?*	'Will they have a surprise?'
	Oni chânt hwy syndod?	'Won't they have a surprise?'
Responses	*Cânt*	'Yes'
	Na chânt	'No'

All varieties of Welsh, apart from a highly literary text, will select the appropriate inflected form of *gwneud* 'to do' (see **294**) as response forms whatever the verb in the interrogative clause:

Interrogative	*A ddarllenwch chi?*	'Will you read?'
	Oni ddarllenwch chi?	'Won't you read?'
Responses	*Gwnaf*	'Yes'
	Na wnaf	'No'
Interrogative	*A gredwn ni?*	'Will we believe?'
	Oni chredwn ni?	'Won't we believe?'
Responses	*Gwnawn*	'Yes'
	Na wnawn	'No'
Interrogative	*A ddarllena'r plant?*	'Will the children read?'
	Oni ddarllena'r plant?	'Won't the children read?'
Responses	*Gwnânt*	'Yes'
	Na wnânt	'No'
Interrogative	*A ddarllenant hwy?*	'Will they read?'
	Oni ddarllenant hwy?	'Won't they read?'

Responses	*Gwnânt*	'Yes'
	Na wnânt	'No'

The *gwneud* response, however, is impossible for certain verbs including *bod* 'to be'; *gwybod* 'know (facts)'; *gallu, medru* 'be able'; *cael* 'have'.

In polite requests *gwneud* 'to do' assumes the function of an auxiliary verb and the following verb-noun is subject to soft mutation:

Interrogative	*A wnewch chi ddarllen?*	'Will you read?'
	Oni wnewch chi ddarllen?	'Won't you read?'
Responses	*Gwnaf*	'Yes'
	Na wnaf	'No'
Interrogative	*A wna'r plant ddarllen?*	'Will the children read?'
	Oni wna'r plant ddarllen?	'Won't the children read?'
Responses	*Gwnânt*	'Yes'
	Na wnânt	'No'
Interrogative	*A wnant hwy ddarllen?*	'Will they read?'
	Oni wnant hwy ddarllen?	'Won't they read?'
Responses	*Gwnânt*	'Yes'
	Na wnânt	'No'

343 The same broad pattern as above is maintained in the periphrastic construction, but the response is supplied by the auxiliary verb *bod* 'to be'. *Yr* is not selected in responses or interrogatives:

Statement	*Yr oedd ef yn darllen*	'He was reading'
Interrogative	*A oedd ef yn darllen?*	'Was he reading?'
	Onid oedd ef yn darllen?	'Wasn't he reading?'
Responses	*Oedd*	'Yes'
	Nac oedd	'No'

The present tense responses are:

Singular:	1	*Ydwyf / ydw*	Plural:	1	*Ydym*
	2	*Ydwyt / wyt*		2	*Ydych*
	3	*Ydyw / ydy*		3	*Ydyn(t)*

The 3 person sing. of the interrogative is realized by *yw/ydyw* and the 3 person pl. by *ydyn(t)*:

Statement	*Y mae ef yn gyrru*	'He is driving'
Interrogative	*A yw ef yn gyrru?*	'Is he driving?'
	Onid yw ef yn gyrru?	'Isn't he driving?'
Responses	*Ydyw*	'Yes'
	Nac ydyw	'No'
Statement	*Y maent hwy'n darllen*	'They are reading'
Interrogative	*A ydynt hwy'n darllen?*	'Are they reading?'
	Onid ydynt hwy'n darllen?	'Aren't they reading?'
Responses	*Ydynt*	'Yes'
	Nac ydynt	'No'
Statement	*Byddi di'n aros*	'You will be staying'
Interrogative	*A fyddi di'n aros?*	'Will you be staying?'
	Oni fyddi di'n aros?	"Won't you be staying?'
Responses	*Byddaf*	'Yes'
	Na fyddaf	'No'
Statement	*Bydd y plentyn yn canu*	'The child will be singing'
Interrogative	*A fydd y plentyn yn canu?*	'Will the child be singing?'
	Oni fydd y plentyn yn canu?	"Won't the child be singing?'
Responses	*Bydd*	'Yes'
	Na fydd	'No'
Statement	*Bydd y plant yn canu*	'The children will be singing'
Interrogative	*A fydd y plant yn canu?*	'Will the children be singing?'
	Oni fydd y plant yn canu?	"Won't the children be singing?'
Responses	*Byddant*	'Yes'
	Na fyddant	'No'
Statement	*Bydd hi'n canu*	'She will be singing'
Interrogative	*A fydd hi'n canu?*	'Will she be singing?'

	Oni fydd hi'n canu?	'Won't she be singing?'
Responses	*Bydd*	'Yes'
	Na fydd	'No'

Statement	*Byddant hwy'n canu*	'They will be singing'
Interrogative	*A fyddant hwy'n canu?*	'Will they be singing?'
	Oni fyddant hwy'n canu?	'Won't they be singing?'
Responses	*Byddant*	'Yes'
	Na fyddant	'No'

344 When the preterite tense is selected in the interrogative clause, the response is *do* 'yes', *naddo* 'no':

Interrogative	*A ddaeth ef?*	'Did he come?'
	Oni ddaeth ef?	'Didn't he come?'
Responses	*Do*	'Yes'
	Naddo	'No'

Interrogative	*A welaist ti'r ras?*	'Did you see the race?'
	Oni welaist ti'r ras?	'Didn't you see the race?'
Responses	*Do*	'Yes'
	Naddo	'No'

Interrogative	*A brynodd hi'r beic?*	'Did she buy the bike?'
	Oni phrynodd hi'r beic?	'Didn't she buy the bike?'
Responses	*Do*	'Yes'
	Naddo	'No'

Interrogative	*A fuost ti'n siopa?*	'Have you been shopping?'
	Oni fuost ti'n siopa?	'Haven't you been shopping?'
Responses	*Do*	'Yes'
	Naddo	'No'

Note
In varieties of northern Welsh, past perfect interrogative clauses may select *do / naddo*. It is also a feature of earlier Biblical prose: *A ydych wedi deall yr holl bethau hyn? Dywedasant wrtho, 'Do'* (1955), *A*

ydych wedi deall yr holl bethau hyn? Dywedasant wrtho, 'Ydym' (1988), 'Have you understood all these things? They told him, Yes' (Matt. 13: 51).

345 When the subject of the present tense of the periphrastic verb is realized by an indefinite noun or a non-personal pronoun such as *neb* 'nobody', *rhai* 'some', *rhywun* 'someone', *rhywrai* 'some persons', *rhywbeth* 'something', the auxiliary verb is realized by *oes*. The response for these clauses is *oes* 'yes', *nac oes* 'no'.

Interrogative	*A oes rhywun yn gweithio?*	'Is someone working?'
	Onid oes rhywun yn gweithio?	'Isn't someone working?'
Responses	*Oes*	'Yes'
	Nac oes	'No'
Interrogative	*A oes plant yn canu?*	'Are children singing?'
	Onid oes plant yn canu?	'Aren't children singing?'
Responses	*Oes*	'Yes'
	Nac oes	'No'

346 When the interrogative clause is contrastive-emphatic, the positive interrogative particle is realized by *ai* (see **341**) and the negative interrogative particle is realized by *onid* (see **340**). Neither particle projects mutation. The response is *ie* 'yes', *nage* 'no':

Interrogative	*Ai dyn a oedd yn rhedeg?*	'Was it a man who was running?'
Responses	*Ie*	'Yes'
	Nage	'No'
Interrogative	*Onid y ferch sy'n canu?*	'Isn't it the girl who is singing?'
Responses	*Ie*	'Yes'
	Nage	'No'
Interrogative	*Ai ei lais a glywaist?*	'Is it his voice that you heard?'
Responses	*Ie*	'Yes'
	Nage	'No'

347 In speech the reply may be emphasized by repetition:

Interrogative	*A oes rhywun yn gweithio?*	'Is someone working?'
Response	*Oes, oes*	'Yes'
Interrogative	*A ddaeth ef?*	'Did he come?'
Response	*Do, do*	'Yes'
Interrogative	*A ddaw ef?*	'Will he come?'
Response	*Daw, daw*	'Yes'
Interrogative	*Ai merch oedd yn canu?*	'Was it a girl who was singing?'
Response	*Ie, ie*	'Yes'

The particle *mi/fe* (see **336**) is normally omitted in replies, but may occur if emphasis is required:

Interrogative	*A ddaw ef?*	'Will he come?'
Responses	*Daw, mi ddaw*	'Yes'
	Daw, fe ddaw	'Yes'

348 *Do, ie, ydyw, naddo, nage, nac ydyw, nac oes,* may occur with sentences which are not formal interrogatives, to express emphasis:

Llwyddaist yn anrhydeddus. Do, yn wir
'You succeeded honourably. Yes, indeed'

Dyma fochyn braf. Ie, braf iawn
'Here is a fine pig. Yes, very fine'

Naddo, ches i ddim cyfle
'No, I didn't have an opportunity'

Nage, nid fel yna mae ei gwneud hi
'No, that is not the way to do it'

Mae Hywel yn fardd. Ydy, yn fardd da iawn
'Hywel is a poet. Yes, a very good poet'

Nid oes un a wna ddaioni, nac oes, dim un
'There is no one who does good, no, not one'
    (Rom. 3: 12)

Ie, drosom yr âi dygyfor y tonnau
'Yes, over us the surging of the waves would go'
    (Ps. 124: 5)

Do, fe fentrais i'r dŵr yr eildro, ond nid i'r dwfn y tro hwnnw
'Yes, I ventured into the water the second time, but not into the deep that time'
   (*Y Faner*, 20/27 Rhagfyr 1991: 11)

Ni bydd neb yn cynnau cannwyll a'i chuddio â llestr neu ei dodi dan y gwely. Nage, ar ganhwyllbren y dodir hi
'Nobody lights a lamp and covers it with a basin or puts in under the bed. No, it is on a candlestick that it is placed'
   (Luke 8: 16)

Non-Predicator Clauses

349 Non-predicator clauses are nominal clauses having the structure C(omplement) + S(ubject).

(i) Non-predicator clauses are often proverbial or didactic in nature and as such are considered as universal present. The complement may be a noun, an adjective or a compared adjective; the subject may be a noun, verb-noun or nominalized clause:

Cyfaill blaidd / bugail diog
   C   S
'A wolf's friend a lazy shepherd'

Castell pawb / ei dŷ
   C   S
'Everyone's castle his house'

Hir / pob aros
 C   S
'Long every waiting'

Hardd / pob newydd
  C   S
'Beautiful all (that is) new'

Llwyr / y dial
  C   S
'Complete the vengeance'

Diau / y byddaf fi gyda thi
 C   S
'Surely I will be with you'

The subject may come between the parts which form the complement:

Haws / dringo / na disgyn
  C—   S   —C
'Easier to climb than descend'

Gwell / angau / na chywilydd
   C—   S   —C
'Better death than shame'

(ii) Other non-predicator clauses refer to actual present time:

Gwell / mynd
  C   S
'(It is) better to go'

Rhaid / mynd
  C   S
'(It is) necessary to go'

When a person marker is required the C-element may be followed by the prep. *i* or *gan* + a noun or the personal form of these prepositions, thus forming a C A(dverb) S structure as follows:

Rhaid i John fynd
'(It is) necessary for John to go, John must go'

Rhaid iddo fynd
'(It is) necessary for him to go, He must go'

Gwell ganddo aros
'He prefers to stay'

Gwell gan John aros
'John prefers to stay'

Hawdd inni gredu
'(It is) easy for us to believe'

Certain common idioms have this structure with *gan*:

da gennyf
'I'm glad'

drwg gennyf
'I'm sorry'

gwell gennyf
'I prefer'

gwaeth gennyf
'I like less'

anodd gennyf
'it's difficult for me'

hawdd gennyf
'it's easy for me'

syn gennyf
'I'm surprised'

rhyfedd gennyf
'it's strange to me, I'm surprised'

hyfryd gennyf
'it's pleasant to me, I'm delighted'

These occur in C S structure as:

Da / gennyf / eich gweld
C   A   S
'I'm glad to see you'

Anodd / gennyf / gytuno
C   A   S
'It's difficult for me to agree'

Hawdd / gennyf / gredu
C   A   S
'It's easy for me to believe'

Note
English requires a tense marker – the copula – for (i) and (ii) above.
Welsh does not.

(iii) An A(dverb) S(ubject) structure is also possible:

I ffwrdd / â chi!
A   S
'Away with you!'

Ymlaen / Llanelli!
A   S
'Forward Llanelli!'

I'r afon / â nhw!
  A   S
'Into the river with them!'

On negation of non-predicator clauses see **337**.

(iv) A verbal form, the copula, may be added to a non-predicator clause to express the category of tense.
    The verb *bod* 'to be' functions as copula.

(a) The copula may occur between the complement and subject thus forming a C(omplement) P(redicator) S(ubject) structure:

Hir / yw / pob aros
  C   P   S
'Long is every waiting!'

Llwyr / fydd / y dial
  C   P   S
'Complete will be the vengeance'

Hawdd / fuasai / inni gredu
  C   P   S
'It would have been easy for us to believe'

Rhaid / oedd / i John fynd
  C   P   S
'John had to go'

P always selects the 3 sing. in this type of construction. See also **279** (i).
    On mutation of *b-* forms of *bod* in copulative clauses see **75**.

(b) The copula also occurs initially and the clause takes the structure P C (A) S; the complement is preceded by the predicative *yn*. P selects the 3 sing. *mae, bydd* etc.:

Bydd / yn anodd / gennyf / gredu
  P   C   A   S
'It will be difficult for me to believe'

Mae / 'n well / mynd
  P   C   S
'It's better to go'

> *Yr oedd / yn rhaid / imi / aros*
> P   C   A   S
> 'It was necessary for me to wait'

On mutation following the predicative *yn* see **54**.

Notes

(1) The predicative *yn* is frequently omitted but the initial consonant of the complement still selects mutation: *bûm newynog . . . bûm ddieithr* (1955), *bûm yn newynog . . . bûm yn ddieithr* (1988) 'I had been hungry . . . I had been a stranger' (Matt. 25: 35); *nid yw ddoeth* (1955) 'he is not wise' (Prov. 20: 1), cf. *Nid yr oedrannus yn unig sydd ddoeth* 'It is not only the aged who are wise' (Job 32: 9). See **280**.

(2) The complement may be preceded by *ys*. This construction is rare in Middle Welsh (see D. Simon Evans, 1964: 139 n.1). The examples that occur in modern texts have a distinctly archaic flavour: *Ys truan o ddyn oeddwn!* 'A wretched man was I!' (Harri Williams, 1978: 30); *Ys cymysg o genedl ydym!* 'A mixed bag of a nation are we!' (*Llais Llyfrau*, Haf 1990: 3).

(c) When the complement is adverbial, it is not preceded by *yn*:

> *Mae / pawb / felly*
> P   S   A
> 'Everyone is like that'

> *Yr oedd / ei wyneb / fel y galchen*
> P   S   A
> 'His face was like lime'

> *Yr oeddent / mor ddu â'r fran*
> P + S   A
> 'They were as black as the crow'

The Verbal Sentence

350 The verb precedes the subject and may be preceded by a particle (see **334–340**).

(i) When the subject is realized by a noun, a demonstrative pronoun (see **236**) or one of the pronominalia (see **238–258**) the 3 sing. of the verb is selected (see **260**).

(ii) The personal ending of the verb may denote the subject (see **222**), but the verb is frequently followed by the auxiliary pronoun (see **221**). An independent pronoun may precede the verbal form (see **212** (iv)).

(iii) Impersonal forms vary for tense only and the agent of an impersonal verb is expressed by the prep. *gan* followed by a noun or by the personal form of the prep.; see **314**.

The Abnormal Sentence

351 In the abnormal sentence an unemphatic subject occupies initial position in an affirmative sentence, followed by an optional relatival particle that causes soft mutation of the following verb (see **72, 325** (ii), **335**). The verb agrees in number and person with the subject. The abnormal construction is found in Middle Welsh (see D. Simon Evans, 1964: 179–81) and examples abound in earlier Biblical prose:

> *A Job a atebodd ac a ddywedodd . . .* (1955)
> 'And Job answered and said . . .'
> > (Job 12: 1)

> *Hwy a welsant y mab bychan gyda Mair ei fam* (1955)
> 'They saw the young boy with Mary his mother'
> > (Matt. 2: 11)

> *A'i ddisgyblion a ddaethant ato* (1955)
> 'And his disciples came to him'
> > (Matt. 8: 25)

For examples of the abnormal construction adv. + *y* + verb see **334** (v).

Although prescriptive Welsh grammarians at the turn of the century discouraged use of the abnormal order, examples do occur in modern texts:

> *Chwi wyddoch na all y rhai sy'n mynd ar bererindod obeithio osgoi trwbwl a pherygl*
> 'You know that the ones who go on pilgrimage can not hope to avoid trouble and danger'
> > (John Bunyan, 1962: 43)

Chwi gofiwch pwy oedd yr hyfforddwr yn sicr
'You will certainly remember who the coach was'
   (*Y Faner*, 27 Hydref 1989: 21)

Chwi welwch fy mhwynt gobeithio!
'You see my point (I) hope!'
   (*Barn*, Hydref 1992: 6)

An unemphatic object may also precede the verb:

Chwi a alwyd o'ch gorchwyl
'You were summoned from your task'
   (Mair Wyn Hughes, 1983: 7)

Some of these examples have a distinct biblical or archaic flavour. The construction has been abandoned in the 1988 translation of the Welsh Bible. The abnormal order, however, is a feature of certain dialects in south Wales (see H. Lewis, 1931: 118–19; C. H. Thomas, 1975/76: 345–66; D. A. Thorne, 1976: 503; P. J. Brake, 1980: 365):

[di nabəðid i pan gweli di ði]
'You'll recognize her when you see her'

[χi wiðoχ χi]
'You know'

In varieties of spoken Welsh the simple independent pronoun usually realizes the subject in the abnormal order and the construction only occurs in affirmative sentences. Modern poetry also retains the feature but the restrictions relating to varieties of spoken Welsh do not operate.

The Mixed Sentence

352 In mixed structure any element of the clause may be marked for emphasis, and elements marked for emphasis appear initially in the clause. When the predicator is realized by an inflected verb and the S-element is marked for emphasis, the relative pronoun *a* occurs between the emphatic S and the verb. The relative pronoun projects soft mutation (see **73**) and the verb is always 3 sing.:

Afon Teifi a orlifodd ei glannau
'(It's) the river Teifi (that) overflowed its banks'

Y ceiliog a ganodd ei gân
'(It's) the cockerel (that) sang its song'

Y ceiliogod a ganodd eu caneuon
'(It's) the cockerels (that) sang their songs'

When O(bject) is emphatic, the relative pronoun occurs between the emphatic O and the inflected verb. The verb always agrees with its subject in person and number except when it is impersonal:

Ci a welodd y ffermwr
'(It's) a dog (that) the farmer saw'

Cath a welais i
'(It's) a cat (that) I saw'

Cath a welwyd
'(It's) a cat (that) was seen'

When A(dverb) is emphatic, the relative particle $y(r)$ precedes the inflected verb. The verb always agrees with its subject in person and number except when it is impersonal:

Ddoe y gweithiodd
'Yesterday he worked'

Ddoe y gweithiwyd
'Yesterday work was done'

Prin y gallech ei chlywed
'Hardly could you hear her'

I'w waith yr aeth
'To his work he went'

The A may be realized by an adjective:

Da y gwnaethost
'Well you did'

Da y'i gwnaethpwyd
'Well was it done'

Mor anrhydeddus y llwyddaist
'So honourably you succeeded'

Swynol y canai hi'r delyn
'Sweetly she played the harp'

When P is marked as emphatic, P is realized by the verb-noun and is followed by all the clause elements that normally follow P, giving the sequence P1 C P2 S. P2 is realized by an appropriate tense of *bod* 'to be' or *gwneud* 'do'; *bod* is preceded by the relative particle *yr* and *gwneud* by the relative pronoun *a*. A may either follow C or occur finally:

Astudio yn y llyfrgell y bydd hi heno
'Study in the library she will tonight'

Darllen y llyfr a wnaeth hi
'Read the book she did'

Darllen y llyfr a wnaed
'(It's) reading the book (that) was done'

Mynd i'r gwely a wnaf fi
'Go to bed I will'

In this construction *bod* 'to be' is a simple time referent, but the choice of *gwneud* implies a deliberate intention.

The 3 sing. present tense of *bod* 'to be' has a relatival form *sydd*, *sy* (see **227**, **280**). When the predicator of the emphatic clause is realized by the present tense of the syntactical verb, *sydd* is selected when S is marked for emphasis:

Arholiadau sydd yn poeni'r plant
'(It's) examinations (that) are worrying the children'

Ci sydd wedi lladd yr oen
'(It's) a dog (that) has killed the lamb'

In other tenses the relative pronoun *a* is selected to precede the auxiliary:

Ci a oedd wedi lladd yr oen
'(It's) a dog (that) had killed the lamb'

Arholiadau a fydd yn poeni myfyrwyr
'(It's) examinations (that) will worry students'

The relative pronoun may be omitted. When O is emphatic and followed by a periphrastic construction with *bod* it is followed by the relative particle *y(r)*, and *bod* 'to be' agrees in person and number with S. A possessive pronoun agreeing in number and gender with O must precede the verb-noun:

Tîm Cymru y byddaf fi'n eu cefnogi
'(It's) the Welsh team I shall support (lit. support them)'

Y ferch y byddem ni'n ei gweld
'(It's) the girl we would see (lit. see her)'

Y bachgen y byddem ni'n ei weld
'(It's) the boy we would see (lit. see him)'

Emphatic A is also followed by the relative particle *y(r)*:

Y prynhawn yma y byddaf fi'n mynd
'(It's) this afternoon (that) I'll go'

Yn y car yr oedd hi'n cysgu
'(It's) in the car (that) she was sleeping'

The Noun Clause

353 When a clause occurs as subject or object of a verb or is in apposition to a noun or pronoun, it is called a noun clause.

(A) Affirmative

The construction selected is dependent upon the tense of the verb in the main clause:

(i) When the verb in the main clause and the verb in the noun clause have the same time referent, or if the action of the noun clause is in the imperfect, the noun clause is introduced by *bod* 'to be':

Gwyddai fod pob un yn y gynulleidfa'n anelu'i wn tua ato
'He knew that every one in the congregation was pointing his gun towards him'
     (John Rowlands, 1965: 7)

Mi rydach chi'n gwybod bod Bob, ein brawd, yn byw yn Sir Fôn
'You know that Bob, our brother, lives in Anglesey'
     (Kate Roberts, 1976: 26)

Rydw i'n credu fod pob un ohonom yn wylo'n fewnol wrth fynd oddi ar y cae
'I believe that every one of us was weeping inwardly leaving the field'
     (R. Gerallt Jones, 1977: 42)

> *Cytunent fod bywyd yn faich*
> 'They agreed that life was a burden'
>> (Jane Edwards, 1976: 87)

On mutation of *bod* see **102**.

The subject of the clause may be expressed by a prefixed pronoun, possibly accompanied by the affixed pronoun:

> *Teimlent eu bod yn gwastraffu eu doniau*
> 'They felt that they were wasting their talents'
>> (Jane Edwards, 1976: 88)

> *Credai ei fod yn clywed sŵn gweryriad ceffyl yn dod o rywle o'r tu cefn i'r adeilad*
> 'He thought that he could hear the sound of a horse's neigh coming from somewhere behind the building'
>> (R. Cyril Hughes, 1976: 162)

> *Credaf eich bod chi'n byw yn y wlad*
> 'I think that you live in the country'

(ii) When the verb in the noun clause is future in time in relation to the verb in the main clause, the noun clause is introduced by *y(r)* followed by an inflected verb. *Y* is selected before consonants, *yr* before vowels and *h-*:

> *Dywedwyd wrthi y byddai'n cael ei symud i ysbyty yn ymyl ei chartref*
> 'She was told that she would be moved to a hospital near her home'
>> (Kate Roberts, 1976: 77)

> *Gwyddai Lisi Evans y byddai ei brecwast yma yn y munud rŵan*
> 'Lisi Evans knew that her breakfast would be here soon'
>> (Kate Roberts, 1976: 75)

> *Rwy'n credu yr hoffai'r gaseg bori ychydig ar y ddôl*
> 'I believe that the mare would like to graze a little on the meadow'
>> (R. Cyril Hughes, 1975: 35)

> *Yr wyf yn gwybod y bydd yma'n fuan*
> 'I know that he will be here soon'

(iii) When the verbal element in the noun clause expresses past tense in time referent to the verb in the main clause, one of two constructions may be selected:

(a) *bod* + *wedi* + verb-noun

Credai fod eu perthynas wedi tyfu'n un agos a chynnes iawn
'She believed that their relationship had developed into a close and warm one'
(R. Cyril Hughes, 1976: 141)

Credai fod perthynas Rhisiart a Chatrin wedi tyfu'n un agos a chynnes iawn
'She believed that Richard and Catrin's relationship had developed into a close and warm one'

Gwelwn ei bod wedi ei siomi'n enbyd
'I could see that she had been sorely disappointed'
(Emyr Humphreys, 1981: 258)

Credaf ei fod ef wedi colli ei ddefaid
'I think that he has lost his sheep'

(b) *i* + subject + verb-noun. The subject may be realized by a personal form of the preposition (see **326** (i)):

Dywedir iddo gael ei enw oherwydd fod y tywod sydd ar y traeth mor llyfn â sidan
'It is said that it got its name because the sand that is on the beach is as smooth as silk'
(T. Llew Jones, 1977: 7)

Dywedir i'r lle gael ei enw oherwydd fod y tywod sydd ar y traeth mor llyfn â sidan
'It is said that the place got its name because the sand that is on the beach is as smooth as silk'

Credaf i mi gyflawni'r gwaith y'm galwyd i'w gyflawni
'I believe that I completed the work that I was called to accomplish'
(Harri Williams, 1978: 7)

Notes
(1) In varieties of northern Welsh *daru* mutated to *ddaru* (see **290**) occurs before the preposition *i*: *Credaf ddaru imi gyflawni'r gwaith* 'I believe that I completed the work'.

(2) The prep. *o* occurs in older constructions; the subject follows the verb-noun governed by the prep. *o* (see **326** (ii)). This construction has been abandoned by the 1988 translation of the Welsh Bible in the following examples:

Yna gwybu Noa dreio o'r dyfoedd oddi ar y ddaear (1955)
A deallodd Noa fod y dyfroedd wedi treio oddi ar y ddaear (1988)
'Then Noah knew that the waters on the earth had subsided'
(Gen. 8: 11)

Hwy a wybuant weled ohono weledigaeth yn y deml (1955)
Deallasant iddo gael gweledigaeth yn y cysegr (1988)
'They realized that he had seen a vision in the temple'
(Luke 1: 22)

(B) Emphasis

The noun clauses described under (i), (ii) and (iii) above are marked for emphasis by *mai* at clause initial. In varieties of southern spoken Welsh *taw* occurs instead of *mai*; *taw* also occurs in the writing of southern authors. Any part of the noun clause other than the verb may be emphasized:

Ni ddywedodd yr hen walch mai gweled Catrin o Ferain oedd ei brif bwrpas
'The old devil did not say that seeing Catrin of Berain was his main purpose'
(R. Cyril Hughes, 1975: 48)

Roeddwn i'n meddwl mai'r Llew Coch oedd eich tafarn chi
'I thought that the Red Lion was your pub'
(John Rowlands, 1978: 17)

Yr oedd yn flin iawn ganddi mai hyhi a achosodd y sgwrs i droi i gyfeiriad Mari Stewart
'She was very sorry that it was she who had caused the conversation to turn towards Mary Stewart'
(R. Cyril Hughes, 1976: 166)

Credaf mai fi oedd yr unig Gymro Cymraeg yng ngwersyll Palemborg

'I believe that I was the only Welsh-speaking Welshman in Palemborg camp'
>(David Roberts, 1978: 7)

Dywedodd wrthi mai dychmygu'r cyfan roedd hi
'He told her that imagining everything she was'
>(Gerhart Hauptman and Heinrich Böll, 1974: 22)

A wyt ti'n tybio mai anrhydeddu dy dad y mae Dafydd wrth anfon cysurwyr atat?
'Do you suppose that it is to honour your father that David sends you comforters?'
>(2 Sam. 10: 3)

Gadewch imi ddatgan taw gwaith caled fydd y cyfan
'Let me declare that hard work it will all be'
>(*Y Faner*, 13/20 Ebrill 1990: 8)

(C) Negative

The predicator of the noun clause is realized by an inflected verb.

(i) *Na(d)* occurs before the verb in negative noun clauses (see **337**); *na* occurs before consonants, *nad* before vowels:

Mi wn i na wnaiff Mr Edwards ddim dweud wrth neb
'I know that Mr Edwards will not tell anyone'
>(Kate Roberts, 1976: 26)

Mi fentra i nad oes neb arall yn rhoi sylw iddi hi
'I wager that no one else gives her attention'
>(Kate Roberts, 1976: 77)

Sylwodd Menna nad oedd hi wedi sôn am ei thad naturiol
'Menna noticed that she had not mentioned her natural father'
>(Marion Eames, 1992: 49)

On mutation following *na* see **87, 115**.
  Nad replaces *mai* in negative emphatic clauses:

Gwyddost nad hawdd yw'r dasg sy'n dy aros
'You know that it is not easy, the task that awaits you'
>(John Bunyan, 1962: 21)

Byddwn yn gwybod nad ei law ef a'n trawodd
'We shall know that it is not his hand that struck us'
(1 Sam. 6: 9)

Note
In varieties of spoken Welsh and in informal texts *mai nad / mai nid*, *taw nad / taw nid* occur; *mai nid* occurs in the 1988 translation of the Welsh Bible:

Datguddiwyd i'r proffwydi hyn mai nid arnynt eu hunain, ond arnoch chwi, yr oeddent yn gweini
'It was disclosed to these prophets that it was not to themselves, but to you, they were ministering'
(1 Pet. 1: 12)

(ii)   *Heb* may be selected as verbal adjunct (see **329** (ii)):

Clywodd fod y car heb ei werthu
'He heard that the car had not been sold'

Clywaf eu bod heb benderfynu
'I heard that they have not decided'

354   The prep. *ar* may introduce a noun clause which is the object of a verb denoting an appeal, request or command, or a noun clause which follows an expression tantamount to an appeal or request:

Gweddïwch bob amser, ar gael eich cyfrif yn deilwng (1955)
'Pray constantly, that you may be accounted worthy'
(Luke 21: 36)

Ar may be followed by the prep. *i* which governs the subject:

Dyma fy ngorchymyn i; Ar i chwi garu eich gilydd (1955)
'This is my commandment; that you love one another'
(John 15: 12)

Gweddïa ar i'r Arglwydd yrru'r seirff ymaith oddi wrthym
'Plead with the Lord that he rid us of the snakes'
(Num. 21: 7)

Gweddïa'n ddi-baid drosom ar yr Arglwydd ein Duw iddo'n gwaredu ni o law'r Philistiaid

'Pray unceasingly for us to the Lord our God that he save us from the hand of the Philistines'
>> (1 Sam. 7: 8)

When the verb or noun in the main clause is normally followed by *ar* in a simple sentence, *ar* may be reproduced to introduce the noun clause:

Gweddïa ar yr Arglwydd ar yrru ohono ef y seirff oddi wrthym (1955)
'Plead with the Lord that he rid us of the snakes'
>> (Num. 21: 7)

The prep. *ar* may be omitted following a verb expressing entreaty:

Yr wyf yn atolwg i chwi . . . roddi ohonoch eich cyrff (1955)
'I implore you . . . that you present your bodies'
>> (Rom. 12: 1)

355 The prep. *am* may introduce the noun clause where the subject is not expressed:

Dywed wrth yr Israeliaid am fynd ymlaen
'Tell the children of Israel that (they) go forward'
>> (Exod. 14: 15)

Am may be followed by the prep. *i* which governs the subject:

Fy marn i yw na ddylem boeni'r rhai o blith y Cenhedloedd sy'n troi at Dduw, ond ysgrifennu atynt am iddynt ymgadw rhag bwyta pethau sydd wedi eu halogi gan eilunod
'My judgement is that we should not make things difficult for those amongst the Gentiles who are turning to God, but we write to them that they abstain from eating things that have been polluted by idols'
>> (Acts 15: 19/20)

Mi rydw i'n gweddïo ar Dduw am iti fod yn hapus
'I pray to God that you may be happy'
>> (John Rowlands, 1965: 75)

When *dweud* expresses a request or command, the command *per se* is imparted by a noun clause introduced by *am*:

Dywedodd un arall wrtho am yfed schnapps
'Another one told him to drink schnapps'
>> (Gerhart Hauptman and Heinrich Böll, 1974: 10)

When the entreaty in the noun clause is negative, it is expressed by *peidio â* + verb-noun:

> *Dywedodd un arall wrtho am beidio ag yfed schnapps*
> 'Another one told him not to drink schnapps'

In earlier texts, however, *na* is selected followed by a verb in the subjunctive (see **311** (iii)):

> *Yr wyf yn atolwg i ti na'm poenech* (1955)
> 'I implore you not to torment me'
>> (Luke 8: 28)

356 Indirect questions are noun clauses:

> *Gofynnais a oedd ganddynt ryw newydd*
> 'I asked whether they had any news'
>> (Kate Roberts, 1976: 25)

> *Hola'r awdur pam y dylem drafferthu i ddarllen cerddi Iolo Goch*
> 'The author asks why we should bother to read the poems of Iolo Goch'
>> (*Y Faner*, 26 Mai 1989: 14)

> *Ni wyddom beth yn union oedd adwaith y tlawd i'w tynged ar y ddaear hon*
> 'We don't know what exactly was the reaction of the poor to their fate in this world'
>> (Geraint H. Jenkins, 1983: 50)

> *Ni wyddwn i ble i droi nac o ble y deuai ymwared*
> 'I didn't know where to turn or from where salvation would come'
>> (Harri Williams, 1978: 31)

> *Ni wyddai neb yn iawn ymhle yr oedd yr arglwydd Cynan*
> 'No one knew where exactly Lord Cynan was'
>> (Rhiannon Davies Jones, 1977: 88)

> *Dwy' ddim yn deall sut y doist ti yma*
> 'I don't understand how you came here'
>> (Emyr Humphreys, 1981: 74)

> *Gofynnodd i'r Dehonglwr beth oedd ei ystyr a phaham y dangoswyd y darlun iddo*

'He asked the Expositor what it meant and why he had been shown the picture'
(John Bunyan, 1962: 21)

357 *Efallai, dichon, hwyrach* 'perhaps' and *diau, diamau* 'doubtless' are followed by a noun clause:

Hwyrach fod arno hiraeth am ei fam
'Perhaps he missed his mother'
(Rhiannon Davies Jones, 1985: 80)

Diau fod cysylltiadau agos Prosser Rhys a Saunders Lewis yng nghyffiniau Aberystwyth ar y pryd yn fantais i'r anturiaeth
'Doubtless the close relations between Prosser Rhys and Saunders Lewis in the Aberystwyth area at the time were of advantage to the venture'
(*Y Faner*, 6 Ionawr 1989: 8)

Pe cysgem yma dichon na chaem ni byth gyfle arall i fynd ymlaen i ben y daith
'If we were to sleep here perhaps we would never have another opportunity to finish the journey'
(John Bunyan, 1962: 72)

Efallai yr arhosaf gyda chwi
'Perhaps I shall stay with you'
(1 Cor. 16: 6)

358 The noun clause may be introduced by *llai na, peidio â* followed by a verb-noun to denote a negative meaning:

Ni allwn lai na rhyfeddu at y cyfoeth ysbrydol sydd yn ei emynau mawr
'We cannot but wonder at the spiritual riches in his great hymns'
(J. Elwyn Hughes, 1991: 85)

Ni allai lai na rhyfeddu at y newid ynddi
'He could not but wonder at the change in her'
(Marion Eames, 1982: 35)

Ni allai beidio â rhyfeddu at y newid ynddi

Note
In an earlier period *amgen na* occurred: *Ni wyddai beirdd y bedwaredd ganrif ar bymtheg amgen na bod yr erthylod hyn yn eiriau*

Cymraeg 'Nineteenth-century poets did not know but that these dreadful forms were Welsh words' (John Morris-Jones, 1925: 25).

The Absolute Phrase

359 The absolute phrase consists of a subject followed by a subordinate predicate. The subject may be either a noun or a personal pronoun. The absolute phrase is always introduced by the conjunction *a(c)*; *a* occurs before consonants, *ac* before vowels. The phrase is wholly independent of the syntax of the sentence to which it is appended. It is frequently equivalent to an adverbial clause, but does not contain a finite verb; it may, however, contain a verb-noun. The absolute phrase may precede or follow the main sentence or it may occur in a parenthesis.

(i)   subject + predicative *yn* + noun or adjective

Nid hawdd fu hi i JWH, ac yntau'n heddychwr, foddhau ei eglwys yn St Albans
'It wasn't easy for JWH, being a pacifist, to please his church in St Albans'
   (*Y Faner*, 30 Mehefin 1978: 8)

Yr oeddwn eisoes yn hen ŵr, a minnau'n blentyn
'I was already an old man, when I was a child'
   (Harri Williams, 1978: 12)

Pwy sydd wedi ei ddifetha ac yntau'n ddieuog?
'Who has destroyed him and he being guiltless?'
   (Job 4: 7)

The predicative *yn* is omitted when *mor* precedes the adjective:

Ac yntau mor esgeulus o'i eiddo, cafodd fod heb ei ddeg ceiniog
'Being so careless of his property, he was left without his ten pence'
   (Irma Chilton, 1989: 12)

Nid oeddent hwy am symud cam o'r fan, a hwythau mor gysurus eu byd
'They did not wish to move a step from there, when they were so well off'
   (John Bunyan, 1962: 12)

(ii) subject + adverb or adverbial phrase

Ac yntau heb waith, ni fedrai fforddio iro llaw y swyddogion
'And being unemployed, he could not afford to grease the palm of the officers'
(Geraint H. Jenkins, 1980: 84)

A ninnau ar drothwy'r unfed ganrif ar hugain, rhyfedd meddwl cynifer o gynlluniau ysgolheigion y Dadeni a gwŷr llên y ddeunawfed ganrif ar eu hôl a erys heb eu gwireddu
'And being (since we are) on the threshold of the twenty-first century, it is strange to think how many of the schemes of the Renaissance scholars and the literati of the eighteenth century following them have not been realized'
(*Barn*, Ebrill 1990: 43)

(iii) subject + adjunct + verb-noun

Ac yntau wedi mynd heibio i oed pensiwn, gwyddai mai un cyfle oedd ganddo
'And having passed pensionable age, he knew that he had one chance'
(*Y Faner*, 30 Mawrth 1979: 3)

Bloeddiodd Twm Twmffat er mwyn sicrhau bod ei neges yn cyrraedd ei nôd, ac yntau heb weld dim ond y swp gwallt
'Twm Twmffat bellowed in order to ensure that his message reached its target, when he had only seen the bundle of hair'
(T. Glynne Davies, 1974: 16)

Yn 1960, a minnau'n paratoi ffilm ar y Fro ar gyfer y BBC, holais wraig ffermdy Gregory am unrhyw hanesion a glywsai am Iolo
'In 1960, when I was preparing a film on the Vale for the BBC, I asked the wife at Gregory farmhouse for any tales that she had heard about Iolo'
(Aneirin Talfan Davies, 1972: 64)

360 The Relative Clause

For the construction of the relative clause see **225–235**.

361 The Adverbial Clause

For the construction of the adverbial clause see **279** (iii), **410–415**, **417** (ii), **418**.

Prepositions, Adverbs, Conjunctions, Interjections

Prepositions

The English equivalents given here do not always express the whole range of meanings of the Welsh preposition.

Conjugated Prepositions

362 Simple Prepositions

(i) These are selected when the object governed by the preposition is a noun or verb-noun:

dan gwmwl	'under a cloud'
dros glawdd	'over a hedge'
i lwyddo	'to succeed'
heb gwmni	'without company'
rhwng bysedd	'between fingers'

On mutation following prepositions see **69, 103, 106, 107, 111.**

(ii) A sub-class of prepositions (simple and compound) inflect to mark person and number, and the 3 sing. gender as well. The sub-class may be divided into groups according to the phonological shape of the affix selected:

Group 1 The prepositions *at* 'to'; *tuag at* 'towards'; *ar* 'on'; *hyd at* 'up to'; *oddi ar* 'from, off'; *am* 'at, about, for'; *tan/dan/o dan* 'under'. See **363.**

Group 2 The prepositions *rhwng* 'between'; *rhag* 'before, over, against'; *er* 'for the sake of, despite'; *heb* 'without'; *yn* 'in'; *o* 'from'; *tros/dros* 'over'; *trwy/drwy* 'through'; *hyd* 'until, till, along'. See **364**.

Group 3 The prepositions *wrth* 'by'; *oddi wrth* 'from'; *gan* 'by, with'. See **365**.

Group 4 The preposition *i* 'to'. See **366**.

Notes

(1) Some prepositions have adverbial forms (see **363**, **364** n. 2, **364** n. 3, **364** n. 5).

(2) Auxiliary pronouns (see **221**) may be selected with prepositions.

(3) Final *-f* in 1 sing. is omitted in informal texts and in varieties of spoken Welsh.

(4) Final *-m* in 1 pl. may be realized as *-n* in informal texts and in varieties of spoken Welsh. See **261**.

(5) Final *-t* in 3 pl. does not occur in natural speech; the selection of final *-t* is a characteristic of standard literary Welsh. See **261** n. 3.

(6) *Tuag at, hyd at, oddi ar* are compound prepositions consisting of two simple prepositions.

363

Preposition	Adverbial form	Stem	Affix Sing.	Pl.
ar	*arnodd*	*arn-*	1 *-af*	*-om*
oddi ar	*oddi arnodd*	*oddi arn-*	2 *-at*	*-och*
at		*at-*	3 *-o* (masc.)	*-ynt*
tuag at		*tuag at-*	*-i* (fem.)	
hyd at		*hyd at-*		
am		*amdan-*		
dan	*danodd*	*dan-*		

Conjugations of the prepositions *ar*, *at*, *am*, *dan*:

ar	Sing.	Pl.
	1 *arnaf*	*arnom*
	2 *arnat*	*arnoch*
	3 *arno* (masc.)	*arnynt*
	arni (fem.)	

at	Sing.	Pl.
	1 *ataf*	*atom*
	2 *atat*	*atoch*
	3 *ato* (masc.)	*atynt*
	ati (fem.)	

am	Sing.	Pl.
	1 *amdanaf*	*amdanom*
	2 *amdanat*	*amdanoch*
	3 *amdano* (masc.)	*amdanynt*
	amdani (fem.)	

dan	Sing.	Pl.
	1 *danaf*	*danom*
	2 *danat*	*danoch*
	3 *dano* (masc.)	*danynt*
	dani (fem.)	

364

Preposition	Stem	Affix		
			Sing.	Pl.
rhwng	*rhyng-*		1 *-of*	*-om*
rhag	*rhag-*		2 *-ot*	*-och*
er	*er-*		3 *-ddo* (masc.)	*-ddynt*
heb	*heb-*		*-ddi* (fem.)	
yn	*yn-*			

Conjugations of the prepositions *rhwng*, *rhag*, *er*, *heb*, *yn*:

rhwng	Sing.	Pl.
	1 *rhyngof*	*rhyngom*
	2 *rhyngot*	*rhyngoch*
	3 *rhyngddo* (masc.)	*rhyngddynt*
	rhyngddi (fem.)	

rhag	Sing.	Pl.
	1 *rhagof*	*rhagom*
	2 *rhagot*	*rhagoch*
	3 *rhagddo* (masc.)	*rhagddynt*
	rhagddi (fem.)	

er	Sing.	Pl.
	1 *erof*	*erom*
	2 *erot*	*eroch*
	3 *erddo* (masc.)	*erddynt*
	erddi (fem.)	

heb	Sing.	Pl.
	1 *hebof*	*hebom*
	2 *hebot*	*heboch*
	3 *hebddo* (masc.)	*hebddynt*
	hebddi (fem.)	

yn	Sing.	Pl.
	1 *ynof*	*ynom*
	2 *ynot*	*ynoch*
	3 *ynddo* (masc.)	*ynddynt*
	ynddi (fem.)	

Notes

(1) *Hyd* inflects in the 3 sing. and pl. only: *ar hyd-ddo*, *ar hyd-ddi*, *ar hyd-ddynt*.

(2) *Trwy/drwy* selects the stem *trw-* for the 1 and 2 sing. and pl. but selects the stem *trwy-* for 3 sing. and pl.: *trwof*, *trwot*, *trwyddo*, *trwyddi*, *trwom*, *trwoch*, *trwyddynt*. Adverbial form: *trwodd*.

(3) *Tros/dros* selects the inflectional affix *-to* (masc.), *-ti* (fem.) in the 3 sing., and *-tynt* in the 3 pl. The stem is *tros-/dros-*: *trosof*, *trosot*, *trosto*, *trosti*, *trosom*, *trosoch*, *trostynt*. Adverbial form: *trosodd*.

(4) *O*, stem *ohon-*, selects the inflectional affix *-o* (masc.), *-i* (fem.) in the 3 sing. and *-ynt* in the 3 pl.: *ohonof*, *ohonot*, *ohono*, *ohoni*, *ohonom*, *ohonoch*, *ohonynt*.

(5) The adverbial form of *heb* is *heibio*.

(6) In varieties of spoken Welsh and in informal texts *-dd-* may occur in the 1 and 2 sing. and pl. of *rhwng*, *rhag*, *heb*, *yn*: *Faswn i ddim yn gadael iddo fynd allan i yfed hebddoch chi eto* 'I would not allow him to go out drinking without you again' (*Y Faner*, 19 Ionawr 1991: 7). Other dialects and informal texts omit *-dd-* in the 3 sing.: *Doedd tŷ Jeroboam fab Nebat yr hwn a wnaeth i Israel bechu ddim yni hi* 'The house of Jeroboam son of Nebat who made Israel sin wasn't in it' (Jane Edwards, 1977: 97).

365

Preposition	Stem	Affix		
		Sing.		Pl.
gan	genn-	1 -yf		-ym
		2 -yt		-ych
	gan-	3 -ddo (masc.)		-ddynt
		-ddi (fem.)		
wrth	wrth-	1 -yf		-ym
		2 -yt		-ych
		3 -o (masc.)		-ynt
		-i (fem.)		

Conjugations of the prepositions *gan*, *wrth*:

gan	Sing.	Pl.
	1 *gennyf*	*gennym*
	2 *gennyt*	*gennych*
	3 *ganddo* (masc.)	*ganddynt*
	ganddi (fem.)	

Notes

(1) The form *gen*, together with the appropriate affixed pronoun, occurs in the 1 and 2 sing. and is acceptable in all save very formal styles of the language: *gen i* for *gennyf*; *gen ti* for *gennyt*.

(2) In varieties of spoken Welsh *gandd-* is often extended to the 1 and 2 pl.: *ganddon* for *gennym*; *ganddoch* for *gennych*.

wrth	Sing.	Pl.
	1 *wrthyf*	*wrthym*
	2 *wrthyt*	*wrthych*
	3 *wrtho* (masc.)	*wrthynt*
	wrthi (fem.)	

366 The conjugation of *i*. This conjugation is anomalous, affixes being selected for the 3 sing and 3 pl. only:

Sing.	Pl.
1 *im, imi*	*in, inni*
2 *it, iti*	*ichwi*
3 *iddo* (masc.)	*iddynt*
iddi (fem.)	

The inflected forms of *i* are accented on the penult. When the pronoun is to be stressed, the preposition and pronoun are written separately in the 1st and 2nd person:

Sing.	Pl.
1 *i mi*	*i ni*
2 *i ti*	*i chwi*

Note
In varieties of spoken Welsh *i fi* may occur in the 1 sing.

367 It has been possible to give only generalized indications of localized variation in this discussion of the prepositions. No comprehensive study listing the literary paradigms and spoken variations exists. Some indication of the variety is to be found in Thomas and Thomas, 1989: 57–60 and in Martin J. Ball, 1988: 159–60. See **212** (vi) n. 1.

Uninflected Prepositions

368 The following prepositions do not have personal forms. Some can be followed by an independent pronoun (see **211**, **212** (iv)). Some compound prepositions can select a prefixed (see **214**) or infixed pronoun (see **217**) to follow the first element and an auxiliary pronoun to follow the second element.

On mutation following the prefixed pronouns see **216**.
On mutation following the infixed pronouns see **219**.

â, ag (*ag* is selected before vowels; *â* occurs before consonants); *gyda(g)* 'with'; *ynghyda(g), ynghyd â* (*ag*) 'together with'; *gyferbyn â* (*ag*) 'opposite'; *gyfarwyneb â* (*ag*) 'facing'; *parth â* (*ag*), *tua(g)* 'towards'. An independent pronoun may follow all of these prepositions apart from *tua*.

On mutation following *â, gyda, tua* see **117**.

achos: see *o achos* below.

am ben 'in addition to, upon', *am fy mhen* 'upon me', *ar ben* 'on top of'; *ar ei phen hi* 'on top of her'; *ar bwys* 'near', *ar dy bwys di* 'near to you'; *ar draws* 'across', *ar fy nhraws* 'across me'; *ar gyfer* 'for', *ar eu cyfer* 'for them'; *ar hyd* 'along', *ar eich hyd* 'along you' (see **364** n.1); *ar ôl* 'after', *ar eich hôl* 'after you'; *ar uchaf* 'upon'; *ar warthaf* 'upon', *ar eu gwarthaf* 'upon them'; *ar gefn* 'on back of', *ar fy nghefn* 'on my back'; *ar fedr* 'on point of'; *ar fin* 'on edge of'; *ar ochr* 'on side of', *ar ei* *ochr* 'on his side'; *ar ymyl* 'on edge of', *ar ei ymyl* 'on its edge'; *ar flaen* 'in front of'.

Note

Ar bwys features in varieties of southern Welsh.

cyn 'before'.

efo 'with'. An independent pronoun may follow.

er mwyn 'for the sake of', *er fy mwyn i* 'for my sake'; *er gwaethaf* 'in spite of', *er fy ngwaethaf* 'in spite of me'.

ers 'for'. It occurs before a noun denoting a period of time past: *ers blwyddyn* 'for a year'; *ers mis* 'for a month'; *ers meityn* 'since some little time'; *ers talwm* 'for a long time past'. See **374**.

erbyn; *yn erbyn* 'by, against', *yn fy erbyn* 'against me'. See **375**.

fel 'like'. An independent pronoun may follow.

ger; *gerbron*, *gerllaw* 'near', *ger ei bron*, *ger ei llaw* 'near to her'.

gerfydd 'by'.

heblaw 'besides'. An independent pronoun may follow.

herwydd 'according to'; *oherwydd* 'on account of', *o'm herwydd* 'on account of me' (see *o achos* etc. below); *yn herwydd* 'because of', *yn ei herwydd* 'because of him'.

is; *islaw* 'below, beneath', *is fy llaw* 'beneath me'.

llwrw 'in the direction of'. In contemporary Welsh it only occurs in expressions like *llwrw fy mhen* 'head foremost'; *llwrw'i gefn* 'backwards'; *llwrw'i din* 'rump first'; *llwrw'i drwyn* 'nose foremost'.

megis 'like, such as'. An independent pronoun may follow.

mewn 'in' (occurs only before an indefinite noun: *mewn car* 'in a car', *mewn llyfrau* 'in books'); *o fewn* 'within', *o'm mewn* 'within me' (see *o achos* etc. below) (*i mewn i* 'into'; *tu mewn i*, *tu fewn i* 'inside'; *o fewn i* 'within', are conjugated like *i*, see **366**).

nes 'until' (before verb-nouns in an adverbial clause or phrase, see **410**): *nes gadael* 'until (I) left', *nes dod* 'until (I) came'. *Nes i*, *hyd nes i* 'until' are conjugated like *i*: *nes imi ddod*, *hyd nes imi ddod* 'until I came'.

When *o* forms the first element of a compound preposition the infixed pronoun can occur between both elements: *o achos*, *oblegid* 'because of', *o'm hachos*, *o'm plegid* 'because of me'; *o ran* 'for the part of', *o'm rhan i* 'for my part'; *o flaen* 'before, in front of', *o'i flaen* 'in front of him'; *o gylch* 'around', *o'i chylch* 'around her'; *o amgylch* 'around', *o'i amgylch* 'around him'.

rhag bron 'in front of', *rhag dy fron* 'in front of you'.

tros/dros, *dros ben* 'over (the top of)', *dros ei phen* 'over her head'.

uwch, *uwchben*, *uwchlaw* 'above', *uwch fy mhen* 'above me'.

wedi 'after' may be followed by:

  (i)   a demonstrative pronoun: *wedi hyn* 'after this'; *wedi hynny* 'after that'.
  (ii) a numeral when time is denoted: *wedi deg (o'r gloch)* 'after ten (o'clock)'.
  (iii) a verb-noun in a periphrastic construction, see **286, 323**.

yn occurs as the first element of several compound prepositions: *ynghylch* 'concerning', *yn ei chylch* 'concerning her'; *ymhlith* 'among', *yn eu plith* 'among them'; *yn ôl* 'according to', *yn dy ôl* 'according to you'; *ymhen* 'at the end of'; *yn wysg* 'in the direction of'; *yn ymyl* 'by the edge of, near', *yn fy ymyl* 'near to me'.

In many of the compound prepositions noted above the noun-element is used metaphorically. When the noun occurs in its literal meaning it is regarded as an ordinary noun governed by a simple preposition.

Examples:

(a) simple prepositions

> *Rydach chi fel dwy efaill*
> 'You are like two twins'
> > (Kate Roberts, 1976: 27)

> *Cyfeiriodd . . . tua'r ffenestr*
> 'He pointed . . . towards the window'
> > (Gerhart Hauptman and Heinrich Böll, 1974: 8)

> *Yr oedd ysgarmes mewn salŵn ddiota*
> 'There was a brawl in a drinking parlour'
> > (Emyr Humphreys, 1986: 111)

> *Nid oeddent yn bwriadu mynd â Gustavchen gyda hwy*
> 'They did not intend taking Gustavchen with them'
> > (Gerhart Hauptman and Heinrich Böll, 1974: 7)

Byddwn yn cael llawer o hwyl efo hwynt
'I used to have a lot of fun with them'
(Kate Roberts, 1976: 24)

(b) compound prepositions

Aeth i eistedd ar y gadair ar bwys y ddesg
'He went to sit on the chair near the desk'
(Ioan Kidd, 1977: 47)

Cynheuwyd y tanau ar ben yr Wyddfa
'The fires were lit on top of Snowdon'
(Rhiannon Davies Jones, 1977: 71)

Rhoddais fy mhregeth gyntaf gerbron f'athrawon
'I delivered my first sermon in front of my teachers'
(Harri Williams, 1978: 82)

Gadawodd gwmwl o fwg drygsawr ar ei ôl
'He left a cloud of evil smelling smoke behind him'
(Emyr Humphreys, 1986: 13)

Mae'r dewis o'u blaenau nhw
'The choice faces them'
(R. Cyril Hughes, 1976: 208)

Ymgrymodd y Prior o flaen y plant
'The Prior bowed in front of the children'
(Rhiannon Davies Jones, 1977: 86)

A yw'n iawn iti deimlo'n ddig o achos y planhigyn?
'Is it right for you to feel angry because of the plant?'
(Jonah 4: 9)

Prepositions in Special Constructions and Idiomatic Expressions

369 â, ag, primary meanings 'with; as'

On the selection of *â/ag* see **368**.

The prep. occurs:

(i) Following verbs containing the prefixes *ym-*, *cyf-* (*cyff-*), *cyd-*
(*cyt-*) (see **138**). For example:

ymweld â 'visit'	*ymdrin â* 'deal with'
ymadael â 'leave'	*ymhel â* 'meddle'

ymwneud â 'deal with'
ymryson â 'contend'
cyfarfod â 'meet'
cyfamodi â 'covenant'
cytuno â 'agree'
cydymffurfio â 'conform'

ymddiddan â 'converse'
ymyrryd â 'interfere'
cyffwrdd â 'touch'
cyfeillachu â 'associate'
cyd-dynnu â 'act unitedly'
cydweithio â 'co-operate'

(ii) Following verbs:

peidio â 'cease'
siarad â 'speak to'
dyweddïo â 'become
    engaged to'
ffarwelio â 'bid farewell to'
dod â 'bring'
methu â 'fail'

llenwi â 'fill'
bwydo â 'feed'
tewi â 'be silent'
priodi â 'marry'
dadlau â 'argue with'
mynd â 'take'
arfer â 'be accustomed to'

Note

In informal texts and varieties of spoken Welsh *â* is often omitted
following *peidio, methu, arfer, priodi*. See **313** (iv).

(iii) With adverbs to express movement:

I ffwrdd â nhw!   'Away with them!'
Allan â chi!   'Out you go!'
Drosodd â thi!   'Over you go!'

(iv) Before the name of an instrument etc., to express how an action
was completed:

Llyfodd ei wefusau â blaen ei dafod
'He licked his lips with the tip of his tongue'
    (Gerhart Hauptman and Heinrich Böll, 1974: 6)

(v) To denote possession:

y gŵr â'r car glas
'the man with the blue car'

y tŷ â'r to coch
'the house with the red roof'

(vi) Following the equative (see **199**).

(vii) To express a state or condition:

brenhinoedd â bodiau eu dwylo a'u traed wedi eu torri i ffwrdd
'kings with their thumbs and great toes cut off'
    (Judg. 1: 7)

370 am, primary meanings 'about; at; in exchange for; because'

The prep. occurs:

(i) Following the verbs:

anghofio am 'forget about'	*aros am* 'wait for'
clywed am 'hear about'	*cofio am* 'remember about'
chwerthin am (*ben*) 'laugh about'	*chwilio am* 'search for'
	diolch am 'thank for'
edrych am 'look for'	*galw am* 'call for'
dweud am 'tell about'	*gofyn am* 'ask for'
disgwyl am 'expect'	*gwybod am* 'know about'
gweddïo am 'pray for'	*meddwl am* 'think about'
hiraethu am 'long for'	*sôn am* 'talk about'
edifarhau am 'repent for'	*dysgu am* 'learn about'
talu am 'pay for'	*siarad am* 'talk about'

Note
See **290** (i) on *darfod am*.

(ii) Following certain nouns:

diolch am 'thanks for'	*pryder am* 'fear for'
awydd am 'desire for'	*hiraeth am* 'longing for'
coffa am 'memory of'	*rheswm am* 'reason for'

(iii) To express the meaning 'for, in exchange for':

> *llygad am lygad a dant am ddant*
> 'an eye for an eye and a tooth for a tooth'
>   (Matt. 5: 38)

(iv) To express the meaning 'for, towards' with verbs denoting movement:

rhuthro am 'rush for'	*rhedeg am* 'run for'
mynd am 'go for'	

Note
To express the meaning 'towards, in the direction of', *at* is selected: *rhuthro at* 'rush towards'; *rhedeg at* 'run towards'; *mynd at* 'go towards'.

(v) To express the meaning 'about':

Rhwym hwy am dy wddf
'Bind them about your neck'
(Prov. 3: 3)

(vi) To express the meaning 'because of':

Y maent hwy'n tybied y cânt eu gwrando am eu haml eiriau
'They think that they shall be heard because they use many words'
(Matt. 6: 7)

(vii) In the compound conjunction *am y*: see **311** (ii) (b).

(viii) In the idiom *am . . . â* 'on the other side of':

Eisteddodd am y tân â mi
'He sat on the other side of the fire from me'

(ix) Preceding a superlative adjective: see **201** (iv).

(x) In a noun clause: see **355**.

(xi) In varieties of northern Welsh in expressions such as:

Am fysedd, am ddwylo diwerth!
'What fingers, what useless hands!'
(Angharad Tomos, 1991: 11)

Mae hi am law
'It is going to rain'

Am barti!
'What a party!'

Am hwyl!
'What fun!'

(xii) As an aspective adjunct: see **286**.

371 ar, primary meaning 'on'

The prep. occurs:

(i) Following the verbs:

blino ar 'get tired of'	*edrych ar* 'look at'
galw ar 'call'	*gweddïo ar* 'pray to'

gweiddi ar 'shout at'	*gwenu ar* 'smile at'
gwrando ar 'listen to'	*sylwi ar* 'notice'
esgor ar 'give birth'	*bodloni ar* 'be satisfied with'
ymosod ar 'attack'	*achwyn ar* 'complain about'
cymryd ar 'pretend'	*annog ar* 'encourage'
aflonyddu ar 'disturb'	*cefnu ar* 'turn one's back on'
dial ar 'avenge'	*diflasu ar* 'have enough of'
crefu ar 'implore'	*dotio ar* 'dote'
ffoli ar 'infatuate'	*myfyrio ar* 'mediate on'
menu ar 'disturb'	*dylanwadu ar* 'influence'
deisyf ar 'beseech'	*lladd ar* 'decry'

(ii) Following an adjective depicting a condition or state:

Mae hi'n ddrwg arnynt
'They are in a bad way'

Mae hi'n dda arnat ti
'You are well off'

Roedd hi'n galed arnaf i
'It was difficult for me'

(iii) Following an adjective describing disposition or temperament:

Roedd hi'n hy arnaf
'She was forward with me'

Mae'n rhy eofn ar ei athrawon
'He is too bold towards his teachers'

Paid â bod yn rhy galed arno
'Don't be too hard on him'

(iv) In adverbial phrases:

ar agor 'open'	*ar ddamwain* 'accidentally'
ar ddisberod 'lost, off the track'	*ar fai* 'at fault'
	ar gerdded 'on the move, away'
ar gael 'available'	*ar goll* 'lost'
ar gof (a chadw) 'noted, recorded'	*ar chwâl* 'dispersed, scattered'
	ar gyfeiliorn 'erring'
ar drai 'ebbing, declining'	*ar ddwywaith* 'on two occasions'
ar wasgar 'dispersed'	*ar brydiau* 'occasionally'
ar waith 'afoot'	*ar unwaith* 'at once'

(v) Following nouns such as:

eisiau 'lack'	*ofn* 'fear'
angen 'need'	*dyled* 'debt'
arswyd 'terror'	*cywilydd* 'shame'
chwant 'desire'	*diwedd* 'end'
bai 'fault'	*pregeth* 'sermon'
math 'sort'	*golwg* 'look'

Examples:

Ni bydd eisiau arnaf
'I shall lack nothing'

Nid oes ofn arnaf
'I am not afraid'

Roedd chwant bwyd arno
'He desired food'

Cywilydd arnat
'Shame on you'

(vi) Following the names of infections and ailments:

Mae'r frech goch arni
'She has measles'

Mae pen tost arnaf i
'I have a headache'

Roedd y ddannoedd arni
'She had toothache'

(vii) With the verb *bod* 'to be' to express arrears or liability:

Yr oedd ar y ffermwr ddwybunt iddo
'The farmer owed him £2'

Faint sydd arnat ti?
'How much do you owe?'

(viii) In a noun clause: see **354**.

(ix) As an aspective adjunct: see **286**.

372 at, primary meanings 'to, for; as far as'

The prep. occurs:

(i) Following the verbs:

dod at 'come to'	*mynd at* 'go to'
anfon at 'send to'	*agosáu at* 'approach'
cyfeirio at 'refer to'	*anelu at* 'aim at'
tueddu at 'be inclined to'	*troi at* 'turn to'
ychwanegu at 'add to'	*dotio at* 'dote'
gogwyddo at 'incline'	

(ii) Following a few nouns:

malais at 'malice towards'	*apêl at* 'appeal to'
serch at 'love for'	*archwaeth at* 'appetite for'
cariad at 'love for'	*llythyr at* 'letter to'

(iii) Following a few adjectives:

agos at 'near to'	*nes at* 'nearer to'

(iv) In some compound prepositions:

tuag at 'towards'	*hyd at* 'as far as'

(v) To express the meaning 'for the purpose of':

dillad at waith 'clothes for work'
moddion at beswch 'medicine for a cough'
esgidiau at chwarae 'boots for playing'

(vi) In idioms:

at ei gilydd 'on the whole'
ac ati 'et cetera'
ati â mi, ni, chi etc. 'on with the job'

373 dros/tros, primary meanings 'over, on behalf of'

The prep. occurs:

(i) Following verbs:

mynd dros 'go on behalf of'	*ateb dros* 'answer for/on behalf of'
eiriol dros 'intercede on behalf of'	*dadlau dros* 'argue on behalf of'

gweddïo dros 'pray for/on behalf of'

ymladd dros 'fight for'

gwylio dros 'watch over'

wylo dros 'weep for/over'

(ii) Following a few nouns:

amddiffyniad dros 'defence for'

esgus dros 'excuse for'

iawn dros 'compensation for'

rheswm dros 'reason for'

meichiau dros 'bail for'

cysgod dros 'shadow over'

sêl dros 'zeal for'

(iii) In idioms:

dros ei grogi
'to save his skin'

cynnig dros ysgwydd
'to offer half-heartedly' (lit. to offer over the shoulder)

374 er, primary meanings 'for; since'

The prep. occurs:

(i) To express the meaning 'in order to, for the sake of', as in *er mwyn*:

gwario punt er arbed ceiniog
'spending a pound in order to save a penny'

er mwyn Cymru
'for the sake of Wales'

er lles 'for the good of'
er cof am 'in memory of'
er clod 'in honour'
er drwg 'for ill'
er anrhydedd 'honoris causa'

(ii) To express the meaning 'however, though, despite' with an equative adjective (see **199** (iii)), noun, verb-noun, absolute adjective:

Er nerth y gwynt dringodd i ben y to
'Despite the power of the wind he climbed to the roof top'

Er chwilio'n ddyfal ni chafwyd hyd i'r bêl
'Despite diligent searching the ball was not discovered'

Er nad oedd esgidiau am ei draed aeth allan i'r eira
'Although there were no shoes on his feet he went out in the snow'

Er yn euog cafodd ei ryddhau'n amodol
'Though guilty he was conditionally discharged'

(iii) To express the meaning 'since' before a word or phrase denoting a specified time or event in the past:

Canmolwn ein Dewiswyr – cawsant gryn dipyn o gerydd a diawlio er 1980
'Let us praise our Selectors – they have received a deal of criticism and cursing since 1980'
    (*Y Faner*, 19 Mawrth 1988: 22)

Roedd y tri ohonynt wedi bod yn aelodau o'n llwyth ni er eu geni
'The three of them had been members of our tribe since their birth'
    (Bryan Martin Davies, 1988: 20)

Dyna'r unig fangre a adnabu mewn gwirionedd er dyddiau ei ieuenctid
'That was the only place that he was acquainted with really since the days of his youth'
    (Rhiannon Davies Jones, 1989: 22)

Note
It is important to distinguish between the use of *er* and *ers*. *Ers* 'for' occurs before a word or phrase denoting a continuing period of time: *Gwrthododd ef a'i fam a'i ddwy chwaer addoli yn eglwys y plwyf ers tair blynedd* 'He and his mother and his two sisters had refused to worship in the parish church for three years' (Rhiannon Davies Jones, 1985: 15); *Rydw i yma ers wythnos ond na fedrwn i ysgrifennu na chopio dim ar y cychwyn* 'I have been here for a week but I could not write nor copy anything at the beginning' (ibid.: 41); *Bythefnos yn ôl buasai farw Martha Hughes, ei ffrind ers deuddeng mlynedd* 'A fortnight ago Martha Hughes, her friend for twelve years, had died' (Kate Roberts, 1972: 22).

(iv) In idioms:

er y byd 'for (all) the world'
er dim 'on no account'
er erioed 'since the beginning'

375 erbyn, primary meaning 'by'

The prep. occurs:

(i) To express the meaning 'by, not later than', with words or phrases referring to time or events or dates:

erbyn diwedd y flwyddyn 'by the end of the year'
erbyn amser cinio 'by lunchtime'
erbyn deg y bore 'by 10 a.m.'

(ii) *Erbyn* + verb-noun expresses the meaning 'by the time, after':

Roedd hi wedi marw erbyn inni gyrraedd
'She had died by the time we arrived'

Bydd hi'n rhy hwyr erbyn imi fynd i'r siop
'It will be too late by the time I go to the shop'

(iii) *Yn erbyn* is selected to express the meaning 'against, opposed to':

Pwysodd yn erbyn y car
'He leaned against the car'

Roedden nhw yn erbyn agor ar y Sul
'They were opposed to Sunday opening'

(iv) With prefixed pronouns:

Yr hwn nid yw yn eich erbyn, drosoch chwi y mae
'The one who is not against you, is for you'
    (Luke 9: 50)

(v) In idioms:

cerdded yn erbyn 'climb, go up'
erbyn yn erbyn 'face to face'

Note
In varieties of spoken Welsh *i'w erbyn e* (*nhw*)/*iddi erbyn e* (*nhw*) occurs, meaning 'to meet him (them)'.

376 gan, primary meanings 'with, by; of, from'

On *can*, *gan* see **126**.

The prep. occurs:

(i) Following verbs:

cymryd gan 'take from'   *prynu gan* 'buy from'

cael gan 'receive from'   *clywed gan* 'hear from'
benthyca gan 'borrow from'   *ceisio gan* 'seek from'

(ii) With forms of *bod* 'to be', to denote title or ownership:

Mae car gwyn ganddi
'She has a white car'

Mae digon o arian gan ei thad
'Her father has plenty of money'

(iii) Following an adjective to express feeling or present an opinion:

Mae'n flin gennyf glywed / Blin gennyf glywed
'I am sorry to hear'

Roedd hi'n dda gennyf dderbyn / Da oedd gennyf dderbyn
'I was happy to accept'

Mae'n ddrwg gennyf / Drwg gennyf
'I am sorry'

Mae'n well gennyf fwyd plaen / Gwell gennyf fwyd plaen
'I prefer plain food'

(iv) Before a noun to denote the agent:

Canwyd anthem gan y côr
'An anthem was sung by the choir'

Trefnwyd y gyngerdd ganddo ef
'The concert was organized by him'

(v) With a verb-noun in a sub-predicate or participle construction
(see **325** (vi)) which denotes an action simultaneous with that of the
main verb and usually forming part of it:

Plygai'r cwc dros y tân gan droi llond crochan o gawl
'The cook leaned over the fire turning a cauldron full of broth'
    (Lewis Carroll, 1982: 53)

Aeth allan gan gau'r drws yn glep
'He went out slamming the door'
    (T. Glynne Davies, 1974: 375)

*Daeth Ioan Fedyddiwr, gan bregethu'r genadwri hon yn
anialwch Judea*
'John the Baptist appeared, preaching this message in the
Judean wilderness'
    (Matt. 3: 1)

A similar construction occurs with *dan*. The action denoted in the sub-predicate is simultaneous with that of the main verb, but usually separate from it:

> *Aeth yn ei flaen dan ganu*
> 'He went on his way singing'
>> (John Bunyan, 1962: 25)

> *Dôi gwraig y Porthor i ben y Garthau i weiddi bod lladron y nos yn dwad dan wau'u sanau yng ngolau'r lleuad*
> 'The Gatekeeper's wife would come to the top of y Garthau to shout that the thieves of the night were coming knitting their stockings in the moonlight'
>> (Rhiannon Davies Jones, 1977: 10)

As some of these examples suggest, the difference between the two constructions has been eroded.

(vi) Before a verb-noun to express the meaning 'because':

> *Gan fod y tywydd yn oer gwisgais fy nghot*
> 'Because the weather was cold I put on my coat'

In a negative clause *gan nad* + verb is selected:

> *Gan nad oedd y tywydd yn dwym gwisgais fy nghot*
> 'Because the weather was not warm I put on my coat'

(vii) In idioms:

> *gan amlaf* 'usually'
> *gan bwyll* 'gently, carefully'
> *gan mwyaf* 'mostly'

377 i, primary meaning 'to, into'

The prep. occurs:

(i) Following verbs to complete the meaning, for example:

addo i 'promise to'	*anfon i* 'send to'
cynnig i 'offer to'	*maddau i* 'forgive'
llwyddo i 'succeed in'	*ymroddi i* 'devote oneself to'
ufuddhau i 'obey'	*cyffelybu i* 'compare to'

> *Fe'i cyffelybir i ddyn call*
> 'He is compared to a wise man'
>> (Matt. 7: 24)

Dylem ni faddau i'n gelynion
'We ought to forgive our enemies'

Rhaid i blant ufuddhau i'w rhieni
'Children must obey their parents'

(ii) To indicate the indirect object of verbs such as *rhoddi* 'give', *caniatáu* 'allow', *dysgu* 'teach', *gadael* 'let, allow', *gofyn* 'ask', *rhwystro* 'prevent', *gorchymyn* 'command', *erchi* 'ask':

Rhoddais fwyd i gath
'I gave food to a cat'

Dysgodd ef ganeuon i mi
'He taught me songs'

The object of the verb may be a verb-noun:

Dysgodd ef inni chwarae rygbi
'He taught us to play rugby'

Caniatewch i'r bobl fynd i mewn!
'Allow the people to go in!'

With *dysgu, gadael, rhwystro* another construction may be selected where *i* occurs before a verb-noun thus making the preceding noun or pronoun direct object:

Mae ef yn dysgu'r plant i nofio
'He is teaching the children to swim'

Mae ef yn eu dysgu i nofio
'He is teaching them to swim'

Dysgodd ef y plant i yrru
'He taught the children to drive'

(iii) In a noun clause expressing a request or command: see **354**.

(iv) In a noun clause which is the subject of a noun-predicate sentence:

Diau i bawb godi'n gynnar y bore hwnnw
'Doubtless everyone got up early that morning'

Gresyn i John gael ei anfon o'r maes
'It is a shame that John was sent from the field'

See **326**.

(v) In a noun clause following verbs of saying, knowing, believing:
see **353** (ii).

(vi) In adverbial clauses following the prepositions *am*, *gan*,
oherwydd, *oblegid*, *o achos*, with the action of the verb-noun in the
past tense, for example:

> *Yr wyf yn ei garu, am iddo gymryd fy maich oddi arnaf*
> 'I love him because he has taken my burden from me'
>   (John Bunyan, 1962: 31)

> *Fe wyddai ei fod yn haeddu hynny gan iddo ymddwyn mor
> fwystfilaidd*
> 'He knew that he deserved that because he had acted so
> brutishly'
>   (T. Glynne Davies, 1974: 74)

Also following *er*, *wedi*, *gyda*, *cyn*, *ar ôl*, *erbyn*, *wrth*, *nes*, *er mwyn*,
rhag, *oddi eithr*, with the tense of the verb-noun varying according to
the context:

> *Wedi i mi gyrraedd yn ôl i'r bwthyn, meddyliais pa mor rhyfedd y
> mae dyn yn ymddwyn weithiau*
> 'After I had returned to the cottage, I thought how strangely
> man acts sometimes'
>   (Rhiannon Davies Jones, 1977: 117)

> *Ar ôl iddi dywyllu, ac ar ôl i'r milwyr fod o gwmpas am y tro olaf
> y noson honno, aeth y ddau frawd i'r twll o dan y wal*
> 'After it had got dark and after the soldiers had been around for
> the last time that night, the two brothers went to the hole under
> the wall'
>   (T. Llew Jones, 1977: 59)

> *Yr oedd yn nosi wrth i Farged gerdded i lawr y mymryn stryd at y
> sgwâr*
> 'It was getting dark as Marged walked down the little street
> towards the square'
>   (T. Glynne Davies, 1974: 59)

> *Fe awn i lawr yno yn awr, rhag iti bryderu'n ofer*
> 'We will go down there now, lest you worry without reason'
>   (R. Bryn Williams, 1976: 30)

(vii) To signify ownership or possession:

Plentyn i mi yw hwn
'This is a child of mine'

Prynais gadair ac iddi gefn uchel
'I bought a chair with a high back'

(viii) With verb-nouns to signify why and wherefore:

Euthum ar wyliau i ymlacio
'I went on holidays to relax'

Aeth at lan yr afon i bysgota
'He went to the riverbank to fish'

Prynwch flawd i wneud rhagor o fara
'Buy flour to make more bread'

(ix) Following *ambell, llawer, aml* before a singular noun: see **191** (ii) n. 2.

(x) In idioms:

i'r dim 'exactly, precisely'
i'r gwrthwyneb 'to the contrary'

(xi) As an aspective adjunct: see **286**.

378 o, primary meanings 'of, out of, by'

The prep. occurs:

(i) Following certain verbs and adjectives to complete the meaning, for example:

argyhoeddi o 'convince of'	*teilwng o* 'worthy of'
amddifadu o 'to deprive of'	*balch o* 'glad of'
cyhuddo o 'accuse of'	*sicr o* 'sure of'
cyfranogi o 'partake of'	*hoff o* 'fond of'
	euog o 'guilty of'

Yr oeddwn wedi eu hargyhoeddi o hynny
'I had convinced them of that'

Cafodd ei gyhuddo o dwyll
'He was accused of fraud'

Y mae'n deilwng o'r wobr
'He is worthy of the prize'

Yr wyf yn hoff o'r gwaith
'I am fond of the work'

Yr oedd yn euog o'r cyhuddiad
'He was guilty of the accusation'

It also occurs after a few nouns:

adnabyddiaeth o 'knowledge of'

arwydd o 'sign of'

gwybodaeth o 'knowledge of'

rhybudd o 'warning of'

llawnder o 'abundance of'

hysbysrwydd o 'notification of'

(ii) In adverbial phrases before a word expressing measure of difference:

mwy o lawer 'much more'
gwell o'r hanner 'better by half'
gormod o bell ffordd 'too much by far'
rhy gul o lawer 'too narrow by far'

(iii) To express division, split, fraction of the whole:

y pedwerydd o'r mis 'the fourth of the month'
yr ail adran o'r gwaith 'the second section of the work'
y cyfan o'r arian 'all the money'
aelod o'r garfan 'a member of the squad'
yr wythfed o Ionawr 'the eighth of January'
y rhan orau o'r rhaglen 'the best part of the programme'
y rhan gyntaf ohoni 'the first part of it'

(iv) Between a word expressing number, size, quality and a definite or indefinite noun:

tri o blant 'three children'
digon o fwyd 'plenty of food'
bwcedaid o ddŵr 'a bucketful of water'
llu o bethau 'many things'
saith o'r merched 'seven of the girls'
pump ohonynt 'five of them'
dull o ysgrifennu 'a style of writing'

Following *rhai* (see **243**), *pawb* (see **247**), *neb* (see **258**), *dim* (see **256**), *cwbl* (see **251**), *peth* (see **245**) the noun is always definite.

(v) To express the meaning 'because, as a result of, with, through' before a verb-noun or noun:

wylo o lawenydd 'crying with joy'
neidio o gynddaredd 'leaping with anger'
Gwnaethant hynny o gariad 'They did that for love'
Aeth hi ato o dosturi 'She went to him out of compassion'
Bu ef farw o yfed gormod 'He died from drinking too much'

(vi) Between a definite abstract noun and a verb-noun in apposition:

y fraint o gadeirio 'the privilege of chairing'
y gelfyddyd o garu 'the art of loving'
y ddefod o wisgo 'the custom of dressing'
yr arfer o ysmygu 'the habit of smoking'
y anrhydedd o siarad 'the honour of speaking'

It also occurs between two abstract nouns in apposition:

y fendith o gwsg 'the blessing of sleep'
y rhinwedd o dawelwch 'the virtue of silence'

(vii) Between two nouns, the second of which describes the first and
refers to material or characteristics:

tŷ o gerrig 'a house of stone'
blows o gotwm gwyn 'a blouse of white cotton'
person o bwys 'a person of importance'
dyn o sylwedd 'a man of substance'

(viii) Between two nouns, to express membership of a group or
nationality:

cyfaill o Fethodist 'a Methodist friend'
plentyn o Gymro 'a Welsh child'
awdur o Sais 'an English author'
milwr o Wyddel 'an Irish soldier'

(ix) The descriptive element may precede the preposition:

da o beth 'a good thing'
cywilydd o beth 'a disgraceful thing'
pwt o lythyr 'a brief letter'
cawr o ddyn 'a giant of a man'
truan o ddyn 'a wretch of a man'
cloben o ferch 'a strapping girl'

(x) To mark the subject of the verb-noun: see **326** (ii).

(xi) Between an adverbial adjective and another adjective:

> *yn hynod o gryf* 'extremely strong'
> *yn rhyfeddol o falch* 'wonderfully happy'
> *yn od o dda* 'fairly good'
> *yn ddychrynllyd o ddrud* 'horribly expensive'
> *yn syndod o gryf* 'surprisingly strong'

379 rhag, primary meanings 'before, against; from; lest'

The prep. occurs:

(i) Following certain verbs, for example:

amddiffyn rhag 'defend from/against'	*achub rhag* 'save from'
	arswydo rhag 'dread'
atal rhag 'keep from, prohibit'	*cysgodi rhag* 'shelter from'
cadw rhag 'save from'	*cuddio rhag* 'hide from'
celu rhag 'hide from'	*diogelu rhag* 'make safe from'
dianc rhag 'escape from'	*ymguddio rhag* 'hide oneself
gwared rhag 'deliver from'	from'

> *Gwared ni rhag drwg*
> 'Deliver us from evil'

> *Aeth i gysgodi rhag y glaw*
> 'He went to shelter from the rain'

> *Mae hi wedi cadw'r wybodaeth rhagom*
> 'She has kept the information from us'

(ii) In a negative purpose clause:

> *Paid â gorwedd rhag iti gysgu*
> 'Do not lie down lest you sleep'

(iii) To express the meaning 'because' before an equative adj.: see **199**.

380 wrth, primary meanings 'by; with; to; because'

The prep. occurs:

(i) Following certain verbs, for example:

addef wrth 'confess'	*dweud wrth* 'tell, say'
cenfigennu wrth 'envy'	*digio wrth* 'be angry with'
disgwyl wrth 'expect'	*trugarhau wrth* 'have mercy on'

glynu wrth 'stick to'   *llefaru wrth* 'speak to'
tosturio wrth 'have pity on'   *sorri wrth* 'be displeased with'

Dywedais wrtho sawl gwaith
'I told him several times'

Tosturiwch wrth y plant
'Have pity on the children'

(ii) To express the meaning 'towards', following certain adjectives, for example:

caredig wrth 'kind to'   *cas wrth* 'nasty to'
tyner wrth 'tender to'   *dig wrth* 'angry with'
creulon wrth 'cruel to'   *tirion wrth* 'gentle with'

Yr oedd yn greulon wrth ei gi
'He was cruel to his dog'

Mae bob amser yn garedig wrthynt
'He is always kind to them'

(iii) With forms of *bod* 'to be' to express diligence, industry, business:

Yr oedd wrth ei waith
'He was at his work'

Mae wrthi yn yr ardd
'He is busy in the garden'

(iv) To express comparison between two things:

Nid yw hwn yn ddim wrth y llall
'This is nothing compared to the other'

(v) To mark the object in a *rhaid* construction:

Mae'n rhaid iddynt wrth olau
'They must have light'

Rhaid i bob gweithiwr wrth gyflog
'Every worker must have a wage'

(vi) In adverbial clauses to express the meaning 'while':

Wrth imi gerdded i'r dref, ystyriais beth a wnawn weddill y dydd
'While I was walking to town, I considered what I would do for the rest of the day'

Wrth gysgu breuddwydiais
'While I was sleeping I dreamed'

(vii) In idioms:

wrthyf fy hun(an) 'by myself, alone'
wrthyt dy hunan 'by yourself'
wrtho'i hunan 'by himself'
wrthi'i hunan 'by herself'
wrthym ein hunain 'by ourselves'
wrthych eich hunain 'by yourselves'
wrthynt eu hunain 'by themselves'

381 wedi, primary meaning 'after'

The prep. occurs:

(i) Before demonstrative pronouns, numerals, and nouns expressing time and incidents:

wedi hynny 'after that'
wedi chwech o'r gloch 'after six o'clock'
wedi'r Pasg 'after Easter'
wedi cwrdd 'after chapel'
wedi'r arholiadau 'after the examinations'
wedi'r ail o'r mis 'after the second of the month'

(ii) Before verb-nouns in an adverbial phrase, and in absolute phrases:

Wedi iddo orffen ei waith, aeth i orffwyso
'After he had finished his work, he went to rest'

Wedi bachu'r pysgodyn, fe'i collodd o'r rhwyd
'Having hooked the fish, he lost it from the net'

Gwadodd ei fod wedi dweud hynny, a minnau wedi ei glywed
'He denied that he had said that, and I having heard him'

(iii) *wedi* + verb-noun may qualify a preceding noun:

plentyn wedi blino 'a tired child'
coeden wedi disgyn 'a fallen tree'

A passive construction also occurs where the possessive pronoun precedes the verb-noun:

wy wedi ei ferwi 'a boiled egg'
dillad wedi eu crasu 'aired clothes'

The construction is made negative by substituting *heb* for *wedi*:

> *coeden heb ddisgyn* 'a tree that has not fallen'
> *dillad heb eu crasu* 'clothes that have not been aired'

On mutation following *heb* see **69**.
Examples:

> *crwyn hyrddod wedi eu lliwio'n goch*
> 'rams' skins dyed red'
>> (Exod. 25: 5)

> *Dyn wedi dychryn yw e*
> 'He is a frightened man'
>> (Idwal Jones, 1978: 75)

> *Pobl wedi marw ydan ninna!*
> 'We are dead people!'
>> (Idwal Jones, n.d.: 45)

(iv) As a verbal adjunct: see **286**.

382 yn, primary meaning 'in, at, into'

The prep. occurs:

(i) Before a definite noun following certain verbs, for example:

cydio yn 'grasp in'	*gafael yn* 'take hold of'
glynu yn 'cling to'	*gorfoleddu yn* 'rejoice in'
llawenychu yn 'rejoice in'	*ymffrostio yn* 'boast about'
ymserchu yn 'cherish'	*ymhyfrydu yn* 'delight oneself in'
ymdrybaeddu yn 'wallow in'	*ymddiried yn* 'trust'
credu yn 'believe in'	*ymaflyd yn* 'wrestle with'

> *Yr wyf yn ymddiried yn llwyr ynddo*
> 'I trust him completely'

> *Credwch yn Nuw*
> 'Believe in God'

> *Gafael ynddo!*
> 'Take hold of him!'

(ii) Before definite nouns:

> *yn yr ardd* 'in the garden'
> *yn Llanfair* 'in Llanfair'

yng Nghwmaman 'in Cwmaman'
ym Machynlleth 'in Machynlleth'

On *yng*, *ym* see **111**.

Mewn must be used before an indefinite noun:

mewn car 'in a car'
mewn lle unig 'in a lonely place'

A noun followed by another in a genitival construction is normally definite:

yn ysgol y pentref 'in the village school'
ym Mhrifysgol Cymru 'in the University of Wales'
yng Ngharchar Caerdydd 'in Cardiff Prison'

The genitival noun may be adjectival, thus forming a noun + adjective relationship (see **68**). The expression is regarded as a compound indefinite noun and is preceded by *mewn*:

mewn cymanfa ganu 'in a singing festival'
mewn siop esgidiau 'in a shoe shop'
mewn bocs pren 'in a wooden box'
mewn cadair freichiau 'in an armchair'

(iii) Before words like *angau* 'death', *paradwys* 'paradise', *uffern* 'hell', *tragwyddoldeb* 'eternity', *pawb* 'everyone', which are deemed definite and are therefore preceded by *yn*. *Dim* 'nothing, anything' vacillates between definite and indefinite:

yn angau 'in death'
ym mharadwys 'in paradise'
ym mhob dim 'in all things'
mewn dim 'in anything'

Distinction is made between *yng ngharchar* 'in prison', *mewn carchar* 'in a prison'. The article is elided in phrases such as

yn tŷ	= *yn y tŷ*	'in the house'
yn gwely	= *yn y gwely*	'in the bed'
yn tân	= *yn y tân*	'in the fire'
yn Gymraeg	= *yn y Gymraeg*	'in Welsh' (see **159** (iii)).

When the noun points to a particular period in the history of a language, refers to quality of usage or to a particular variety of a language it is regarded as indefinite and preceded by *mewn*:

mewn Cernyweg Canol 'in Middle Cornish'
mewn Cymraeg llafar 'in spoken Welsh'
mewn Almaeneg safonol 'in standard German'

(iv) With the pronominalia *un* (see **240**), *unrhyw* (see **242**), *rhyw* (see **241**), *rhai* (see **243**) the selection of *yn* or *mewn* is dependent on the exact meaning:

Clymwch y ci mewn un man diogel
'Tie the dog in one safe place'

Mae lle ichi yn un o'r seddau blaen
'There is room for you in one of the front seats'

Mae hi yn yr ardd yn rhywle
'She is in the garden in some place'

Cuddiwch ef mewn rhyw le diogel
'Hide it in some safe place'

(v) With *pwy* and *pa* (see **235**):

Ym mhwy wyt ti'n gallu ymddiried?
'In whom are you able to confide?'

Ym mha adran wyt ti'n gweithio?
'In which section are you working?'

(vi) With nouns and adjectives as a predicative particle:

Lladdasom bawb ym mhob dinas, yn ddynion, gwragedd a phlant
'We killed everybody in every city, men, women and children'
        (Deut. 3: 6)

Trodd yn sarff
'It became a serpent'
        (Exod. 3: 4)

Gwnaf eu dyfroedd yn groyw
'I will make their waters sweet'
        (Ezek. 32: 14)

Y maent yn gwneud eu phylacterau'n llydan
'They make their phylacteries broad'
   (Matt. 23: 5)

See also **278, 359**.
On mutation following the predicative *yn*, see **50, 54**.

(vii)   As a verbal adjunct: see **278, 286**.

(viii)   With verb-nouns as a predicative particle:

Yr wyf wedi diffygio'n gweiddi
'I am weary of shouting'
   (Ps. 69: 3)

See also **325** (vi).

Adverbs

Introduction

383   Only a few simple adverbs occur in Welsh. Many of the following forms are derived from adverbial expressions but function as simple adverbs.

384   Adverbs of time:

beunos 'every night'	*beunydd* 'every day'
heddiw 'today'	*heno* 'tonight'
echnos 'the night before last'	*byth/fyth* 'ever'
trennydd 'the day after tomorrow'	*eleni* 'this year'
trannoeth 'the following day'	*doe/ddoe* 'yesterday'
echdoe 'the day before yesterday'	*(y)fory* 'tomorrow'
y llynedd 'last year'	*eto* 'again'
tradwy 'two days hence'	*gynt* 'formerly'
cynt 'previously'	*yn awr/nawr* 'now'
yr awron/(y)rŵan 'now'	*wedyn* 'afterwards'
weithiau 'sometimes'	*yna* 'then'
weithian/weithion 'now'	*mwy* 'any more'
bellach/mwyach 'any longer'	*toc* 'soon'
yrhawg 'in future, for a long time to come'	*chwap* 'in a moment'

Examples:

Gwelais eneth hardd heddiw
'I saw a beautiful girl today'
    (Harri Williams, 1978: 72)

Mi fyddwch yn y pentref chwap
'You will be in the village in a moment'
    (Aneirin Talfan Davies, 1976: 30)

Gyda'r wawr drannoeth, trefnodd Duw i bryfyn nychu'r planhigyn, nes iddo grino
'At dawn the next day, God prepared a worm to weaken the plant, until it withered'
    (Jonah 4: 7)

Yr oeddent hwy a'u plant i mewn ac allan beunydd yn ei thŷ
'They and their children were in and out of her house every day'
    (Kate Roberts, 1972: 23)

Ymgeisiodd chwech eleni
'Six entered (the competition) this year'
    (J. Elwyn Hughes, 1991: 56)

Gwyddai ei bod yn rhy hwyr yrŵan i ychwanegu neb o bwys
'She knew that it was too late now to add anyone of note'
    (R. Cyril Hughes, 1975: 56)

Note
Byth, erioed
Byth functions as a non-perfective time adverb, as a marker of continuation, and as a perfective time adverb:

Ni fydd John byth yn gwybod
'John will never know'

Dydy'r hen chwaraewr byth yn blino ar straeon hen chwaraewyr eraill
'The former player never tires of the tales of other former players'
    (R. Gerallt Jones, 1977: 44)

Ni fyddai hi byth yn mynd ar gyfyl na chapel na llan
'She would never go near chapel or church'
    (T. Glynne Davies, 1974: 46)

Erioed functions as a perfective time adverb and as a marker of exclamation or surprise:

> *Ni wnaethai'r un ohonynt erioed osgo at roi unrhyw help ariannol iddi*
> 'Not one of them had ever made a gesture towards assisting her financially'
>> (Kate Roberts, 1972: 21)

> *Buasai ef farw cyn imi erioed weld y Berffro*
> 'He died before I ever saw Berffro'
>> (Rhiannon Davies Jones, 1977: 9)

> *Ni fedrais i erioed ystyried meddwyn o fyfyriwr yn arwr*
> 'I could not ever consider a drunken student a hero'
>> (John Jenkins, 1978: 127)

> *Ni fûm i erioed cyn oered wrth wylio rygbi*
> 'I had never been as cold when watching rugby'
>> (*Y Faner*, 14 Rhagfyr 1990: 21)

> *Fe ganwn ni fel na chanasom erioed o'r blaen*
> 'We will sing as we have never sung before'
>> (*Y Faner*, 19 Ionawr 1991: 21)

> *Rwyt ti mor real i mi rŵan ag y buost ti erioed*
> 'You are as real to me now as you have ever been'
>> (Angharad Tomos, 1991: 62)

> *Dydy John erioed yn gweithio!*
> 'John is never working!'

> *Fydd John erioed wedi cyrraedd mewn pryd!*
> 'John will never have arrived in time!'

385 Adverbs of place, manner and measure:

acw 'yonder'	*ddim* 'at all'
adref, tua thref 'home(wards)'	*allan* 'out'
gartref 'at home'	*draw* 'yonder'
hefyd 'also'	*hwnt* 'yonder'
(*yn*) *hytrach* 'rather'	*lled* 'fairly'
oll 'altogether'	*prin* 'hardly'
ynteu 'then, or else'	*uchod* 'above'
isod 'below'	*ymaith* 'away'

ymlaen 'forward, on'

dyna 'there is/are, that is, there are'

modd bynnag/fodd bynnag 'whatever, however'

dyma 'here is/are, this is, these are'

efallai/nid hwyrach 'perhaps'

ysywaeth 'alas, more's the pity'

Examples:

Câi gipolwg eto ddiwedd y prynhawn, cyn gyrru adref i'w fyngalo di-blant
'He would take a look again at the end of the afternoon, before driving home to his childless bungalow'
(Urien William, 1974: 22)

Draw mi welwn gribau Eryri
'Yonder I could see the peaks of Snowdonia'
(Rhiannon Davies Jones, 1977: 202)

Gwneud y cas yn gasiach, y clên yn gleniach a'r blêr yn fleriach ydyw tuedd y ddiod gadarn, ysywaeth
'The tendency of strong drink is to make the bitter more bitter, the affable more affable and the negligent more negligent, alas'
(Idwal Jones, n.d.: 38)

Nid hwyrach yr arhosaf gyda chwi (1955)
Efallai yr arhosaf gyda chwi (1988)
'I may stay with you'
(1 Cor. 16: 6)

Anfonodd ef adref
'He sent him home'
(Mark 8: 26)

Ni allent adael Gustavchen gartref gyda nain
'They could not leave Gustavchen at home with granny'
(Gerhart Hauptman and Heinrich Böll, 1974: 9)

386 Many adverbial expressions consist of a preposition followed by a noun, for example:

ar ôl 'after, behind'

o gwbl 'at all'

gerllaw 'nearby'

rhag llaw 'henceforth'

i maes 'out'

i fyny(dd) 'upwards'

ar led 'abroad'

i waered 'downwards'

rhag blaen 'at once'

i ffwrdd 'away'

yn ôl 'back'	*o gwbl* '(not) at all'
yn gwbl 'completely'	*ar frys* 'hastily'

In some expressions the article precedes the noun:

o'r neilltu 'on one side'	*ar y neilltu* 'separately,
o'r herwydd 'on that account'	individually'
o'r diwedd 'at last'	*o'r bron* 'completely'
i'r lan 'upwards'	*o'r blaen* 'previously'

Notes

(1) *I mewn* 'inside' consists of two prepositions.
(2) In informal texts and varieties of spoken Welsh *i* is often omitted before *lan, mewn, maes, ffwrdd, fyny(dd)*.

Examples:

Safai pysgotwr arall gerllaw a galwodd hwnnw arno
'Another fisherman was standing nearby and that one called to him'
    (Gerhart Hauptman and Heinrich Böll, 1974: 4)

Byddai i ffwrdd am ddeuddydd neu dri
'She would be away for two or three days'
    (Jane Edwards, 1976: 59)

Gwibiodd ei fys i fyny ac i lawr y colofnau
'His finger sped up and down the columns'
    (Urien William, 1974: 25)

Tyrd lan i'r gwely, nghariad i
'Come up to bed, my love'
    (R. Gerallt Jones, 1977: 40)

387 The preposition *yn* + adjective may form an adverb, for example:

yn dda 'well'	*yn well* 'better'
yn gyflym 'quickly'	*yn llawen* 'happily'
yn rhwydd 'easily'	*yn wresog* 'warmly'

On soft mutation following *yn* see **54**.

When *yn* is compounded with the adjective nasal mutation occurs (see **333** (ii)):

yn bell	*ymhell*	'far'
yn gynt	*ynghynt*	'sooner'

yn gyntaf	*ynghyntaf*	'firstly'
yn gudd	*ynghudd*	'secretly'
yn glwm	*ynghlwm*	'tied'

For example:

Ymhen deugain diwrnod fe ddymchwelir Ninefe
'Within forty days Nineveh shall be overthrown'
   (Jonah 3: 4)

Cerddodd at y drws, a gadwyd ynghau gan gortyn a dwy hoelen
'He walked towards the door that was kept shut by cord and two nails'
   (Georges Simenon, 1973: 7)

Prepositions other than *yn* may precede the adjective, for example:

ar fyr 'in short'
trwy deg 'fairly'
trwy deg neu hagr 'by fair (means) or foul'
trwy iawn 'by right'

388 The demonstrative pronouns *hyn*, *hynny* connect to prepositions to form adverbs (see **237**).

389 A preposition + the article or pronoun + superlative adjective may form an adverb (see **201** (iv)).

390 A superlative adjective without *yn* may function adverbially (see **201** (iii)).

391 Nominal groups expressing time, measure or duration are frequently used adverbially, for example:

diwrnod 'day'	*nos* 'evening'
dydd 'day'	*prynhawn* 'afternoon'
ennyd 'interval'	*wythnos* 'week'
bore 'morning'	*tridiau* 'three days'
prynhawn 'afternoon'	*modfedd* 'inch'
mis 'month'	*troedfedd* 'foot'
milltir 'mile'	*llathen* 'yard'

Examples:

Mae Mati a minnau am fynd i'r dref ddydd Mercher i brynu blows a het a menig
'Mati and I wish to go to town on Wednesday to buy a blouse and a hat and gloves'
   (Kate Roberts, 1976: 27)

Fis yn ôl fe symudsom ni yma o Gaerdydd
'A month ago we moved here from Cardiff'
(R. Gerallt Jones, 1977: 50)

Dwy flynedd yn ddiweddarach yr oedd llanc arall o'r enw Francis wedi saethu ati
'Two years later another youth called Francis had shot at her'
(T. Glynne Davies, 1974: 32)

Bwytaodd stêc deirgwaith yr wythnos er mwyn adfer ei ynni rhywiol
'He ate steak three times a week in order to restore his sexual energy'
(Harri Prichard Jones, 1978: 39)

Gwnâi hynny mewn lle rhyfedd iawn, ar lan y môr, ddiwrnod trip yr Ysgol Sul
'She was doing that in a very strange place, at the sea side, the day of the Sunday School outing'
(Kate Roberts, 1972: 22)

Roedd y criw gant y cant y tu cefn iddo
'The gang were one hundred per cent behind him'
(Jane Edwards, 1976: 90)

On mutation in the nominal group see **83**.

392 The adjectives *iawn* 'very', *odiaeth* 'extremely', *aruthr* 'very', *ofnadwy* 'terribly', *rhyfeddol* 'remarkably', *digon* 'mainly' etc., function adverbially following another adjective:

> *mawr iawn* 'very big'
> *hardd odiaeth* 'extremely beautiful'
> *drwg ofnadwy* 'terribly bad'
> *gwych ryfeddol* 'remarkably fine'
> *cywir ddigon* 'mostly correct'

On mutation of the adverbial adjective see **89**.

393 In periphrastic constructions (see **198**) *mor, mwy, mwyaf* are adverbs:

> *gwaith mwy deniadol*
> 'more attractive work'
>
> *cwmni mor ddymunol*
> 'such pleasant company'

y daith fwyaf cofiadwy
'the most memorable journey'

Adverbial expressions may be formed by *mwy na/fwy na*:

Er imi wrando'n astud ni allwn ei glywed fwy na chynt
'Although I listened intently I could not hear him more than before'

394 *Llai* 'smaller', *lleiaf* 'smallest', *eithaf* 'uttermost' (see **195**), *digon* 'enough' are adverbial preceding absolute adjectives:

llai gwreiddiol 'less original'
eithaf da 'quite good'
digon agos 'near enough'

395 The conjunction *ond/onid* occurs in adverbial expressions:

ond odid 'probably'
onid e 'otherwise'

Examples:

Fe gytunir, ond odid, eu bod yn dangos nodwedd arddullegol y gallai ein llenorion wneud mwy ohoni nag a wnaethant hyd yn hyn
'It is agreed, probably, that they show a stylistic characteristic that our writers could adopt more than they have done so far'
  (*BBCS*, 26, 1974–6: 23)

Gwell inni frysio onid e collwn y bws
'We had better hurry otherwise we will miss the bus'

396 Expressions such as *mae'n debyg* 'it is likely', *debyg (iawn)* 'probably', *decini* 'I suppose' function adverbially:

Pwrpas hyn, mae'n debyg, oedd dangos pa mor ffiaidd oedd y tai
'The purpose of this, probably, was to show how disgusting the houses were'
  (*Barn*, Tachwedd 1990: 38)

Debyg iawn, 'doedd Lora ddim mewn gwirionedd yn golygu'r hyn a ddywedai
'Very probably, Lora did not in reality mean what she was saying'
  (T. Glynne Davies, 1974: 245)

Hyn, decini, fu profiad eraill
'This, I suppose, had been the experience of others'
(*Taliesin*, Gorffennaf 1992: 26)

397 (i) In expressions such as *bloeddio canu* 'joyfully sing', *chwipio rhewi* 'freeze hard', *snwffian crio* 'snuffle, whimper', *gwichian chwerthin* 'giggle', *mwmian canu* 'hum', *treisio bwrw* 'pour (rain)' which consist of verb-noun + verb-noun, the first verb-noun acts as an intensifier and thus has an adverbial function.
Examples:

Bydd y mynyddoedd a'r bryniau'n bloeddio canu o'ch blaen
'The mountains and the hills shall joyfully sing before you'
(Isa. 55: 12)

Roedd y ferch yn beichio crio
'The girl was sobbing'
(John Rowlands, 1978: 115)

Beichio crio yr oedd hi y bore hwnnw
'She was sobbing that morning'
(Rhiannon Davies Jones, 1987: 128)

Yr oedd y crio wedi troi yn igian crio
'The crying had developed into convulsive sobbing'
(T. Glynne Davies, 1974: 136)

Dechreuodd Dici huno cysgu
'Dici started to snooze'
(Kate Roberts, 1972: 70)

(ii) On the adverbs *go, rhy, hollol, pur* see **90**.

(iii) On the adverb *tra* see **124**.

(iv) On the construction adverbial adjective + *o* + adjective see **378** (xi).

(v) On adverbial interrogatives see **235** (vi).

(vi) On adjectives functioning adverbially in a mixed sentence see **352**.

(vii) On adjectives functioning adverbially preceding other adjectives, nouns, verb-nouns, verbs in loose compounds see **332**.

Conjunctions

Introduction

398 Conjunctions may be either co-ordinating or subordinating. Co-ordinating conjunctions connect like to like, two or more words or clauses or sentences. Subordinating conjunctions introduce subordinate clauses.

(i) Co-ordinating

399 A(c) 'and'

The conjunction *ac* is pronounced [ag].

A occurs before consonants; *ac* is used before vowels and also before the negatives *ni, na*; *mor* 'as'; *felly* 'so, thus'; *fel* 'like'; *megis* 'as'; *mwyach* 'henceforth'; *mewn* 'in'; *mai* 'that'; *meddaf* 'I say'; *mae, sydd* 'is'; the particles *mi, fe*; a consonantal *i*:

> *dŵr a halen* 'water and salt'
> *ceffyl a chart* 'horse and cart'
> *cig a gwaed* 'flesh and blood'
> *gwlad ac iaith* 'country and language'
> *bywyd a gwaith* 'life and work'

On mutation following *a* see **118**.

A(c) is selected:

(i) To link co-ordinating main clauses:

> *Rhwymwch ei draed a'i ddwylo a bwriwch ef i'r tywyllwch eithaf*
> 'Bind his feet and his hands and throw him into the outer darkness'
>> (Matt. 22: 13)

> *Caewch eich ceg ddiddannedd, nain, a rhowch ochenaid o weddi i'r Forwyn dros daeogion Penlla'r-gaer!*
> 'Close your toothless mouth, grandmother, and whisper a prayer to the Virgin for the serfs of Penlla'r-gaer!'
>> (Rhiannon Davies Jones, 1977: 31)

> *Mae poen yn costio ac mae aberth yn costio*
> 'Pain costs and sacrifice costs'
>> (Rhiannon Davies Jones, 1985: 78)

On the use of the verb-noun instead of an inflected verb in a serial co-ordinating clause see **325** (iv).

In biblical prose the conj. *a(c)* frequently occurs at the beginning of serial co-ordinating sentences:

> *A phan welodd Ioan lawer o'r Phariseaid a'r Sadwceaid yn dod i'w bedyddio ganddo, dywedodd wrthynt* ... *A pheidiwch â meddwl dweud wrthych eich hunain* ... *Ac y mae'r fwyell eisoes wrth wraidd y coed*
> 'And when John saw many of the Pharisees and Sadducees coming to be baptized by him, he told them ... And do not presume to say to yourselves ... And the axe is already at the roots of trees'
> (Matt. 3: 7–9)

(ii) To introduce the absolute phrase (see **359**).

400 Neu 'or'

> *dau neu dri* 'two or three'
> *melyn neu las* 'yellow or blue'
> *haearn neu ddur* 'iron or steel'
> *ennill neu golli* 'win or lose'

On mutation following *neu* see **84**.

Clauses linked by *neu* are co-ordinating:

> *Ni chymerai honno unrhyw ddiddordeb neu fe ddywedai rywbeth dwl, diddim*
> 'That one did not show any interest or she would say something foolish, insignificant'
> (Kate Roberts, 1972: 25)

> *Eisteddai'r hen wraig yn fud neu dywedai ei phader mewn llais gwan, crynedig*
> 'The old woman would sit silently or she would pray in a weak, shaky voice'
> (Gerhart Hauptman and Heinrich Böll, 1974: 10)

In biblical prose the conj. *neu* occurs at the beginning of serial co-ordinating sentences:

> *Oherwydd sut y gwyddost, wraig, a achubi di dy ŵr? Neu sut y gwyddost, ŵr, a achubi di dy wraig?*

'Because how do you know, wife, whether you will save your husband? Or how do you know, husband, whether you will save your wife?'

(1 Cor. 7: 16)

Note
Verbs are not mutated following *neu: Dos allan neu bydd ddistaw!*
'Go out or be quiet!'

401 Ond 'but'

Ond is selected to link co-ordinating main clauses:

Gall siarad yn ddiddiwedd am weddi a ffydd ac edifeirwch, ond ni ŵyr ddim amdanynt
'He can speak incessantly about prayer and faith and repentance, but he knows nothing about them'
(John Bunyan, 1962: 42)

'Roeddwn i wedi fferru wrth eistedd cyhyd ger y ffynnon, ond trech chwilfrydedd na synnwyr
'I had frozen sitting for so long near the well, but curiosity is stronger than sense'
(Rhiannon Davies Jones, 1977: 44)

It frequently occurs at the beginning of serial co-ordinating sentences:

Ond byddai'r sawl a alwai Herr Kielblock yn ddyn diog yn gwneud camgymeriad. Ni fedrai neb weithio yn fwy diwyd nag ef. Ond pan ddôi'r hwylio i ben, gan gymaint y rhew, ni phryderai ddim
'But the person who would call Herr Kielblock a lazy man would be making a mistake. No one could work more assiduously than he. But when the sailing finished because of the accumulation of ice, he would not worry at all'
(Gerhart Hauptman and Heinrich Böll, 1974: 3)

Yr oedd ein tadau yn addoli ar y mynydd hwn. Ond yr ydych chi'r Iddewon yn dweud mai yn Jerwsalem y mae'r man lle dylid addoli
'Our fathers worshipped on this mountain. But you Jews say that it is in Jerusalem that the place for worship is'
(John 4: 20)

Dim ond 'nothing but' (see **81**) and *neb ond* 'no one but' often occur in negative sentences:

> *Nid oes yma ddim ond adar gwylltion*
> 'There is nothing here but wild birds'

> *Ni welwyd neb ond plant yn y goedwig*
> 'No one but children were seen in the wood'

Dim and *neb* are frequently omitted:

> *Nid oes yma ond adar gwylltion*
> *Ni welwyd ond plant yn y goedwig*

Ond often follows *pawb, pob un, y cwbl, i gyd, oll* etc., to express the meaning 'except, apart from':

> *Gwelais bawb ond fy mam*
> 'I saw everybody apart from my mother'

> *Maen nhw i gyd ond un yn bresennol*
> 'They are all present apart from one'

402 Namyn 'but'

Namyn may occur with numerals (see **203** n. 4):

> *cant namyn un* 'a hundred but one' (= 99)
> *y deugain erthygl namyn un* 'the 39 articles'

Namyn also connects other forms:

> *Bu adeg pan nad oedd milwyr o Gymry yn enwog am ddim namyn eu blerwch*
> 'There had been a time when Welsh soldiers were famous for nothing but their disarray'
> (Marion Eames, 1982: 23)

403 Eithr 'except, but'

Eithr links co-ordinating phrases:

> *Dynes â llygaid i weled oedd hi eithr â gwefusau i gau yn dynn rhag i'w thafod siarad â phawb yn ddiwahaniaeth*
> 'She was a woman with eyes to see but with lips to close tight lest her tongue talk to all and sundry'
> (Kate Roberts, 1972: 20)

It may also introduce serial co-ordinating sentences in narrative. In the 1988 translation of the Welsh Bible *eithr* has been replaced by *ond* in the following examples:

Clywsoch ddywedyd gan y rhai gynt, Na ladd . . . Eithr yr ydwyf fi
yn dywedyd i chwi . . . (1955)
Clywsoch fel y dywedwyd wrth y rhai gynt, Na ladd . . . Ond 'rwyf
fi'n dweud wrthych . . . (1988)
'You have heard our forefathers say, Do not commit murder . . .
But I tell you . . .'
    (Matt. 5: 21–2)

A hwy a osodasant ddwylo arnynt hwy . . . Eithr llawer o'r rhai a
glywsant y gair a gredasant (1955)
Cymerasant afael arnynt . . . Ond daeth llawer o'r rhai oedd wedi
clywed y gair yn gredinwyr (1988)
'And they arrested them . . . But many of those who had heard
the word believed'
    (Acts 4: 3–4)

404 Na(c)

Na(c) connects words and phrases in negative sentences.
    Na occurs before consonants, *nac* occurs before vowels:

Hiraethwn am fannau lle nad oedd gwynt na therfysg na haint na
phla
'I longed for places where there was no wind or terror or disease
or plague'
    (Rhiannon Davies Jones, 1985: 78)

Yr wyf yn gwbl sicr na all nac angau nac einioes, nac angylion na
thywysogaethau, na'r presennol na'r dyfodol, na grymusderau
nac uchelderau na dyfnderau, na dim byd arall a grewyd, ein
gwahanu ni oddi wrth gariad Duw
'I am convinced that neither death nor life, nor angels nor
principalities, nor the present nor the future, nor powers nor
heights nor depths, nor anything created, can separate us from
the love of God'
    (Rom. 8: 38–9)

Na(c) may occur before the first word in the series:

Ni all na llenorion na haneswyr na gwleidyddwyr y dyfodol
fforddio ei hanwybyddu
'Future authors or historians or politicians cannot afford to
ignore her'
    (*Taliesin*, Tachwedd 1989: 33)

Ni bydd arnynt angen na golau lamp na golau haul
'They will not need the light of lamp or the light of sun'
   (Rev. 22: 5)

Na(c) does not occur before the negative particles *ni, na* or the particles *mi, fe*.
On mutation following *na* see **116**.

405 Â, ag 'as'

Â is selected before consonants, *ag* occurs before vowels.
   They occur:

(i)   Following the equative degree of the adjective (see **199**).

(ii)   Preceding a relative clause (see **199**).

(iii)   Preceding a verb-noun (see **199**).

(iv)   Preceding an adverbial clause with *pe* and *pan* (see **199**).

(v)   Following words with prefixes *cyf-, cy-, cyd-* (see **138**):

Yr oedd ei gruddiau yn gyfliw â'r rhosyn
'Her cheeks were the same colour as the rose'

maent yn gydradd â'i gilydd
'they are equal to each other'

rhoddodd gymaint ag a oedd ganddo
'he gave as much as he possessed'

daeth cynifer ag a oedd yno ymlaen
'as many as were there came forward'

On mutation following *â* see **117**.

406 Naill ai . . . neu (ynteu) see **238** (iv).

407 Na(g) 'than'

Na is selected before consonants, *nag* occurs before vowels.
   It is used:

(i)   Following a comparative adjective (see **200** (i)):

Gwell yw llochesu yn yr Arglwydd nag ymddiried mewn tywysogion
'It is better to find refuge in the Lord than to trust in princes'
   (Ps. 118: 9)

Gwell yw parch nag arian ac aur (1988)
'Esteem is better than silver or gold'
    (Prov. 22: 1)

Na(g) may be repeated if the comparison refers to more than one object:

Gwell yw ffafr dda nag arian, ac nag aur (1955)
    (Prov. 22: 1)

(ii) Before a relative clause (see **234**).

On mutation following *na* see **116**.

408 Oherwydd, oblegid, canys, (o) achos 'because, since, for'

These are used to link co-ordinating sentences:

Cafodd geiriau ei gŵr gryn ddylanwad ar ei wraig, canys cododd yn sydyn ar ei thraed a dechreuodd ddawnsio o amgylch yr ystafell
'Her husband's words had great influence on his wife, because she got to her feet suddenly and started to dance around the room'
    (Gerhart Hauptman and Heinrich Böll, 1974: 5)

Ni ddywedais i ddim, oblegid yr oedd y capel wedi rhoi gwres canolog efo oel imi
'I didn't say anything, because the chapel had given me oil central heating'
    (Kate Roberts, 1976: 25)

Diolchwch i'r Arglwydd oherwydd da yw
'Give thanks to the Lord for he is good'
    (Ps. 118: 1)

Ni phrynais anrheg iddi o achos yr oedd y siopau i gyd wedi cau
'I did not buy her a present because all the shops had closed'

Note
Oherwydd, oblegid, (o) achos also occur as prepositions: see **368**.

409 Ys

Ys is used:

(i) Preceding the simple inflected forms of the verb *dweud* 'state, say' and *galw* 'call' to express the meaning 'as':

> *Heb fod ymhell o ganol Caerdydd saif y Carchar: 'Jail Caer-dydd', ys dywed y baledi*
> 'Not far from the centre of Cardiff stands the Prison: "Cardiff Jail" as the ballads say'
> > (Urien William, 1974: 19)

> *Ys dywedwyd, prif bwrpas y fenter yw astudio'r Gofod*
> 'As has been said, the venture's main aim is to study Outer Space'
> > (*Y Faner*, 14 Gorffennaf 1989: 16)

> *y Brenin Alltud (ys gelwir ef yn 'Mewn Dau Gae')*
> 'the Exiled King (as he is called in "Mewn Dau Gae")'
> > (R. Geraint Gruffydd, 1988: 112)

(ii) Preceding the 1 sing. pres. indic. of *gwybod* 'know, wonder' in an interrogative clause:

> *Oes 'na rywfaint yn hwn, ys gwn i?*
> 'Is there anything in this, I wonder?'
> > (Alun Jones, 1989: 33)

> *Ys gwn i a fyddech chi'n cytuno ei fod yn codi cwestiwn go sylfaenol?*
> 'I wonder whether you would agree that it raises a rather basic question?'
> > (*Golwg*, 20 Rhagfyr 1990: 26)

Note
In informal texts and varieties of spoken Welsh, the vowel frequently disappears and the consonant is appended to the following verb:

> *Sgwn i a oedd e'n cael ei ben blwydd bob mis neu rywbeth?*
> 'I wonder whether he used to have his birthday every month or something?'
> > (*Golwg*, 15 Hydref 1992: 14)

(ii) Subordinating

410 The following prepositions are used as conjunctions to introduce subordinating adverbial clauses of time, place, cause, purpose
etc.:

am 'because'	*wrth* 'while'
gan 'since'	*erbyn* 'by the time'
oblegid 'because'	*fel* 'so that'
oherwydd 'because'	*megis* 'as, just as'
o achos 'because'	*er mwyn* 'for the sake of'
er 'although'	*hyd* 'as far as'
rhag ofn 'lest'	*cyn* 'before'
rhag 'lest'	*gyda* 'as soon as'

The following nouns and adjectives are also used to introduce subordinating adverbial clauses (see **232, 235**):

pryd	*hyd nes*
pryd bynnag	*cymaint ag*
lle	*modd*
nes	

An affirmative clause is introduced by *y*, a negative clause is introduced by *na*.
   Examples:

Er nas gwelai ond yn anaml iawn, hwy oedd ei arwyr
'Although he only saw them infrequently, they were his heroes'
   (Urien William, 1974: 22)

*Fe hyrddiais innau ei llaw a'r cwpan ar draws yr ystafell nes yr
oedd darnau o grochenwaith Ewenni'n sglefrian o gwmpas y
llaw*
'I hurled her hand and the cup across the room until there were
pieces of Ewenni pottery skating across the room'
   (R. Gerallt Jones, 1977: 34)

*Lle'r oedd Barry John yn llifo'n ddiymdrech dros y ddaear mae
Phil yn gwibio fel arian byw*
'Where Barry John used to flow effortlessly across the surface
Phil darts like quicksilver'
   (R. Gerallt Jones, 1977: 48)

*Fel y nesaem at y cylch gwelwn y cerrig anferth fel cewri byw yn
ymestyn tua'r ffurfafen*

'As we drew near to the circle I could see the massive stones like live giants stretching towards the heavens'
(Rhiannon Davies Jones, 1977: 21)

Penliniais innau'n ufudd gan na feiddiwn groesi Gwladus
'I knelt obediently because I dared not cross Gwladus'
(Rhiannon Davies Jones, 1977: 22)

Estyn dy ddisgl, Angharad, rhag ofn y bydd hi'n sâl
'Pass your bowl, Angharad, in case she is (lit. will be) ill'
(Rhiannon Davies Jones, 1977: 113)

Gwnaeth gais am blwyf er mwyn cael ei ordeinio, ond am na chafodd y plwyf a ddymunai, tynnodd ei gais yn ôl
'He applied for a parish in order to be ordained, but because he did not have the parish that he desired, he withdrew his application'
(Harri Williams, 1978: 18)

Ni fyddai hi byth yn mynd ar gyfyl na chapel na llan, er y byddai'n gweddïo bob nos a bore
'She would never go near chapel or church, although she prayed every night and morning'
(T. Glynne Davies, 1974: 46)

Aros di yno hyd nes y clywi di Dewi a Chybi yn siarad â thi
'You wait there until you hear Dewi and Cybi speaking to you'
(J. G. Williams, 1978: 9)

Aros di nes y daw hi'n ôl!
'You wait until she returns!'
(Gweneth Lilly, 1981: 66)

Mor fychan yw cyflog athro yn Nepal fel na eill fyw heb iddo roi gwersi i unigolion gyda'r nos
'A teacher's salary in Nepal is so small that he cannot live without giving lessons to individuals in the evening'
(Beti Rhys, 1988: 61)

Y is frequently omitted:

Cerddais i mewn i gae gwair nes byddai'r ffordd yn glir
'I walked into a hayfield until the road would be clear'
(Emyr Humphreys, 1981: 317)

See also **311** (ii) (b).

Notes

(1) *Megis* and *fel* may be followed by *ag*: *ni a gawn ei weled ef megis ag y mae* (1955), *cawn ei weld ef fel y mae* (1988) 'we will see him as he is' (John 3: 2); *yr oedd fel ag yr oedd* 'he was as he was'.

(2) The equative adj. *cymaint ag* (see **194**, **199**) becomes *yn gymaint ag* 'in as much as' as a conj.: *yn gymaint ag i chwi beidio â'i wneud i un o'r rhai lleiaf hyn, nis gwnaethoch i minnau chwaith* 'in as much as you did not do it to one of the least of these, you did not do it for me' (Matt. 25: 45).

(3) (*Hyd*) *nes* may be followed directly by the verb-noun or by *i* + verb-noun: *Ymbalfalai ynddi nes dod o hyd i Pfennig* 'She would grope inside till she would discover a Pfennig' (Gerhart Hauptman and Heinrich Böll, 1974: 4); *Fe arhosaf nes iti ddod yn ôl* 'I will stay until you come back' (Judg. 6: 18).

411 Pan 'when'

(i) When *pan* occurs in an affirmative clause it is followed immediately by the verb:

Fe fyddai Rhisiart o'i gof pan glywai am y briodas anghymarus hon
'Richard would be angry when he would hear of this incongruous wedding'
    (R. Cyril Hughes, 1976: 120)

Pan oedd ar ganol cael bath, fe ganodd y ffôn
'While he was in the middle of having a bath, the phone rang'
    (John Rowlands, 1978: 88)

Mi fydd yn gaffaeliad mawr iawn inni pan ddaw o atom ni
'He will be a great asset to us when he comes to us'
    (J. G. Williams, 1978: 158)

On mutation following *pan* see **94**.
    When the infixed object pronoun (see **217**) is selected it is attached to a particle *y* which follows *pan*:

pan y'm clywai clust (1955)
'when the ear heard me'
    (Job 29: 11)

Serial subordinate clauses following one introduced by *pan* can be linked by *y* thus avoiding repetition of *pan*:

Gwyn eich byd pan y'ch gwaradwyddant ac y'ch erlidiant (1955)
'Blessed are you when they abuse you and persecute you'
   (Matt. 5: 11)

This construction has been abandoned in the above examples in the 1988 translation of the Welsh Bible:

Gwyn eich byd pan fydd dynion yn eich gwaradwyddo a'ch erlid
'Blessed are you when men abuse you and persecute you'
   (Matt. 5: 11)

Note
A construction with a prefixed pron. following *pan* is antiquated: *pan ei dygasoch adref, chwythais adref* (1955), *pan ddygwch y cynhaeaf adref, yr wyf yn chwythu adref* (1988) 'when you would bring home the harvest, I blast home' (Hag. 1: 9).

(ii) The present subjunctive may occur following *pan* when the action of the verb is indefinite (see **311** (ii)). In the following examples the 1988 translation of the Welsh Bible has abandoned the subjunctive and selected the indicative:

Pan edrychwyf ar y nefoedd, gwaith dy fysedd (1955)
Pan edrychaf ar y nefoedd, gwaith dy fysedd (1988)
'When I look at the heavens, the work of your fingers'
   (Ps. 8: 3)

pan agorwyf eich beddau (1955)
pan agoraf eich beddau (1988)
'when I open your graves'
   (Ezek. 37: 13)

pan ddihunwyf (1955)
pan ddihunaf (1988)
'when I awake'
   (Ps. 17: 15)

(iii) On the 3 sing. pres. indic. of *bod* following *pan* see **283**.

(iv) In negative clauses *pan* is followed by *na(d)*; *na* occurs before consonants, *nad* before vowels.

Pan na chafodd ateb, gwthiodd y drws yn bwyllog
'When he didn't have a reply, he pushed at the door carefully'
   (Idwal Jones, 1977: 73)

Un anhydrin oedd Gwenllian pan na fyddai'r Tywysog ei hun o gylch y lle
'Gwenllian was an obstinate one, when the Prince himself wasn't about the place'
(Rhiannon Davies Jones, 1977: 174)

Aeth i ddwyn yr arian pan nad oedd neb yn edrych
'He went to steal the money when no one was looking'

412 Er pan 'since'

Fuom ni ddim mewn priodas, er pan briododd tad Ceinwen, nac i ffwrdd yn unlle ac mae naw mlynedd er pan gawsom ni ddillad newydd
'We haven't been in a wedding, since Ceinwen's father got married, or away somewhere either and it's nine years since we had new clothes'
(Kate Roberts, 1976: 27)

Aeth llawer o amser heibio er pan fûm yn teimlo mor hyfryd iach a chryf
'A lot of time has passed since I felt so pleasantly fit and strong'
(J. G. Williams, 1978: 11)

413 Tra 'while'

(i) *Tra* is followed immediately by the verb:

Bydd dyfodol Cymru'n ddiogel tra llwydda'r Blaid
'The future of Wales will be secure while Plaid prospers'
(John Jenkins, 1978: 173)

Ni fedrai neb weithio yn fwy diwyd nag ef tra oedd gwaith i'w wneud
'No one could work more diligently than he while there was work to be done'
(Gerhart Hauptman and Heinrich Böll, 1974: 3)

Tra y also occurs:

Gwthiodd ei ddwylo yn ddwfn i'w bocedi tra y gafaelodd hi yn ei fraich
'He pushed his hands deep into his pockets while she held his arm'
(Emyr Humphreys, 1986: 110)

Ceisiwch yr Arglwydd tra y gellir ei gael (1955)
'Seek the Lord while he is still to be found'
    (Isa. 55: 6)

The 1988 translation of the Welsh Bible omits *y* following *tra*.

(ii) In earlier biblical texts *tra* is frequently followed by the subjunctive mood and may project soft mutation. In the 1988 translation of the Welsh Bible the radical follows *tra* and the subjunctive mood is replaced by the indicative mood in the following examples:

Canaf i'r Arglwydd tra fyddwyf fyw: canaf i'm Duw tra fyddwyf (1955)
Canaf i'r Arglwydd tra byddaf byw, rhof foliant i Dduw tra byddaf (1988)
'I will sing to the Lord as long as I live, I will praise my God all my life'
    (Ps. 104: 33)

Gelwch arno tra fyddo yn agos (1955)
Galwch arno tra bydd yn agos (1988)
'Call upon him while he is near'
    (Isa. 55: 6)

Y ffôl tra tawo a gyfrifir yn ddoeth (1955)
Tra tawa'r ffôl, fe'i hystyrir yn ddoeth (1988)
'While the fool holds his peace, he is thought wise'
    (Prov. 17: 28)

(iii) In a negative clause *tra na(d)* occurs:

Tra na byddom yn edrych ar y pethau a welir, ond ar y pethau ni welir (1955)
'While we look not at the things that are seen, but at the things that are not seen'
    (2 Cor. 4: 18)

Note
The adverb *tra* and the prefix *tra-* project spirant mutation (see **124, 139**).

414 Oni(d), hyd oni(d) 'until'

Onid, hyd onid occur before vowels: *oni, hyd oni* occur before consonants:

Dangoswch farwolaeth yr Arglwydd oni ddelo (1955)
'Proclaim the death of the Lord until he comes'
(1 Cor. 11: 26)

Dyma'r seren a welsant ar ei chodiad yn mynd o'u blaen hyd oni ddaeth hi ac aros uwchlaw'r man lle 'roedd y mab bychan
'This is the star which they had seen at its rising going ahead of them until it reached and stopped above the place where the young child was'
(Matt. 2: 9)

The infixed pronoun may be attached to *oni*:

Pa wraig a chanddi ddeg dryll o arian, os cyll hi un dryll, ni olau gannwyll, ac ysgubo'r tŷ, a cheisio yn ddyfal hyd onis caffo ef? (1955)
'What woman who has ten silver pieces, if she loses one piece, does not light a candle and sweep the house carefully till she has found it?'
(Luke 15: 8)

On mutation following *oni*, *hyd oni* see **93, 123**.

415 Os, o(d), oni(d), pe(d) introduce conditional clauses.

(i) In earlier prose *os* and *o(d)* occur; *o* occurs before consonants, *od* before vowels:

Os gofynnwch ddim yn fy enw i, mi a'i gwnaf. O cherwch fi cedwch fy ngorchmynion (1955)
Os gofynnwch unrhyw beth i mi yn fy enw i, fe'i gwnaf. Os ydych yn fy ngharu i, fe gadwch fy ngorchmynion i (1988)
'If you ask anything in my name, I will do it. If you love me you will obey my commandments'
(John 14: 14–15)

Od ymdrech neb, hefyd, ni choronir ef onid ymdrech yn gyfreithlon (1955)
Os yw dyn yn cystadlu mewn mabolgamau, ni all ennill y dorch heb gystadlu yn ôl rheolau (1988)
'If a person competes, also he will not be crowned unless he has competed lawfully'
(2 Tim. 2: 5)

Os has supplanted *o(d)* in contemporary prose and in the 1988 translation of the Welsh Bible.
On mutation following *o* see **120**.

(ii) *Os* normally precedes the verb, but if emphasis is required on some element of the clause other than the verb, *os* will precede the element requiring emphasis:

> *Os oes ofn arnoch chi, byddai'n well i chi fynd*
> 'If you are afraid, it would be better for you to go'
>> (Emyr Humphreys, 1981: 289)

> *Os 500 o gopïau oedd y cyfanswm a gyhoeddwyd yn yr argraffiad hwn, yna amhosibl fod llawer o'r werin yn cael copïau*
> 'If 500 copies were the total published in that edition, then it is impossible that many common people had copies'
>> (Gwyn Thomas, 1971: 92)

> *Os Mab Duw wyt ti, dywed wrth y cerrig hyn am droi'n fara*
> 'If you are the Son of God, tell these stones to become bread'
>> (Matt. 4: 3)

Os y may occur before the verb in informal texts and varieties of spoken Welsh:

> *Fe ddaw deddf os y gweithredwn i gael un*
> 'Legislation will come if we act to have it'
>> (*Y Faner*, 23 Chwefror 1990: 18)

> *Hwyrach na ddaw Robert yn ôl hyd G'lan Gaea', os y daw o o gwbl*
> 'Perhaps Robert will not return until All Saints' Day, if he returns at all'
>> (Rhiannon Davies Jones, 1985: 21)

(iii) Examples occur in earlier biblical prose of placing *os* before an element other than the verb when no emphasis is intended. The clauses have abnormal sentence structure (see **351**) and the construction has been abandoned in the 1988 translation of the Welsh Bible:

> *Os myfi a af. . . mi a ddeuaf drachefn* (1955)
> *Os af. . . fe ddof yn ôl* (1988)
> 'If I go . . . I shall return'
>> (John 14: 3)

> *Os chwychwi a fedrwch roddi rhoddion da . . .* (1955)
> *Os ydych chwi yn rhoi rhoddion da i'ch plant* (1988)
> 'If you are able to give good gifts . . .'
>> (Matt. 7: 11)

In varieties of spoken Welsh and in literary texts *mai* or *taw* frequently occurs between *os* and the element selected for emphasis:

> *Os taw'r Bontfaen a ystyrir yn 'brif-ddinas' y Fro, y pentref hwn*
> *yw ei chalon*
> 'If Cowbridge is considered the "capital" of the Vale, this village
> is its heart'
>> (Aneirin Talfan Davies, 1972: 59)

> *Os mai ti, syr, a'i cymerodd ef, dywed wrthyf lle y rhoddaist ef i*
> *orwedd* (1988)
> *Syr, os tydi a'i dygaist ef, dywed i mi pa le y dodaist ef* (1955)
> 'If it is you, sir, who removed him, tell me where you have laid
> him'
>> (John 20: 15)

(iv) The conjunction *o* and the negative *nid* are combined to form a
conj. *oni(d)* 'if not, unless'. *Oni* occurs before consonants, *onid*
before vowels:

> *Oni fyddwch yn sefydlog, ni'ch sefydlogir*
> 'Unless you will be firm, you will not be established'
>> (Isa. 7: 9)

> *Oni wrandewi ar lais yr Arglwydd dy Dduw . . . daw arnat yr holl*
> *felltithion hyn* (1955)
> 'Unless you obey the voice of the Lord your God . . . all these
> maledictions shall come to you'
>> (Deut. 28: 15)

In varieties of spoken Welsh and in literary texts *os na(d)* may be
selected instead of *oni(d)*:

> *Dydy pobol ifanc heddiw ddim yn fodlon os na chân nhw falu a*
> *dinistrio*
> 'Young people today are not content if they are not allowed to
> wreck and destroy'
>> (Eigra Lewis Roberts, 1980: 93)

> *Os na fyddi'n gwrando ar lais yr Arglwydd dy Dduw . . . fe ddaw*
> *i'th ran yr holl felltithion hyn* (1988)
> 'Unless you obey the voice of the Lord your God . . . all these
> maledictions shall come to you'
>> (Deut. 28: 15)

Onid is the negative form corresponding to *os* which occurs before elements (other than verbs) requiring emphasis:

> *Dylid newid trefn y rhaglen rhagblaen ac adolygu llyfrau Cymraeg yn unig. Onid e, beth yw pwrpas rhaglenni Cymraeg?*
> 'The order of the programme should be changed at once to review only Welsh books. If not, what is the purpose of Welsh programmes?'
> (*Y Faner*, 27 Medi 1991: 8)

> *Os daw â ffrwyth y flwyddyn nesaf, popeth yn iawn; onid e, cei ei dorri i lawr*
> 'If it yields fruit next year, all well and good; if not you may cut it down'
> (Luke 13: 9)

(v) *Os* introduces conditional clauses that contain implications as to the truth or falsehood of the premise. *Pe(d)* introduces conditional clauses that express doubt or false supposition. *Pe* occurs before consonants, *ped* before vowels:

> *Pe dôi rhyfel ar fy ngwarthaf, eto, fe fyddwn yn hyderus*
> 'Though a war would come upon me, yet, I would be confident'
> (Ps. 27: 3)

> *Ped adwaenit ti ddawn Duw . . .* (1955)
> 'If you knew the gift of God . . .'
> (John 4: 10)

> *Mae hi'n sicr na phoenwn i . . . ped enillai Cymru ym Mharis*
> 'It is certain that I would not worry . . . if Wales were to win in Paris'
> (*Y Faner*, 21 Chwefror 1992: 22)

(vi) The verb following *pe(d)* is in the imperfect subjunctive or the pluperfect (see **312**).

(vii) The infixed pronoun may be affixed to *pe* (see **218** (b), **312**).

416 When *pe* is bound to forms of the verb *bod* 'to be' the following forms occur:

Imperfect Tense

Sing.		Pl.	
1	*pe bawn*	*pe baem*	
2	*pe bait*	*pe baech*	
3	*pe bai*	*pe baent*	

Pluperfect Tense

1	*pe buaswn*	*pe buasem*
2	*pe buasit*	*pe buasech*
3	*pe buasai*	*pe buasent*

The above forms are commonly contracted:

Imperfect Tense

	Sing.	Pl.
1	*petawn*	*petaem*
2	*petait*	*petaech*
3	*petai*	*petaent*

Pluperfect Tense

1	*petaswn*	*petasem*
2	*petasit*	*petasech*
3	*petasai*	*petasent*

Examples:

Petaent yn fy eillio, yna byddai fy nerth yn pallu
'If they shaved me, then my strength would fail'
(Judg. 16: 17)

Petai'n gwenu, byddai peryg i'w wyneb gracio
'If he smiled, his face would be in danger of cracking'
(John Rowlands, 1978: 36)

Fe fyddai'n dda gen i petaech chi'n mynd i'r clinic rwan ac yn y man i gael pob gofal
'I would be glad if you were to go to the clinic occasionally to have every care'
(Islwyn Ffowc Elis, 1970: 16)

Pe baent i gyd yn un aelod, lle byddai'r corff?
'If the whole were one organ, where would the body be?'
(1 Cor. 12: 19)

Pe bai fy nhad a'm mam yn cefnu arnaf, byddai'r Arglwydd yn fy nerbyn
'If my father and my mother were to forsake me, the Lord would accept me'
(Ps. 27: 10)

. *Pe na(d)* occurs in a negative clause:

Diffygiaswn, pe na chredaswn (1955)
'I would have fainted, had I not believed'
(Ps. 27: 13)

Da fuasai i'r dyn hwnnw pe nas ganesid ef
'It would be better for that man if he had never been born'
(Matt. 26: 24)

Cofier nad ef fyddai'n ddewis cyntaf y wlad pe na fyddai Fabio Gomez yn chwarae yn Yr Eidal
'Remember that he would not be the country's first choice were Fabio Gomez not playing in Italy'
(*Y Faner*, 23 Tachwedd 1990: 21)

If emphasis is required the element to be emphasized can occur between *pe* and the verb:

a phe rhy fychan fuasai hynny, myfi a roddaswn iti fwy o lawer (1955)
'and had this been too small, I would give you much more'
(2 Sam. 12: 8)

pe deillion fyddech, ni byddai arnoch bechod (1955)
'if you were blind, you would be without sin'
(John 9: 41)

In the 1988 translation of the Welsh Bible this construction has been abandoned:

A phe buasai hynny'n rhy ychydig, buaswn wedi ychwanegu cymaint eto
(2 Sam. 12: 8)

Pe baech yn ddall, ni byddai gennych bechod
(John 9: 41)

Fel and *megis* can be followed by *pe*:

I'w cyfarfod, gan sefyll bron yn union o'u blaenau fel pe bai ar fin siarad â nhw, fe ddaeth dyn blonegog tew
'To meet them, standing almost directly in front of them as though he were about to speak to them, came a fat greasy man'
(T. Glynne Davies, 1974: 294)

Eisteddai Angela ar y gwely yn ei ffrog wen laes, wedi croesi ei choesau, yn union fel petai'n hysbysebu dodrefn llofft
'Angela sat on the bed in her long white frock, having crossed her legs, exactly as though she were advertising bedroom furniture'
(John Rowlands, 1978: 85)

Cerddai'n ofalus megis petai wedi neweidio'i goes
'He walked carefully as though he had injured his leg'

417 Mai

(i) *Mai* occurs in noun clauses to mark emphasis (see **353** (B), (C)).

(ii) *Fel mai* occurs:

Yr oedd y tywydd mor stormus fel mai ychydig a ddaeth i'r cyfarfod
'The weather was so stormy that few came to the meeting'

418 Po

Po is deemed a conjunction before a superlative adjective expressing the meaning 'the sooner . . . the better' etc.:

Gorau po gyntaf y dychweli
'The sooner you return the better'

See **201** (ii).

Note
Po is an alternative form of *bo*, 3 sing. pres. subj. of *bod* 'to be' (see **277**).

419 Ynteu 'then, else'

Ynteu is an earlier form of the 3 sing. conjunctive pron. *yntau* (see **211** (c)) and occurs as a conjunction:

O ble, ynteu, y daeth y feistrolaeth hon ar y tair iaith?
'From where, then, did this mastery of the three languages come?'
(*Llên Cymru* 16: 10)

Pam, ynteu, yr aeth yn ysbail?
'Why, then, has he been despoiled?'
(Jer. 2: 14)

Beth ynteu a ddylem ei wneud?
'What then should we do?'
　　(*Taliesin*, Tachwedd 1989: 6)

Interjections

420 The following simple interjections occur and are often followed by a noun in the vocative: *a, ha, hai, o, ho, och, ach, ych, ha-ha, o-ho, wfft, gwae, ust, twt, pw, wel, ow,* etc.
Examples:

O na bawn wedi cyrraedd oedran ymddeol
'Oh that I had not reached retiring age'
　　(*Barn*, Mawrth 1990: 2)

Ust! dyma lais fy nghariad
'Hark! here is my beloved's voice'
　　(S. of S., 2: 8)

Ha, wŷr doethion (1955)
'O, wise men'
　　(Job 34: 2)

O genhedlaeth gwiberod (1955)
'O brood of vipers'
　　(Matt. 3: 7)

Gwae wlad yr adenydd chwim
'Woe the land of speedy wings'
　　(Isa. 18: 1)

Och! Twrf pobloedd lawer
'Ah! The thunder of many peoples'
　　(Isa. 17: 2)

421 Interjectional forms and expressions often originate in other parts of speech and form phrases and sentences, for example:

Bore da!	'Good morning!'
Prynhawn da!	'Good afternoon!'
Dydd da i chi!	'Good day to you!'
Croeso!	'Welcome!'
Bendith arnat!	'Bless you!'

Rhad arno!	'A blessing upon him!' (sarcastically)
Rhag cywilydd!	'For shame!'
Myn f'enaid i!	'By my soul!'
Myn cythraul!	'By a demon!'
Myn gafr!	'By a goat!'
Myn uffern!	'By hell!'
Er mwyn dyn!	'For goodness sake!'
Neno'r dyn!	'In God's name!' (euphemism for *Yn enw Duw!*)
Bobl bach!	'Good gracious!' (lit. 'Little people!')
Hawyr bach!	'Heavens!'
Gwyn fyd!	'Would to heaven!'
Yr achlod iddynt!	'Fie upon them!'
Atolwg!	'Pray!'
Wfft iddo!	'Shame on him!'
Gwae fi!	'Woe am I/unto me!'
Duw a'n helpo!	'May God help us!'
Duw a'n catwo!	'May God keep us!'
Wele!	'Behold!'
Gresyn mawr!	'A great pity!'
Wir!	'Really!'
Dyna drueni!	'A great pity!'
Druan ohonom!	'Pity us!'
Ysywaeth!	'Alas!', 'Unfortunately!' (contracted from *yssy(d) waeth* 'which is worse')
Henffych!	'Hail!' (see **292**)

Appendices

ael	n.f.	brow	
ail	adj. and n.m.	like; second	
bae	n.m.	bay	
bai	n.m.	fault	
bar	n.m.	bar	
bâr	n.m.	anger	
budd	n.m.	benefit	
bydd	3 sing. future tense *bod* 'to be'		
cae	n.m.	field; brooch	
cau	v.n.	to close	
cau	adj.	hollow	
cael	v.n.	to have	
caul	n.m.	curd; rennet	
caledi	n.m.	hardship	
caledu	v.n.	to harden	
cam	n.m.	step; wrong	pl. *camau*
camre	n.m.	footsteps; journey	
can	n.m.	flour	
can	adj.	white	

can	adj.	hundred	
cân	n.f.	song	
cân	3 sing. present tense *canu* 'to sing'		
cannu	v.n.	to whiten	
canu	v.n.	to sing	
car	n.m.	car	
câr	n.m.	kinsman; friend	
carpedi	n.pl.	carpets	
carpedu	v.n.	to carpet	
cartref	n.m.	home	
gartref	adv.	at home	
adref	adv.	homewards	
ci	n.m.	dog	
cu	adj.	dear	
cil	n.m.	corner; cud; wane	
cul	adj.	narrow	
claear	adj.	lukewarm	
claer	adj.	bright	
clai	n.m.	clay	
clau	adj.	swift	
clos	n.m.	close; yard	pl. *closydd*
clos	n.m.	breeches	pl. *closau*
clòs	adj.	close	
côr	n.m.	stall; choir	pl. *corau*
cor	n.m.	dwarf	pl. *corrod*
corryn	n.m.	spider	pl. *corynnod, corrod*
corun	n.m.	crown of the head	pl. *corunau*
crud	n.m.	cradle	
cryd	n.m.	fever	
cynghorau	n.pl.	councils	
cynghorion	n.pl.	counsels	
Cymru	n.f.	Wales	
Cymry	n.pl.	Welshmen	
Cymraeg	n.m.f.	Welsh (language)	
Cymraeg	adj.	in Welsh	
Cymreig	adj.	pertaining to Wales	

cymun	n.m.	communion	
cymuno	v.n.	to take communion	
cymynn	n.m.	bequest	
cymynnu	v.n.	to bequeath	
cymynu	v.n.	to hew	
cyn	prep.	before	
cŷn	n.m.	chisel	
cynnau	v.n.	to light	
gynnau	n.pl.	guns	
gynnau	adv.	a short while ago	
chwaeth	n.m.	taste	
chwaith	adv.	neither	
chwith	adj.	left; sad	
chwyth	n.m.	blast	
dol	n.f.	doll	pl. *doliau*
dôl	n.f.	meadow	pl. *dolydd*
dug	n.m.	duke	
dug	3 sing. preterite tense *dwyn* 'to carry'		
dig	adj.	angry	
dwg	3 sing. present tense *dwyn* 'to carry'		
esgid	n.f.	shoe, boot	
esgud	adj.	quick	
ewin	n.m.f.	nail; claw; hoof	
ewyn	n.m.	foam	
ffraeo	v.n.	to quarrel	
ffrio	v.n.	to fry	
gefail	n.f.	smithy	pl. *gefeiliau*
gefel	n.f.	tongs	pl. *gefeiliau*
glân	adj.	clean; pure	
glan	n.f.	shore	
glyn	n.m.	glen	
glŷn	3 sing. present tense *glynu* 'to adhere'		
gwain	n.f.	sheath	pl. *gweiniau*
gwaun	n.f.	moor	pl. *gweunydd*
gwâl	n.f.	lair	pl. *gwalau*
gwal	n.f.	wall	pl. *gwaliau, gwelydd*

gwâr	adj.	gentle; civilized	
gwar	n.m.f.	nape of the neck	
gwarchae	v.n.	to besiege	
gwarchod	v.n.	to guard; to baby-sit	
gwiw	adj.	worthy; meet	
gwyw	adj.	withered	
gŵn	n.m.	gown	pl. *gynnau*
gwn	n.m.	gun	pl. *gynnau*
gwn	1 sing. present tense *gwybod* 'to know'		
gŵydd	n.m.	presence	
gŵydd	n.f.	goose	
gwŷdd	n.pl.	trees	
gŵyr	3 sing. present tense *gwybod* 'to know'		
gŵyr	adj.	crooked	
gwŷr	n.pl.	men	
hael	adj.	generous	
haul	n.m.	sun	
hud	n.m.	magic	
hyd	n.m.	length	
hyd	prep.	to; till; as far as	
hun	n.f.	sleep	
hun	pron.	self	
hyn	adj. and pron.	this	
hŷn	adj.	older	
hin	n.f.	weather	
llen	n.f.	curtain; sheet; veil	
llên	n.f.	literature	
lli	n.m.	flood	
llu	n.m.	host	
llifiau	n.pl.	saws	
llifogydd	n.pl.	floods	
llin	n.m.	flax	
llun	n.m.	picture	pl. *lluniau*
llyn	n.m.	lake	pl. *llynnoedd*
lliw	n.m.	colour	pl. *lliwiau*
llyw	n.m.	ruler; rudder	pl. *llywiau*

llus	n.pl.	bilberries	
llys	n.m.	court; slime	
llwythau	n.pl.	tribes	
llwythi	n.pl.	loads	
mae	3 sing. present tense *bod* 'to be'		
mai	conj.	that	
maeth	n.m.	nourishment	
maith	adj.	long	
melin	n.f.	mill	
melyn	adj.	yellow	
mil	n.f.	thousand	pl. *miloedd*
mil	n.m.	animal	pl. *milod*
mul	n.m.	mule	pl. *mulod*
mor	adv.	so, as	
môr	n.m.	sea	
nad	negative particle		
nâd	n.f.	cry	
nith	n.f.	niece	pl. *nithoedd*
nyth	n.f.	nest	pl. *nythod*
peri	v.n.	to cause	
pery	3 sing. present tense *parhau* 'to continue'		
pin	n.m.	pine	
pìn	n.m.	pin	
pridd	n.m.	soil	
prudd	adj.	sad	
prif	adj.	chief	
pryf	n.m.	insect	
prydau	n.pl.	meals	
prydiau	n.pl.	times	
pwysau	n.m.	weight	
pwysi	n.pl.	lbs.	
rhiw	n.f.	hill	
rhyw	n.f.	sort; sex	
rhyw	adj.	some; certain	
rhu	n.m.	roar	
rhy	adv.	too	
rhy	3 sing. present tense *rhoi* 'give'		

rhudd	adj.	red	
rhydd	adj.	free	
rhydd	3 sing. present tense *rhoddi* 'give'		
sir	n.f.	county	
sur	adj.	sour	
syr	n.m.	sir	
sudd	n.m.	juice	
sydd	3 sing. relative form present tense *bod* 'to be'		
taer	adj.	earnest	
tair	adj.	three (fem.)	
tal	adj.	tall	
tâl	n.m.	payment; forehead	
tâl	3 sing. present tense *talu* 'to pay'		
ti	pron.	you	
tu	n.m.	side	
tŷ	n.m.	house	
ton	n.f.	wave	pl. *tonnau*
tôn	n.f.	tune	pl. *tonau*
twr	n.f.	crowd; heap	pl. *tyrrau*
tŵr	n.f.	tower	pl. *tyrau*
ymladd	v.n.	to fight	
ymlâdd	v.n.	to tire oneself	
yntau	pron.	he also	
ynteu	conj.	or; otherwise	

423 Proverbs

Note
Welsh alphabetical ordering is adopted in this section.

A arddo diroedd a gaiff ddigonedd
He who tills the land will have plenty

A bryn gig a bryn esgyrn
He who buys meat buys bones

A chwilia fwyaf am fodlondeb a fydd bellaf oddi wrtho
He who searches most for satisfaction will be furthest from it

A ddarlleno, ystyried
He who reads, let him reflect

A ddwg wy a ddwg fwy
He who steals an egg will steal more

A fo ben bid bont
He who would be leader let him be a bridge

A fo byw yn dduwiol a fydd marw yn ddedwydd
He who leads a godly life will die happy

A fynno barch, bid gadarn
He who desires respect, let him be steadfast

A fynno Duw, a fydd
What God wills will be

A fynno glod, bid farw
He who desires fame, let him die

A fynno iechyd, bid lawen
He who would be healthy, let him be cheerful

A gâr a gerydd
He who loves chastises

A geir yn rhad a gerdd yn rhwydd
What is got cheaply goes cheaply

A wnêl dwyll, ef a dwyllir
He who deceives shall be deceived

A ystyrio, cofied
He who reflects, let him remember

Adar o'r unlliw hedant i'r un lle
Birds of a feather flock together

Adeiniog pob chwant
Every desire is fleeting

Adfyd a ddwg wybodaeth, a gwybodaeth ddoethineb
Adversity brings knowledge, and knowledge wisdom

Adwaenir dyn wrth ei gyfeillion
A man is recognized by the friends he keeps

Adwaenir ffôl wrth ei wisg
The fool is recognized by his dress

Aeddfed angau i hen
Death is ripe for the old

Afal pwdr a ddryga'i gyfeillion
A rotten apple spoils the others

Afalau'r nos, cnau'r bore, os ceri'th iechyd
If you cherish good health, eat apples at night and nuts in the morning

Afrad pob afraid
Everything needless is waste

Angau'r euog ydyw'r gwir
The death of the guilty is truth

Angel pen ffordd, a diawl pen tân
An angel abroad, and a devil at home

Angen a ddysg i hen redeg
Necessity teaches the old to run

Angor diogel yw gobaith
Hope is a safe anchor

Ail fam, modryb dda
A good aunt is a second mother

Allwedd tlodi, seguryd
Idleness is the key to poverty

Am y tywydd gorau tewi
It is best to be silent about the weather

Aml cogau, aml ydau
Many cuckoos, abundance of corn

Aml yw haint ym mol hen
The old has many afflictions

Amlach ffŵl na gŵr bonheddig
There are more fools than gentlemen

Amlwg gwaed ar farch gwinau
Blood is conspicuous on a bay horse

Amser yw'r meddyg
Time is the doctor (healer)

Amynedd yw mam pob doethineb
Patience is the mother of wisdom

Anaml elw heb antur
Profit is rare without a venture

Annoeth, llithrig ei dafod
The unwise has a ready tongue

Anodd iacháu hen glefyd
It is difficult to cure an old ailment

Anwylach bywyd na bwyd
Life is dearer than food

Arfer yw hanner y gwaith
Practice is half the work

Arfer yw mam pob meistrolaeth
Practice is the mother of every mastery

Asgre lân, diogel ei pherchen
Safe is the owner of a clear conscience

Athro da yw amser
Time is a good teacher

Awel y canolddydd a ddwg law yn ebrwydd
A breeze at noon brings rain soon

A wrthodo gyngor rhad a brŷn edifeirwch drud
He who refuses inexpensive advice buys a costly repentence

Bach hedyn pob mawredd
The seed of all greatness is small

Bach pob dyn a dybio ei hun yn fawr
Small is everyone who considers himself great

Bedd a wna bawb yn gydradd
The grave makes everybody equal

Benthyg dros amser byr yw popeth a geir yn y byd hwn
Everything one has in this world is only borrowed for a short time

Blasus pob peth a gerir
Everything one loves is tasty

Blodau cyn Mai, gorau na bai
Flowers before May, better without them

Blwyddyn o eira, blwyddyn o lawndra
A year of snow, a year of plenty

Blys geneth yn ei llygaid, blys bachgen yn ei galon
A girl's desire in her eyes, a boy's desire in his heart

Bolaid ci a bery dridiau
A dog's fill lasts three days

Bonheddig pob addfwyn
Every meek person is courteous

Brawd mogi (mygu) yw tagu
Choking is brother to suffocating (i.e. it is all the same)

Brawd yw celwyddog i leidr
The liar is brother to the thief

Brenhines pob camp, cyfiawnder
Righteousness is the queen of all feats

Brenin pob llyffant ar ei domen ei hun
Every toad is a king on his patch

Brenin y bwyd yw bara
Bread is the king of all foods

Bu weithiau heb haf; ni bu erioed heb wanwyn
Sometimes there has been no summer; but always there has been a spring

Bychan y tâl cyngor gwraig, ond gwae y gŵr nas cymero
A wife's advice is not worth much, but woe to the husband who doesn't take it

Bydd olaf i fyned trwy ddŵr dwfn
Be the last one to go through deep water

Byr ei hun, hir ei hoedl
Sleep little, live long

Byr yw Chwefror, ond hir ei anghysuron
February is short but its discomforts are long

Byw i arall yw byw yn iawn
To live for others is to live properly

Cadarna'r mur po arwa'r garreg
The rougher the stone, the stronger the wall

Cadw dy ardd, ceidw dy ardd dithau
Keep thy garden and thy garden will keep thee

Cadw dy dafod i oeri dy gawl
Keep thy tongue to cool thy broth

Cadw yn graff a ddysgych
Keep securely what you learn

Cael rhad Duw, cael y cyfan
To have God's blessing is to have everything

Cais ddedwydd yn ei gartref
Seek the happy at home

Cais ddoeth yn ei dyddyn
Seek the wise in his homestead

Cais ffrwyn gref i farch gwyllt
Seek a strong bridle for a wild horse

Call dros awr, cyfoethog dros fyth
Wise for an hour, rich for ever

Call pob un yn ei farn ei hun
Everyone is wise in his own opinion

Canmol dy fro a thrig yno
Praise thy country and stay there

Canmoled pawb y bont a'i dyco drosodd
Let everyone praise the bridge that has brought him over

Câr cywir yn yr ing fe'i gwelir
A friend in need is a friend indeed

Cariad yw mam pob dwyfoldeb
Love is the mother of all godliness

Cas athro heb amynedd
Hateful is an impatient teacher

Cas chwerthin heb achos
To laugh without cause is abhorrent

Cas dyn a ddirmygo Dduw a dyn
Hateful is he who despises God and man

Cas dyn ni chredo neb, na neb yntau
Hateful is he who believes no one, and whom no one believes

Cas fydd un enllibiwr gan y llall
One slanderer is hated by another

Cas gŵr na charo'r wlad a'i maco
Hateful is the man who does not love the country that has reared him

Cas yw'r gwirionedd lle nis carer
Truth is hateful where it is not loved

Castell pawb ei dŷ
Everyone's castle is his home

Ceffyl da yw ewyllys
The will is a good horse

Ceiniog a enillir ydyw'r geiniog a gynilir
A penny saved is a penny gained

Ceir llawer cam gwag trwy sefyll yn llonydd
Many a false step is made by standing still

Celf orau yn y tŷ, gwraig dda
A good wife is a home's best piece of furniture

Celwydd sydd yn marchogaeth ar ddyled
Untruth rides on debt

Cenedl heb iaith, cenedl heb galon
A nation without a language, a nation without a heart

Cenfigen yw gwraidd pob cynnen
Jealousy is the root of all strife

Cennad hwyr, drwg ei neges
A late messenger brings bad news

Clust doeth a lwnc wybodaeth
A wise ear swallows information

Clydwr dafad yw ei chnu
A sheep's shelter is its fleece

Clyw a gwêl ac na ddywed ddim
Listen and look and say nothing

Craffach un llygad llysfam na dau lygad mam
A stepmother's eye is keener than a mother's two eyes

Cred air o bob deg a glywi, a thi a gei rywfaint bach o'r gwir
Believe one-tenth of what you hear and you will get a small grain of truth

Crefftwr tafod hawdd ei nabod
It is easy to recognize a glib talker

Crochaf yr afon, lleiaf y pysgod
The louder the river, the fewer the fish

Cura'r haearn tra fo'n boeth
Strike the iron while it is hot

Cwsg yw bywyd heb lyfrau
A life without books is a sleep

Cydwybod euog a ofna ei gysgod
A guilty conscience is afraid of its shadow

Cydymaith asyn ei glustiau
A donkey's companion is his ears

Cyfaill blaidd, bugail diog
A lazy shepherd is the wolf's friend

Cyfaill da cystal â cheffyl
A good friend is as good as a horse

Cyfoeth pob crefft
Every craft is wealth

Cyfoethog pob bodlon
Every contented person is wealthy

Cyfyng ac eang yw dewis
Every choice is both narrow and wide

Cymydog da ydyw clawdd
A hedge makes a good neighbour

Cynt y cwrdd dau ddyn na dau fynydd
Sooner will two men meet than two mountains

Cynt y cwymp dâr na miaren o flaen y gwynt
An oak will fall sooner than a bramble bush in the wind

Cyntaf ei og, cyntaf ei gryman
First with the harrow, first with the sickle

Cysur pob gwyryf – cusan
Every maiden's comfort – a kiss

Chwedl a gynydda fel caseg eira
A tale increases like a rolling snowball

Chwefror garw; porchell marw
A rough February; a dead pigling

Chwerthin a wna ynfyd wrth farw
The fool will laugh while dying

Chwynnwch eich gardd eich hun yn gyntaf
Weed your own garden first

Da gadael pob da fel y mae
Leave well alone

Da yw dant i atal tafod
A tooth is useful to check the tongue

Darllenwch ddynion yn gystal â llyfrau
Read men as well as books

Dedwydd pob di-falch
Every modest person is happy

Deuparth gwaith ei ddechrau
Beginning is two-thirds of work

Deuparth llwyddiant, diwydrwydd
Two-thirds of success, diligence

Diflanna geiriau, ond erys gweithredoedd
Words vanish but actions remain

Dim glaw Mai, dim mêl Medi
No rain in May, no honey in September

Diogi a rhinwedd, dwyrain a gorllewin
Idleness and virtue are like east and west (poles apart)

Diwedd pob peth yw cyffes
Confession is the end of everything

Doeth a wrendy; ffôl a lefair
The wise listens; the fool talks

Doeth pob tawgar
Wise every lover of silence

Doethaf naid, naid dros fai
The wisest jump is to jump over a fault

Drych i bawb ei gymydog
A man's neighbour is his mirror

Dwla dwl, dwl hen
The most foolish fool is an old fool

Dyfal donc a dyr y garreg
Persistent blows break the stone

Dyled ar bawb ei addewid
Everyone who promises is in debt

Dyn a chwennych, Duw a ran
Man proposes, God disposes

Dyngarwch yw'r dawn gorau
Philanthropy is the best of all gifts

Eglwys cybydd, ei gist
A miser's church is his money-chest

Egni a lwydd
Exertion will succeed

Eli i bob dolur yw amynedd
Patience is an ointment for every sore

Enfys y bore, aml gawodau
Rainbow in the morning, frequent showers

Enw da yw'r trysor gorau
A good name is the best of treasures

Esgeulus pob hen
The old are neglectful

Etifeddiaeth werthfawr ydyw gair da
A good word is a valuable inheritance

Euog a wêl ei gysgod rhyngddo â'r haul
The guilty sees his shadow between himself and the sun

Ewyn dwfr yw addewid mab
A son's promise is just foam

Fallai yw hanner y ffordd i felly
'Perhaps' is half-way to 'yes'

Fe gwsg galar, ni chwsg gofal
Grief sleeps, care sleeps not

Fel yr afon i'r môr yw bywyd dyn
Man's life is like the river flowing to the sea

Ffawd ar ôl ffawd a wna ddyn yn dlawd
Misfortune after misfortune makes a man poor

Ffôl pawb ar brydiau
Everyone is foolish at times

Ffolog sydd fel llong heb lyw
The fool is like a rudderless ship

Ffon y bywyd yw bara
Bread is the staff of life

Ffordd nesaf at olud, talu dyled
The next road to wealth is to pay one's debt

Ffynnon pob anffawd, diogi
The fount of all misfortune is laziness

Gaeaf gwyn, ysgubor dynn
A white winter, a full barn

Gair drwg a dynn y drwg ato
One bad word attracts more to it

Gair mam a bery'n hir
A mother's advice lasts long

Gall y gwaethaf ddysgu bod yn orau
The worst can learn to be best

Gan bwyll y mae mynd ymhell
Going slowly going far

Gelyn yw i ddyn ei dda
A man's wealth is his enemy

Gellir yfed yr afon ond ni ellir bwyta'r dorlan
One can drink the river but one cannot eat the bank

Genau oer a thraed gwresog a fydd byw yn hir
Cold lips and warm feet mean a long life

Gloddest awr a newyn blwyddyn
An hour's festivity, a year's famine

Gnawd i feddw ysgwyd llaw
It is customary for a drunkard to shake hands

Gochel gyfaill a elo'n feistr
Beware of a friend who becomes a master

Gorau aml, aml gardod
The best frequency, frequent alms

Gorau arfer, doethineb
Wisdom is the best of practices

Gorau caffaeliad, enw da
A good name is the best acquisition

Gorau cannwyll, pwyll i ddyn
Discretion is man's best candle

Gorau cof, cof llyfr
The best memory is that of a book

Gorau coll, enw drwg
The best of all losses, a bad name

Gorau cyfoeth, iechyd
The best wealth is health

Gorau Cymro, Cymro oddi cartref
The best Welshman is the exile

Gorau chwedl gwirionedd
Truth is the best of all tales

Gorau doethineb, tewi
The best wisdom is silence

Gorau gwraig, gwraig heb dafod
The best wife is a wife without a tongue

Gorau haelioni, rhoddi cardod
The best generosity, giving alms

Gorau nawdd, nawdd Duw
The best protection, the protection of God

Gorau prinder, prinder geiriau
The best scarcity is the scarcity of words

Gorau trysor, daioni
The best treasure is goodness

Gorau un tlws, gwraig dda
A good wife is the best gem

Gormod o ddim nid yw dda
Too much of anything is not good

Gorwedd yw diwedd pob dyn
Death is the end of all

Gwae a fag neidr yn ei fynwes
Woe to the person who nurtures a serpent in his bosom

Gwae leidr a fo weledig
Woe to the thief who is seen

Gwaethaf gelyn, calon ddrwg
A wicked heart is the worst of all enemies

Gweddw crefft heb ei dawn
Craft is useless without talent

Gwell amcan gof na mesur saer
A smith's guess is better than a carpenter's measure

Gwell bach mewn llaw na mawr gerllaw
Better the small in the hand than the large nearby

Gwell bachgen call na brenin ffôl
A wise boy is better than a foolish king

Gwell benthyg nag eisiau
It is better to borrow than to be in need

Gwell bygwth na tharo
It is better to threaten than to strike a blow

Gwell câr yn y llys nag aur ar fys
A friend in the court is better than a gold ring on one's finger

Gwell ci da na dyn drwg
A good dog is better than a wicked man

Gwell cydwybod na golud
A conscience is better than riches

Gwell cymydog yn agos na brawd ymhell
Better a neighbour at hand than a distant brother

Gwell digon na gormod
Enough is better than too much

Gwell Duw yn gâr na holl lu daear
God as a friend is better than all the world's people

Gwell dysg na golud
Better learning than wealth

Gwell goddef cam na'i wneuthur
Better suffer wrong than do it

Gwell gwegil câr nag wyneb estron
Better a kinsman's back than a stranger's face

Gwell hanner na dim
Better half than nothing

Gwell hwyr na hwyrach
Better late than never (later)

Gwell mam anghenog na thad goludog
A needy mother is better than a rich father

Gwell migwrn o ddyn na mynydd o wraig
A small man is better than a huge woman

Gwell pwyll nag aur
Prudence is better than gold

Gwell un awr lawen na dwy drist
One happy hour is better than two sad ones

Gwell yr heddwch gwaethaf na'r rhyfel gorau
Better the worst peace than the best war

Gwers gyntaf doethineb; adnabod ei hunan
Wisdom's first lesson; know thyself

Gwerth dy wybodaeth i brynu synnwyr
Sell your knowledge to buy sense

Gwisg orau merch yw gwylder
Modesty is a girl's best dress

Gwna dda unwaith, gwna dda eilwaith
Do good once, do good twice

Gŵr dieithr yw yfory
Tomorrow is a stranger

Gŵr heb bwyll, llong heb angor
A man without discretion, a ship without anchor

Gwybedyn y dom a gwyd uchaf
The dung fly rises highest

Gwybydd fesur dy droed dy hun
Know the length of your own foot

Gwyn y gwêl y frân ei chyw
The crow sees its young white (faultless)

Gwynfyd herwr yw hwyrnos
A robber's bliss is eventide

Hardd ar ferch bod yn ddistaw
A girl's virtue is silence

Hawdd cymod lle bo cariad
Reconciliation is easy where there is love

Hawdd cynnau tân ar hen aelwyd
It is easy to kindle a fire on an old hearth

Hawdd dweud, caled gwneud
It is easy to say, but hard to act

Haws bodloni Duw na diafol
It is easier to please God than the devil

Haws dywedyd mawr na gwneuthur bychan
It is easier to say much than to do a little

Heb Dduw, heb ddim
Without God, without anything

Heb ei fai, heb ei eni
He who is without fault is not born (No one is perfect)

Heb wraig, heb ymryson
Without a wife, without strife

Hedyn pob drwg yw diogi
Idleness is the seed of all evil

Hen bechod a wna gywilydd newydd
An old sin brings fresh shame

Hir ei dafod, byr ei wybod
A long tongue but little knowledge

Hir pob aros
Every waiting is long

Hir yn llanc, hwyr yn ŵr
If one remains long as a lad he will marry late

Hwde i ti a moes i minnau
Take for yourself and give to me

Hwy pery clod na hoedl
Praise lasts longer than life

Ionawr cynnes, Mai oer
A warm January, but a cold May

Llawer gwir, gwell ei gelu
Many a truth is best hidden

Lle bo dolur y bydd llaw
Wherever there is a wound there will be a hand

Llon colwyn ar arffed ei feistres
The pup is happy in the lap of its owner

Llwm yw'r ŷd lle y mae'r adwy
The corn harvest is poor where there is a gap in the hedge

Llysywen mewn dwrn yw arian
Money is an eel in the fist

Mae ffôl yn ymlid ei gysgod
The fool pursues his shadow

Mae pont i groesi pob anhawster
There is a bridge to cross every difficulty

Mae rhagluniaeth yn fwy na ffawd
Providence is mightier than fate

Mae'r diawl yn dda wrth ei blant
The devil is kind to his children

Mam ddiofal a wna ferch ddiog
A neglectful mother rears a lazy daughter

Meddu pwyll meddu'r cyfan
To have discretion is to have everything

Meddwl agored, llaw agored
An open mind, an open hand

Meistr pob gwaith yw ymarfer
Practice is master of all work

Mwyaf poen yw poen methu
The greatest pain, the pain of failure

Na ddeffro'r ci a fo'n cysgu
Do not wake the sleeping dog (Let sleeping dogs lie)

Nac adrodd a glywaist rhag ei fod yn gelwyddog
Don't repeat what you heard in case it is false

Nac yf ond i dorri syched
Don't drink except to quench your thirst

Nerth cybydd yw ei ystryw
Cunning is the miser's strength

Nerth gwenynen, ei hamynedd
Patience is the strength of the bee

Nes penelin nac arddwrn
Nearer elbow than wrist (Blood is thicker than water)

Ni all neb ddwyn ei geraint ar ei gefn
No one can carry his relations

Ni cheir da o hir gysgu
No good comes from long sleep

Ni cheir gan lwynog ond ei groen
A fox only gives one its pelt

Ni chyll dedwydd ei swydd
The happy will not lose his job

Ni ddaw doe byth yn ôl
Yesterday will not return

Ni ddaw henaint ei hunan
Old age does not come alone

Ni ddychwel cyngor ynfyd
A fool's advice will not return

Ni ellir prynu parch
No one can buy respect

Ni ŵyr dyn ddolur y llall
One man knows not another's pain

Nid athro ni ddysg ei hunan
No one is a teacher unless he teaches himself

Nid aur popeth melyn
All that glitters is not gold

Nid byd, byd heb wybodaeth
A world without learning is no world

Nid call, adrodd y cyfan
It is not wise to tell everything

Nid deallus ond a ddeall ei hunan
One is not intelligent unless one understands oneself

Nid doeth a ymryson
He is not a wise man who argues

Nid eir i annwn ond unwaith
One only goes once to hell

Nid hawdd bodloni pawb
It is not easy to please everyone

Nid hwy oes dyn nag oes dail
A man's life is not longer than that of leaves

Nid o fradwr y ceir gwladwr
A traitor will never become a patriot

Nid oes ar uffern ond eisiau ei threfnu
Hell needs only to be organized

Nid rhodd rhodd oni bydd o fodd
No gift is a gift unless it is from the heart

Nid rhy hen neb i ddysgu
No one is too old to learn

Nid tegwch heb wragedd
There is no beauty without women

Nid wrth ei big y prynir cyffylog
It is not by its beak that a woodcock is bought

Nid yw'r hoff o lyfr yn fyr o gyfaill
He who loves books is not bereft of friends

Nid yw rhinwedd byth yn mynd yn hen
Virtue never grows old

O ddau ddrwg gorau y lleiaf
Of two evils choose the lesser

Oedran a ŵyr fwy na dysg
Old age knows more than learning

Oer yw'r cariad a ddiffydd ar un chwa o wynt
Cold is the love that is put out by one gust of wind

O gyfoeth y daw gofid
From wealth comes trouble

O mynni brysurdeb, cais long, melin a gwraig
If you want to be busy, seek a ship, mill, and a wife

Oni byddi gryf, bydd gyfrwys
If you lack strength be cunning

Oriadur yw meddwl dyn, a rhaid ei ddirwyn bob dydd
Man's mind is a watch that needs winding daily

Os rhôi barch ti gei barch
If you give respect you will receive it

Pawb a fesur arall wrtho'i hunan
Everyone measures others by himself

Pawb yn aros yr amser, a'r amser nid erys neb
Everybody waits for the time but time waits for no one

Pert pob peth bach ond diawl bach
Everything small is pretty except a small devil

Perth hyd fogel, perth ddiogel
A hedge up to one's midriff is a safe hedge

Peswch sych, diwedd pob nych
A dry cough is the end of every ailment

Po callaf y dyn, anamlaf ei eiriau
The wiser the man, the fewer his words

Po dynnaf fo'r llinyn, cyntaf y tyr
The tighter the rope, the sooner it breaks

Po fwyaf y cwsg, hwyaf yr einioes
The longer one sleeps, the longer one lives

Pob sorod i'r god ag ef
Throw all rubbish into the bag

Pob un a gâr lle ceir arian
All will love where there is money

Prinder gorau, prinder geiriau
The best scarcity, scarcity of words

Pritaf o bob prŷn, edifeirwch
The dearest buy of all, repentance

Prŷn wael, prŷn eilwaith
Buy a poor thing, buy a second time

Rhaid cariad yw cerydd
Chastisement is essential to love

Rhaid cropian cyn cerdded
One must crawl before walking

Rhaid i'r dderwen wrth gysgod yn ifanc
The oak needs some shelter when young

Rhaid wrth lwy hir i fwyta gyda'r diafol
One needs a long spoon to sup with the devil

Rhed cachgi rhag ei gysgod
A coward flees from his shadow

Rhy hwyr galw doe yn ôl
It is too late to recall yesterday

Rhydd i bob meddwl ei farn, ac i bob barn ei llafar
Everyone has a right to his opinion, and a right to express it

Seguryd ni fyn sôn am waith
Idleness does not want to mention work

Selni rhai yw eu hiechyd
Good health to some is an ailment

Sylfaen pob rhinwedd – gwirionedd
The foundation of virtue is truth

Taer yw'r gwir am y golau
Truth is eager for the light

Tafl garreg at fur, hi a neidia at dy dalcen
Throw a stone at a wall and it will rebound on your forehead

Tebyg i ddyn fydd ei lwdwn
Like father, like son

Tecaf fro, bro mebyd
The finest place is one's own neighbourhood

Trech cariad na'r cyfan
Love surpasses everything

Trech gwlad nag arglwydd
A country is mightier than a lord

Trech serch nag arfau dur
Love is mightier than weapons of steel

Tri brodyr doethineb: a wrendy, a edrych, a daw
Three brothers of wisdom: he who listens, he who looks, he who is silent

Trwy dwll bach y gwelir goleuni
Light is seen through a small hole

Trydydd troed i hen ei ffon
The third foot of the aged is his stick

Twyllo arall, twyllo dy hunan
To deceive another is to deceive thyself

Ufudd-dod ydyw llwybr bywyd
Obedience is the path of life

Un celwydd yn dad i gant
One lie is a father to a hundred

Utgorn angau yw peswch sych
A dry cough is the trumpet of death

Y ci a gyfarth ni fratha
The dog which barks does not bite

Y doeth ni ddywed a wŷr
The wise does not say all he knows

Yf dy gawl cyn oero
Drink thy broth before it gets cold

Y fesen yn dderwen a ddaw
The acorn will grow into an oak

Y groes waethaf yw bod heb yr un
The worst cross is to be without one

Y gwaith a ganmol y gweithiwr
The worker is praised by his work

Y llaw a rydd a gynnull
The hand which gives gathers

Y mae gweithred yn well na gair
Actions are better than words

Ymhob clwyf y mae perygl
There is danger in every wound

Ymhob pen y mae 'piniwn
In every head there is an opinion

Ym mhob gwlad y megir glew
In every country a hero is bred

Y mwyaf ei fost, lleiaf ei orchest
The greater the boast, the least in accomplishment

Yn yr hwyr y mae adnabod gweithiwr
One recognizes a worker in the evening

Yr afal mwyaf yw'r pydraf ei galon
The largest apple is the most rotten

Yr euog a ffy heb neb yn ei erlid
The guilty flees without any pursuer

Yr hen a ŵyr, yr ieuanc a dybia
The old knows, the young surmises

Bibliography

The main bibliographical sources for the study of Welsh are *Bibliotheca Celtica* and *Llyfryddiaeth Cymru, A Bibliography of Wales*, published by the National Library of Wales, Aberystwyth; *The Year's Work in Modern Language Studies*, published by the Modern Humanities Research Association; *Studia Celtica* 1– (1966–), 'A list of books, articles, etc. concerning various aspects of the Celtic languages received at the National Library of Wales, Aberystwyth'. A section on the Celtic languages is included in *Linguistic Bibliography*, published by the Permanent International Committee of Linguists.

All examples from literary sources are acknowledged and translated. To celebrate the fourth centenary of the translation of the Bible into Welsh a new translation of the complete Bible appeared in 1988; quotations from biblical texts are from this 1988 version but on occasion forms which appear in an earlier version are also noted. Some quotations have been taken from grammars of the Welsh language.

(A) Biblical Books

Books of the Old Testament:
Gen., Exod., Lev., Num., Deut., Josh., Judg., Ruth, 1 and 2 Sam., 1 and 2 Kgs., 1 and 2 Chr., Ezra, Neh., Esther, Job, Ps., Prov., Eccles., S. of S., Isa., Jer., Lam., Ezek., Dan., Hos., Joel, Amos, Obad., Jonah, Mic., Nahum, Hab., Zeph., Hag., Zech., Mal.

Books of the New Testament:
Matt., Mark, Luke, John, Acts, Rom., 1 and 2 Cor., Gal., Eph., Phil., Col., 1 and 2 Thess, 1 and 2 Tim., Titus, Philem, Heb., Jas., 1 and 2 Pet., 1 and 2 John, Jude, Rev.

(B) Dictionaries

Collins Spurrell Welsh Dictionary (1991). Glasgow: HarperCollins.
Geiriadur Prifysgol Cymru: A Dictionary of the Welsh Language (1950–). Cardiff: University of Wales Press.
Evans, H. Meurig 1981: *Y Geiriadur Cymraeg Cyfoes*. Llandybïe: Hughes a'i Fab.
Evans, H. Meurig and Thomas, W. O. 1958: *Y Geiriadur Mawr*. Llandysul: Gwasg Gomer.

The School of Education and the Language and Literature Committee of the Board of Celtic Studies of the University of Wales have since 1930 published basic lists of specialized terms, for example, Grammatical Terms (1930), Mathematics (1957), The Theatre (1964), Office and Business (1970), Economics and Econometrics (1976), Medical (1976).

(C) Grammars and Other Works on Language

Anwyl, Edward 1897: *Welsh Grammar*. London: Swann, Sonnenschein & Co. Ltd.
Awbrey, G. M. 1984: Welsh. In Peter Trudgill (ed.), *Language in the British Isles*. Cambridge: Cambridge University Press.
Ball, Martin J. (ed.) 1988: *The Use of Welsh*. Clevedon: Multilingual Matters.
Ball, Martin J. and Müller, Nicole 1992: *Mutation in Welsh*. London: Routledge.
Brake, Phylip J. 1980: Astudiaeth o Seinyddiaeth a Morffoleg Tafodiaith Cwm-ann a'r Cylch. Unpublished M.A. thesis (University of Wales).
Davies, Cennard 1988: Cymraeg Byw. In M. J. Ball (ed.), pp. 200–10.
Davies, Evan J. 1955: Astudiaeth Gymharol o Dafodieithoedd Dihewyd a Llandygwydd. Unpublished M.A. thesis (University of Wales).
Davies, J. J. G. 1934: Astudiaeth o Gymraeg llafar ardal Ceinewydd. Unpublished Ph.D. thesis (University of Wales).
Evans, D. Simon 1964: *A Grammar of Middle Welsh*. Dublin: Dublin Institute of Advanced Studies.
Evans, J. J. 1946: *Gramadeg Cymraeg*. Aberystwyth: Gwasg Aberystwyth.
Fife, J. 1986: Literary vs. colloquial Welsh: problems of definition. *Word*, 37: 141–51.
Fife, J. and Poppe, E. (eds) 1991: *Studies in Brythonic Word Order*. Amsterdam: Benjamins.

Fynes-Clinton, O. H. 1913: *The Welsh Vocabulary of the Bangor District*. Oxford: Oxford University Press.

Jackson, K. H. 1953: *Language and History in Early Britain*. Edinburgh: Edinburgh University Press.

Jenkins, Myrddin 1959: *A Welsh Tutor*. Cardiff: University of Wales Press.

Jones, C. M. 1987: Astudiaeth o iaith lafar Y Mot (Sir Benfro). Unpublished Ph.D. thesis (University of Wales).

Jones, Dafydd Glyn 1988: Literary Welsh. In M. J. Ball (ed.), pp. 125–71.

Jones, Morris 1972: The items Byth and Erioed. *Studia Celtica*, 7: 92–119.

Jones, Robert Owen 1967: A Structural Phonological Analysis and Comparison of Three Welsh Dialects. Unpublished M.A. thesis (University of Wales).

Lewis, Henry 1931: *Datblygiad yr Iaith Gymraeg*. Caerdydd: Gwasg Prifysgol Cymru [Cardiff: University of Wales Press].

Lewis, Henry 1943: *Yr Elfen Ladin yn yr Iaith Gymraeg*. Caerdydd: Gwasg Prifysgol Cymru [Cardiff: University of Wales Press].

Lewis, Henry and Pedersen, Holger 1937: *A Concise Comparative Celtic Grammar*. Göttingen: Vandenhoeck & Ruprecht.

Morgan, T. J. 1952: *Y Treigladau a'u Cystrawen*. Caerdydd: Gwasg Prifysgol Cymru [Cardiff: University of Wales Press].

Morris-Jones, J. 1913: *A Welsh Grammar: Historical and Comparative*. Oxford: Oxford University Press.

Morris-Jones, J. 1925: *Cerdd Dafod*. Rhydychen: Gwasg Clarendon [Oxford: Clarendon Press].

Morris-Jones, J. 1931: *Welsh Syntax*. Cardiff: University of Wales Press.

Phillips, Vincent H. 1955: Astudiaeth o Gymraeg llafar Dyffryn Elái a'r cyffiniau. Unpublished M.A. thesis (University of Wales).

Richards, Melville 1938: *Cystrawen y Frawddeg Gymraeg*. Caerdydd: Gwasg Prifysgol Cymru [Cardiff: University of Wales Press].

Thomas, Beth and Thomas, Peter Wyn 1989: *Cymraeg, Cymrâg, Cymraeg ... Cyflwyno'r Tafodieithoedd*. Caerdydd [Cardiff]: Gwasg Tâf.

Thomas, C. H. 1975/76: Some phonological features of dialects in southeast Wales. *Studia Celtica*, 10/11: 345–66.

Thomas, C. H. 1982: Registers in Welsh. *International Journal of the Sociology of Language*, 35: 87–115.

Thorne, D. A. 1971: Astudiaeth Seinyddol a Morffolegol o Dafodiaith Llangennech. Unpublished M.A. thesis (University of Wales).

Thorne, D. A. 1976: Astudiaeth Gymharol o Ffonoleg a Gramadeg Iaith Lafar y Maenorau oddi mewn i Gwmwd Carnwyllion yn Sir Gaerfyrddin. Unpublished Ph.D. thesis (University of Wales).

Thorne, D. A. 1980: Cyfosod yn y Gymraeg: camre cyntaf mewn diffinio. *Bwletin y Bwrdd Gwybodau Celtaidd*, 29: 53–65.

Thorne, D. A. 1984: Sylwadau ar rai treigladau. *Bwletin y Bwrdd Gwybodau Celtaidd*, 31: 74–86.

Thorne, D. A. 1985: *Cyflwyniad i Astudio'r Iaith Gymraeg*. Caerdydd: Gwasg Prifysgol Cymru [Cardiff: University of Wales Press].

Watkins, T. A. 1961: *Ieithyddiaeth: Agweddau ar Astudio Iaith*. Caerdydd: Gwasg Prifysgol Cymru [Cardiff: University of Wales Press].

Watkins, T. Arwyn 1977/78: Y Rhagenwau Ategol. *Studia Celtica*, 12/13: 349–66.

Watkins, T. Arwyn 1991: The function of cleft and non-cleft constituent orders in modern Welsh. In J. Fife and E. Poppe (eds), pp. 229–351.

William, Urien 1960: *A Short Welsh Grammar*. Llandybïe: Christopher Davies.

Williams, Stephen J. 1959: *Elfennau Gramadeg Cymraeg*. Caerdydd: Gwasg Prifysgol Cymru [Cardiff: University of Wales Press].

Williams, Stephen J. 1980: *A Welsh Grammar*. Cardiff: University of Wales Press.

(*D*) *Newspapers, Journals and Periodicals*

Barddas
Barn
BBCS (*Bulletin of the Board of Celtic Studies*)
Golwg
Llais Llyfrau
Llên Cymru
Sbec
Studia Celtica
Taliesin
Y Cymro
Y Faner
Y Traethodydd

(*E*) *Literary Texts*

Ap Gwilym, Gwyn 1979: *Da o Ddwy Ynys*. Abertawe [Swansea]: Christopher Davies.

Bowen, Geraint (ed.) 1970: *Y Traddodiad Rhyddiaith*. Llandysul: Gwasg Gomer.

Bowen, Geraint (ed.) 1972: *Ysgrifennu Creadigol*. Llandysul: Gwasg Gomer.

Bowen, Geraint (ed.) 1976: *Y Traddodiad Rhyddiaith yn yr Ugeinfed Ganrif*. Llandysul: Gwasg Gomer.

Bromwich, Rachel and Evans, D. Simon 1988: *Culhwch ac Olwen*. Caerdydd: Gwasg Prifysgol Cymru [Cardiff: University of Wales Press].

Bunyan, John 1962: *Taith y Pererin*, addaswyd gan Trebor Lloyd Evans [*Pilgrim's Progress*, adapted by Trebor Lloyd Evans]. Llandysul: Gwasg Gomer.

Carroll, Lewis 1982: *Anturiaethau Alys yng Ngwlad Hud*, trosiad gan Selyf Roberts [*Alice's Adventures in Wonderland*, translated by Selyf Roberts]. Llandysul: Gwasg Gomer.

Carroll, Lewis 1984: *Trwy'r Drych a'r Hyn a Welodd Alys Yno*, trosiad gan Selyf Roberts [*Through the Looking Glass*, translated by Selyf Roberts]. Llandysul: Gwasg Gomer.

Chilton, Irma 1989: *Mochyn Gwydr*. Llandysul: Gwasg Gomer.

Davies, Aneirin Talfan 1972: *Bro Morgannwg 1*. Llandybïe: Christopher Davies.

Davies, Aneirin Talfan 1976: *Bro Morgannwg 2*. Llandybïe: Christopher Davies.

Davies, Bryan Martin 1988: *Gardag*. Llandybïe: Christopher Davies.

Davies, T. Glynne 1974: *Marged*. Llandysul: Gwasg Gomer.

Dürrenmatt, Friedrich 1958: *Yr Adduned*, Cyfieithiad o *Das Versprechen*, gan Robat Powell [translation of *Das Versprechen*, by Robat Powell]. Caerdydd [Cardiff]: Yr Academi Gymreig.

Eames, Marion 1982: *Y Gaeaf Sydd Unig*. Llandysul: Gwasg Gomer.

Eames, Marion 1992: *Y Ferch Dawel*. Llandysul: Gwasg Gomer.

Edwards, Hywel Teifi 1980: *Gŵyl Gwalia*. Llandysul: Gwasg Gomer.

Edwards, Hywel Teifi 1989: *Codi'r Hen Wlad Yn Ei Hôl*. Llandysul: Gwasg Gomer.

Edwards, Jane 1976: *Dros Fryniau Bro Afallon*. Llandysul: Gwasg Gomer.

Edwards, Jane 1977: *Miriam*. Llandysul: Gwasg Gomer.

Edwards, Jane 1980: *Hon, Debygem, ydoedd Gwlad yr Hafddydd*. Llandysul: Gwasg Gomer.

Edwards, Jane 1989: *Blind Dêt*. Llandysul: Gwasg Gomer.

Eirian, Siôn 1979: *Bob Yn Y Ddinas*. Llandysul: Gwasg Gomer.

Elis, Islwyn Ffowc 1970: *Y Gromlech Yn Yr Haidd*. Llandysul: Gwasg Gomer.

Elis, Islwyn Ffowc 1971: *Eira Mawr*. Llandysul: Gwasg Gomer.

Evans, Ray 1986: *Y Llyffant*. Llandysul: Gwasg Gomer.

Evans, T. Wilson 1983: *Y Pabi Coch*. Llandysul: Gwasg Gomer.

George, Delyth 1990: *Islwyn Ffowc Elis*. Caernarfon: Gwasg Pantycelyn.

Gruffudd, Robat 1986: *Y Llosgi*. Talybont: Gwasg y Lolfa.

Gruffydd, R. Geraint (ed.) 1988: *Y Gair ar Waith*. Caerdydd: Gwasg Prifysgol Cymru [Cardiff: University of Wales Press].

Hauptman, Gerhart and Böll, Heinrich 1974: *Carnifal*, cyfieithiad J. Elwyn Jones [*Carnival*, translated by J. Elwyn Jones]. Y Bala: Gwasg y Sir.

Hughes, J. Elwyn 1989: *Cyfansoddiadau a Beirniadaethau Dyffryn Conwy a'r Cyffiniau*. Llandysul: Gwasg Gomer.

Hughes, J. Elwyn 1991: *Cyfansoddiadau a Beirniadaethau Bro Delyn*. Llandysul: Gwasg Gomer.

Hughes, Mair Wyn 1983: *Yr Un Yw'r Frwydr*. Llandysul: Gwasg Gomer.

Hughes, Mair Wyn 1989: *Caleb*. Llandysul: Gwasg Gomer.

Hughes, R. Cyril 1975: *Catrin o Ferain*. Llandysul: Gwasg Gomer.
Hughes, R. Cyril 1976: *Dinas Ddihenydd*. Llandysul: Gwasg Gomer.
Humphreys, Emyr 1981: *Etifedd y Glyn*, trosiad Cymraeg gan W. J. Jones [Welsh translation by W. J. Jones]. Llandysul: Gwasg Gomer.
Humphreys, Emyr 1986: *Darn o Dir*, trosiad Cymraeg gan W. J. Jones [Welsh translation by W. J. Jones]. Penygroes: Gwasg Dwyfor.
Hywel, Emyr 1973–4: *Gwaedlyd y Gad*. Y Bontfaen: Brown a'i Feibion.
Hywel, Emyr 1989: *Dyddiau'r Drin*. Llandybïe: Cyhoeddiadau Barddas.
Jenkins, Geraint H. 1980: *Thomas Jones yr Almanaciwr*. Caerdydd: Gwasg Prifysgol Cymru [Cardiff: University of Wales Press].
Jenkins, Geraint H. 1983: *Hanes Cymru yn y Cyfnod Modern Cynnar 1530–1760*. Caerdydd: Gwasg Prifysgol Cymru [Cardiff: University of Wales Press].
Jenkins, John (ed.) 1978: *Fy Nghymru i*. Abertawe [Swansea]: Christopher Davies.
Johnson, Dafydd 1989: *Iolo Goch*. Caernarfon: Gwasg Pantycelyn.
Jones, Alun 1981: *Pan Ddaw'r Machlud*. Llandysul: Gwasg Gomer.
Jones, Alun 1989: *Plentyn y Bwtias*. Llandysul: Gwasg Gomer.
Jones, Dic 1989: *Os Hoffech Wybod . . .* Caernarfon: Gwasg Gwynedd.
Jones, Elwyn 1978: *Picell mewn Cefn*. Llandysul: Gwasg Gomer.
Jones, Harri Prichard 1978: *Pobl*. Llandysul: Gwasg Gomer.
Jones, Idwal 1977: *Llofrudd Da*. Llanrwst: Llyfrau Tryfan.
Jones, Idwal 1978: *Dirgelwch yr Wylan Ddu*. Llanrwst: Llyfrau Tryfan.
Jones, Idwal 1979: *Gari Tryfan v Dominus Gama*. Llanrwst: Llyfrau Tryfan.
Jones, Idwal n.d.: *Y Fainc*, Llanrwst: Llyfrau Tryfan.
Jones, John Gruffydd 1981: *Cysgodion ar y Pared*. Llandysul: Gwasg Gomer.
Jones, Marian Henry 1982: *Hanes Ewrop 1815–1871*. Caerdydd: Gwasg Prifysgol Cymru [Cardiff: University of Wales Press].
Jones, Rhiannon Davies 1977: *Llys Aberffraw*. Llandysul: Gwasg Gomer.
Jones, Rhiannon Davies 1985: *Dyddiadur Mari Gwyn*. Llandysul: Gwasg Gomer.
Jones, Rhiannon Davies 1987: *Cribau Eryri*. Caernarfon: Gwasg Gwynedd.
Jones, Rhiannon Davies 1989: *Barrug y Bore*. Caernarfon: Gwasg Gwynedd.
Jones, R. Gerallt 1977: *Triptych*. Llandysul: Gwasg Gomer.
Jones, T. Llew 1977: *Lawr ar lan y Môr: Storïau am Arfordir Dyfed*. Llandysul: Gwasg Gomer.
Jones, T. Llew 1980: *O Dregaron i Bungaroo*. Llandysul: Gwasg Gomer.
Kidd, Ioan 1977: *Cawod o Haul*. Llandysul: Gwasg Gomer.
Lewis, Robin 1980: *Esgid yn Gwasgu*. Llandysul: Gwasg Gomer.
Lewis, Roy 1978: *Cwrt y Gŵr Drwg*. Talybont: Gwasg y Lolfa.
Lilly, Gweneth 1981: *Gaeaf y Cerrig*. Llandysul: Gwasg Gomer.
Lilly, Gweneth 1984: *Orpheus*. Llandysul: Gwasg Gomer.

Lloyd, D. Tecwyn 1988: *John Saunders Lewis: Y Gyfrol Gyntaf*. Dinbych: Gwasg Gee.

Llwyd, Alan 1984: *Gwyn Thomas*. Caernarfon: Gwasg Pantycelyn.

Llwyd, Alan 1991: *Gwae Fi Fy Myw*. Caernarfon: Cyhoeddiadau Barddas.

Morgan, Derec Llwyd 1972: *Barddoniaeth T. Gwynn Jones*. Llandysul: Gwasg Gomer.

Morgan, Derec Llwyd 1983: *Williams Pantycelyn*. Caernarfon: Gwasg Pantycelyn.

Nicholas, W. Rhys (ed.) 1977: *Cyfansoddiadau a Beirniadaethau Wrecsam*. Llandysul: Gwasg Gomer.

Nicholas, W. Rhys (ed.) 1984: *Cyfansoddiadau a Beirniadaethau Llanbedr Pont Steffan*. Llandysul: Gwasg Gomer.

Nicholas, W. Rhys (ed.) 1988: *Cyfansoddiadau a Beirniadaethau Casnewydd*. Llandysul: Gwasg Gomer.

Owen, John Idris 1984: *Y Tŷ Haearn*. Llandysul: Gwasg Gomer.

Rhys, Beti 1988: *Crwydro'r Byd*. Dinbych: Gwasg Gee.

Roberts, David 1978: *I'r Pridd heb Arch*. Llandysul: Gwasg Gomer.

Roberts, Eigra Lewis 1980: *Mis o Fehefin*. Llandysul: Gwasg Gomer.

Roberts, Eigra Lewis 1981: *Plentyn yr Haul*. Llandysul: Gwasg Gomer.

Roberts, Eigra Lewis 1988: *Cymer a Fynnot*. Llandysul: Gwasg Gomer.

Roberts, Kate 1972: *Gobaith a Storïau Eraill*. Dinbych: Gwasg Gee.

Roberts, Kate 1976: *Yr Wylan Deg*. Dinbych: Gwasg Gee.

Roberts, Wil 1985: *Bingo*. Penygroes: Gwasg Dwyfor.

Rowlands, John 1965: *Ieuenctid yw Mhechod*. Llandybïe: Christopher Davies.

Rowlands, John 1972: *Arch ym Mhrâg*. Llandybïe: Christopher Davies.

Rowlands, John 1978: *Tician Tician*. Llandysul: Gwasg Gomer.

Simenon, Georges 1973: *Maigret'n Mynd Adre*, trosiad gan Mair Hunt [*L'Affaire Saint-Fiacre*, translated by Mair Hunt]. Caerdydd [Cardiff]: Gwasg y Dref Wen.

Thomas, Gwyn 1971: *Y Bardd Cwsg a'i Gefndir*. Caerdydd: Gwasg Prifysgol Cymru [Cardiff: University of Wales Press].

Thomas, Gwyn 1987: *Alun Llywelyn-Williams*. Caernarfon: Gwasg Pantycelyn.

Thomas, Ned 1985: *Waldo*. Caernarfon: Gwasg Pantycelyn.

Thomas, Rhiannon 1988: *Byw Celwydd*. Llandysul: Gwasg Gomer.

Tomos, Angharad 1991: *Si Hei Lwli*. Talybont: Gwasg y Lolfa.

William, Urien (ed.) 1974: *Storïau Awr Hamdden*. Llandybïe: Christopher Davies.

Williams, Anwen P. 1976: *Antur Elin a Gwenno*. Llandysul: Gwasg Gomer.

Williams, Harri 1978: *Y Ddaeargryn Fawr*. Llandysul: Gwasg Gomer.

Williams, J. E. Caerwyn 1975– : *Ysgrifau Beirniadol*. Dinbych: Gwasg Gee.

Williams, J. G. 1978: *Betws Hirfaen*. Dinbych: Gwasg y Gee.

Williams, Marcel 1990: *Diawl y Wenallt*. Talybont: Gwasg Lolfa.

Williams, Rhydwen 1979: *Gallt y Gofal*. Abertawe [Swansea]: Christopher Davies.

Williams, R. Bryn 1973: *Agar*. Caernarfon: Llyfrfa'r M.C.

Williams, R. Bryn 1976: *Y Gwylliaid*. Abertawe [Swansea]: Christopher Davies.

Williams, Waldo 1956: *Dail Pren*. Aberystwyth: Gwasg Aberystwyth.

Index